GEND

and

JUSTICE

in

FAMILY LAW

DISPUTES

BRANDEIS SERIES ON GENDER, CULTURE, RELIGION, AND LAW

Series editors: Lisa Fishbayn Joffe and Sylvia Neil

This series focuses on the conflict between women's claims to gender equality and legal norms justified in terms of religious and cultural traditions. It seeks work that develops new theoretical tools for conceptualizing feminist projects for transforming the interpretation and justification of religious law, examines the interaction or application of civil law or remedies to gender issues in a religious context, and engages in analysis of conflicts over gender and culture/religion in a particular religious legal tradition, cultural community, or nation. Created under the auspices of the Hadassah-Brandeis Institute in conjunction with its Project on Gender, Culture, Religion, and the Law, this series emphasizes cross-cultural and interdisciplinary scholarship concerning Judaism, Islam, Christianity, and other religious traditions.

GENDER

and

JUSTICE

in

FAMILY LAW DISPUTES

Women,
Mediation,
AND
Religious
Arbitration

EDITED BY Samia Bano

BRANDEIS UNIVERSITY PRESS · Waltham, MA

Brandeis University Press
An imprint of University Press of New England
www.upne.com
© 2017 Brandeis University
All rights reserved
Manufactured in the United States of America
Designed by Vicki Kuskowski
Typeset in Scala by Westchester Publishing Services

Library of Congress Cataloging-in-Publication Data

Names: Bano, Samia, editor.
Title: Gender and justice in family law disputes : women, mediation,
    and religious arbitration / Samia Bano, Editor.
Description: Waltham, Massachusetts : Brandeis University Press,
    2017. | Series: Brandeis series on gender, culture, religion,
    and law | Includes bibliographical references and index.
Identifiers: LCCN 2016038576 (print) | LCCN 2016038724 (ebook) |
    ISBN 9781512600346 (cloth : alk paper) | ISBN 9781512600353
    (pbk. : alk. paper) | ISBN 9781512600360 (epub, mobi & pdf)
Subjects: LCSH: Matrimonial actions. | Dispute resolution (Law) |
    Divorce mediation—Religious aspects. | Religious minorities—
    Legal status, laws, etc.
Classification: LCC K672 .G46 2017 (print) | LCC K672 (ebook) |
    DDC 346.01/5—dc23
LC record available at https://lccn.loc.gov/2016038576

5 4 3 2 1

CONTENTS

PART TWO

Mediation and Religious Arbitration
in Different National Contexts

FOREWORD

Lisa Fishbayn Joffe

The topic of this book, the implementation of Sharia law in Europe, North America, and Australia, is a women's issue—not just because Sharia law can be a source of discrimination against women, but because the way it is applied has a dramatic impact on the intimate and economic lives of Muslim women. The tenets of Sharia law guide the marital and family lives of many people, whether they live in nations in which Islamic law is enforced by the state or in secular democracies where Islamic clergy are sought out by those who voluntarily subject themselves to their authority to deal with family disputes.

Liberal democracies struggle to understand and accommodate this religious and legal pluralism within their borders. Many citizens, recent immigrants, and members of long-standing religious minorities alike have legal lives that are regulated by both the laws of the state and norms of their religion. These overlapping legal fields are most apparent in the context of family law. While some religions treat a divorce in civil courts as sufficient to dissolve a religious marriage, many do not. Catholicism does not recognize divorce, so Catholics seeking to remarry within the church must seek an annulment there. Some branches of Judaism recognize civil divorce as sufficient to end a marriage, but Orthodoxy and the Conservative/Masorti movement do not. Jews wishing to remarry in the Jewish faith must secure a Jewish divorce (a *get*) before a rabbinical court. Islam also requires delivery of an Islamic divorce in order to terminate a marriage.

Samia Bano's excellent anthology, *Gender and Justice in Family Law Disputes*, discusses both push and pull factors leading women to seek the services of religious mediators and arbitrators. A general trend toward the privatization of justice and cuts to legal services in the name of austerity have led the United Kingdom and other nations to require mediation before divorcing spouses become eligible for legal aid to hire an attorney or to decline to support family law litigation altogether. Religious bodies have stepped up to fill the gap left by the retreating state. Conversely, religious norms mean that access to religious divorce is often more important to women than it is to men. Jewish men who remarry and have children under civil law without getting a religious divorce are subject to disapproval, but no lasting harm attaches to them or their offspring. Jewish women who remarry civilly without a religious divorce are considered adulterers, and any children they have will be classed as *mamzerim* and ineligible to marry into the Jewish community. Bano demonstrates that securing an Islamic divorce is of similar import to Muslim women. While men retain the right to enter into polygamy by taking additional wives, women cannot be free to remarry unless and until their Islamic marriages have been dissolved. The conduct and content of proceedings in religious courts are a women's issue, as women seek out their services because they require a declaration of their divorced status in order to move on with their lives.

This anthology makes a valuable contribution to the literature on the operation of Sharia law in Western democratic nations. Against the backdrop of anxiety in the United States, Canada, and the United Kingdom about the prospects of foreign law being implemented, the authors present a broad set of materials discussing the ways in which real "Sharia courts" operate in practice. Particular attention is given to developments in the United Kingdom because it has a much more developed and diverse set of institutions applying Sharia than other Anglo-American legal systems, but case studies also include India, Canada, the United States, Australia, Italy, and Finland. The contributors include academics, activists, and lawyers who handle Islamic divorce cases. They describe the variation in Islamic law practice between Sharia councils serving different immigrant communities and applying different schools of Islam.

This work is illuminating for those who study the working of religious courts in secular states. These analyses describe the factors that make some Sharia councils dangerous for women, because they apply conservative conceptions of Islam and collaborate with families and community elders to coerce women to accept polygamy or domestic violence and to surrender hard-won rights to property and maintenance that they enjoy under civil law. However, they also describe stories of incremental innovations and improvements, as feminist advocates have worked to make these bodies more amenable to women. This could mean altering the physical space of the courts to shield women from exposure to a hostile ex-husband or family members seeking to apply pressure. It could mean changing the personnel of the Sharia council to include female support workers who accompany a woman through the process and advocate on her behalf. It could even mean changing the practices of the council to better harmonize the principles of Islamic and civil law, for example, by treating a husband's consent to a civil divorce as implied consent to end the Islamic marriage. It may also require that spouses who have married only in a religious ceremony go through a civil marriage to ensure that the spouses have all the legal rights to which they are entitled.

The mission of the Brandeis Series on Gender, Culture, Religion, and Law is to create opportunities for scholars and activists from different religious traditions working toward greater equality under religious law to share insights and best practices. Many of the initiatives described in these essays describe practices that have been adopted or could be adopted by those seeking to reform the rabbinical court divorce process as well. The book also suggests how Muslim feminists are seeking to learn from the successes of Jewish feminists, for example, by seeking amendments to the Divorce (Religious Marriages) Act (the English *get* law) in order to make it applicable to Muslim divorces. This law, developed to assist women denied a divorce under Jewish law, allows a judge to refuse to declare a civil divorce complete until the spouses have dissolved their religious marriage. A similar law passed in Canada as an amendment to its Divorce Act has been used successfully by both Jewish and Muslim Women for more than twenty-five years. Contributors to this volume also suggest how Muslim communities and religious leaders can learn from Jewish models for integrating commitments to religious law with living within and obeying the laws of nations that do not share their faith.

This book will be of wide interest and suitable for course adoption in a number of disciplines. Scholars of legal pluralism will be intrigued by the various concrete examples of how religious law is integrated with secular law. Scholars of legal processes, civil procedure, and negotiation will be interested in this examination of the application of doctrines of alternative dispute resolution to the religious family law context. Scholars of multiculturalism will read these texts with a view to understanding how rights to culture, religion, and personal equality are balanced in these cases.

GENDER
and
JUSTICE
in
FAMILY LAW
DISPUTES

Women, Mediation, and Religious Arbitration

THINKING THROUGH GENDER AND JUSTICE IN FAMILY LAW DISPUTES

Samia Bano

THIS BOOK DRAWS UPON empirical research and a theoretically informed critical analysis to investigate the diverse, complex, and contested experiences of women using mediation and religious arbitration to resolve family and matrimonial disputes in minority, ethnic, and religious communities. At the heart of the debates addressed in this book lie questions of justice, tolerance, equality, rights, and "harm." Feminists and postcolonial scholars in particular have shown that the dominant features of alternative dispute resolution (ADR) are often characterized by male-dominated and patriarchal modes of governance and control. This represents a significant challenge to the family law field and one that has failed to critically engage the related questions of mediating across cultural and religious differences. Instead ADR in the family law context is often understood as the conflictual relationship between the informal and formal spheres and the clash of non-Western versus Western approaches. Very little, however, is understood about the interaction between the formal and informal spheres and, significantly, the "mutually constitutive relationship between informal and formal spheres and the accompanying politico-cultural relations of conflict resolution" (Brigg 2008, 52). Reflection on the question of how power and governance operate reveals that the traditional assumptions of ADR as consent versus freedom are unsettled, challenged, and in need of further scrutiny and critique. Furthermore, an emphasis on the elements of consent coercion, harm, and ADR as an empowering tool for women not only demonstrates the problematic aspects of such ADR but produces a more nuanced critical analysis in relation to the ways in which mediation and religious arbitration are infused with power relations acting as important mechanisms of liberal governance. Again, as Brigg points out, "The operation of informal governance facilitates the workings of sovereign power and vice versa" (2008, 55). This valuable critique raises urgent questions about whether the emergence of new and localized privatized forms of mediation and religious arbitration produce harms to and discrimination against women based on illiberal and unequal practices and informal decision-making processes. What, for example, are the boundaries of consent and coercion within community and family dispute resolution mechanisms? Do such bodies discriminate against women? Is justice being administered in the shadow of the law? What is the response of the state in different national jurisdictions? What are the lived experiences of women using mediation and religious arbitration to resolve family and matrimonial disputes? Is there a need for a "reconceptualization of the law-religion-women nexus" (Ashe and Helie 2014, 140)?

In the post-9/11 era in Europe as well as North America and Australia, new methods of family law dispute resolution have generated heated debate and controversy. Islamophobia, xenophobia, and anti-immigrant rhetoric have all played central roles in vilifying Islamic practices as "premodern," "backward," and "patriarchal" (Razack 2008; Sayyid and Vakil 2010). Muslim migrations to the West, in particular, have engendered a large body of scholarship exploring, analyzing, and critiquing the argument that Muslim communities are in essence unable to integrate into Western political, social, economic, legal, and intellectual practices, leading to the construction of popular narratives of Muslims as representing a form of "non-European otherness" (Hesse and Sayyid 2006, 18). Indeed, the migration, settlement, and integration of all minority ethnic communities into Western state democracies have led to fierce debates over the emergence of social and public policies that aim to accommodate and recognize different forms of minority ethnic pluralism(s). One feature of this process is what Estin (2008, x) refers to as the advent of the "multicultural family," one that is shaped by multiple cultural and legal frameworks, overlapping with the complexities of hybrid and contested identities based on cultural, religious, and ethnic affiliations. Liberal political philosophers in particular have produced a large body of scholarship theorizing the relationship between identity, norms and normativity, rights, justice, and state recognition and the relationship to human rights legal instruments and mechanisms (Kymlicka 1995; Parekh 2000; Taylor 2007). More recently the focus has been on the detrimental effects of multiculturalism on majority and minority communities. The current popular discourse on the failure of multiculturalism that has led to segregated communities, communities living parallel lives, and a failure to forge a common national identity, one that is based on shared norms and values. But to what extent do multicultural policies and discourses shape ADR practices in minority community contexts? This volume addresses this question, with a core interest in the issues of gender, justice, and equality, drawing on important insights from the United Kingdom, India, the United States, Australia, and Europe. It is the first collection of essays to bring together a group of feminist legal scholars and family law practitioners to explore in depth the experiences of women using mediation and religious arbitration to resolve family and matrimonial disputes.

Over the years legal scholars and practitioners have recognized the role played by culture and, more recently, religion in the resolution of matrimonial and family law disputes. What we see emerging now are not only new forms of legal cultures, but also new forms of informal and formal adjudication developing within groups, communities, networks, and nation-states. Significantly, this increasing privatization of marital disputes takes shape both *outside* the traditional adversarial framework of family law and *inside* state law process and practice. For feminist scholars and legal practitioners, these new methods raise a number of fundamental questions relating to citizenship, personhood, and agency as well as the extent to which the privatization of ADR mechanisms may undermine traditional conceptions of justice, "equality before the law," and "common citizenship" (see Yuval-Davis 2011). In addition, they raise questions about whether ADR mechanisms might increase citizen participation in civil society as well as their more general effect on changing patterns of state governance in resolving marital disputes. In Britain, for example, community and family mediation mechanisms that seek to resolve matrimonial disputes both outside the framework of state law and in conjunction with state law mechanisms have emerged. Research by feminist socio-legal scholars underscores the emergence of Sharia councils within diasporic Muslim communities that act as mechanisms to resolve matrimonial disputes within the family, home, and local communities (Shah-Kazemi 2001; Bano 2012). In Britain, this development has been followed by the establishment of the Muslim Arbitration Tribunal (MAT), which operates as a civil law mechanism under the auspices of the Arbitration Act 1996 to produce decisions that may be enforced and relied on in the civil courts. Within British Muslim communities, then, there is currently a three-tiered approach to resolving matrimonial disputes: (1) state law, (2) unofficial community mediation (e.g., Sharia councils), and (3) the Muslim Arbitration Tribunal.

In the United States, while most states allow religious arbitration as long as civil family law procedures are followed, more than a dozen have banned the use of Sharia courts. For example, in 2012 in Dearborn County, Michigan, opponents launched a vitriolic anti-Islamic campaign to abolish such practices. A Michigan Republican, Dave Agena, well known for his inflammatory anti-Islam remarks, introduced an "anti-sharia bill" (HB4769) to the state legislature that ultimately died in committee.[1] The introduction of religious arbitration services has provoked similar reactions in other Western nations. In 2003 in Canada, Syed Mumtaz Ali's announcement that the Islamic Institute of Civil Justice planned to offer arbitration services to families in accordance with Islamic law in marital disputes under Canada's 1991 Arbitration Act provoked a firestorm of protest. As the premier, Dalton McGinty, concluded, "There will be no Sharia law in Ontario. There will be no religious law in Ontario. There will be one law for all Ontario."[2]

In many countries the state has renewed efforts to develop ADR mechanisms involving the use of arbitration, mediation, conciliation, and other collaborative legal initiatives across national boundaries. In Canada, for example, the 1991 Arbitration Act opened the door to religious and other forms of arbitration outside the courts, and in the United States there has been an even longer history of using arbitration and mediation in an effort to bypass crowded court calendars and save money (Sander 1985; Menkel-Meadow 2003, 2013, 2015). Moreover, in many nations, these initiatives have arisen specifically to meet the needs of varied religious communities, particularly those of observant Jews and Muslims. As a result, cross-cultural mediation mechanisms such as Islamic councils have come to the fore in determining the use and delivery of arbitration services. Unsurprisingly, these developments require that the challenges of gender inequality, discrimination, and harm be addressed.

For some, the emergence of new forms of family law dispute resolution mechanisms is understood as part of a wider liberal response to the challenges presented by immigration and the settlement of migrant communities of diverse religious and cultural backgrounds in Western liberal democracies. Questions of rights and demands for recognition of community rights are framed as "multicultural challenges," which, in turn, give rise to important questions about power, authority, agency, choice, and capacity. For instance, should the state or a religious minority community have the ultimate authority in granting a divorce? Are women who work through religious tribunals to get a divorce acting autonomously? Or are they succumbing to the pressures of non-Western religious models of family life? There is now a rich body of scholarship that draws our attention to the social, political, and philosophical dimensions of minority rights and the ways in which the state accommodates cultural and religious differences while respecting group rights. For the legal scholar Ayelet Shachar, the right balance between "the accommodation of minority group traditions, on the one hand, and the protection of individuals' citizenship rights, on the other" is what holds together liberal societies (2001, 1). This balance has been tested extensively in relation to the practice of cultural and religious beliefs of religious communities located in the West and their potential effects upon women as "at-risk" group members.

At the same time, feminist theorists have grappled with reconciling Western interpretations of sexual equality and autonomy and women's agency, on the one hand, with cultural and religious differences, on the other (Mahmood 2004). Postcolonial feminists, for example, utilize the intersectionality framework to capture the differential experiences of women occupying multiple identity locations. Feminist analyses of the murky division between public and private life offer important insights into the feminist goals of autonomy, equality, and women's capacity for decision making. For example, feminist interpretations of autonomy encourage women to make personal choices that include the autonomy of "being" and the right to go against what is considered the norm (Benhabib 1992; Fineman 2004; Mahmood 2004). In this collection of essays, our contributors draw upon feminist theory, intersectionality,

Muslim feminist literature, empirical research, and legal practice to come to a better understanding of the ways in which women living in diverse cultural and religious communities access, utilize, and negotiate different mechanisms of ADR as forms of mediation and religious arbitration. We see how culture and religion can also be used as sites for locating the agency of women where cultural norms and cultural practices act as tools of representation and power, but in different contexts and locations identity can be expressed through cultural and religious practices. This volume also addresses the ways in which religiously observant women can be represented as devoid of agency and subjectivity in debates on universal liberal discourse on equality, justice, and freedom.

Family law is an important area for analyzing claims about the multicultural accommodation of cultural and religious norms and the potential effects on vulnerable group members. Some Western feminists have evinced skepticism about Muslim women's use of religious tribunals, for instance, arguing that such behavior constitutes acquiescence to patriarchal structures rather than an autonomous choice (Abu-Lughod 2015). This volume provides important insights into the ways in which women's agency, autonomy, and personal decision-making capabilities are expressed through formal and informal marital dispute resolution mechanisms and as part of women's social and legal lived realities. Although the resolution of family disputes through mediation has a long history around the globe, scholars have paid little attention to its effects on users or its effectiveness. In addition, the emergence of religious arbitration in the United Kingdom, Europe, Asia, and the United States (among other contexts) in family law disputes has led to increasing concern about the fact that alternative dispute resolution mechanisms in general and mediation in particular are gaining momentum in legal practice and political theory without accompanying critique or scrutiny. By filling this empirical gap, the chapters in this volume provide an in-depth critique and analysis of the particular ways mediation and religious arbitration take shape across contemporary family law jurisdictions in Europe, the United States, India, and Australia. Furthermore, they analyze the dividing line between contemporary family mediation and more recent forms of religious arbitration in order to better understand the complexities and diversities embedded in these processes nationally and transnationally. At the same time, they do so with attention to both academic research and the reflections of legal practitioners and feminist activists who work in this area and engage with the cultural, social, political, and institutional contexts of ADR practices.

Mediation is traditionally understood as a process that assists parties in pre- and post-divorce settlements to produce the best possible outcomes for all parties involved. Moreover, it can take place both with and without state assistance and recognition. Alternative avenues for religious dispute resolution, on the other hand, such as the Jewish *beth din* and the Muslim Arbitration Tribunal, use existing civil law mechanisms to produce agreements by both parties subject to safeguards in the public interest. Yet the terms *mediation* and *religious arbitration* are often presented as interchangeable and overlapping privatized forms of dispute resolution. Further, they are often perceived by users to be situated outside the traditional framework of legal dispute resolution. Yet as we saw in the 2013 England and Wales Supreme Court decision in which the court ruled to uphold a rabbinical authority's arbitration decision on child custody in a divorce proceeding (*AI v. MT* 2013), the state concurred with a religious authority in a marital dispute. Despite this recent decision, both mediation and religious arbitration continue to occupy a contested arena in law whereby competing legal and social discourses interact to produce a wide array of new disputing mechanisms and outcomes for its users. Yet scholars have paid little attention to the ways such agreements are forged and how issues of fairness, consent, justice, and protection of women as potentially vulnerable users take shape during the process.

On the other hand, legal practitioners now discuss extensively the increasing move toward implementing a nonadversarial approach to resolving matrimonial disputes in national and transnational family law contexts. For example, in England the Children and Families Act 2014 made it obligatory for all couples in England and Wales to attend a mediation meeting before submitting an application for divorce to the court. S10 (1) of this act states, "Before making a relevant funding application, a person must attend a family mediation information and assessment meeting." The state therefore clearly expects family law disputes to be resolved outside the adversarial court process. But the extent to which newer forms of mediation and religious arbitration spaces are emerging to resolve matrimonial disputes, and the ways in which they are increasingly being occupied by a new kind of faith-based approach among minority religious communities, warrant further scrutiny. In contributing to this new area of research, this volume explores the relationship between women's experiences using faith-based dispute resolution mechanisms and contemporary debates on religious identity, multiculturalism, citizenship, and equality before the law. Framed as sites where family law matters are resolved according to personal religious systems of law, these bodies have often emerged within the "private" sphere of local community and developed frameworks that are characterized by specific cultural and religious norms and values. Furthermore, self-governing religious bodies that act as councils and tribunals in matters of family law not only challenge the assumed centrality of state law mechanisms, but also open up the question of resolving matrimonial disputes in multicultural nation-states in cross-cultural settings.

Mediation has also been scrutinized by feminist theorists for many years. In the late twentieth century, for example, feminist scholarship from multiple theoretical traditions converged around skepticism regarding the use of mediation to resolve matrimonial disputes. For many, the theoretical promise of resolving disputes in a fair, open, and nonadversarial process failed to match up to the experience of mediation. Instead, the process ultimately reproduced unequal power relations and patriarchal social practices reflecting the subordinate position that women occupy in wider society. Mediation, such feminists argue, can increase rather than reduce the level of harm and violence directed toward vulnerable participants, particularly women (Booth 2008). Furthermore, the impact on women living in racialized minority communities can be particularly detrimental. As Patel points out: "Ironically, the current promotion of faith based projects in all areas of civil society will compromise the gender equality agenda for black and minority women in particular. It will divert women away from the legal justice system into the hands of religious conservative and fundamentalist leaders. The cry of religious discrimination can and will be used to claim access to control over resources, whilst at the same time it will serve to perpetuate discrimination against women and other sub groups and to deter state intervention in family matters" (2008, 15). So what insights can be drawn from national and international jurisdictions and the multiplicity of mediation and religious arbitration practices? Has the move from multiculturalism to "multifaithism" (Patel 2008, 10), for example, led to an erosion of women's rights?

Feminist criticisms of mediation therefore relate to broader issues of social, cultural, and historical relationships and unequal power relations that result in unfair bargaining practices and outcomes for vulnerable parties. Yet over the past forty years, the practice of resolving matrimonial disputes outside the sphere of formal legal adjudication and the emergence of new forms of mediation practices have gained renewed impetus among legal practitioners, policymakers, and feminist lawyers and activists.

The contributors to this volume seek to better understand the social and lived realities of mediation in family law disputes. At the same time, they investigate the rise of religious arbitration as a complex, contested process somewhere amid the constitutive relations of community, law, and state. In doing so they pose a series of questions: How do community processes and the state overlap and/or contest one another in family law dispute resolution? If mediation and religious arbitration manifest in different ways in law and community, what are their effects on women? What kinds of ADR practices are formed and what kinds of enforcement mechanisms, state legal processes, or community-based processes can protect women against coercive social and cultural pressures? What forms do mediation and religious arbitration take within nations and across national borders? How do personal laws, state laws, and community dispute resolution processes such as Sharia councils and the Muslim Arbitration Tribunal overlap and/or contest one another in Britain, Canada, and other nations? What kinds of enforcement mechanisms shape such family law dispute resolution processes internationally? And finally, to what extent do family law dispute resolution mechanisms protect *all* women in culturally and religiously diverse communities against coercive social and cultural pressures?

This volume considers whether feminist perspectives on mediation and religious arbitration are able to capture the complex ways in which mediation and ADR processes are conceived and understood by women who experience them in the broader context of social, cultural, and historical processes. In doing so, it builds upon existing scholarship on questions of religious integration into Western European societies that remain at the forefront of current social and political analyses. It also draws on recent feminist scholarship to explore how these processes are taking shape in the field of family law both nationally and internationally and raises important questions about women's agency, autonomy, and personal decision-making capabilities.

At the same time, the volume locates debates on mediation and religious arbitration within the wider context of liberal rights discourse and community demands for formal recognition of religious arbitration tribunals as state-recognized bodies for resolving matrimonial disputes. At the same time, the important questions of sovereignty and judicial autonomy cannot be ignored, leading to new forms of legal state governance. As Ashe and Helie explain, "The toleration of judicial autonomy in such bodies in itself manifests a striking sharing of sovereignty. And the ceding to religious bodies of a central feature of governmental sovereignty—the judicial power—becomes particularly problematic when that power is utilized in order to enforce religious law that conflicts with fundamental principles of the civil law" (2014: 142).

In recent years, for example, the *renewed* visibility of religious communities in Europe, the United States, Canada, and Australia has led to increased discussions of identity and belonging. In England, this has been described as part of a "crisis of multiculturalism" in Western democratic societies, a crisis that has led to segregated communities rather than the successful integration of minority communities into mainstream societies (Bano 2012).

Drawing on original empirical data and critiquing existing research, this collection of essays analyzes the language of community rights and claims for legal autonomy in matters of family law. Drawing upon critiques of power, dialogue, and positionality to explore how multiple spaces in law and religious communities can potentially empower *and* restrict women at different times and in different contexts, it also opens up the conceptual space in which we can see in evidence the multiple legal and social realities in operation, within the larger context of state law, liberal multiculturalism, and human rights discourse. In this way, it also provides an important contribution to current debates on increasing the use of mediation and religious arbitration in family law and understanding the dynamics of relationality and cultural diversity in new forms of mediation and religious arbitration practices. In a wider context it explores the conceptual challenges that the rise of a faith-based dispute resolution process poses to secular/liberal notions of law, human rights, and gender equality. In addition, the collection considers the ways in which women with multiple social, legal, and political identities are able to utilize multiple systems of family law in their everyday lives.

Overview of This Volume

The chapters in Part One critically engage the concepts of *mediation* and *religious arbitration*, providing new insights into policy-oriented approaches. These chapters discuss empirical research and practitioner experience in the development of new mediation practices that raise important questions of power, capacity, and effectiveness. For example, Lisa Webley draws on her extensive empirical research on mediation and religious arbitration (for a number of public bodies and organizations) to question the ways in which the terms *mediation* and *religious arbitration* are often used interchangeably in practitioner settings and how religious norms and values are leading to new ways of resolving family law disputes. In particular she considers the controversial issue of whose norms should be applied in reaching a decision, taking into account mediator stance, issues of consensual decision making, what interest the state and society have more broadly in privately ordered disputes, and when (A)DR becomes dispute resolution performed by self-appointed judges using a parallel and sometimes covert and subconscious set of norms that are not easily susceptible to scrutiny, challenge, or appeal. We see here the multiple ways in which mediation and ADR have been shaped, challenged, and contested in the English legal context.

My chapter introduces critiquing notions of power, agency, and mediation within feminist legal theory. In particular it examines the contribution of feminist scholarship to our understanding of how women's agency, autonomy, and capacity can be expressed in different ways and in multiple settings. Two key questions are posed. First, to what extent does a critique based on intersectional and feminist ethics of care contribute to a conceptual understanding of women's religious subjectivity and agency and women's use of mediation and religious arbitration? Second, does the increasing privatization of family law disputes provide evidence of the emergence of new cross-cultural mediation mechanisms encapsulating new forms of legal cultures in family law disputes within British Muslim communities that can be both supported and challenged by state law relations? The chapter makes it clear that while religious mediation and arbitration may emanate an emancipatory aura in resolving matrimonial disputes, the consequences for those who use them and for those who are asked to recognize them are often difficult and contradictory.

In her chapter, Pragna Patel, director of London's Southall Black Sisters, challenges the rise of religious arbitration as a direct attack on access to justice for women living within minority communities and an eroding of citizenship rights. The key questions addressed in this chapter are: How can justice be protected by ever increasing religiously motivated claims-making in a neoliberal political context, and more important, what are the consequences of state legal aid being withdrawn from the most vulnerable in society, most often women and children? Drawing on an intersectional feminist critique of politics, Patel cautions against the resolution of family law disputes by ADR processes. The work of Southall Black Sisters demonstrates that the demand for the accommodation of non-state legal orders within the formal legal system is inextricably connected to the rise of religious fundamentalism and neoliberalism, both of which seek to privatize justice for their own ends.

Whether religious arbitration constrains or enables women's autonomy and creates gender-equitable outcomes is a theme that comes up in many chapters in this volume. Sarah Beskine, an English solicitor, provides insights based on her experience as a family law lawyer into mediation and religious arbitration in the British legal context as well as the potential repercussions for women living in minority communities. At the forefront of new changes to family law provisions, she investigates how women from Muslim and Jewish communities navigate mediation, religious arbitration, and civil law to resolve matrimonial disputes.

The following three chapters focus specifically on official and unofficial dispute resolution mechanisms operating within Muslim communities in Britain. Critiquing the distinctions between what is understood as mediation and as religious arbitration, the contributors explore the ways in which different forms of dispute resolution manifest in different contexts with the emergence of new models of Muslim dispute resolution. For example, addressing the difficulties of obtaining a *khula*, the Muslim declaration that a marriage has ended, from Sharia councils, Saher Tariq's chapter examines a mediation service in England, Islamic Divorce & Khula, that operates on the principle that women who want to obtain a khula are entitled to get one. This organization, run by a family lawyer, offers free mediation services and takes the position that a civil divorce fulfills all the requirements of a khula. In its view, if a civil divorce is granted, a khula will follow. Such an approach effectively complicates the division between mediation and religious arbitration and ensures that women do not have to go to a Sharia council and then go through the civil process of divorce as well. As Tariq points out, this approach has been used successfully by English civil courts.

While Tariq's chapter points to the advantages of mediation services, Rehana Parveen's chapter considers ways to improve the process of religious arbitration for Muslim women inside Sharia councils themselves. Through an analysis of divorce cases as well as fieldwork and interviews, Parveen takes us into one of the biggest mosques in Birmingham in England to see how imams who work with the Islamic Judiciary Board handle divorce and other martial disputes. Her research prompts a number of important recommendations for improving this process—specifically, that women serve as support workers in the imam's office by taking family histories from the women seeking help. Many of the women Parveen interviewed said they would feel more comfortable talking with a women about personal matters and found the initial meeting intimidating because their husband was present when they were asked whether they wanted to consider reconciliation. In her argument, many of the needs of British Muslim women could be met by the inclusion of female support workers, a more structured timetable, the provision of clearer information, a screening process with suitable measures to address issues of vulnerability, the updating of service users throughout, and the presentation of written reasons for any final determination.

While Parveen proposes changes inside Sharia councils that could benefit Muslim women, Shaista Gohir and Nazmin Akthar-Sheikh, who head the Muslim Women's Network UK, propose even broader changes. On the one hand, they point to numerous hurdles that Sharia councils can put in the way of women wishing to obtain a divorce and criticize imams for their lack of training in mediation. On the other hand, trained mediators often know little about Muslim communities or cultural values. Their solution is to improve the training of mediators by involving female Muslim mediators. In their view, this would promote inclusivity and diversity within the process and empower Muslim women both as service providers and as service users. Currently, the Muslim Women's Network UK is exploring the possibility of a model divorce service that, if not entirely women-led, would include participation by women and apply Islamic principles on a gender-equitable basis as well as adhere to principles of fairness and best interests as required by the family and equality laws of England and Wales. The organization's ultimate goal is to replace Sharia councils with this alternative service.

As these chapters show, even within one nation there is variation in the kinds of services available to Muslim women seeking divorce. At the same time, the authors are all concerned with gender equity for women, and some have developed new solutions that effectively combine forms of religious arbitration with mediation. Much like the other chapters in the volume, they highlight the particular ways that religious arbitration takes shape across contemporary family law jurisdictions. Further, they help us to understand the varied ways women living in diverse religious communities access, utilize, and negotiate alternative dispute resolution as forms of mediation and religious arbitration.

The chapters in Part Two of the book examine mediation and religious arbitration in different national and transnational contexts. Bringing together contributors from a range of national contexts and jurisdictions, these chapters offer insights into and a critical analysis of the factors that distinguish the social, legal, and political in relation to matrimonial dispute resolution mechanisms. The legal scholar Wendy Kennett, for example, compares the historical development of Jewish and Muslim religious institutions in resolving familial disputes in the United States and Canada. Significantly, the Jewish *batei din* and Muslim Sharia councils bear many similarities. Both of these institutions serve community members, specifically women, who wish to obtain divorce. Because Jews immigrated to the United States and Canada much earlier than Muslims did, they have had a longer time to establish their communities, consolidate their religious institutions and practices, and develop political clout. (Orthodox Jews in New York, for example, have considerable influence in the state legislature.) By contrast, Muslim groups who came later and supported religious arbitration were slower to mobilize, and their opponents were numerous and vociferous, particularly in the media. While some Jewish and Christian groups took advantage of Canada's 1991 Arbitration Act to facilitate religious dispute resolution without arousing public concern, when the spokesperson for the Islamic Institute of Civil Justice announced in 2003 that the institute planned to offer religious arbitration services to Muslim families, there was enormous public outcry. Subsequently, a judge was asked to review the Arbitration Act and in that review (culminating in the Boyd report) found that it ensured an appropriate balance between respect for minority groups and protection of individual rights. Initially, it seemed that the Canadian government would adopt the report's recommendations, but the public debate subsequently moved toward pitting civic secularism along with women's rights against the accommodation of religion in the public sphere (Selby and Korteweg 2012). Ultimately, the 1991 Arbitration Act was amended to exclude religious family arbitration from its scope, thereby excluding not only Muslim but also Jewish and Christian arbitration from state legal recognition. As Kennett points out, the measure that was ostensibly designed to protect Muslim women may actually have disadvantaged Orthodox Jewish women because they rely on religious arbitration for prenuptial agreements to protect their personal assets in the case of divorce.

Debates about women's autonomy and the accommodation of religion in the public sphere also take place in other countries, but in very different contexts and with other kinds of institutional support. India, for example, does not have a uniform civil code, but rather recognizes religious laws of majority Hindu and minority Christian, Muslim, and Parsi religious communities. The Indian state has also adopted the "shared adjudication model," in which the state splits its adjudicative authority with ethno-religious groups in the governance of marriage and divorce. What this means is that in India, unlike Canada, state courts, caste, and sect councils, doorstep courts, and religious clergy and civil society actors adjudicate in matters of marriage and divorce. While there have been debates about establishing a uniform law as a tool of modernization, secularism, and gender equality, most Indian feminists have come to realize that a uniform civil code was central to the Hindu Right's ideology of a common family and Hindu nationalism. Consequently, most women's groups have dropped demands for a uniform civil code and other legislative reforms and are currently working with forms of informal dispute resolution.

Within this national context, Gopika Solanki's chapter examines the role a secular Muslim women's feminist collective, Awaaz-e-Niswaan (AEN), plays in assisting Muslim women with marital disputes by intervening in religious family laws and negotiating with clergy. For Solanki, AEN provides an important site for investigating Muslim women's agency in the context of the dispute resolution process. In contrast to arguments that presume a restrictive notion of agency, Solanki's research on Muslim women's decisions and their work with and support from AEN women over time provides examples of what she terms "agency in process." In other words, agency is a capacity and a process shaped by personal, relational, and social contexts that can change over time. As Solanki finds, AEN often provides different interpretive grounds than do family members or religious law, an opportunity to learn about varied choices through dialogue with other women, and a sense of belonging in women's networks. As her research shows, women who participate in AEN not only develop different understandings about their choices (i.e., leave an abusive relationship or get a divorce), but may also become participants in feminist social movements.

While India has a pluralist legal system, nations such as Australia recognize only state law in divorce. Though some government initiatives have emerged to enhance access to the Australian legal system's services for people of culturally diverse backgrounds and to develop a more inclusive approach to family law service delivery, calls for the recognition of Islamic religious arbitration are considered controversial and have not been implemented. How, then, do Australian Muslim women resolve familial disputes? In their chapter, the legal scholars Ghena Krayem and Farrah Ahmed outline a variety of informal community-based mediation practices for resolving familial dispute that they term "Islamic community processes." These practices are implemented by a range of actors, from community-based organizations and Muslim women's organizations to imams. As Krayem and Ahmed find, women's organizations such as the Muslim Women's Association (MWA) play an important role in Islamic community processes in Australia. When a woman with family difficulties walks through the front door of the MWA office, she is interviewed and a case plan is made for her, which, depending on her circumstances, can involve counseling and/or dealing with social security issues, immigration issues, and housing (particularly when women are leaving an abusive situation). Community organizations often provide referrals and counseling, while informal, nonpermanent groupings of imams typically work together with families toward dispute resolutions. As many Muslim women in their study reported, although imams may be helpful, they do not have full knowledge of Australian law and are unable to provide legal advice. As Krayem and Ahmed point out, when Muslim women are not satisfied with the outcome, they have the option of turning to the formal legal system for resolution of their dispute. Indeed, several of the women interviewed had chosen to seek a lawyer's advice and initiate proceedings in the family courts when community processes failed. As the authors argue, their choice of forum reflects an aspect of these processes that is often ignored, namely the agency that Muslim women exercise as they navigate through these formal and informal processes.

Other chapters challenge the mutually exclusive binaries of religious versus state law by highlighting the dynamic and nuanced ways in which religious institutions such as mosques understand and conduct dispute resolution work in relation to the state legal system and how the goals and practices of dispute resolution work are mixed, with complex implications for the relation between the state and faith-based legal systems, on the one hand, and for gender equality, on the other. For example, in Finland Somali Muslim women seeking help with family disputes are most likely to go to local mosques for assistance. As the chapter by the legal scholars Mulki Al-Sharmani, Sanna Mustasaari, and Abdirashid A. Ismail shows, mosques in Finland favor an integrated system of dispute resolution that combines mosques and state legal institutions. Mosque interviewees applied norms in multiple and mixed ways, such as blending Islamic juristic doctrines with cultural practices of particular ethnic communities and interpreting and applying Islamic law in varied ways. In cases where an agreement on divorce was reached between two parties, some mosques required the disputants to secure a civil divorce from state courts before the religious divorce was granted, to ensure that the two processes were linked.

The outcomes of this process for Muslim women in Finland were mixed. Many of these women emphasized the lack of coordination between mosques and organizations dealing with families in conflict. Some worried that when a family crisis is handled by state, municipal, or nongovernmental organizations (NGOs) providing counseling to families, conflict would escalate and the possibilities for an amicable agreement would be diminished. They also felt that the xenophobia toward Muslims in Finnish public discourse diminished trust when family conflicts were taken to secular institutions without coordination with families and mosques. In fact, women who took disputes to Finnish agencies did so only when other dispute resolution mechanisms failed. On the other hand, mosque interviewees believed these challenges could be mitigated if secular institutions coordinated with them. For example, several imams suggested that practitioners providing counseling services, such as municipalities, NGOs, women's shelters, or the police, needed to contact mosques and involve them in the conflicts that were reported to them. Imams also believed that such an approach would encourage positive attitudes among the immigrants toward the work of these institutions and would improve the effectiveness of alternative mechanisms of dispute resolution. As Al-Sharmani, Mustasaari, and Ismail argue, support from the state in the form of offering mosques financing, premises, and education about Finnish society, laws and mediation skills, and psychology would help resolve some of these issues.

In her chapter, the legal scholar Maria Federica Moscati considers dispute resolution from yet another national context and with a very different group—gay Catholics in Italy. In the contemporary Italian context, the Catholic Church's disapproval of homosexuality and same-sex unions limits the range of available mechanisms for the resolution of disputes between same-sex partners. The intrusion of the Vatican into the debate about allowing same-sex unions in Italy is one of the reasons for the lack of legal protection of same-sex unions in Italy. Because their relationships do not have legal recognition in Italy, same-sex partners have limited access to formal adjudication and its institutions—courts of law—for the resolution of their family disputes. Consequently, same-sex Catholic partners often turn to Catholic third-party interventions such as informal help from Catholic gay and lesbian groups, meetings with members of the clergy or a religious order or with a religious mediator, and mediation at diocesan family counseling associations.

The empirical and lived reality of mediation and religious arbitration points to a complex and contested internal and external logic of governance and power creating new social and legal spaces for interests to compete and a blurring of boundaries between the private and public spheres. Conceptually grounded in the language of rights, self, and empowerment, the chapters of this book document, critique, and problematize both the dangers and the emancipatory possibilities of such new forms of alternative dispute resolution in the family law context. This empirical, critical-theoretical approach locates the normative standards of ADR mechanisms fused with the imagined community, minority rights, and multiculturalism. Feminist critiques in particular address the problem of mediation and religious arbitration that is based on exclusionary and "immutable" group-based religious characteristics effectively excluding female service users from equal participation. The rise of mediation and religious arbitration across the world today means that these inquiries are imperative. As these chapters convincingly argue, the process of ADR can be closed, exclusive, and discriminatory but also flexible, multifaceted, and differentiated according to needs, obligations, and responsibilities. The work presented in the chapters forms the basis of future work and the start of new and critical engagements with the rise of mediation and religious arbitration and the experience of women.

Notes

1. "Anti Sharia Law Supporters Push for Action on Michigan House Bill Targeting Islamic Ideology," *Huffington Post*, 26 November 2012; http://www.huffing tonpost.com/2012/11/26/anti-sharia-law-michigan-house-bill_n_2192221.html.

2. "One Law for All Ontarians," *Toronto Star*, 14September 2010; http://www .thestar.com/opinion/editorialopinion/2010/09/14/one_law_for_all_ontarians .html.

Bibliography

Abdi, Cawo (2015). *Elusive Jannah: The Somali Diaspora and a Borderless Muslim Identity.* Minneapolis: University of Minnesota Press.

Abu-Lughod (2013). *Do Muslim Women Need Saving?* Cambridge, MA: Harvard University Press.

Ashe, Marie and Anissa Helie (2014). "Realities of Religico-Legalism: Religious Courts and Women's Rights in Canada, the United Kingdom, and the United States." *University of California, Davis Journal* 20: 2.

Bano, Samia (2012). *Muslim Women and Shari'ah Councils: Transcending the Boundaries of Community and the Law.* London: Palgrave.

Benhabib, Seyla (1992). *Situating the Self: Gender, Community, and Postmodernism in Contemporary Ethics.* New York: Routledge.

Booth, P. (2008). "Judging Sharia." *Family Law* 22: 11.

Brigg, Morgan (2008). *The New Politics of Conflict Resolution.* London: Palgrave Macmillan.

Estin, L. Ann (2008). *The Multicultural Family.* London: Ashgate.

Fineman, Martha (2004). *The Autonomy Myth: A Theory of Dependency.* New York: New Press.

Hesse, Banor and Sayyid, Salman (2006). "The Post-Colonial Political and the Immigrant Imaginary." In Nasreen Ali, Vrinder Kalra, and Salman Sayyid (eds.), *A Post-Colonial People: South Asians in Britain,* 13–32. London: Hurst.

Kibria, Nazil (2011). *Muslims in Motion: Islam and National Identity in the Bangladeshi Diaspora*. New Brunswick, NJ: Rutgers University Press.

Kymlicka, Will (1995). *Toleration and Its Limits in Multicultural Citizenship*. Oxford: Oxford University Press.

Mahmood, Saba. *The Politics of Piety: The Islamic Revival and the Feminist Subject*. Princeton, NJ: Princeton University Press, 2004.

Menkel-Meadow, Carrie (2003). *Mediation, Theory, Policy Practice*. London: Ashgate.

Menkel-Meadow, Carrie (2013). "Regulation of Dispute Resolution in the United States of America: From the Formal to the Informal to the 'Semi-Formal.'" In Felix Steffek, Hannes Unberath, Hazel Genn, Reinhard Greger, and Carrie Menkel-Meadow (eds.), *Regulating ADR and Access to Justice at the Crossroads*, 419–49. Oxford: Hart.

Menkel-Meadow, Carrie (2015). "Mediation, Arbitration and Alternative Dispute Resolution." University of California–Irvine School of Law Research Paper 2015-59.

Morgan, L (1991). "Women and the Knife: Cosmetic Surgery and the Colonization of Women's Bodies." *Hyapatia* 6(3): 25–53.

Parekh, Bhikhu (2000). *Rethinking Multiculturalism, Cultural Diversity and Political Theory*. Cambridge: Cambridge University Press.

Patel, Pragna (2003). "Shifting Terrains: Old Struggles for New?" in R. Gupta (ed.), *Homebreakers to Jailbreakers*, 35–52. London: Zed Books.

Patel, Pragna (2008). "Faith in the State? Asian Women's struggles for Human Rights in the UK." *Feminist Legal Studies* 16(1): 9–36.

Pew Research Center (2011a). *The Future Global Muslim Population: Projections for 2010–2030* (Forum on Religion and Public Life, Pew–Templeton Global Religious Futures Project). Washington, DC: Pew Research Center.

Pew Research Center (2011b). *American Muslim Report 2011*. Washington, DC: Pew Research Center.

Razack, Sherene (2008). *Casting Out: The Eviction of Muslims from Western Law and Politics*. Toronto: University of Toronto Press, 2008.

Sander, Frank (1985). "Alternative Methods of Dispute Resolution: An Overview." *Florida Law Journal* 37: 1.

Sayyid, Salman and Vakil, Abdoolkarim, eds. (2010). *Thinking Through Islamophobia: Global Perspectives*. London: Hurst, 2010.

Selby, Jennifer A. and Korteweg, Anna C. (2012). "Introduction: Situating the Sharia Debate in Ontario." In Anna C. Korteweg and Jennifer A. Selby (eds.), *Debating Sharia: Islam, Gender Politics, and Family Law Arbitration*, 12–31. Toronto: University of Toronto Press.

Shachar, Ayelet (2001). *Multicultural Jurisdictions*. Cambridge: Cambridge University Press.

Shah-Kazemi, Sonia Nurin (2001). *Untying the Knot: Muslim Women, Divorce, and the Shariah*. Oxford: Nuffield Foundation.

Taylor, Charles (2007). *A Secular Age*. Cambridge, MA: Harvard University Press.

Yuval-Davis, Nira (2011). *The Politics of Belonging: Intersectional Contestations*. Thousand Oaks, CA: Sage.

PART ONE

Mediation
and
Religious Arbitration
in the
United Kingdom

1

When Is Mediation Mediatory and When Is It Really Adjudicatory?

RELIGION, NORMS, AND DECISION MAKING

Lisa Webley

FAMILY PROBLEMS—INCLUDING THE BREAKDOWN of formally and informally recognized intimate relationships, disputes about money, property, and children, intergenerational and parent(s)–child conflict, and domestic violence—are among the most common disputes liable to require third-party help (Genn 1999, 2000; Trinder et al. 2014). These problems are often multifaceted and interconnected, and the narrative between the disputants may be highly contested, emotionally charged, and at the heart of individuals' identity, beliefs, and values. The issues are frequently reframed over time as family members uncouple and recouple, children mature, and the dynamics between the generations shift; additional parties may enter, be the focal point of, and exit the dispute as time elapses (Ekeelaar, Maclean, and Beinart 2000; Ingelby 1988; Davis 1988; Webley 2010a). And it is often difficult for family members to seek support from those closest to them given that the dispute has arisen within kinship groups, sometimes restricting their access to guidance within the family and engendering a reluctance to seek help from a wider circle of support so as to keep family disharmony private from the local community.

It is, therefore, unsurprising that people turn to third-party professionals to seek advice about where they stand, what they should do, and how they may settle their family problems. Not everyone will seek recourse to law, but some will consider it an essential step when children, property, and money are at stake and they feel thoroughly disempowered. Few people will be able successfully to navigate without a lawyer's help the complex legal provisions and procedural rules that bedevil a family justice system designed for a different age in which legal advice, assistance, and advocacy were largely funded through the legal aid scheme (Webley 2015b). Those who feel more confident of their ability to negotiate with family members may be looking for third-party help to facilitate the negotiation process, with or without reference to law. Where the factual basis of the problem is accepted by all sides, negotiations may center on developing creative, practical, and mutually acceptable solutions that allow for closure. Where the factual basis is in dispute and people's values and identities appear to be at odds, there is the thorny issue of whose norms are to be applied in pursuit of the resolution. Historically, in England and Wales when the views of professionals were sought, those professionals would assert the prevailing legal norms to reach an outcome (Webley 2015b). Increasingly, as private ordering is championed by the state, the norms to be used may be agreed upon by the parties or overtly or covertly imposed by one or more of the parties or by a third party. The norms may have some relationship to law; they may be personal values or religious and/or cultural norms, and they may be held in common by all concerned, by the parties if not the third party, or not shared by any (Shah-Kazemi 2000). Consequently, the settlement or judgment may not be one that corresponds to current legal precedent and practice. Should the parties be permitted to bargain away their legal rights in pursuit of a settlement that corresponds to their cultural expectations of family life and childrearing? Does society have an interest in a private settlement, and does it have a procedural interest in knowing how the settlement was derived and a substantive interest in the content of the outcome?

These questions will be addressed in later chapters in this volume and from a variety of perspectives. This chapter aims to set the scene for what follows. In the first section of the chapter I seek to uncover some of the common confusions in the lexicon of dispute resolution to provide a platform from which we may interrogate our stance on family mediation (and in later chapters on family arbitration) in an increasingly culturally heterogeneous society and at a time when family mediation has become a mandatory condition for access to the family justice system in England and Wales (introduced by the Children and Families Act 2014, s 10). In the second section, I examine the contested terrain of mediation, the mediator's role and identity in the family justice context, with reference to mediator neutrality and impartiality. Some conclude that there is a need for a nuanced and developed appreciation of the role of reflexivity in the mediation project and for and by mediators, in place of mediator neutrality, so as to guard against subconscious bias and the subordination of gender and other power dynamics within the mediation environment. This provides a basis for considering the role of mediators and what they contribute to a site of struggle as regards gender, equality, and justice. The third section considers the controversial issue of whose norms should be applied in reaching a decision, taking into account the mediator's stance, issues of consensual decision making, what interest the state and society more broadly have in privately ordered disputes, and when the (alternative) dispute resolution becomes dispute resolution performed by self-appointed "judges" using a parallel and sometimes covert and subconscious set of norms that are not easily scrutinized, challenged, or appealed. In short this chapter addresses when mediation is truly mediatory and when it is really adjudicatory or complicit in the dominant party's narrative such that any settlement is not consensual, fair, or just according to the law or purported mediation practice.

Dispute Resolution: Modes, Means, Ideologies

Much of the discourse on (alternative)[1] dispute settlement[2] conflates a number of key components of dispute settlement such that it can be difficult to ask fundamental questions about the extent to which each mode can deliver fairness. There is often an elision of one or more of the following:

> the *mode of dispute determination or settlement* (court adjudication, arbitration, mediation, third-party negotiation, negotiation between the parties with periodic third-party advice, negotiation purely between the parties, or a combination of these modes); with

> the *theoretical framework* underpinning the mode of dispute resolution (adversarialism, mutualism/consensus, or other); and

the *role that third parties* may be playing within the dispute (partisan, neutral, or both, facilitator or decision maker, or both); and

the *approaches that they are adopting* in the dispute (facilitative, evaluative, transformative, adopted overtly or covertly as regards the parties, consciously or subconsciously by the third-party professional); with

the *professional affiliation of the third-party professional* (lawyer, non-lawyer, other, a range of professional affiliations); with

the *norms (and whose norms) to be used in the decision-making process to reach the determination or settlement* (law, familial values, cultural norms, religious norms, a combination; shared by the parties and the third party/parties, the parties only, one party and the third party, not shared by any); and finally with

resolution by means of *public ordering or private ordering* ideologies.

Many of these components interconnect, overlap, and/or map onto other components more commonly than do others; for example, court adjudication is often associated with lawyers acting as partisans (increasingly less so with the rise of self-represented litigants; see Moorhead and Sefton 2005; Williams 2011; Trinder et al. 2014), and court adjudication has been heavily associated with adversarialism (see examples in Lewis 2000, 6–7), although this too is something of a myth in family law cases (see Davis 1988: 47–61; Ingelby 1988, 43–6; Eekelaar, Maclean, and Beinart 2000, 182–89; Webley 2010a). Mediation is most frequently associated with a neutral third-party facilitator, the theory of mutualism or consensus-based settlement, and the ideology of private ordering, acceptance of plural viewpoints, and mutual respect (although there are contrary narratives; see Dingwall, 1988; Greatbatch and Dingwall 1989; Dingwall and Greatbatch 1991; Mulcahy 2001). These overlaps and intersections only add to the level of complexity and the possibility of misrecognition in the assessment of procedural and substantive equality and fairness, by whom and for whom. This is all the more difficult in a context where many family disputes are settled behind closed doors at home, in a community center, in a professional's office, or in a closed court and when few written records are available for public scrutiny and analysis. In addition, many professionals are now dual or triple qualifying as lawyers, as mediators, and as arbitrators too, and switching between modes, roles, approaches, affiliations, and norms depending on context (Webley 2010a). The aforementioned components are not mutually exclusive, and thus the parties may employ them consecutively or concurrently. It is easy to see how heuristics develop to describe the bundle of attributes associated with different modes of dispute resolution, even if—as we shall see later in this chapter—these heuristics mask great variations in combination and lead to some problematic assumptions about autonomy and justice, fairness and equality.

Perhaps one of the most apparent dichotomies to address is that of adversarialism linked to public ordering via the courts and mutualism linked to private ordering via mediation, because although the dichotomy is rarely expressed in such explicit terms, much of the discourse is constructed through these lenses. Adversarialism in an English and Welsh context assumes a degree of equality of arms between the parties by means of their legal representatives; the latter advocate robustly from a partisan position on their clients' behalf in front of an independent judge free from bias who then adjudicates, after hearing both sides, by applying legal norms to reach a reasoned judgment that is susceptible to appeal. Adversarialism has been linked to autonomy, "rationality," and the assertion of a right against another's position; it is argued to be outcome orientated (see Cockburn 2005) within a context of procedural fairness and has been criticized, particularly in a family law context, as hostile and destructive (see Finlay 1993, 65–69; Milne 1988, 27; cf. Felstiner and Sarat 1998). Consequently, the picture created is one of masculinist competitive lawyers forcefully asserting their clients' legal rights in a public arena, to the detriment of others within the family, so as to achieve a win at all costs, even if empirical evidence does not bear this out in England and Wales (see Webley 2010a, b; Eekelaar, Maclean, and Beinart 2000; Eekelaar and Maclean 2009; Eekelaar and Maclean 2013; Mulcahy 2006; Trinder et al. 2014). Further, this picture, were it ever true, is fast becoming outdated: court adjudication in even the most frequent of family disputes is becoming a rarity and then one that is dominated by self-represented litigants rather than legally represented parties (nearly two-thirds of all divorces involve a negotiated property and financial agreement rather than an adjudicated outcome; see earlier in the chapter for details of research on self-represented litigants).[3] Yet critics of legal professional involvement in family law problems argue that as lawyers are trained in the adversarial paradigm they carry this over into *inter partes* negotiations too, and consequently recourse to law is always recourse to adversarialism; recent British studies undermine this contention and are suggestive of a much more nuanced approach by family lawyers such that they engage in a range of approaches more akin to those ascribed to mediation (see the following section) than to legal practice (Eekelaar, Maclean, and Beinart 2000; Maclean and Eekelaar 2009; Trinder et al. 2014). There continues to be much debate about the role that law and lawyers do and should play in the settlement of family disputes.

Mutualism or consensus-driven decision making, in contrast, is an altogether more appealing theory, more commonly discussed in the context of peace studies (Barak 2005) and associated more closely with feminism and the ethic of care (Cockburn 2005, 73). Mutualism embodies cooperation between all involved in the dispute, operating from a stance of mutual respect, growth, and development through relationship and negotiation (Barak 2005). It is process focused but designed where possible to give rise to a durable outcome that is acceptable to all involved in the situation (Cockburn 2005, 73, 78). Discussions take place in private, are conducted using a shared, negotiated frame of reference and norms, and are facilitated by a neutral third party acceptable to all those involved in the discussions. Thus it is easy to see why mediation has been linked to mutualism given the seeming similarities between the process (neutral third-party facilitator) and the lack of an imposed set of substantive norms to guide decision making (no imposition of family law as the tool). On the face of it, then, mediation should be able to accommodate a plurality of viewpoints, and it should engender a greater chance of equality and fairness for women and vulnerable parties than does recourse to law, given its links with feminism (assuming recourse to law is adjudication or in the shadow of adjudication), especially if a process founded on mutualism can also assist individuals to learn more about themselves and their family members along the way.

In the following section, I shall consider mediation in more detail in order to examine some of the ways in which mediation may provide a more inclusive mode of dispute settlement for families who do not fit within dominant family ideal-types and whose values and beliefs may not be positively supported by current law and practice. I shall also examine the extent to which a more powerful party may overbear a weaker one in the absence of an adept and reflexive mediator and, further, how a focus on mediator "neutrality" coupled with confidentiality within the paradigm of private ordering may mask subconscious bias and negate some of mediation's advertised benefits.

The Mediation Professional Project, Equality, and Fairness

Family mediation has been given a range of definitions; most appear to coalesce around a number of key elements: the process is voluntary, flexible, and confidential, and it is facilitated by an impartial and/or neutral third person with the aim of the parties negotiating a consensual settlement to meet their needs (Boulle and Nesic 2001, 4–6; Folberg and Taylor 1984; Davis and Roberts 1998; Mackie 1991; Bartsch 1999, 540). Some definitions of mediation are augmented to take in aspects of mutualism, including active engagement with the importance of mutual respect so as to provide the parties with a developmental opportunity to see conflict and their needs differently (Richards 1997; Foster and Kelly 1996). These augmented definitions, in part, take in some of the differing approaches to mediation (discussed later). Others have preferred to adopt definitions that view mediation as a set of tasks and roles (S. Roberts 1988; Gulliver 1977, 26–31), some of which may be more interventionist than others (Roberts 1988, 144). But at its core, family mediation involves one or more mediators facilitating and/or directing negotiations between the parties (negotiating alone or with their representatives present), which take place face-to-face or with the parties in separate rooms with the mediator(s) shuttling between them. Thus there are many ways of doing mediation, which change the process and experience of mediation quite considerably. Further, as mediation is not a reserved professional activity outside the state-funded sector, anyone who wishes to practice as a family mediator may do so without training, accreditation, supervision, ethical compliance, public scrutiny, appeal, or challenge (see Webley 2010a, b). It is not immediately obvious who is and who is not regulated in the absence of one national register of family mediators. Therefore, although the definition given here is an important marker of mediation practice, it does not bind all who claim to practice mediation, but nor is all legal work reserved for admitted legal professionals in England and Wales, and there is growing disquiet that parties may be seeking legal help from less than ideally qualified and regulated family lawyers (Webley 2015a; Trinder et al. 2014).

Not only do family mediators select from a range of ways to do mediation, they also make choices about how they approach their mediation practice (in toto or for particular clients). A range of terms are used to distinguish between the different approaches, many of which are set up as dichotomous: the *conceptualist approach* (ideological and aspirational) and the *descriptive approach* (the day-to-day practice of mediation) (Boulle and Nesic 2001, 4–6; M. Roberts 1992); the *settlement-oriented approach* and the *transformative approach* ("Test Design Project" 1995, 4–6; Honeyman 1993). And, in turn, the settlement approach is closely associated with the *narrow approach* focused on specific issues and the *broad approach* that addresses conflict more generally with the transformative (Riskin 1996). Further, family mediation may be *facilitative* (to facilitate the negotiations only) or *evaluative* (to provide an assessment of the options for settlement and an assessment of merits; Haynes 1994), sharing similarities with Roberts's *direct intervention* approach, as distinct from *therapeutic intervention*, similar in type to forms of transformative mediation (S. Roberts, 1988, 144). These labels render as binaries approaches that occur on a scale. There is evidence to suggest that the mediator approach has a direct effect on settlement (Pearson and Thoeness 1988, 212; Donohue, Drake, and Roberto 1994) and that mediators may not be aware of how interventionist they are being (Greatbatch and Dingwall, 1989) or upfront with the parties about how they are evaluating and framing the options and steering the negotiation toward particular outcomes (Mulcahy 2001, in a community rather than family mediation context). This array of approaches underlines that when we talk of family mediation we are not all necessarily talking about the same thing. The heuristics we use are inadequate to the tasks of describing the diversity of practices on offer to potential parties to mediation and of holding mediators to account for their practice and the impact that may have on outcomes and not just on process.

A range of factors are implicated in the success of family mediation sessions, including the willingness of the parties to negotiate with each other and their ability to do so in light of the power dynamics between them. It is generally considered important that the parties be relatively power balanced or that any imbalance be capable of redress by the mediator such that there is a reasonable prospect of equal bargaining to afford the opportunity of a consensual and fair settlement (for the range of factors see S. Roberts 1996). Domestic violence is one of the most challenging forms of power imbalance to address, and it not necessarily easy to detect at intake stage, although triage questionnaires are often employed and there is training in when it is appropriate to mediate and how to manage mediation in the context of domestic violence (Hester and Pearson 1997; Thoennes, Salem, and Pearson 1995). That having been said, overt and obvious attempts to counteract power imbalances offend the core definition of family mediation: mediator impartiality and/or neutrality (Ingelby 1988, 53), yet failure to intervene to counterbalance power discrepancies may reinforce an imbalance, creating an unfair, nonconsensual settlement that also offends mediation's goals (Dingwall 1988, 151; Greatbatch and Dingwall 1989; Taylor 1997; Mulcahy 2001; Astor 2007). Where power imbalance is not corrected, negotiations are dominated by the stronger party's norms and needs, but mediator intervention risks imposing a framework on the parties too unless intervention is undertaken knowingly, strategically, and reflexively so as to steer the process rather than the outcome. The seeming impossibility of integrating impartiality and a duty to counterbalance unfair power dynamics has led some to call for approaches to practice that actively manage power relationships (through activist, transformative narrative mediation: Harper 2006; McEwen 1993; Haynes 1994; Astor 2007; Field 2000; Douglas and Field 2006). More controversially, others argue that mediators should focus on power relationships and if necessary move away from the fictional terminology of neutrality and impartiality in favor of developed reflexivity in their professional encounters more in keeping with that undertaken by psychosocial professionals (Astor 2007; Wall, Stark, and Standifer 2001; for evidence that this practice is already in use in another context see Mulcahy 2001).

But if the mediator is to take an interventionist stance, to evaluate the options and set down hard ground rules to mitigate against power imbalances, to what extent has the family mediator stepped from her role into a decision-making one? Were a family mediator to intervene without informed consent and generate and/or evaluate the options before the parties against her own normative framework, she would become a quasi-adjudicator during that phase of the mediation, someone who is not formally acting as a decision maker but who may have a palpable influence on the final settlement. To what extent does her role differ from that of a judge in a Family Dispute Resolution hearing other than as regards the norms that are being used to evaluate the strength of each party's position? The normative framework employed in mediation will be considered next.

Family Disputes: Private Interests, Public Interests

The family justice landscape has changed markedly since the early 1980s. Policymakers and politicians incrementally have shifted from an ideology of family justice through the application of law, assisted by and overseen by legal professionals with final recourse to the courts, to an ideology of private ordering and private responsibility for dispute settlement where recourse to the family justice system is largely a choice with cost consequences borne by the parties (Webley 2015b). Some arenas of family dispute have been more susceptible to private ordering given the relative dearth of family law tailored to those situations—cohabitation disputes, for example. Private ordering has, however, been incentivized for all forms of family dispute—through reform of divorce procedure (the special procedure), then divorce practice (mandatory mediation introduced first in the context of legal aid reforms), and through the introduction of child support calculations and redress mechanisms, (dis)incentives for seeking state-supported assistance with child support disputes, and restriction on the court's jurisdiction in this regard (Child Support Act 1991, Child Maintenance Service). Over time legal aid has been withdrawn for all but the most exceptional family law problems (Legal Aid Sentencing and Punishment of Offenders Act 2012, about 210,000 fewer people now having access to legal advice and assistance as a result of changes to family legal aid; see Cookson 2011, 50). This is a corollary of the shift from universalism to neoliberalism that has at its core individualism, choice, and personal responsibility (Jessop 2003). The state has retreated and there has been a reduction in the role of establishment institutions such as the old professions in favor of a greater role for market-based service provision (Webley 2015a). Notions of universal justice have been replaced by those of personal choice and personal responsibility for any resulting problems and for their resolution. It is thus unsurprising that family mediators have been welcomed into the family dispute arena, that state funding for family mediation services has been increased as funding for legal help has been reduced, and that family mediation information and assessment meetings are the main gatekeeper route through which disputants must walk prior to gaining access to a family court judge.[4]

Family problems are now viewed as predominantly private sphere problems, to be privately and largely informally settled away from the glare of the law and the law's imposition of values. Some argue that it is essential that settlements be legally compliant, however reached, in order to reduce the risk of long-term inequality going unchallenged. Others argue that the state's privatization of justice is an abdication of responsibility and an erosion of the principle of the rule of law (for a discussion see Genn 2012). Some may be more sanguine about this development, perhaps because they suspect that many agreements will be made in a way that conforms to law even if it is not determined by a judge, others because they consider the loose weave of family law to encompass such a range of possibilities that even a judge attempting to apply the law faithfully would be faced with a great diversity of options (see, e.g., the analysis of family law in this regard in O'Donovan 1993, 10–29). Critics of family law, such as O'Donovan and Naffine, argue that family law privileges the public over the private, and this reinforces conservative notions of the family through the overt or covert application of legal norms (O'Donovan 1993, 41) and preserves white male dominance and supports its values and structures (Naffine 1990, 148). This may be a liberating opportunity for the parties to determine their dispute according to their shared values (on the importance of culture see Shah-Kazemi 2000). It may be a bulwark against conservatism and homogeneity and may encourage creative, equal, individualized solutions fit for a diversity of family forms.

As discussed earlier in this chapter, power imbalances are considered by some to be inherent in family mediation given the gendered nature of family life and the gendered consequences of conflict—earning imbalances, childrearing responsibilities—and collective ones that are too complex to be redressed via private ordering (on gender and mediation see Slaughter 2000, 44; on gender and power more generally see Oldersma and Davis 1991, 12). Some mediation proponents indicate that when power imbalances are great, mediators should insist that the parties take legal advice before finalizing any agreement (Finlay 1993, 70–74; S. Roberts 1996). However, exceptional access to (self-funded) legal advice will not address Slaughter's suggestion that without a partisan professional on one's side, and a lawyer at that, it may not be possible to redress the inequality of bargaining power that is inherent in many opposite-sex familial disputes. The findings of Davis, Cretney, and Collins (1994) add some weight to this contention even within *inter partes* solicitor-facilitated negotiations. Legislative provisions may go some way to counterbalance the risks to more vulnerable parties, if harnessed (although note the concerns of O'Donovan 1993, ch. 2, as regards the gendered nature of law). But there is no requirement that the parties be informed of or make use of law as part of their negotiations, and therefore any protection afforded by law may be lost in a private ordering context. Public legal understanding is far from extensive, and the speed of family reform makes it difficult for all but the most devoted family law follower to keep abreast of developments. Davis et al.'s findings on the prevalent folk myths concerning legal entitlement on divorce bear this out. They showed that male clients were much more likely than female clients to overestimate their "entitlement" and that the power struggles played out by the couple during their relationship transferred to their approaches to each other and the negotiations in respect of their divorce (Davis, Cretney, and Collins 1994, ch. 3). Solicitors spent considerable time managing the expectations of their own clients so as to move them to a position where they would accept a sensible deal in keeping with legal principles. But the greater the legal input into the family mediation process, the further it strays from its theoretical underpinnings of mutualism and private ordering and the closer it comes to collaborative law practice undertaken in round table meetings between lawyers and their clients negotiating face-to-face to reach an amicable settlement according to law. In the absence of legal representation, it cannot be assumed that the parties are well informed about the law when weighing different settlement options, and the family mediator cannot provide legal advice. But if she is adopting an evaluative approach she may nonetheless give her view of the relative merits of the available options and subconsciously reframe the discussion in order to privilege some over others, her norms over theirs.

Did public ordering fulfill an important function in society, and has the public an interest in being able to see the law applied, and its effects, to challenge the law and its application if it appears unfair? Fiss would argue yes. To him, settlement (by any means) is a decision to strike a bargain, to make peace, to maximize party interests rather than to reach justice. He argues that the parties undermine the law and the values it embodies whenever they choose to settle (1984, 1075–85; on rational adjudication, Bentham, and the importance of adjudication see Twining 1993, 382–85; for a contrary view see Finlay 1993). But this is a minority view, and for many the importance of transparency and the opportunity of challenge are fundamental notions of justice. Family justice is founded on the principle that the outcomes of family disputes are resolved fairly for the parties as against the legal normative framework. Eekelaar (2000, 9) contends that family law is undergirded by three kinds of assumptions: the predictive assumptions about what is considered likely to happen, the normative assumptions about what the majority of the population considers should happen, and the value assumptions of policymakers indicating what ought to happen. Family disputes are increasingly regulated through value assumptions of how disputes should be resolved in procedural terms; in substantive terms the law places considerable reliance on normative and value assumptions in respect of children, finance, and property. It is difficult to gain a sense of how many settlements are reached with reference to family law, as most settlements are private and may not be recorded formally or informally in a way that allows outside scrutiny. It could be argued that all dispute outcomes are negotiated in the shadow of the law (Mnookin and Kornhauser 1979); it is just that some are in full shade while others are barely obscured by shadow. There is some evidence to suggest that the opportunity to scrutinize and challenge outcomes is important to some (see Finlay 1993), but this is further evidence of the important role played by adjudication rather than recourse to law per se (solicitor negotiations are similarly private). There are equal opportunities for mediation agreements and solicitor-negotiated agreements to be scrutinized by the court and become a matter of public record as consent orders, if the parties choose to formalize those kinds of agreement. Where mediation or solicitor-negotiated agreements are converted into court orders by consent, they will be subject to similar public scrutiny as to the outcome, if not the reasons for the settlement and the norms used to reach the agreement. Thus the issue is not normative in the sense of whose norms are applied; rather, it is an issue of public adjudication versus private settlement and whether any agreements reached are reached through genuinely informed consent.

Norms, Gender, Equality, and Justice

It is highly unlikely that any negotiation will be played out with full equality of bargaining power between the parties to the problem, and historically the law has been used (however ineffectively) to provide an equality of arms between them with reference to legal professionals employing legal norms to negotiate on their behalf and at a cost affordable to many by virtue of access to legal aid. The courts have been available for intractable disputes; judgments have been open to public scrutiny (until recently) and subject to appeal. As long as the legal norms are considered reflective of families' norms, and the legal professionals and the legal system function in a gender-neutral way, recourse to law offers a backstop protection while providing for meaningful negotiation in the shadow of the law (Galanter 1984, 368). This is private ordering, but private ordering employing public principles. We know, however, that law is only as fair as the society within which it operates, and legal professionals, including judges, are socialized within the system and its values; there are many examples of women suffering discrimination at the hands of a legal system designed by men for men (as described in this chapter, O'Donovan and Naffine have suggested in the past that law has gone a long way to restrict female emancipation and to impose a conservative model of family relations on women; on more recent gender-equality polities and legislation and a weakening of male dominance within the institutions that have supported hegemonic masculinity (see Connell 2005). Recourse to law and legal professional help has not provided a complete answer to gender and other forms of inequality.

Mutualism holds out the promise of an alternative theoretical framework through which all parties may be empowered to reach positive, personalized settlements in keeping with their culture, religion, and values. It is a compelling narrative yet to be fully realized through family mediation offered over short time frames, by a range of very differently qualified people who are hampered by the shibboleth of neutrality and impartiality that conceals the mediator stance even from the mediator's view. Dominant forms of current family mediation practice provide family mediators with inadequate tools to redress power imbalances, support the parties in their development, or curtail their ability to incorporate their perspectives into the decision-making process. Public ordering may be only as good as the content of the norms that the legal system applies;

similarly, private ordering is only as good as the quality of mediators' abilities to recognize and actively reflect on their biases. Private ordering may be an effective means by which women's voices can be heard, their experiences respected, and their needs met away from institutions that have been implicated in the subordination of women (Naffine 1990; O'Donovan 1993). But if inequality is, in part, a product of gender relations within the household and employment, the state's normalization of male violence, and patriarchal cultural institutions and practices propagated via the media, religion, and education, which frame women within the confines of patriarchy (Walby 1990), then private ordering may be yet another arena in which male dominance can be reasserted, and this time away from the glare of public scrutiny or challenge.

The structures, processes, and attitudes that lead to gender inequality are contested within feminist scholarship (Beasley 1999), but it does require significantly more consideration in the light of state incentives for private ordering in a seemingly deregulated, consumerist environment. If private ordering really is to be positioned within an unregulated, informal, and confidential context, concerns about equal bargaining power, whose norms are applied, mediator neutrality, and/or mediator reflexivity will persist. But private ordering does have a lot to offer those whose cultures the law is blind to; it allows family members to live and settle their disputes according to their values, with reference to law to the extent that they choose. A lack of imposed institutional and institutionalized norms may further the postmodern feminist project to value diversity and support movement toward a society that celebrates difference and in which equality is achievable, regardless of sex, gender, class or sexuality (on stratified inequality see Bottero and Irwin 2003; Rosenfeld 2002; Skeggs 1997). Where power imbalances are largely absent or can be counteracted by an effective, competent, reflexive mediator, where consent is genuine, decision making informed, and settlement clearly consensual, family mediation has a lot to offer by way of equality and fairness, whether it delivers on legal justice or not.

Notes

1. I have bracketed "alternative" as it is unclear whether mediation and arbitration remain real alternatives to the dispute resolution mechanism held up as the standard model—adjudication. Instead they may more properly be

categorized on a three-dimensional plotted chart of dispute resolution mechanisms that take into account many of the factors that I address in this section of the chapter. For a more detailed discussion see Twining (1993).

2. I have chosen the phrase *dispute settlement* as a compromise (mooted by Tillet 1999, 4–6), although there are definitional difficulties with this. *Resolution* implies a degree of finality about the issues under discussion that is not borne out by the empirical literature on the trajectory of family disputes. *Dispute* is also problematic, and some commentators favor the term *decision making* to indicate that there may be no real dispute (Boulle and Nesic 2001, 7), but rather a series of issues that need to be addressed with the help of a third party. However, as will become apparent later in the chapter, *decision making* is a loaded term in the context of mediation: while it appears to suggest that this rests solely and yet jointly with the parties, it may subtly be exercised by the mediator or by one of the parties such that the consensual character of decision making is undermined. In addition, the term *party* is more appropriate to contexts involving legal proceedings; however, it is difficult to find a neutral term that explains those individuals who are directly involved in the decision making related to the end of their relationship. Relational terminology (*couple, former couple*) did not encompass a sufficient range of familial relationships; "each side" was rejected as too partisan and contrary to the spirit of family mediation. Thus I have continued with the phrase *the parties* while acknowledging that this is not a neutral term and tends toward the legal paradigm.

3. There were 28,542 petitions filed for divorce and 29,197 decrees absolute made in January–March 2014 but only 10,259 financial remedy (formerly "ancillary relief") cases started and 8,098 cases with a disposal in January–March 2014, demonstrating that nearly two-thirds of all divorces involve a negotiated property and financial agreement rather than an adjudicated outcome (Ministry of Justice, *Court Statistics Quarterly Report, January to March 2014*). For figures on the rise of self-represented litigants after the legal aid reforms see Webley (2015b).

4. This change came into force on 22 April 2014 following the introduction of s10 of the Children and Families Act 2014 and follows a similar requirement with respect to access to court adjudication on divorce. There is some early anecdotal evidence to suggest that some courts are not enforcing this requirement, particularly where the parties are unrepresented; see Trinder et al. (2014).

Bibliography

Astor, H. (2007). "Mediator Neutrality: Making Sense of Theory and Practice." *Social and Legal Studies* 16: 221.

Barak, G. (2005). "A Reciprocal Approach to Peacemaking Criminology: Between Adversarialism and Mutualism." *Theoretical Criminology* 9(2): 131.

Bartsch, H.-J. (1999). "Council of Europe: Legal Co-operation in 1998–9." *Yearbook of European Law* 19(1): 533–45.

Beasley, C. (1999). *What Is Feminism? An Introduction to Feminist Theory*. Thousand Oaks, CA: Sage.

Bottero, W. and Irwin, S. (2003). "Locating Difference: Class, 'Race' and Gender, and the Shaping of Social Inequalities." *Sociological Review* 51(4): 453.

Boulle, L. and Nesic, M. (2001). *Mediation Principles Process Practice*. London: Butterworths.

Chancer, L. S. and Watkins, B. X. (2006). *Gender, Race, and Class: An Overview*. Oxford: Blackwell.

Cockburn, T. (2005). "Children and the Feminist Ethic of Care." *Childhood* 12(1): 71.

Connell, R. (1987). *Gender and Power: Society, the Person and Sexual Politics*. Cambridge: Polity Press.

Connell, R. (2001). *The Men and the Boys*. Berkeley, NSW: Allen & Unwin.

Connell, R. (2005). *Masculinities*, 2d ed. Cambridge: Polity Press.

Cookson, G. D. (2011). *Unintended Consequences: The Cost of the Government's Legal Aid Reforms*. London: King's College London.

Davis, G. (1988). *Partisans and Mediators: The Resolution of Divorce Disputes*. Oxford: Clarendon Press.

Davis, G., Cretney, S. M., and Collins, J. (1994). *Simple Quarrels: Negotiations and Adjudication in Divorce*. Oxford: Clarendon Press.

Davis, G. et al. (2000). *Monitoring Publicly Funded Family Mediation: Final Report to the Legal Services Commission*. London: Legal Service Commission.

Davis, G. and Roberts, M. (1998). *Access to Agreement: A Consumer Study of Mediation in Family Disputes*. Milton Keynes: Open University Press.

Dingwall, R. (1988). "Empowerment or Enforcement?" In R. Dingwall and J. Eekelaar (eds.), *Divorce Mediation and the Legal Process*, 150–67. Oxford: Oxford University Press.

Dingwall, R. and Eekelaar, J., eds. (1988). *Divorce Mediation and the Legal Process*. Oxford: Oxford University Press.

Dingwall, R. and Greatbatch, D. (1991) "Behind Closed Doors: A Preliminary Report on Mediator/Client Interaction in England." *Family Court Review* 29(3): 291.

Donohue, W. A., Drake, L., and Roberto, A. J. (1994). "Mediator Issue Intervention Strategies: A Replication and Some Conclusions." *Mediation Quarterly* 11: 261.

Douglas, K. and Field, R. (2006). "Looking for Answers to Mediation's Neutrality Dilemma in Therapeutic Jurisprudence." *eLaw Journal* 13(2): 177.

Eekelaar, J. (2000). "Uncovering Social Obligations: Family Law and the Responsible Citizen." In M. Maclean (ed.), *Making Law for Families*, ch. 2. Oxford: Hart.

Eekelaar, J. and Maclean, M. (2013). *Family Justice: The Work of Family Judges in Uncertain Times.* Oxford: Hart.

Ekeelaar, J., Maclean, M., and Beinart, S. (2000). *Family Lawyers: The Divorce Work of Solicitors.* Oxford: Hart.

Felstiner, W. L. F. and Sarat, A. (1988). "Negotiation between Lawyer and Client in an American Divorce." In R. Dingwall and J. Eekelaar (eds.), *Divorce Mediation and the Legal Process*, ch. 2. Oxford: Oxford University Press.

Field, R. (2000). "Mediation Praxis: The Myths and Realities of the Intersection of Mediator Neutrality and the Process of Redressing Power Imbalances." 5th National Mediation Conference, Australia. http://www.apmec.unisa.edu.au /events/conference2000/field.pdf, accessed 20 October 2009.

Finlay, H. A. (1993). "Family Mediation and the Adversary Process." *Australian Journal of Family Law* 7: 63.

Fiss, O. (1984). "Against Settlement." *Yale Law Journal* 93: 1073.

Folberg, J. and Taylor, A. (1984). *Mediation: A Comprehensive Guide to Resolving Conflict Without Litigation.* San Francisco: Jossey-Bass.

Foster, N. J. and Kelly, J. B. (1996). "Divorce Mediators: Who Should Be Certified?" *University of San Francisco Law Review* 30: 667.

Galanter, M. (1984). "World of Deals: Using Negotiation to Talk about Legal Process." *Journal of Legal Education* 34: 368.

Genn, H. (1999). *Paths to Justice: What Do People Think about Going to Law?* Oxford: Hart.

Genn, H. (2012). "What Is Civil Justice For? Reform, ADR, and Access to Justice." *Yale Journal of Law and the Humanities* 24: 397.

Greatbatch, D. and Dingwall, R. (1989). "Selective Facilitation: Some Observations on a Strategy used by Divorce Mediators." *Law and Society Review* 23: 613.

Grillo, T. (1991). "The Mediation Alternative: Process Dangers for Women." *Yale Law Journal* 100(6): 1545.

Gulliver, P. (1977). "On Mediators." In I. Hamnett (ed.), *Social Anthropology and Law*, 15–52. London: Academic Press.

Harper, C. (2006). "Mediator as Peacemaker: The Case for Activist Transformative-Narrative Mediation." *Journal of Dispute Resolution* 2006(2): 595.

Haynes, J. (1994). *The Fundamentals of Family Mediation.* Albany: Albany State University and New York Press.

Hester, M. and Pearson, C. (1997). "Domestic Violence and Mediation Practices: A Summary of Recent Research Findings." *Family Mediation* 7(1): 10.

Honeyman, C. (1993). "A Consensus on Mediators' Qualifications." *Negotiation Journal*, 289.

Ingelby, R. (1988). "The Solicitor as Intermediary." In R. Dingwall and J. Eekelaar (eds.), *Divorce Mediation and the Legal Process*, ch. 3. New York: Oxford University Press.

Jessop, R. B. (2003). "From Thatcherism to New Labour: Neo-Liberalism, Workfarism, and Labour Market Regulation." In H. Overbeek (ed.), *The Political Economy of European Employment: European Integration and the Transnationalization of the (Un)Employment Question*, 137–53. London: Routledge.

Karlberg, M. (2005). "The Power of Discourse and the Discourse of Power: Pursuing Peace through Discourse Intervention." *International Journal of Peace Studies* 10(1): 1.

Lewis, P. (2000). *Assumptions about Lawyers in Policy Statements: A Survey of Relevant Research*. No. 1/2000. London: Lord Chancellor's Department.

Mackie, K. (1991). *A Handbook on Dispute Resolution*. London: Routledge.

Maclean, M. (2010). "Editorial—Family Mediation: Alternative or Additional Dispute Resolution?" *Journal of Social Welfare and Family Law* 32(2): 105.

Maclean, M. and Eekelaar, J. (2009). *Family Advocacy: How Barristers Help Victims of Family Failure*. Oxford: Hart.

Maclean, M. and Eekelaar J. (2013). *Managing Family Justice in Diverse Societies*. Oxford: Hart.

Maclean, M., Eekelaar J., and Bastard, B., eds. (2015). *Delivering Family Justice in the 21st Century*. Oxford: Hart.

Maclean, M. and Kurczewski, J. (2011). *Making Family Law: A Socio Legal Account of Legislative Process in England and Wales, 1985 to 2010*. Oxford: Hart.

McEwen, C. (1993). "Competence and Quality." *Negotiation Journal*, 313.

Milne, A. (1988). "The Nature of Divorce Disputes." In J. Folberg and A. Milne (eds.), *Divorce Mediation, Theory and Practice*, 27–44. New York: Guildford Press.

Ministry of Justice (2014). *Court Statistics Quarterly Report, January to March 2014*. Ministry of Justice Statistical Bulletin, 19 June.

Mnookin, R. H. and Kornhauser, L. (1979). "Bargaining in the Shadow of the Law: The Case of Divorce." *Yale Law Journal*, 88(5): 950.

Moorhead, R. and Sefton, M. (2005). *Litigants in Person: Unrepresented Litigants in First Instance Proceedings*. DCA Research Series 2/05. London: Department for Constitutional Affairs.

Mulcahy, L. (2001). "The Possibility and Desirability of Mediator Neutrality: Towards an Ethic of Partiality." *Social and Legal Studies* 10: 505.

Mulcahy, L. (2005). "Feminist Fever? Cultures of Adversarialism in the Aftermath of the Woolf Reforms." In J. Holder and C. O'Cinneide (eds.), *Current Legal Problems, 2005*, 215–34. Oxford: Oxford University Press.

Naffine, N. (1990). *Law and the Sexes: Exploration in Feminist Jurisprudence*. London: Allen & Unwin.

O'Donovan, K. (1993). *Family Law Matters*. London: Pluto Press.

Oldersma, J. and Davis, K. (1991). "Introduction." In K. Davis, M. Leijenaar, and J. Oldersma (eds.), *The Gender of Power*, 1–18. London: Sage.

Pearson, J. and Thoeness, N. (1988). "Divorce Mediation: An American Picture." In R. Dingwall and J. Eekelaar (eds.), *Divorce Mediation and the Legal Process*. New York: Oxford University Press.

Richards, C. (1997). "The Expertise of Mediating." *Family Law*, January, 52.

Riskin, L. L. (1996). "Understanding Mediator Orientations, Strategies and Techniques: A Grid for the Perplexed." *Harvard Negotiation Law Review* 1: 7.

Roberts, M. (1992). "System of Selves? Some Ethical Issues in Family Mediation." *Mediation Quarterly* 10: 11.

Roberts, S. A. (1996). "The Path of Negotiations." *Current Legal Practice* 49: 108.

Roberts, S. (1988). "Three Models of Family Mediation." In R. Dingwall and J. Eekelaar (eds.), *Divorce Mediation and the Legal Process*, 144–50. Oxford: Oxford University Press.

Roberts, S. A. (1983). "Mediation in Family Disputes." *Modern Law Review* 46(5): 537.

Rosenfeld, R. (2002). "What Do We Learn about Difference from the Scholarship on Gender?" *Social Forces* 81(1): 1.

Sarat, A. and Felstiner, W. L. F. (1995). *Divorce Lawyers and Their Clients: Power and Meaning in the Legal Process*. New York: Oxford University Press.

Shah-Kazemi, S. N. (2000). "Cross-Cultural Mediation: A Critical View of the Dynamics of Culture in Family Disputes." *International Journal of Law Policy Family* 14(3): 302–25.

Skeggs, B. (1997). *Formations of Class and Gender*. London: Sage.

Slaughter M. M. (2000). "Martial Bargaining: Implications for Legal Policy." In M. Maclean (ed.), *Making Law for Families*, ch. 3. Oxford: Hart.

Spelman, E. (1988). *Inessential Woman*. Boston: Beacon Press.

Sullivan, O. (2004). "Changing Gender Practices with the Household: A Theoretical Perspective." *Gender and Society* 18(2): 207.

Taylor, A. (1997). "Concepts of Neutrality in Family Mediation: Contexts, Ethics, Influence and Transformative Process." *Mediation Quarterly* 14: 215.

"Test Design Project Performance-Based Assessment: A Methodology for Use in Selecting, Training and Evaluating Mediators" (1995). National Institute for Dispute Resolution. http://www.convenor.com/uploads/2/3/4/8/23485882/method.pdf, accessed 27 June 2016.

Thoennes, N., Salem, P., and Pearson, J. (1995). "Mediation and Domestic Violence Current Policies and Practices." *Family Court Review* 33(1): 6.

Tillet, G. (1999). *Resolving Conflict: A Practical Approach*, 2d ed. Sydney: Sydney University Press.

Trinder, L., Hunter, R., Hitchings, E., Miles, J., Moorhead, R., Smith, L., Sefton, M., Hinchly, V., Bader K. and Pearce, J. (2014). *Litigants in Person in Private Family Law Cases.* London: Ministry of Justice

Twining, W. (1993). "Alternative to What? Theories of Litigation, Procedure and Dispute Settlement in Anglo-American Jurisprudence: Some Neglected Classics." *Modern Law Review* 56(3): 380.

Walby, S. (1990). *Theorizing Patriarchy.* Oxford: Blackwell.

Waldman, E. (1993). "The Role of Legal Norms in Divorce Mediation: An Argument for Inclusion." *Virginia Journal of Social Policy & the Law* 1 (1): 87.

Wall, J. A., Stark, J. B., and Standifer, R. L. (2001). "Mediation: A Current Review and Theory Development." *Journal of Conflict Resolution* 45(3): 370.

Webley, L. C. (1998). *A Review of the Literature on Family Mediation in England and Wales, France, Ireland, Scotland and the United States.* London: Lord Chancellor's Advisory Committee on Legal Education and Conduct.

Webley, L. (2010a). *Adversarialism and Consensus? The Professions' Construction of Solicitor and Family Mediator Identity and Role.* New Orleans: Quid Pro Books.

Webley, L. (2010b). "Solicitors as Imagined Masculine, Family Mediators as Fictive Feminine and the Hybridisation of Divorce Solicitors." In R. Mortensen, F. Bartlett, and K. Tranter (eds.), *Alternative Perspectives on Lawyers and Legal Ethics: Reimagining the Profession,* 132–50. Sydney: Routledge-Cavendish.

Webley, L. (2010c). "Gate-Keeper, Supervisor or Mentor? The Role of Professional Bodies in the Regulation and Professional Development of Solicitors and Family Mediators Undertaking Divorce Matters in England and Wales." *Journal of Social Welfare and Family Law* 32(2): 119–33.

Webley, L. (2015a). "Legal Professional De(re)regulation, Equality, and Inclusion, and the Contested Space of Professionalism Within the Legal Market in England and Wales." *Fordham Law Review* 83(5): 2349–67.

Webley, L. (2015b). "When Is a Family Lawyer, a Lawyer?" In M. Maclean, J. Eekelaar, and B. Bastard (eds.), *Delivering Family Justice in the 21st Century,* ch. 17. Oxford: Hart Bloomsbury.

Williams, K. (2011). *Litigants in Person: A Literature Review.* Research Summary 2/11. London, Ministry of Justice. https://www.gov.uk/government/uploads/system/uploads/attachment_data/file/217374/litigants-in-person-literature-review.pdf, accessed 27 June 2016.

2

Agency, Autonomy, and Rights

MUSLIM WOMEN AND ALTERNATIVE DISPUTE RESOLUTION IN BRITAIN

Samia Bano

TODAY IT IS COMMONLY HELD that Western democratic states are in the midst of a renewed religious revival, a revival that seems most evident among minority ethnic and religious communities whose very visible display of religious symbols, clothing, faith-based schools, and demands for the recognition of religious practice and belief not only challenges the liberal values of toleration, free speech, and equality before the law but also, and most important perhaps, poses a challenge to the very basis on which Western secular societies are understood to function as cohesive, stable, and liberal. Indeed the European story of migration, settlement, and the development of the state management of ethnic, cultural, and religious diversity produces important yet contested narratives about the rise of religious identity, secularism, and the limits of recognition and accommodation of personal family law systems in Western liberal societies. In Europe, therefore, the position of minority ethnic groups and the question of state responsibility to ensure the successful integration of minority groups into mainstream society have recently come under sustained attack from all along the political spectrum. This renewed questioning of the place of religious belief and practice is also framed as part of a wider debate on the benefits of multiculturalism and cultural pluralism to liberal societies versus its divisive and detrimental impacts upon European societies (Modood 2007).

46

In recent times, the increased consciousness of cultural and religious difference has also complicated the field. The relationship between secularism, multiculturalism, and religion is problematic in its negotiation of relations between the state and ethnic and religious groups, but is one understood to be crucial to a better understanding of how such relations can be managed and developed. In social and political theory, *multiculturalism* is a relatively new concept that can be traced to the mid-twentieth century with the deployment of state strategies to manage ethnic difference generated by increased migration. In Britain, multiculturalism has been framed and articulated largely around questions of cultural identity and the forging of a common national identity.

The diversity of religious belief systems in European states has also long raised critical questions about how far diverse religious practices can be accommodated in the public sphere, as well as the extent to which state and religion should be separated. One of the key points of contention between the religious and secular is the argument that rights to equality and autonomy are enshrined in secular human rights principles and law and that, in contrast, religious doctrine often fails to promote these rights or actively undermines them. This has generated conflicts between the notions of secularism and the religious and the place of the latter in public civic life, a conflict that has also been described as permanent and intractable but also important for testing the limits of democracy, human rights, and the role of the state. For example, is there a conflict between traditional and/or orthodox religious belief systems and thought and secular values in Western liberal democracies? To what extent is there a clash between "secular" values of human rights, in particular women's equality and autonomy, and religious ideas, norms, and values? To what extent do concepts such as equality, dialogue, justice, and autonomy operate as theoretical engagements framing relations of power between state law and minority religious groups? What are the processes of contestation, conflict, and overlapping sites of power?

In this chapter I draw upon these debates and questions to consider the ways in which notions of agency, power, and autonomy are constituted in current debates on mediation and religious arbitration, as markers for women as decision makers. I do this not only in relation to critiques of normativity and the cultural and social norms that may underpin such forms of dispute resolution, but also and more importantly within the wider context of feminist legal critiques, multiculturalism and liberal "rights" debates. In doing so I pose two key questions. First, to what extent does an intersectional and feminist ethics of care critique contribute to our conceptual understanding of women's religious subjectivity and agency and their use of mediation and religious arbitration? Second, does this increasing privatization of family law disputes provide evidence of the emergence of new cross-cultural mediation mechanisms that encapsulate new forms of legal cultures in family law disputes within British Muslim communities that may be both supported and challenged by the state?

I consider these questions from three angles. First, I sketch the historical and current landscape of Western feminist engagements with religion, drawing attention in particular to an increased consciousness of multiculturalism and secularism in recent years. These factors add complexity to what started in feminist thought as a more simple critique of religious patriarchy. Second, I consider the ways in which core liberal values such as agency, autonomy, and equality have dominated the agenda, both in Western feminism and in broader cultural contexts, and the critique offered by intersectional and feminist ethics of care analyses. Postcolonial feminists, for example, have long offered a strong critique of the way in which liberal values collapse into a simplistic binary analysis of, for instance, consent versus coercion. Such values often mask their own cultural heritage in the name of universalism, meaning that visibly noncomplying *cultures* are seen as the source of the problem, rather than, for instance, male dominance or patriarchy. Finally, I look at the ways in which these debates have played out in the context of some specific and high-profile issues—namely the emergence of Muslim mediation and religious arbitration in the United Kingdom. I suggest that alternatives to the binaries that have structured discussion about agency and equality are beginning to be replaced by more nuanced and reflective markers of autonomy, agency, and power reflecting the personal narratives of women's lives and thereby providing new insights.

Religion and Western Feminism

The relationship between religious women and feminism can at best be described as difficult and protracted but also vital and necessary to feminist scholars and feminist activists seeking a better understanding of the lives of religious women who choose to live their lives as part of their faith communities. As Failinger et al. (2013, x) point out:

> Feminist legal scholars have, until recently, mostly avoided the study of the difficult place in which religious women find themselves—pulled apart by family expectations for their lives, feminist critiques of their choices, and religious demands on their consciences and loyalties. . . . . They have a hard time seeing why any self-respecting woman would wear a chador, or acknowledge her husband as head of the household, or agree to stay home full-time to raise children and care for the household when she has a college education and the prospect of public life.

While putting aside the fixed characteristics this assigns to women (and hence reflecting only one interpretation of the wide array of lived experiences of religious life), it also illustrates the potential and real polarization of feminist and religious perspectives. Indeed, feminist scholars have long critiqued the role of women inherent in religious ideology and religious practice (Sahgal and Yuval-Davis 1992). Under the project of gaining equality, feminist scholars have historically charted the ways in which religious doctrine served to entrench the inferior legal status of women in Western societies in the eighteenth and nineteenth centuries. Historically, feminist scholars have therefore focused on the patriarchal nature of religion and the limits that religious practice and belief can impose on women, thereby in effect limiting women's autonomy, choice, and rights in both the public and private spheres (see Sharma 1994). Within mainstream feminism the focus has therefore been on the ways in which the institutions of the family, home, and motherhood in monotheistic religions (Islam, Christianity, and Judaism) entrench patriarchal conditions for women members. More specifically, control of women's sexuality and reproductive roles is deemed crucial to promoting and preserving religious ideologies to the extent that any transgression by individual community members is deemed threatening and unacceptable. This critique intensified with the advent of second-wave feminism in the 1960s and 1970s, which documented women's departure from traditional religions and the impact of secularization, leading to the emergence of new religions and forms of spirituality (Woodhead and Helas 2005).

Most important, however, such critiques also emerged within black and ethnic minority feminist groups in Britain. Organizations such as Southall Black Sisters, Newham Asian Women's Project, and the Black Women's Collective drew on intersectional feminist frameworks to challenge racism and sexism and to challenge intra- and inter-communal power relations within families and communities to which they belonged. In Britain, for example, the organization Women Against Fundamentalism was set up in 1989 following the Rushdie affair to challenge the rise of religious orthodoxy and fundamentalism within minority religious communities. Julia Bard (1992: 1), a member, explained:

> WAF's work from the start has been based on the conviction that while fundamentalism appears in different forms in different religions and in different political contexts, all of them have at the heart of their agendas the control of the lives, minds and bodies of women. This is expressed in terms of "family values," a constellation of supposedly immutable ideas which place men at the head of the family, bestowing on it its status as well as its income, and which define women as the conveyors of morality and tradition to the next generation. A non-conformist or rebellious woman, according to this view, will endanger the future of the community as a whole which is thus entitled to coerce her to "do her duty" or throw her out.

Male religious leaders' control of women, their denial of women's rights to freedom, choice, and autonomy, and their role in defining acceptable patterns of female behavior, therefore, underpin many feminist critiques and campaigns. These critiques have led to a new form of scholarship that casts light on the relationship—both current and historical—between women, religion, and society). In turn feminist theologians have also drawn attention to the marginalization of women in dominant patriarchal religions, most often Christianity, Judaism, and Islam. Today, in the West, there is also a great deal of scholarly interest in understanding the nature of religion and the religious experience. Demanding reform in religious doctrine, feminist theology has produced important and challenging scholarship (Mir-Hosseini et al. 2015). Historically, women's religious experience has been measured by attendance at places of worship, frequency of prayer, study of religious texts, and adherence to religious doctrines or texts. Much of this scholarship focuses not only on issues concerning the rise and/or decline of religiosity and religious practice but on the growing influence of secularism and secularization upon religion and its consequences. Woodhead and Heelas (2005), for instance, draw on the emergence of *coexistence theory* within Christianity, which points to new and different forms of Christianity that have emerged under secularism, primarily evangelical and charismatic Christianity. Thus, far from being a constraining influence on feminism, religion has for many acted as a stimulus to new thinking about the status of women in society and law. Katherine Young (1987: 6) warns, however, that studies on women and religion cannot "be summed up by the descriptions of Chinese footbinding, Hindu *sati*, Muslim *purdah* and Christian witchcraft" but must instead seek to uncover the nuances in challenges to religious power and authority in order to explore alternative narratives. In her recent work the Muslim feminist scholar Ziba Mir-Hosseini, along with other Muslim feminist scholars, has produced groundbreaking scholarship that argues "for an egalitarian construction of family laws from within Muslim legal tradition" (Mir-Hosseini et al. 2015, 3).

Feminist theology has also, therefore, been a focus of possible reform in the monotheistic religions. For example, ideological developments embracing feminist principles of equality, nondiscrimination, and human rights have been expressed by Christian, Muslim, and Jewish feminists. In Islam, for example, the emergence of Islamic feminism (Mir-Hosseini et al. 2015) has led to debates on reformulating Islamic principles from a universal human rights perspective. But, although there have been a number of family reforms in various Muslim-majority societies (Welchman 2009), conflict remains over notions of equality and the persistence of patriarchy.

Today, feminist literature also explores the relationship between feminism, multiculturalism, and religion in the lives of religiously diverse women living in minority communities. More specifically, the focus has been on the relationship between religion, women's issues, gender roles, and culture; and feminism has been at the forefront of attempts to understand the experience of religious women's lives in a complex and nuanced way. In their introduction to a special issue of *Feminist Review*, Avtah Brah and Lyn Thomas (2011: 2) explain that the emergence of "secular spiritualties" challenges the old binaries of "religion and tradition" versus "modernity and secularism." They insist that, in order to better understand what meanings women attach to these new religious understandings, it is necessary to pay closer attention to the narratives of the women themselves.

Throughout history, the circumscribed values that underpin Western conceptions of law and justice have strongly influenced how law is perceived and understood by contemporary feminist political and legal theorists. I start from fairly common premises within critical theory, that traditional notions of legal objectivity and legal neutrality simply do not exist and that the operation and effects of law cannot be understood in isolation from the social, moral, and political context in which law operates (Davies 2002).

In describing how law deals with questions of justice, political philosophers analyze the fragmented nature of legality and the relations between normative orders and individual rights (Dworkin 1986). Law is an important potential source of power, and the pursuit of justice in response to the challenges presented by diverse cultural and religious communities reveals contradictory practices. The *effects* of a plural and multicultural society on the development of English law have been extensively documented over the past twenty years by anthropologists, sociologists, and increasingly legal scholars (Malik 2012). The debate over the nature of this interaction is often characterized as a clash of a given set of values, identity, and interest claims by state law and the demands of minority religious communities. This in turn gives rise to central and difficult questions regarding the appropriate level and type of legal accommodation to be afforded and protected.

Contemporary liberal thinkers, shaping the terms of liberal values in Western societies and the postcolonial world, have advanced a rather conservative agenda. Significantly, they have done so in and through liberal rights discourse rather than in opposition to it (Kapur 2005, 19). For many of these thinkers, the focus on religious women serves as a yardstick to consider the conflict between the rights of religious communities and the rights afforded by the liberal state. As Shireen Razack (2008: 86) points out, "Women's bodies have long been the ground on which national difference is constructed. When the Muslim woman's body is constituted as simply a marker of a community's place in modernity and an indicator of who belongs to national community and who does not, the pervasiveness of violence against women in the West is eclipsed. Saving Muslim women from the excesses of their society marks Western women as emancipated." Violence against women in the West is not seen as "cultural" because of the universalism associated with Western values. Indeed, the heightened visibility of Muslim women only serves to underline the narrative of Western women's freedom.

It is important, therefore, to begin with the recognition that religious and faith-observant women belong to many diverse communities and their lived experiences must thus be understood as complex, strategic, and at times contradictory (Afshar 2005; Bano 2012). While current feminist scholarship maintains the critique of patriarchy, as discussed earlier, it has also moved beyond this concern, using a wide range of methodological approaches and conceptual frameworks to capture the experiences of all women, including religious women. Drawing on the feminist conceptual frameworks of *intersectionality, complementarity, feminist ethics of care*, and *feminist standpoint theory*, new insights have emerged, as will be discussed in what follows.

Mediation and Personal and Group Autonomy

Self-governing religious bodies that act as unofficial tribunal bodies in matters of family law not only challenge the assumed centrality of state law mechanisms in resolving matrimonial disputes but also open up the question of relationality in law and developing policies to resolve matrimonial disputes in multicultural Britain via a cross-cultural setting (see Bano 2013a).

For many scholars, the question of personal autonomy and choice underpins debates on the recognition and state accommodation of personal systems of law in Britain. These debates fall largely within two spectrums of scholarly work. The first can be described broadly as orientalist discourses that accord Muslim women little if any agency and personal choice as members of Muslim families and communities (see, e.g., the critiques by Razack 2008), and the second points to the fact that all debates on equality and free choice are in effect partial and incomplete, as choice in this context is simply circumscribed by other multiple variables that include family and community relations, class, notions of belonging, and identity. The extent, therefore, to which free choice can be expressed at any one time and context is flawed, and all choices are made as part of personal and strategic decision making in the face of conflicting and competing demands.

In her work Ahmed (2013) questions the norms underpinning current debates on choice and autonomy for Muslim women living their lives as part of their faith communities and questions whether religious norms do in fact harm personal autonomy. Instead, she argues that personal autonomy can be enhanced through its positive associations with religious group autonomy (2013, 34). Defining group autonomy as "a religious group having a level of freedom from external (usually state) control, as well as the ability to govern itself through minimally democratic institutions of governance" (2014, 37) she insists that religious alternative dispute resolution (RADR) can in fact help facilitate and represent the interests of the individual via this process in order to promote personal autonomy within a wider group autonomy. She explains, "If religious individuals feel alienated from their state representatives, RADR might give them the opportunity to be governed instead, at least in family matters, by those who they feel represent them better their co-religionists. Group members and their leaders share a religion and therefore (one might expect) some values, goals and cultural attributes. So RADR, by enhancing group autonomy, might improve the representation of individual group members in family matters relating to their religion" (2013, 37).

Such links between personal and group autonomy have long been documented within British Muslim communities in relation to community organizing and mosque formations (Gillat-Ray 2010; Abbas 2014). Yet how Muslim women have been able to exercise agency and autonomy using community mechanisms to resolve family law disputes remains an important question. One of the key criticisms leveled against mediation and all forms of religious arbitration is that they offer a "privatized version of justice" whereby the formal protections offered by formal law are simply lost and this puts the lives of women at risk. For Ahmed, however, the key to preventing harm and coercion within religious groups is to ensure that deliberative processes are in place within the groups in order to ensure that all voices are heard. This commitment to democratic and participatory representation embodying deliberative features of consent and debate guarantees that collective decision making and group autonomy takes place (Ahmed 2013, 44) and in turn opens the key spaces that help prevent community coercion and harm.

While patriarchy and gender inequality are not, of course, unique to Muslim communities but are endemic to multiple and diverse groups, networks, and organizations, patriarchal assumptions and biases may

nevertheless exist within localized religious dispute resolution mechanisms, raising important questions ranging from the extent to which
women's voices are heard within religious arbitration mechanisms to
whether such groups have the ability, capacity, and desire to embed
democratic values of procedural representation into their organizations.
Furthermore, the precarious contexts on which such organizations
may operate notwithstanding financial insecurity, competition for local
resources, and the capacity and ability to develop inclusive and deliberative decision-making processes can mean that they are simply unable to
provide democratic functioning processes. Added to this complexity is
the fact that some normative religious systems of belief and groups may
align themselves with conservative interpretations of Islam that challenge the very idea of Muslim women acting as religious scholars, mediators, and arbitrators and thereby excluding large sections of the Muslim
populations. This itself poses a challenge to the role of religious groups
in multicultural societies operating in complex and diverse ways and
based on complex dialogic power relations with the local state, community, and family relations.

Over the past three decades, feminist theorists have grappled with the
question of how to reconcile Western interpretations of sexual equality
and the autonomy of women's agency with cultural and religious difference. Debates have focused largely on a clash of values in which liberal
notions of equality, free will, and choice have been deemed "progressively
modern" and open to all, while the continued adherence of women belonging to minority communities to religious and traditional ties has been
presented as illiberal, backward, and a barrier to the enhancement of
women's rights. In these debates, the law and juridical liberalism (e.g.,
antidiscrimination legislation) serve as the starting point for enhancing
the rights of all women. Admittedly this dichotomous approach of Western liberalism versus traditional practice and the universal applicability
of "Western modernity" with the ideas of Enlightenment to non-Western
traditions and in non-Western contexts has been a subject of intense critique. Postcolonial theorists such as Gayatri Spivak (1988) and Chandra
Mohanty (1991) were among the first to challenge the ahistorical, over-
generalized constructions of Muslim women as members of minority religious communities. Basing themselves in both a postcolonial
and feminist critique, they challenged the epistemological roots of Western scholarship that focused on the subordinated position of women

belonging to minority, ethnic, and religious communities. Going against the grain of traditional Western feminism, Spivak (1988, 25) highlights the hierarchical positions of power that Western feminists occupy and the need to critique feminist "subject positions." A failure to do so, she suggests, renders many preexisting feminist arguments simply inadequate and limited. Perspectives like these also emerge in the scholarship on agency. Framing the question of individual agency in terms of the extent to which Western democratic principles can be applied within non-Western societies (and the idea of human rights interconnected to Western liberal democracy) raises the rhetoric of a "clash of civilizations." A key debate in human rights literature is the conceptualization of cultural human rights.

However, providing cultural rights is not simply a matter of making provisions for multiple sets of personal and family civil laws based on the idea that religions and cultures are unchanging and nondiverse. These same laws have been used by men to subordinate women in their communities (Purkayastha 2009, 292). It is therefore necessary to start from the perspective of diversity and more nuanced contestation *within* specific communities rather than to simply look at conflict between broader (and male-defined) versions of culture. In turn, questions of agency and autonomy inevitably arise.

Feminist writing provides many avenues for conceptualizing multiple identities and multiple forms of inequality (Cooper 2004). Feminist political theorists, such as Nancy Fraser and Iris Young, approach the question by considering a matrix of factors—both social and structural—that position women in particular contexts. Fraser (1989) links social relations to distinct economic and cultural societal structures and to related forms of redress (recognition and redistribution). She approaches oppression as a process whereby social collectivities operate along a spectrum from injustices of distribution to those of recognition. For Fraser, therefore, the issue of multiple identity raises a number of key questions: "Which identity claims are rooted in the defense of social relations of inequality and domination? And which are rooted in a challenge to such relations? . . . Which differences . . . should a democratic society seek to foster, and which, on the contrary, should it aim to abolish?" (1989, 65).

For many feminist *legal* scholars, the focus has also been squarely on the question of equality and subordination in the context of the ways in which legal regulations construct, and respond to, intersecting orders of inequality. This approach ultimately draws upon the work of legal feminists such as Catharine MacKinnon (1987) and others, who maintain that the law tends to reflect masculine values: many of the values around which the law is built, including its assumption of an individualistic "reasonable" person, are those used and valued by men. Scholars such as Patricia Williams (1988) and Kimberley Crenshaw (1989) use the concept of intersecting identities (in this case race, class, and gender) to illustrate how the law and legal relations fail to grasp the complexities of black women's lives. For example, juridical liberalism expressed via legislation such as antidiscrimination legislation remains inadequate in its understanding of the position of minority ethnic women who may be situated in multiple social locations. As such, these laws simply fail to effectively redress the claims of discrimination.

Feminist interpretations of autonomy encourage women to make personal choices that include the autonomy of being and the right to go against what is considered the norm. This raises a number of important questions relating to how we understand autonomy, choice, and agency and whether ultimately autonomy and equality can ever be reconciled. As Charusheea (2004, 197) questions, "Can we conceive of worlds in which women act differently from men, attain different outcomes based on criteria we do not ourselves agree with, and yet do so as autonomous choosing beings expressing a desired identity for themselves?"

As we can see from this brief discussion, feminist engagements with issues of choice and definitions of agency can be underpinned by broad and sometimes false distinctions. It is simplistic to contrast belonging to a religious group, and the constraints this may bring, with the autonomy of opting out. The critique of such either/or choices is now well documented, and for the past two decades feminist theorists have been grappling with the criticism that their analyses of women's oppression are ethnocentrically universalist. As Anne Phillips (2007) points out, while there is broad agreement in principle that ethnocentric universalism is to be avoided, there is also much disagreement about how we can achieve this without falling into debates on cultural relativism.

Feminist Theory and Critiques of Mediation

Feminist critiques of mediation and religious arbitration point both to the positive attributes one can experience in resolving disputes outside the formal adversarial legal framework(s) and to the potential and detrimental consequences for women's human rights, autonomy, and safety. More important, questions of choice, consent, and women's vulnerability underpin feminist critiques. Mediation, therefore, has been conceptualized and understood as transformative and empowering but also potentially dangerous and oppressive. So is mediation essentially an "oppressive" dispute resolution process that inhibits and denies women agency and is based on patriarchal normative frameworks while reinforcing patriarchal values? In this part of the chapter I draw on feminist legal theory to consider this question and the ways in which intersectional and feminist ethics of care approaches may produce alternative and more insightful analyses.

At its core, intersectionality challenged the early feminist claim that feminism spoke for all women with a singular universal voice. In her pioneering work, Kimberley Crenshaw (1989) demonstrated how the experience of law is experienced by black women via multiple dimensions and modalities of social relations and subject formations. Gender, therefore, could no longer be seen as a single category on which feminist scholarship and practice based its conceptual understandings of women's experience and life stories, but now it could be understood in the ways in which gender intersects and confronts other categories and identities that illustrate the complexities of women's lives. At its heart, therefore, intersectionality challenges the language of essentialism. As Joanne Conaghan (2009, 23) explains, "Just as women's experiences were overlooked through the 'universalisation' of men's, so also were the experiences of women of colour eclipsed by feminist attendance to white women's interests and concerns: the 'woman' of feminism was, for most purposes, white; whiteness was part of the 'essence' of womanhood which feminism represented." Such challenges by black feminist scholars, such as Crenshaw (1989), introduced notions of difference, complexity, and "the invocation of women's individual and shared experience as the epistemological base of feminist theoretical knowledge" (Conaghan 2009, 23).

Imagining mediation as part of intersectional faith identities signals the subject's capacity to use multiple legal forums (see Grabham et al. 2009). A feminist ethics of care approach in mediation, for example, produces new paradigms in which the voices of women and other vulnerable groups are central to dispute resolution processes. As Alberstein (2009, 13) notes, "The new logic of relational thinking, which defines the self and the other as inherently connected and responsible for each other, provides challenges for formalistic and individualistic perceptions of law and has inspired new developments that incorporate the new world-view." Ethics of care as a paradigm of feminist thought and action raises important questions of justice, responsibility, and individual actions (see Gilligan 1982). Therefore, a feminist ethics of care approach to mediation overcomes the problems of individualism versus collectivism because it entails a more comprehensive understanding of the nuanced notions of self and of other.

Feminist scholars (Lichtenstein 2000; Baruch Bush and Folger 2005) have long recognized that mediation can be a positive and constructive process for women. The characteristics of collaboration, cooperation, bargaining, and consensus decision making are understood to be integral to feminist values of recognition, voice, value, choice, and ethics. As Field (2006, 49) points out: "The focus of mediation on the facilitation of constructive consensual decision-making and cooperative problem solving is aligned with the feminist principle that women as individuals are important to group processes. These aspects of mediation support an understanding of the process as a good dispute resolution process for women." The emphasis on parties taking responsibility for their decisions is also considered a positive development for women. This potentially allows women important spaces to challenge gendered inequalities and to ensure that the mediation process can incorporate their interests and needs. Mediation can therefore be part of a process of social change contributing to a positive change in women's lives. As Field (2006, 51) notes, "This sits well with the feminist goal to circumvent the continued patriarchal oppression of women through achieving social change; and contrasts with determinations imposed by courts that are inherently restricted by the gendered limitations of legal remedial norms. In mediation, importantly, women are in a situation where pursuit of their own outcome priorities is expected, and is integrated into the overall objective of a consensus-based outcome. Mediation can therefore be considered a good dispute resolution process for women in the context of post separation disputes."

Mediation is therefore described as empowering for women in that it gives them a voice and a space that captures their personal experiences based on personal narratives and emotions. This fits in well with feminist principles of self-expression and empowerment as well as with a feminist ethics of care. Carol Smart (1992) points out, for example, that mediation can provide alternative "resistant discourses" where concerns for needs and interrelationships can form an important part of the dispute resolution process but also a challenge to the adversarial legal process that is based on patriarchal norms and values (that perceive emotion and care as subordinate values). In this way mediation can be understood as part of a feminist approach to resolving disputes and working to promote the best interests of women by allowing women an opportunity to speak and, most important, to be heard.

Furthermore, state law remains an important part of the mediation process that continues to offer protections to vulnerable parties (most often women) whose experience of mediation may prove difficult and oppressive and/or who may choose not to opt for mediation in the first instance. State responsibility to protect vulnerable parties therefore is not only not abandoned. Further protections embedded in the mediation process, such as ensuring that all couples seek independent legal advice before taking part in the mediation process and that all agreements are rubber-stamped via court orders prior to the enforcement of agreements, allow a space for legal formalism in what is traditionally seen as part of legal pluralism. As Field (2006, 53) argues, "Mediation *can* be good for women; it can be said to display inherently feminist values and principles, and as a result it can be used to make a positive contribution to the feminist goal of working to discontinue male oppression of women, particularly in the context of post-separation disputes."

Feminist scholars have, however, also warned of the dangers of trying to resolve marital disputes outside the protection of formal law. This may include situations where cultural norms deny women decision-making authority or where the mediator is not neutral and yet still provides the normative framework for discussion—situations that can transform the nature of the discussion and curtail the autonomy of the disputant. Roberts (2008) raises the concern that negotiations might well occur in private "without the presence of partisan lawyers and without access to appeal." Numerous studies point to the fact that official mediation places women in a weak bargaining position and encourages them to accept a settlement considerably inferior to one that they might have obtained had they gone through the adversarial process. In their study of mediation and divorce, Greatbach and Dingwall (1993, 203) found that mediators do not act in a neutral way: they guide participants toward particular outcomes, with the consequence that there is a strong imbalance of power—the parties are not equal and cannot respond in an equal way. Furthermore, Bottomley and Conaghan (1993, 45) remind us that mediation "has not arisen in a vacuum and is not practised in one" and that we need to explore the dynamics of power underpinning this process. Thus, we can say that mediation promotes a particular familial ideology that is based on social control and patriarchal norms and values, and operates through subliminal, covert forms of power and coercion. In contrast, formal law provides protection against abuse in the private sphere, and so in response to the move toward private legal ordering, critics argue that mediation fails to deliver on the key issue of justice. Eekelaar (2000) describes this development of social and legal norms as one that

> exists within society [as] a network of social norms which is for-mally independent of the legal system, but which is in constant interaction with it. Formal law sometimes seeks to strengthen the social norms. Sometimes it allows them to serve its purposes with-out the necessity of direct intervention; sometimes it tries to weaken or destroy them and sometimes it withdraws from enforce-ment, not in an attempt to subvert them, but because countervail-ing values make conflicts better resolved outside the legal arena.

Feminists have extensively critiqued this tenuous relationship between family and state intervention across a wide spectrum of disciplines. For example, Thornton (1991, 120) points out that unofficial family media-tion ensures that the state absolves itself of responsibility to adequately protect vulnerable women. She explains: "In mediating interests which appear to be irreconcilable, the task of the liberal state is made easier if there are some areas conceptualised as 'private' with which it does not have to grapple." In other words, privatized family mediation allows the state to avoid intervention on the grounds of respecting cultural and reli-gious difference. For organizations such as Southall Black Sisters, the multiculturalists treat racial-minority women in a way that they would not treat white women—that is, ignoring the violence directed against them in the interest of respecting culture.

Yet it is precisely the fact that women have such divergent experiences of family mediation that renders problematic any proposals to develop family mediation as a more formalized process that suits the specific needs of minority ethnic communities. There seems to be an inherent conflict between recognizing identities as multiple and fluid and formulating social policy initiatives that are based on specific cultural practices, precisely because cultural and religious practices are open to change, contestation, and interpretation. At the very least, we must ensure that mechanisms are in place so that those who choose not to participate in such processes are not compelled to do so. It is in this context that concerns have been raised about how such proposals will lead to delegating rights to communities to regulate matters of family law, which is effectively a move toward some form of cultural autonomy. Maclean (2000, 67) rightly asks, "What are the implications for family justice of this move towards private ordering? Is this form of 'privatisation' safe?" Undoubtedly, in this context formal law provides protection against abuse in the "private" sphere—the sphere in which this legal ordering operates. Maclean (2000, 67) goes on to ask: "Is it dangerous to remove disputes from the legal system with the advantage of due process, plus protection of those at the wrong end of the far from level playing field, and visible negotiation and settlement which takes place of not in court than in the shadow of the law?"

Muslim Alternative Dispute Resolution Mechanisms in Britain and the Experience of Muslim Women

I now turn to describing the development of community and family mediation mechanisms in Britain that seek to resolve matrimonial disputes outside the frame work of state law processes and then draw on the experiences of Muslim women.

The work of Shah-Kazemi (2001) and Bano (2013a, b) illustrates the emergence of Sharia councils within diasporic Muslim communities that act as mechanisms to resolve matrimonial disputes within the family, home, and local communities. This development has been followed by the emergence of the Muslim Arbitration Tribunal (MAT), which operates as a civil law mechanism under the auspices of the Arbitration Act 1996 to produce decisions that may be enforced and relied on in the civil courts. Within British Muslim communities we therefore currently have a three-tiered approach to resolving matrimonial disputes, involving state law, unofficial community mediation (Sharia councils), and the new MAT.

In Britain, Sharia councils can be traced to a diverse set of social, political, and religious developments in civil society. The formation of Islamic religious organizations and their engagement with the state have been characterized by the practice of multiculturalism and the development of "multicultural" state policies to accommodate cultural and religious "difference." And, in the past two decades, a growing number of scholars have explored the changing and contested nature of this relationship, which has revealed a new discursive space of engagement, contestation, and negotiation between minority ethnic communities and the state. One way of viewing this new relationship has been the claim that cultural and religious communities actively seek to avoid interaction and possible conflict with the secular state and hence retreat to the privatized sphere of local Muslim communities where matrimonial disputes are resolved according to principles of Muslim family law.

More recent research has explored the comparative nature of religious councils and tribunals operating in Britain. A 2011 study entitled *Social Cohesion and Civil Law: Marriage, Divorce and Religious Courts in England and Wales*, led by Gillian Douglas, looked specifically at the relationship between religion, divorce, and access to law. The study focused on the work of three tribunals, the Birmingham Sharia Council, the London Beth Din of the United Synagogue, and the National Tribunal for Wales of the Roman Catholic Church. It found both diversity and commonalities between these three mechanisms of dispute resolution, but each sought to avoid conflict with state law in matters of family law. The authors found the process of resolving disputes to be more open and flexible rather than based on rigid religious laws.

The Muslim Arbitration Tribunal that was set up in June 2007 aims to settle disputes in accordance with religious Sharia law. The authority of this tribunal rests with the Arbitration Act 1996, which permits civil matters to be resolved in accordance with Muslim law and within the ambit of state law. For many, this process of resolving disputes may provide the ideal forum that allows the arbitrating parties to resolve disputes according to English law while fulfilling any obligations under Islamic law. One advantage of arbitration, it is argued, is that the parties can achieve some level of autonomy in the decision-making process. This, coupled with the informal setting, lower costs, flexibility, and time efficiency, means that for some it may prove an attractive alternative to the adversarial court system in England and Wales. However, there remain real concerns about whether this process can restrict women's equality and about issues of fairness and justice in family law. Shachar (2001, 573) points out succinctly that "the vision of privatised diversity in its fully-fledged 'unregulated islands of jurisdiction' variant poses a challenge to the superiority of secular family law by its old adversary: religion." This vision of privatized diversity can be applied to the new MAT if we understand privatized diversity as a model in which to achieve and possibly separate the secular from the religious in the public space, in effect encouraging individuals to contract out of state involvement and into a traditional non-state forum when resolving family disputes. This would include religious tribunals arbitrating according to a different set of principles than those enshrined in English law. This approach was advocated by the archbishop of Canterbury, Dr. Rowan Williams (2008, 2), who stated that "there are ways of looking at marital disputes, for example, which provide an alternative to the divorce courts as we understand them. In some cultural and religious settings they would seem more appropriate." He also suggested that the recognition of Sharia in Britain is "unavoidable" and advised that we need to find a "constructive accommodation" of Sharia in the law. Although he was careful not to restrict his general argument to Muslims, but more broadly to all those belonging to religious communities, the focal point was Muslims and the recognition of Sharia in English law. Lord Phillips, CJ (2008: 4) added further weight to the argument when he stated, "There is no reason why principles of Sharia law, or any other religious code, should not be the basis for mediation or other forms of alternative dispute resolution." Both speakers suggested that Islamic mechanisms of family disputes could perform a function not dissimilar to that of the Jewish *beth din* courts that deal with matters relating to marriage and divorce. For Shachar (2008, 580) there are real concerns about individuals being expected to live "as undifferentiated citizens in the public sphere, but remain free to express our distinct cultural or religious identities in the private domain of family and communal life." For her and many other liberal scholars, the issue surrounds the contentious question of where private identity and life ends and public identity begins. She quite rightly points out that if we are expected to express personal identities in the private sphere, at which point in the public sphere do they cease to be so?

In 2011 a private member's bill, the Arbitration and Mediation Services (Equality) Bill, was introduced by Baroness Cox in the House of Lords. This bill generated considerable media attention, as it aimed to make clear the limits of arbitration and make amendments to the Arbitration Act to ensure its compliance with the Equality Act 2010 while seeking to outlaw discrimination on the grounds of sex. Clause 7 of the bill proposes amending the Courts and Legal Services Act 1990 so as to criminalize anyone "falsely claiming legal jurisdiction" or who "otherwise falsely purports to adjudicate on any matter which that person knows or ought to know is within the jurisdiction of the criminal or family courts." Although the bill does not specifically mention Islamic law, it was widely believed to target Muslim communities and to attempt to limit the powers of organizations such as the MAT and Sharia councils. But for many scholars it raised the question of the extent to which state law should intervene in religious councils and tribunals. Though the bill itself failed in its second reading in 2012, Baroness Cox has made clear she intends to reintroduce it to Parliament in the near future. For the purposes of this chapter such developments raise important questions about the limits of personal and group autonomy in such dispute resolution processes. This is now discussed in relation to critiques of mediation.

Mediation and the Experience of British Muslim Women

The normative framework of these bodies is based on a specific set of cultural and religious norms and values that can exclude alternative interpretations and discourse on "Muslim disputing." Women can be both represented in and excluded from various processes of religious dispute resolution. Existing scholarship on the experience of Muslim women using Sharia councils illustrates that those councils that insist that all women seeking religious divorce participate in reconciliation and mediation sessions may serve to reinforce inequality and disadvantage for some women who may already be disempowered in the family and community (Grillo 1991). In this context, feminist and Muslim feminist concerns about negotiating settlements in such privatized spaces where women may have no access to the protection of state law must be seriously addressed. Such concerns cannot be simply understood or framed as part of the debates on "community rights" under the liberal multiculturalist framework but instead must be understood in relation to debates on agency, power, and decision making both in minority communities and among citizens within public civic spaces (Yuval-Davis 2011).

Muslim mediation and arbitration mechanisms can also be imbued with patriarchal relations of power (see Walby 1990) in which gendered power relations are produced and enacted in these community participation processes. But we know that power is not uniformly distributed. Foucault (1990, 95) points to power relations and sites of resistance: "Power relationships . . . depend on a multiplicity of points of resistance: these play the role of adversary, target, support or handle in power relations. The points of resistance are present everywhere in the power network." Existing scholarship (see Bano 2012) suggests that there are sites of resistance within Sharia councils on occasions when, for example, a female counselor may challenge the authority of a particular religious scholar and seek to promote alternative interpretations, albeit in subtle ways. Yet such resistance can also be controlled and maintained within the boundaries of the council. Hence, the female counselor may be consigned to the periphery of the disputing process, her role reduced to one of observer rather than active participant in the decision-making process. By contrast, the position of male religious scholars in the councils is both strategic and negotiated to produce gendered narratives of the role of women in Islam (as mothers, wives, and daughters). Such gendered cultural practices are endemic in the councils and promote the idea that women cannot occupy positions of power in the local community or serve as voices of authority in the local Muslim community. This is not to suggest that such culturalized interpretations of Islam and what it means to be a Muslim woman in British society are neither contested nor unchallenged. However, the space in which women are able to engage in a transformative dialogue within the councils remains limited and tightly controlled.

The evidence suggests that power within Sharia councils is conceptualized in multiple ways, from controlling the boundaries of the Muslim community and homogenizing Muslim identity to sustaining the ideology of the essentialized construction of the Muslim family. Empirical data about Sharia councils thus reveal how these bodies continually seek to reorganize their *administrative* processes to respond to local pressures and the dominant state legal culture while seeking to remain loyal to the specific normative values of Islamic jurisprudence that underpin these models of dispute resolution. What this means in practice is that these bodies model dispute resolution processes on state law mechanisms of governance, emulating processes of rules, procedures, and oversight and promoting "personal choice" as a key component in resolving marital disputes in this space, while staying committed to the ethos and principles of Islamic law and jurisprudence. Nagel and Snipp (1993) describe this process as "ethnic reorganization" that "occurs when an ethnic minority undergoes a reorganization of its social structure, redefinition of ethnic group boundaries, or some other change in response to pressures or demands imposed by the dominant culture."

Official family mediation occupies an intermediate legal and social space at the boundary of state law and non-state forms of ordering (Santos 1987). This conceptual space between state law and personal law is contested, whereupon state law and personal law struggle to establish control (see Abel 1984; Fitzpatrick 1992). This is a process whereby unofficial mediation marks the site on which to resolve marital disputes from the perspective of Muslim religious law. Because of the centrality of gender relations in Muslim family law and in particular the position of women in relation to marriage and divorce, attempts to strengthen or develop unofficial mediation bodies raise questions about the position and autonomy of women who use these bodies to resolve marital disputes.

Yet it is also accepted that the large number of women using these bodies testifies to the argument that "cross-cultural mediation" must also be addressed. In her study Shah-Kazemi (2000, 304) argues that "negotiations within the domain of marital disputes assume a very particular complexity as the dynamics of both gender and identity-defining normative ethics shape the setting in which the negotiations take place." In other words, Shah-Kazemi argues that a Western human rights approach to notions of justice, equality, choice, and rights for Muslim women inevitably obscures the normative orders on which this form of dispute resolution is based. She explains, "Members of the community who consider themselves to be practising Muslims (and the degrees of adherence vary considerably) are keen to involve the intervention of outsiders with religious authority in their marital disputes in an attempt to ensure that the dispute be resolved within a common normative framework" (2000, 307). Critical of adopting a neutral approach to mediation, she argues that "the insistence upon 'neutrality' as a notion in mediation parlance, even when that is contrary to the common ethical framework shared by the parties, results in the imposition of outsiders as mediators to the exclusion of community members, at the expense of achieving the ideal of genuine community mediation" (2000, 319). This study is invaluable for its insights into the complex dynamics of power within families and communities. Women are involved in the process of dispute resolution, and the participation of family members does indeed challenge the assumed hegemonic position of the mediator. For this we are given unique insight into the dynamics of dispute resolution within minority ethnic communities. Yet this community "self-definition" can quite easily fall into the "charybdis of cultural relativism" (Anthias 2002, 275). Clearly, this argument is premised on fixed understandings of culture, identity, and religion. It embraces Sharia councils as creating a new discursive legal space constructed by community members but fails to engage in debates about how they may sanction power within their boundaries of community, personal law, and individual decision making.

A better understanding of this process of unofficial dispute resolution can challenge the binary oppositions of multiculturalism versus feminism, secular versus religious practice, and universalism versus cultural relativism. Current multicultural literature has been extensively critiqued by feminist political theorists, who point to the unresolved tensions and inequalities multiculturalism imposes on women and argue that multiculturism ultimately preserves cultural and religious expression within the framework of cultural relativism, essentialism, and identity politics leading to the disadvantage of women. For many these tensions are most clearly visible in relation to Islam and its "subordinating" effects upon Muslim women (see Okin 1999). While Western women are presented as "enlightened" and bearers of liberal ideals such as equality and non-discrimination, the Muslim female subject is presented as the "other," a victim of cultural and religious practices and thus unable to realize her human rights. Yet such understandings of Islam and Islamic family practice in the West and the so-called demands Islam imposes on the individual, the group, and the state have been challenged from several directions (Modood 2007). One such argument is that Muslim women have been able to negotiate within Muslim families and communities, and thus group membership of the Muslim community (*umma*) does not in itself violate their autonomy or undermine their citizenship rights as individuals within Western societies. Indeed, the very real potential for Muslim women to renegotiate their positions within family, home, local community, and wider society has now given rise to a growing recognition among some feminist liberal theorists that to posit feminism and multiculturalism as oppositional and in conflict leads to a false and misleading dichotomy. The evident inadequacy of viewing Islamic practice as that of insider/outsider not only relegates women in minority cultural/ religious communities to the role of victims but most importantly denies them agency, autonomy, and choice as subjects of their own communities. Thus the experience of women from minority cultural/ religious communities is objectified in pursuance of a liberal political agenda (see Razack 2004).

Traditional legal pluralist scholarship continues to characterize the practice of minority religious personal law systems as a cultural clash whereby the dominant legal system proves irreconcilable to the demands of minority communities located in the West. Such arguments are largely understood as a continuum of conflict and accommodation or a conflict-oriented spectrum whereby the complicated balance between law, religious belief, and personal autonomy is consistently disrupted. This type of scholarship recognizes the plurality of law and dispute resolution processes but equally defines cultural and religious practice as fixed, unchanging, and homogeneous. This discourse of conflict and incompatibility insufficiently engages with processes of change and transformation that open the way for new contestations and developments. As Estin (2008, 8) points outs, "Beyond the work that all families carry out, the multicultural family navigates a complicated balance of tradition and change, home and diaspora, community and autonomy. These families absorb many tensions born of transformation, and pose in turn new challenges for legal orders premised on more stable community membership and identity." Thus communities symbolize the transformation of change, settlement, and diaspora, and they cannot be viewed as fixed, natural social entities; rather, they emerge in specific historical conditions and usually have shifting and contested boundaries, depending on different political projects that include and exclude different categories of people. Moreover, one cannot assume that the members of any community are homogeneous, have the same attachment to the community and its culture, religion, and tradition, or even understand them in the same way, and we must take into account unequal intra-communal as well as inter-communal power relations and competing political projects. Finally the notions of faith and religion have to be understood in an inclusive way, as faith is a syncretic as well as a multilayered construct (see Yuval-Davis 2006).

Religious mediation and arbitration may therefore emanate an emancipatory aura in resolving matrimonial disputes; the consequences for those who use them and for those asked to recognize them are more difficult and contradictory. Analysis of Sharia councils, for example, as official mediation bodies must take into account unequal intra-communal as well as inter-communal power relations and competing political projects. Moreover, this intersectional analysis should include consideration of the fact that mere recognition by the state of particular people as "community leaders" introduces a new element of power that affects intra- as well as inter-communal relations. This might create a tendency to perceive the views of some unelected representatives and leaders of a community as reflecting the views of most of its members, or at least the authentic way members of such a community should view things (Patel 2008).

The right to religious freedom and religious expression underpins discussions of human rights, citizenship, and equality in liberal democracies throughout the Western world. Further, the impact of secularization on women's religiosity raises questions of the personal autonomy, choice, and consent of women belonging to religious communities. Debates over the legal limits of state intervention into the private lives of individuals and the extent to which liberal principles of equality, nondiscrimination, and individual autonomy are manifested in law also raise important questions regarding religious freedom and belief in the context of civic society. These discussions have interfaced with feminist legal theory in order to explore the ways, and extent to which, religious practice and belief limit women's lives, in both the public and private spheres. More recently, feminist scholars have documented and investigated the tensions inherent in much Western political theory regarding the norma-tive values that underpin the liberal state and the difficulties associated with the social and legal regulation of minority and majority commu-nities (e.g., A. Phillips 2007). This literature conceptualizes our under-standing of equality, difference, and rights, while seeking to provide a clearer framework regarding the relationship between individuals' diverse systems of belief, religious activity, and the state.

However, many Muslim women today also live intersectional lives in which their experiences of discrimination may lie on many different fronts. Feminist paradigms relating to the issue of agency and the role of women in family mediation processes reflect in part new and emerging concepts of agency, autonomy, choice, and decision making. These con-versations among feminist scholars take shape within wider debates on intersectionality, feminist narrative theory, postcolonial and decolonial debates, and the effects of liberal and neoliberal legal regimes on women living in minority communities. Scholars such as Ann Phillips have addressed the question of the extent to which agency can be understood in complex, plural, and multicultural contexts. Feminist engagements with agency, autonomy, and decision making "can no longer be under-stood through dichotomies of male domination and female subordina-tion. Instead, inequalities are emerging along generational, class and racial lines where structural divisions amongst women are as significant as divisions between men and women" (A. Phillips 2007, 2).

And what are the moral values embodied in the mediation process? It has been long recognized that mediation occupies both a challenging and contested space within the frameworks of law and dispute resolution. Alberstein (2013) points out that to understand how mediation operates we must consider the "internal ethical and procedural mechanisms in place" that can in fact also prevent unjust mediatory outcomes. She cau-tions against "the image of mediation as a private, contractual phenom-enon, settlement-driven bargaining based on power relations," arguing that this has resulted in a condemnation of the process as an oppressive mechanism that reinforces the inequalities between the parties (2009, 5). Instead, if mediation is understood to be part of a critique of legal formal-ism and communication discourse rather than situated within a liberal rights discourse, it is both transformative and empowering. Furthermore, mediation models can mirror the expectation of its users; for example, the past couple of decades have witnessed a shift away from the rational scientific models of mediation toward a more interpretive paradigm of mediation with a focus on personal narratives and storytelling. The parties lie at the heart of the mediation process. As Alberstein (2009, 5) argues, "Narratives are the materials from which mediation is made, and cultural analysis is a basic tool of mediation work. Under the interpretive paradigm of mediation the reality of the conflict does not exist outside the perceptions of the parties, and the parties themselves are relatedly reconstituted through the process of mediation." Mediation can therefore be understood as part of a process of personal transformation for each party, with the positive change being reflected in the resolution of the dispute. Personal narratives play a crucial role in the process of transformation—alternative stories set forth the conditions on which alternative ways of seeing can be achieved. A re-narrating of personal stories can help transform the conditions on which disputes can be resolved, and new social and cultural perspectives are then taken into account. As Alberstein (2009, 7) points out, "When parties choose to re-narrate their conflict according to new cultural perspectives, they become more aware of progressive legal developments, which often reflect new cultural perceptions. The mediation process helps parties to overcome their exaggerated entitlement perceptions, and through this process, they internalize a more advanced legal regime."

While traditional understandings of mediation and religious arbitration have played a significant role in determining and fixating the subjective experiences of women as one and the same for all, a more nuanced, intersectional, and ethics of care analysis can produce more complex and insightful narratives. Investing in this process makes it possible to draw on the personal narratives of women who choose to use family law alternative dispute resolution (ADR) mechanisms.

Feminist scholarship and the emergent understanding of the lives of Muslim women via an intersectional and feminist ethics of care analysis have yielded insights into these women's personal narratives and the ways in which mediation and ADR processes can be reformulated to suit their needs. Yet given the continued problems of intra- and inter-community power relations and the role of women in the family, home, and community, we must recognize that the protections offered by formal state law remain strategically important and necessary for ensuring that nonadversarial approaches to resolving disputes do not inadvertently create social conditions of violence, coercion, and pressure or put women's safety at risk. In a liberal society the balancing of minority rights must be based on genuine consent and a commitment of choice and the ability to negotiate and renegotiate in multiple and conflicting ways—a true commitment to feminist justice and equality.

Bibliography

Abbas, T. (2014). "British Muslims: From Cultural Assimilation to Social Integration." In S. Yasmin and N. Markovic (eds.), *Muslim Citizens in the West: Spaces and Agents of Inclusion and Exclusion.* Farnham: Ashgate.

Abel, R. L. (1982). *The Politics of Informal Justice: The American Experience.* New York: Academic Press.

Afshar, H. (2005). "Behind the Veil." In H. Moghissie (ed.), *Women and Islam: Critical Concepts in Sociology.* London. Routledge.

Ahmed, F. (2013). "Religious Norms in Family Law: Implications for Group and Personal Autonomy." In M. Maclean and J. Eekelaar (eds.), *Managing Family Justice in Diverse Societies.* Oxford: Hart.

Alberstein, M. (2009). "The Jurisprudence of Mediation: Between Formalism, Feminism and Identity Conversations." *Cardozo Journal of Conflict Resolution* 11(1): 1–28.

Anthias, F. (2002). "Beyond Feminism and Multiculturalism: Locating Difference and the Politics of Location." *Women's Studies International Forum,* 25(3): 275–86.

Bano, S. (2012). *Muslim Women and Shari'ah Councils: Transcending the Boundaries of Community and Law.* London: Palgrave Macmillan.

Bano, S. (2013a). "Muslim Dispute Resolution in Britain: Towards a New Framework of Family Law Governance?" In M. Maclean and J. Eekelaar (eds.), *Managing Family Justice in Diverse Societies.* Oxford: Hart.

Bano, S. (2013b). "In the Name of God? Religion and Feminist Legal Theory." In Margaret Davies and Vanessa Munro (eds.), *The Ashgate Research Companion to Feminist Legal Theory.* Farnham: Ashgate.

Barlas, A. (2006). *Believing Women in Islam: Unreading Patriarchal Interpretations of the Qu'ran.* Austin: University of Texas Press.

Baruch Bush, R. A. and Folger, J. P. (2005). *The Promise of Mediation: Responding to Conflict Through Empowerment and Recognition.* New York: Wiley.

Bottomley, A. and Conaghan, J. (1993). *Feminist Legal Theory and Legal Strategy.* Oxford: Blackwell.

Brah, A. and Thomas, L. (2011). "Religion and Spirituality." *Feminist Review* 97: 1–4.

Charushleea, S. (2004). "Postcolonial Thought, Postmodernism, and Economics: Questions of Ontology and Ethics." In S. Charushleea and E. Zein-Elabdin (eds.), *Postcolonialism Meets Economics*. London: Routledge.

Conaghan, J. (2009). Intersectionality and the Feminist Project in Law." In E. Grabham, D. Cooper, J. Krishnadas, and D. Herman (eds.), *Intersectionality and Beyond: Law, Power and the Politics of Location*. London: Routledge.

Cooper, D. (2004). *Challenging Diversity: Rethinking Equality and the Value of Difference*. Cambridge: Cambridge University Press.

Crenshaw, K. (1989). "Demarginalising the Intersection of Race and Sex: A Black Feminist Critique of Antidiscrimination Doctrine." In *Feminist Theory and Antiracist Politics*. University of Chicago Forum, 139. Chicago: University of Chicago Press.

Davies, M. (2002). *Asking the Law Question: The Dissolution of Legal Theory*. Sydney: Lawbook Co.

Douglas, G. F., Gillat-Ray, S., Doe, N., Sandberg, R., and Khan, A. (2011). *Social Cohesion and Civil Law: Marriage, Divorce and Religious Courts*. Cardiff University.

Dworkin, R. (1986). *Law's Empire*. London: Fontana.

Eekelaar, J (2000). "Uncovering Social Obligations: Family Law and the Responsible Citizen." In M. Maclean (ed.), *Making Law for Families*. Oxford: Hart.

Estin, L. Ann (2008). *The Multicultural Family*. London: Ashgate.

Failinger, M., Schiltz, Elizabeth R., and Stabile, Susan J. (2013). *Feminism, Law and Religion*. Farnham: Ashgate.

Field, R. (2006). "Using the Feminist Critique of Mediation to Explore 'the Good, the Bad and the Ugly': Implications for Women of the Introduction of Mandatory Family Dispute Resolution in Australia." *Australian Journal of Family Law* 20(5): 45–78.

Fitzpatrick, P. (1992). *The Mythology of Modern Law*. London: Routledge.

Foucault, M. (1990). *The History of Sexuality: An Introduction*, vol. 1. London: Penguin.

Fraser, N. (1989). *Unruly Practices: Power, Discourse and Gender in Contemporary Social Theory*. Cambridge: Polity Press.

Gillat-Ray, S. (2010). *Muslims in Britain: An Introduction*. Cambridge: Cambridge University Press.

Gilligan, C. (1982). *In a Different Voice*. Cambridge, MA: Harvard University Press.

Grabham, E., Cooper, D., Krishnadas, J., and Herman, D., eds. (2009). *Intersectionality and Beyond: Law, Power and the Politics of Location*. London: Routledge.

Greatbach, D., and Dingwall, R. (1993). "Who Is in Charge? Rhetoric and Evidence in the Study of Mediation." *Journal of Social Welfare and Family Law* 17: 199–206.

Grillo, T. (1991). "The Mediation Alternative: Process Dangers for Women." *Yale Law Journal* 100(6): 1545–610.

Kapur, R. (2005). *Erotic Justice, Law and the New Politics of Postcolonialism*. London: Glass House Press.

Lichtenstein, M. (2000). "Mediation and Feminism: Common Values and Challenges." *Mediation Quarterly* 18(1).

Maclean, M., ed. (2000). *Making Law for Families*. Oxford: Hart.

Malik, M. (2012). *Minority Legal Orders in the UK: Minorities, Pluralism and Law*. London: British Academy.

MacKinnon, C. (1987). *Feminism Unmodified: Discourses on Life and Law*. Cambridge, MA: Harvard University Press.

Mir-Hosseini, Z., Al-Sharmani, M., and Rumminger, J. (2015). *Men in Charge? Rethinking Authority in Legal Tradition*. London: Oneworld.

Modood, T. (2007). *Multiculturalism: A Civic Idea*. Cambridge: Polity Press.

Mohanty, C. (1991). "Under Western Eyes: Feminist Scholarship and Colonial Discourse." In C. T. Mohanty, A. Russo, and L. Torres (eds.), *Third World Women and the Politics of Feminism*. Indianapolis: Indiana University Press.

Mohanty, C. (1997). *Feminist Genealogies, Colonial Legacies, Democratic Futures*. New York: Routledge.

Nagel, J. and Snipp, C. (1993). "Ethnic Reorganization: American Indian Social, Economic, Political and Cultural Strategies for Survival." *Ethnic and Racial Studies* 16(2): 203–35.

Okin, S. (1999). *Is Multiculturalism Bad for Women?* Princeton, NJ: Princeton University Press.

Patel, P. (2008). "Faith in the State?" *Asian Women's Struggles for Human Rights in the UK* 16(19): 9–36.

Phillips, A. (2007). *Multiculturalism without Culture*. Princeton, NJ: Princeton University Press.

Phillips, Lord Justice (2008). "Equality before the Law." Speech at East London Muslim Centre, 3 July.

Purkayastha, B. (2009). "Transgressing the Sacred–Secular, Public–Private Debate." In A. Narayan and B. Purkayastha (eds.), *Living Our Religions: Hindu and Muslim South Asian American Women Narrate Their Experiences*. Sterling: Kumarian Press.

Razack, S. (2004). "Imperiled Muslim Women, Dangerous Muslim Men and Civilised Europeans: Legal and Social Responses to Forced Marriages." *Feminist Legal Studies* 12(2): 129–74.

Razack, S. (2008). *Casting Out: The Eviction of Muslims from Western Law and Politics*. Toronto: University of Toronto Press.

Roberts, M. (2008). *Mediation in Family Disputes: Principles of Practice*, 4th ed. Farnham: Ashgate.

Sahgal, G. and Yuval-Davis, N., eds. (1992). *Refusing Holy Orders: Women and Fundamentalism in Britain*. London, Virago Press.

Santos, B. de Sousa (1987). "A Map of Misreading: Toward a Postmodern Conception of Law." *Journal of Law and Society* 14(93): 279–302.

Shachar, A. (2001). *Multicultural Jurisdictions, Cultural Differences and Women's Rights*. Cambridge: Cambridge University Press.

Shachar, A. (2008). "Privatizing Diversity: A Cautionary Tale from Religious Arbitration in Family Law." *Theoretical Inquiries in Law* 9(2): 573–607.

Shah-Kazemi, N. S. (2000). "Cross-Cultural Mediation: A Critical View of the Dynamics of Culture in Family Disputes." *International Journal of Law, Policy and Family* 14(3): 302–55.

Shah-Kazemi, N. S. (2001). *Untying the Knot: Muslim Women, Divorce and the Shariah*. Oxford: Nuffield Foundation.

Sharma, A. (1994). *Our Religions: The Seven World Religions*. New York: HarperCollins.

Smart, C. (1992). *Feminism and the Power of Law*. London: Routledge.

Spivak, G. (1988). "Can the Subaltern Speak?" In N. Nelson and L. Grossberg (eds.), *Marxism and the Interpretation of Culture*. Chicago: University of Illinois Press.

Thornton, M. (1991). "The Public/Private Dichotomy: Gendered and Discriminatory." *Journal of Law and Society* 18(4): 38–52.

Walby, S. (1990). *Theorizing Patriarchy*. Oxford: Wiley-Blackwell.

Welchman, L. (2009). "Family, Gender and Law in Jordan and Palestine." In Kenneth M. Cuno and Manisha Desai (eds.), *Family, Gender, and Law in a Globalizing Middle East and South Asia*. Syracuse, NY: Syracuse University Press.

Williams, P. (1988). "On Being the Object of Property." *Signs* 14(1): 5–24.

Williams, R. (2008). "Civil and Religious Law in England: A Religious Perspective." *Ecclesiastical Law Journal* 10(3): 262–82.

Woodhead, L. and Heelas, M. (2005). *The Spiritual Revolution: Why Religion Is Giving Way to Spirituality*. Oxford: Blackwell.

Young, K. K. (1987). "Introduction." In A. Sharma (ed.), *Women in World Religions*. Albany: State University of New York Press.

Yuval-Davis, N. (2006). "Intersectionality and Feminist Politics." *European Journal of Women's Studies* 13(3): 193–209.

3

The Growing Alignment
of Religion and the Law

WHAT PRICE DO WOMEN PAY?

Pragna Patel

> In a world divided by differences of nationality, race,
> colour, religion and wealth, the rule of law is one of the
> greatest unifying factors, perhaps the greatest.... It
> remains an ideal, but an ideal worth striving for, in the
> interest of good government and peace at home and in
> the world at large
>
> —*Lord Bingham 2006*

THE PRINCIPLE OF THE RULE OF LAW begs the question: How do
we safeguard access to justice for the most vulnerable among us? That is
the key question that has preoccupied us at Southall Black Sisters (SBS)
in the past five years or so.[1] Of course, access to justice has always been a
central concern, given that we have long recognized the law as a key, albeit
contested, site of feminist resistance. We have used the law in a variety
of ways to ensure that the most marginalized and vulnerable can exercise their right to equality, justice, and fairness in civil and criminal proceedings. We seek to lay bare the class, race, and gender norms that
reproduce inequality and legitimate exclusionary and discriminatory outcomes for various groups, including black and black minority women.
Our campaigns have challenged the ways in which laws are constructed
around male norms of behavior (P. Patel 2003). They have also highlighted gaps in the law that prevent state scrutiny from being brought to

bear on atrocities and violations committed in the private sphere of the family (M. Patel and Siddiqui 2003). We have protested against failures to take account of unequal power relations within minority communities for fear of "offending" cultural sensibilities (Siddiqui 2005). In other words, we have sought to challenge the supposed neutrality of the law that often offers legal protection in ways that paradoxically reinforce normative and essentialist assumptions of gender, culture, and agency, thus perpetuating the very subordination and victimization that it seeks to remedy. Our attempts to hold the law to account in this sense remain unfinished business.

However, the struggle to access justice has now reached a crisis point. The ever widening shadow of neoliberalism and the rise and dominance of fundamentalist religious identity politics have left us struggling on two interlinked fronts. First, we are compelled to challenge the removal of legal aid from a huge range of civil and criminal proceedings.[2] The government's "reforms" of legal aid are strongly located in a fiscal context that reiterate some of the key overarching aims of the present government: localism, alternative dispute resolution strategies, deficit reduction, and deregulation. Taken together these measures are destroying one of the great pillars of the welfare state. They have forced SBS into leading or supporting legal and political challenges against various legal aid cuts that have an impact not only on individual rights but also on our demands for institutional accountability in the face of abuses of power that seem to be growing rather than diminishing.

This development is directly linked to the challenges that we face on the second front: the increasing privatization of justice and the adoption of a "faith-based" approach to framing and addressing minority issues in the context of austerity and a shrinking welfare state. In the process, the religious Right—fundamentalists and "moderates" alike—have been given the opportunity to influence and shape law and social policy with reference to a regressive religious identity that they have come to define. In the United Kingdom, fundamentalists and "moderates" have made a concerted attempt to operate largely within already established secular, liberal, democratic institutions precisely to lay bare their limitations but for reasons that are entirely different from those of feminists. Unlike SBS and others who have used the law to eradicate the silences in the law in respect of gender bias and other forms of inequality, those on the religious right use the law to perpetuate gender bias and to silence those who seek to dissent from traditional and religious norms. The growing emphasis placed on religious identity has in turn led to demands for the recognition of non-state (minority) legal orders that most clearly have an impact on the human rights outcomes of women, sexual minorities, and other vulnerable groups in minority communities.

It is against this economic and political backdrop that the demand for the recognition of non-state legal orders must be discussed, bearing in mind that the formal legal system represents the final safety net for the most vulnerable minority women: they live in contexts where they are subjected to internal sources of control and power that compete with the state for ultimate legitimate authority over their lives. This is one of the key dilemmas facing black and minority women today.

From Multiculturalism to Multi-Faithism

In the United Kingdom, historically, the struggle for the human rights of black and minority women, especially South Asian women, has also involved a robust challenge to the politics of multiculturalism (P. Patel and Siddiqui 2010). By the 1990s, the multicultural approach (which had by then become a tool of national policy across a range of issues) had lost its radical edge and lapsed into a form of identity politics that drew upon and gave political life to very conservative and religious identities. For minority women, multiculturalism amounted to cultural relativism and nonintervention in domestic violence and other harmful practices, and was therefore a highly contested approach. What was at stake was the struggle for community representation at the political level, a struggle that has been won largely by predominantly religious fundamentalist and conservative forces that use religion as the basis for social identity and mobilization.

This slide from multiculturalism to "multi-faithism" started in the aftermath of the Rushdie affair, but accelerated under successive governments following 9/11, the London bombings, and civil unrest in northern cities in 2001. A new social contract has since emerged between religious leaderships and the British state in which a degree of communal autonomy amounting to less state interference in respect of family matters has been granted to minorities in return for political acquiescence— in other words, the maintenance of public order. This is reflected, for example, in the increasing acceptance of demands made to the state to accommodate, among other things, faith-based schools, religious dress codes, and religious laws governing family matters (as discussed later). The new multi-faith framework has reduced a complex web of social, political, and cultural processes to purely abstract and "authentic" religious values that are determined largely by fundamentalist religious forces often masquerading as moderates. The term *moderate* in the British context is misleading since there is nothing moderate in the way an extreme Islamist agenda that mirrors the classic contours of European fascism is pursued in Britain without respect for the rights of women and sexual minorities. The result is a defeat of the equality paradigm and the rapid desecularization of public culture and spaces (P. Patel and Siddiqui 2010).

Ironically, it was precisely the progressive secular spaces and not faith-based leaderships or groups within minority communities that gave rise to the emergence of campaigns and organizations within minority communities and helped create normative shifts on gender and social justice. Yet these very spaces are now supplanted by state-backed fundamentalist and authoritarian religious bodies, which present themselves as moderate and even progressive while maintaining power and hegemony over the communities that they claim to represent. For example, the East London Mosque and the London Muslim Centre are now key players in the provision of local services in East London. But both have links with the fundamentalist Jamaati-i-Islami movement,[3] whose members have recently been indicted and convicted for war crimes committed in support of the Pakistani army during the Bangladeshi war of independence in 1971 (Sahgal 2004). The Jamaati-i-Islami movement remains active in Bangladesh, where it also has a vigorous and violent youth wing. Yet these bodies have positioned themselves as the key representatives of Muslims in Tower Hamlets and receive considerable support from local and national state organizations and a range of other organizations for their work with, among others, the youth and women (Eade and Garbin 2002; Bhatt 2006).[4] These developments have strengthened religious identity politics and prevented a culture of citizenship and human rights from taking root in minority communities.

The Decline of Legal Aid and the Rise of Mediation

In the United Kingdom, the legal aid system was created in 1949 as a central component of the postwar settlement.[5] It reflected the recognition that a citizen is entitled to legal representation in order to access the courts, so that his or her voice can be heard properly and effectively. Behind the right of representation and access to the courts is a much broader concept of the right to equal protection of the law (Mansfield 2011): a principle that is also reflected in the European Convention of Human Rights, itself a part of the postwar settlement following the previous horrific collapse of civilized values.

By the late 1990s, reforms were introduced that discouraged litigation and placed alternative dispute resolution and mediation at the heart of the civil justice system.[6] At the same time, successive governments have sought to save hundreds of millions of pounds by severely tightening the criteria for eligibility for legal aid. The consequence, as we have seen in SBS and reported elsewhere, has been an unprecedented number of litigants in person in the criminal and civil justice systems attempting to navigate the complexities of the courts entirely alone (Davies 2014). The majority of those who are unrepresented are undoubtedly those who have the least ability to represent themselves and present the greatest vulnerability, and are therefore more in need of legal advice and representation than others.

These developments have forced the judiciary to voice its concerns about the impact of legal aid cuts and the ability of the courts to ensure justice for all parties,[7] as the cases cause delays, clog the court system, lead to miscarriages of justice, and threaten to undermine key principles of the rule of law. There has, for example, been a steady rise in family cases where increasingly outraged judges have ordered the government to pay the costs of representation for vulnerable litigants in person, who are ineligible for legal aid and therefore "trapped in a system which is neither compassionate or even humane" (Hyde 2015).

Our casework at SBS reveals an unrepresented but growing group of vulnerable and abused women who face enormous obstacles in obtaining legal aid in family proceedings, despite the existence of a legal aid exception to the rule to disallow legal aid in family matters for victims of domestic violence.[8] Many women find themselves just above the financial threshold for legal aid or do not possess the requisite time-bound evidence of abuse necessary to qualify for legal aid; some have been failed by institutions that have not recorded their reports of violence properly, while others have no evidence because they have not been able to make reports to the relevant bodies due to personal, cultural, and religious constraints. In consequence, more and more domestic violence victims find themselves face-to-face with their abusers in court or in circumstances where their rights are compromised and costs are awarded against them.

Since 1998, all governments have vigorously promoted mediation on the basis that it is more cost effective than court litigation.[9] Recent legal aid reforms, for example, have led to the introduction of compulsory pre-court mediation in disputes concerning children as well as financial and property arrangements. Before accessing the courts, a couple is legally required to attend a publicly funded (if appropriate) mediation information and assessment meeting (MIAM) for assessment as to whether the matter is suitable for non-court mediation.[10] The MIAM process recognizes that not all cases are suitable for mediation: for example, domestic violence cases are theoretically exempt from MIAM, although this is not always the reality in practice since the evidential threshold for such exemption by proof of domestic violence is the same as that needed to qualify for legal aid. MIAM mediators are, however, qualified and accredited members of the Family Mediation Council (FMC) and have to meet ethical and quality standards that ensure impartiality, confidentiality, and fairness, all of which are enshrined in the FMC's code of practice. In addition, the FMC trained mediators have to be alert to agreements made outside the framework of the law, or to power disparities between participants, and to take steps if these matters are likely to render the entire process unfair.[11] Lawyers can also override mediation where it is deemed to be against the legal interest of their client.

It is clear, therefore, that even where mediation is directed as an alternative to litigation, it operates under the rubric of the law and is underscored by key civil law principles and the rule of law itself. In his now famous lecture in 2006, Lord Bingham outlined the core tenets of the rule of law that are necessary for the proper functioning of a democratic society. They include the need for accessibility and certainty in the law, the absence of arbitrary decision making, equal application of the law, procedural fairness, and compliance with international legal and human rights obligations (Lord Bingham 2006). In other parts of the world where mediation has played a significant role in the formal legal system, it is often also subject to fundamental principles of civil law and constitutional and human rights guarantees (Chowdhury 2012).[12]

However, the incessant push toward mediation to lower legal aid costs brings with it serious problems for abused black and minority women who are disproportionately affected. By the time they engage with the formal legal system, many have already been subject to often traumatizing and ultimately unsuccessful informal mediation meetings involving family relatives and community elders whose main aim is to uphold family "honor" and to keep the matter "private" at all costs. In a significant number of cases that proceed to litigation, family pressure on women to discontinue legal proceedings never ceases. What happens, then, when the state itself pushes women into the hands of unaccountable religious and community-based forms of mediation that lie outside the formal legal system and the rule of law altogether?

Legal Pluralism?

The demand for legal pluralism in the United Kingdom and indeed elsewhere (in effect, parallel legal systems of governance based on customs, codes, and traditions) more often than not springs from conservative and fundamentalist forces in minority communities, but they also enjoy the support of many who consider themselves progressive and on the left of the political spectrum. Advocates argue that modern plural democracies like the United Kingdom should entertain the demand for the recognition of non-state laws because in some instances they are regarded as more legitimate than state laws (Malik 2012). It is said that the accommodation of non-state laws is necessary to counter the imposition of "muscular" (presumably meaning liberal-secular) values of the dominant state on minority groups in the United Kingdom. Some suggest that a new form of "multicultural citizenship" should evolve, allowing for an interaction between, for example, "Sharia" laws and the formal legal system based on the inclusion of marginal groups through dialogue and mutual understanding (Modood 2008). But these assertions should be closely questioned since they gloss over any analysis of patriarchal power and other social dynamics within minority communities in which dominant groups monopolize the terms of the "dialogue" within as well as outside the community. As with state laws, non-state laws do not exist in a power vacuum; they are enmeshed in a complex web of interlinked social, cultural, and religious norms that operate along various axes of power, including those pertaining to caste, gender, class, and sexuality. In a context where religious identity politics is increasingly defining new social relations, demands for the right to be governed by "Sharia" laws cannot escape ethical questions about the nature and implications of such demands. Who has membership of community and do non-state legal orders really enjoy universal legitimacy and authority?

The family is the site most closely governed by fundamentalist-driven non-state legal orders, mainly because of the centrality that is given to women's role in reproduction and socialization in the preservation of collective identity (Yuval-Davies and Sahgal 1992). Religious power (as a separate source of non-state power) regulates women and shapes their rights, privileges, and responsibilities in the family, leading to significant human rights consequences. The state does not have a monopoly on social control mechanisms. Demands for the recognition of non-state legal systems must therefore be located within contemporary political and social processes that seek to shore up elitist religious and patriarchal power in minority communities—a power base that is even less amenable to challenge and to accountability measures than that of the state.

It is no accident that efforts to build parallel legal systems coincide neatly with the rise of religious fundamentalism and political (Salafi/Wahhabi) Islam in particular. There has been a concerted effort by religious fundamentalists to put pressure on the United Kingdom and other European governments to align secular so-called Western laws with Muslim religious beliefs that are deemed absolute and superior to civil law and, indeed, to the rule of law itself.[13] These advocates and their supporters also attempt to conceal or play down the fact that wherever religious laws governing family and personal relations operate, there are movements led by women and human rights activists demanding their reform or repeal for being incompatible with human rights values. In Ontario, Canada, in 2003, for example, a coalition of feminists of Muslim and non-Muslim backgrounds defeated an attempt by self-styled Muslim leaders backed by the government of Ontario to establish a Muslim arbitration tribunal for governance in family matters in accordance with "Sharia" principles (Shahrzad and El-Kassem 2007).

The critical starting point in any discussion of the legitimacy of non-state laws must therefore be the impact that they have on the most marginalized in our communities, such as women, children, and sexual and other religious minorities. Can non-state legal orders afford protection and dispense justice in compliance with the rule of law, or are they a more structured means by which the dynamics of power are hidden and social criticism is suppressed?

Shariafication by Stealth

At the heart of the debate on religion and the law today is the tension between the rights and fundamental freedoms of the individual, on the one hand, and the rights of minorities to religious freedom and educational and cultural rights, on the other. In the domestic arena, the politics of multi-faithism has allowed the demand for freedom of religion to overshadow and undermine the demand for freedom from religion, which comes mainly from marginalized women and other vulnerable groups within minority communities. For example, Muslim fundamentalists and "moderates" have mounted what can be described as a two-pronged pincer-like maneuver that is based ostensibly on the demand for religious tolerance but is in reality a bid for religious privilege and power in which the control of female sexuality is central.

Indeed, the demand for the right to manifest religion has focused largely on the female body, ranging from the imposition of dress codes (Hélie 2012) to demands for gender segregation in public spaces and religious governance in family matters (as described later). Taken together, they reveal the ideological roots of gendered practices. On the one hand, they seek to ensure that religious codes are normalized within the legal system, and, on the other, they seek to formalize a parallel legal system through the establishment of alternative religious forums for dispute resolution in family matters. This process of "shariafication by stealth" of the legal apparatus involves making state law and policy "Sharia" compliant. If successful, it will undoubtedly lead other religions to demand the same level of accommodation.[14]

The attempt to "normalize" so-called Sharia principles within the legal system and the wider public culture can be discerned from cases like that in 2006 of Shabina Begum,[15] a young Muslim girl who sought unsuccessfully to assert her right to wear the *jilbab* to school.[16] She argued that wearing the jilbab was integral to her Muslim beliefs but, in reality, her case masked a profoundly gender-discriminatory agenda driven by fundamentalist forces. Those supporting or sympathizing with Shabina Begum's legal challenge justified it by reference to her right to assert "Muslim female agency" and "choice," while ignoring the lack of "choice" that would have been imposed on the majority of other Muslim girls at the school who did not want the jilbab institutionalized as a Muslim dress code or to be judged by a strand of religion that they did not sign up for.[17]

Cases like these show how the language of "female agency," "choice," and "human rights" is co-opted to reinforce the right to "manifest religion" in ways that extend absolute control over women and others.

Toward the end of 2012, against a backdrop of growing gender segregation imposed by religious forces at public events in universities, Universities UK (UUK), the governing body of British universities, issued guidance that permitted gender segregation of women at university events in order to accommodate the religious beliefs of external speakers.[18] The guidance, presented in the form of a case study, purported to provide advice in contexts in which the right to manifest religion clashes with gender equality. However, far from addressing the question of sex discrimination, the guidance merely legitimized gender apartheid. SBS and others successfully challenged it on the grounds that it violated the equality and nondiscrimination principles enshrined in the equalities (the Equality Act 2010) and human rights law, the product of long and hard campaigning by feminists, racial minorities, and other marginalized groups in society. This was followed by a formal investigation by the Equalities and Human Rights Commission, which found the guidelines to be unlawful.[19] Many dismissed the matter as "a fuss about nothing" and reduced our protests to "mere hyperbole" or "Islamophobia" and "an attack on yet another Muslim practice": views expressed not only by Islamists and conservatives but also by elements of the Left and those who regard themselves as antiracists and feminists (Penny 2013).

Learning nothing from the debacle, the Law Society, a body representing the interests of the legal profession, followed the UUK's lead by issuing guidance to lawyers on how to prepare "Sharia-compliant" wills. The guidance endorsed so-called Sharia succession rules and reminded solicitors of the core principles of "Sharia." It accepted without question the inherent discrimination that exists in Islam (as indeed in other religions) against women and children born outside of marriage. It endorsed discrimination between women and men, Muslims, non-Muslims, "illegitimate" and "legitimate" children, and adopted and non-adopted children.[20]

The Law Society did not consider how it could possibly pronounce on what exactly constitutes "Sharia." What was purported to be Sharia law was in essence fundamentalist and illiberal interpretations of Muslim laws that are vigorously contested by women throughout the world (Zainah 2004).[21] In effect, the Law Society waded into Islamic doctrinal territory by promoting a "Sharia-compliant" legal culture instead of a rights-based culture, thereby blurring the crucial line between law based on religious norms and law based on equality and human rights norms. Disturbingly, the guidance was part of a wider program of training courses developed by the Law Society to encourage "Sharia" compliance in respect of family, children, property, and financial settlements in minority communities. This guidance too was withdrawn following protests and the threat of legal action by SBS and other campaigning groups, such as One Law for All, on the grounds of equality (Equality Act 2010) and human rights laws (Human Rights Act 1998).[22] But there is no room for complacency given that there is a growing appetite in the United Kingdom for a central role of religion in public and legal spaces.

Parallel Legal Systems

In the United Kingdom, the demand for family matters to be governed by "Sharia" laws and through informal religious dispute resolution forums has seen support from influential parts of the British establishment. For instance, in February 2008, the archbishop of Canterbury argued that the application of some aspects of "Sharia" in Britain "seemed unavoidable."[23] His comments were echoed by prominent members of the judiciary, including Lord Phillips, then the lord chief justice, who stated that "there is no reason why principles of Sharia law or any other religious code should not be the basis for mediation or other forms of alternative dispute resolution."[24] He added that there was "widespread misunderstanding" of the nature of "Sharia" laws and that the principles of "Sharia" law could play a role in some parts of the English and Welsh legal system as long as they complied with the law of the land.

A closer examination of the workings of Sharia councils and the Muslim Arbitration Tribunal, two of the most visible forms of religious dispute resolution systems in minority communities, reveals serious failings that flout principles of the rule of law and undermine the rights of women and other minorities in fundamental ways. These forums use "Sharia" laws in highly selective ways; while not seeking to impose strict criminal codes that would entail cruel, inhuman, and degrading forms of punishment (presumably because they know that there is no public appetite for such laws as an alternative to the criminal law), they nevertheless seek state sanction for imposing civil and family codes that accord women lesser social and legal status than men.

Sharia councils in the United Kingdom emerged as informal, self-organized systems of religious arbitration and mediation in the 1970s and 1980s and were closely tied to the development of Muslim organizations and mosques that follow a range of schools of Islamic jurisprudence. In practice, there is considerable variation in interpretation and opinions across the many Sharia councils that exist in the United Kingdom, reflecting a range of customs and traditions (Bano 2012). Some of those who sit on the councils are clearly fundamentalists and have publicly endorsed female genital mutilation, wife beating, and stoning for adultery as obligatory in Islam.[25] As our own research (as described later) and other reports have shown, others are a little less literalist but are nevertheless socially conservative, even if they outwardly profess to adhere to the principles of equality.[26]

A body of emerging evidence shows that Muslim women are not well served by Sharia councils, which appear to function primarily as means of exercising control over female autonomy and policing the boundaries of religious and community affiliation. The emphasis is centrally on mediation for the purposes of reconciliation, even if this conflicts with gender equality. For example, on a question of domestic violence, a leading "judge" at a London Sharia council stated:

> It depends on the situation. We have to look at the bigger picture. Why? Because so many women who have been divorced they regret it after that. We see it. I saw it in the Islamic Sharia Council. They regretted that. And because they regret, yeah, sometimes we tell that you have to be careful. And there is in all legal theories, there is something called the small problem that can be overlooked to avoid bigger problems, small harm that can be overlooked for a bigger harm. So we apply the same thing. (Council of Ex-Muslims of Britain 2014)

In her study of Sharia councils, Samia Bano (2012) recounts the overwhelmingly negative experiences of the Muslim women who engaged with various Sharia councils. Most of her interviewees described the pressure, obstacles, discrimination, and hostility they faced in their attempts to seek a divorce or obtain a resolution to their family problems.

In many respects, the Muslim Arbitration Tribunal (MAT) follows a pattern of decision making similar to that of the Sharia councils, except that it makes use of the Arbitration Act 1996 to pronounce "legal" judgments in matrimonial (divorce), child (residence/access/custody), domestic violence, forced marriage, and inheritance cases. On the face of it, the MAT seeks to present itself as a formalized professional, quasi-legal body that adheres to formal legal rules of engagement and to nondiscriminatory principles. However, a closer examination of the MAT website shows that there is nothing in its operation to suggest that it is any different, irrespective of what it publicly states and irrespective of the views of some individuals associated with it. It is unequivocal as to its real objective, which is to resolve civil disputes in accordance with "Islamic Sacred Law,"[27] which is by its very nature immune to state scrutiny.

The prime concern of the MAT is to achieve reconciliation between women seeking a divorce and their husbands even where there is evidence of abuse and violence. Indeed, reconciliation is viewed as a moral duty (to preserve the sanctity of religious values) and as a religious obligation (many claim that a divorce cannot be pronounced without reconciliation). But evidence shows that the MAT's approach to family matters flies in the face of established good practice and leads to profoundly unequal outcomes and violations of rights in which the state by its acquiescence is implicated.

All too often, as the MAT's own website, SBS, and other research by, for example, Bano shows, in such religious forums women's claims of abuse are negated or minimized and women are humiliated, blamed, and told to try harder to make their marriage work. Divorces initiated by women are delayed and pressure is exerted on women to waive their entitlements to children, property, and finances following the breakdown of a marriage. A particularly disturbing practice proudly displayed on the MAT website is a willingness to intervene in criminal proceedings in domestic violence cases, while publicly stating that it is "unable to deal with criminal offences." The MAT is clearly confident of its position, power, and influence in effecting reconciliations with abusive partners and then using these to persuade the Crown Prosecution Service to "reconsider" charges, irrespective of the offenses committed or the associated risks.[28]

Similar problems abound in respect of the MAT's approach to forced marriage. In the MAT report "Liberation from Forced Marriage," for instance, the MAT states that the practice of forced marriage is a "cultural" practice that has to be distinguished from "Islamic" values.[29] However, the problem with this approach is that it fails to acknowledge the perception and reality of those who are forced into a marriage, often through a combination of interchangeable cultural and religious norms and practices. The MAT explicitly states that its judges are left to "form an opinion on the basis of the individual before them" but without undertaking any risk assessments. The report distinguishes between "appropriate free will marriages" ("where the man and the woman have met at work or are friends through links between their families or indeed are blood related through their families") and "inappropriate free will marriages" (marriages that take place after prolonged courtship/cohabitation by the couple; this is deemed to be inappropriate in the light of Islamic laws).[30] This distinction clearly gives license to Muslim "judges" and "scholars" of Islam to strictly regulate female sexuality (deemed permissible only if related to the family) and to reproduce the subjugation of women in the family on the basis of what they consider to be authentic versions of Muslim values. It is clear, then, that religious fundamentalists are determined not only to oppose human rights norms but also to roll back existing norms on the grounds that "true" or "authentic" religious values are corrupted by cultural practices, which in effect mean greater and not lesser control and surveillance over women's lives.

There is also evidence that the MAT undermines the legal rights of women in other ways. For example, in one case involving inheritance of family property following the death of parents, a woman was given less than her brothers because religious laws deemed that she should not have equal rights to inheritance and that she should instead be dependent on her brothers for financial support (One Law for All 2010). Similar patterns of women's human rights violations within such parallel legal systems are echoed in other studies elsewhere (Canadian Council of Muslim Women 2007).[31]

It would seem that the sole aim of the MAT is to present itself to the state as a legitimate mediator on family matters in an attempt to oust the position of minority women's organizations that have historically campaigned against domestic violence and forced marriage on feminist principles and that have sought accountability from the very people who now seek to preside over such cases. Complicity of the state in processes that allow religious tribunals like the MAT to sanitize the pursuit of an illiberal agenda by appearing to adhere to the formal rules of the Arbitration Act 1996 does enormous damage to feminist campaigns for due diligence and state accountability to extend to gender-related crimes committed in the private sphere. By shifting responsibility for delivering justice to privatized bodies, the state clearly abrogates from its role as an enabler of human rights and instead increases the sphere of influence of non-state actors; individual family members, religious organizations, and fundamentalist groups are allowed to violate women's rights with impunity.

Parallel Legal Systems: The Experience on the Ground

Far from exercising cultural or religious autonomy, the vast majority of minority women who use non-state legal systems are compelled to do so mainly out of social compulsion, but also due to lack of knowledge of their legal rights or lack of alternative support systems, often in circumstances where there is no legal aid and the wider legal system has let them down.

Findings from a recent SBS study of twenty-one abused women of various religious backgrounds, who engaged with Sharia councils and other religious authorities, suggest that they are exercising a highly constrained form of agency and choice in contexts in which the stranglehold of religion has left them little room to maneuver.[32] The study came out of growing concern within SBS casework about the gendered impact of the entrenchment of the multi-faith approach in law and social policy and, in particular, the rise of religious forms of alternative dispute resolution within minority communities. All the respondents were aged between twenty-five and fifty, had largely South Asian but also African backgrounds, and had fled abusive husbands and in-laws. Some had been born and brought up in the United Kingdom, while others had arrived as spouses of British nationals or through other immigration routes. Many were living in women's refuges or had obtained alternative social housing in West London, Rotherham, and Newcastle, after having received support from women's domestic violence projects in their areas. Many of the women were in the process of resolving their marital and related problems, including obtaining protection orders and regularizing their immigration status. For the overwhelming majority, the decision to flee abuse had led to their isolation, deterioration of their mental health, and a drop in their living standards. They were therefore vulnerable, and their well-being, if not their lives, was continuously at risk. In seeking out this cohort of women in particular, our aim was to assess the impact of religious arbitration decisions on the most severely marginalized within society to assess whether the exercise of female choice and agency varies depending on the socioeconomic background as well as social practices and political ideologies in which they are located. The study examined the reasons women sought recourse from religious authorities and the outcomes of such engagement.

We found that not a single woman in our study chose to use religious arbitration forums to seek redress in respect of violence, children, property, or financial matters. The only area where roughly half sought religious intervention was that of divorce. But even here their reasons were often complex and had more to do with the fact that, unlike their husbands, they could not declare unilateral divorce and therefore had to seek religious permission to end their marriage. Unlike Jewish women, theoretically, Muslim women do not need the consent of their husbands to obtain a divorce, but they do need approval for a religious divorce from a religious scholar. Sharia councils have therefore developed a divorce "service" to meet this "need," although ironically the existence of this need is a fairly recent phenomenon that appears to coincide neatly with the rise of political Islam. From around 1970 to the mid-1990s, many of the Muslim women that we assisted were content with a civil divorce only and did not seek a religious divorce.

Some women sought a religious divorce because they had never registered their marriage in the first place and so could not obtain a civil divorce. Others sought a religious divorce following automatic referrals by community organizations that worked on the problematic assumption that a religious divorce was of paramount importance to their identity as Muslim women. Significantly, the majority of women who sought a religious divorce did so only after obtaining a civil divorce, which indicates that they regarded the civil system as very relevant to their lives. Some, on the other hand, remained skeptical about the entire process of seeking a religious divorce. The following excerpts reveal the difficulties experienced by a number of women:

> To be honest, I'm not really a religion person; I am Muslim, right, but I don't know the history, why they need it, need to know that you're divorced, but I think it's wrong. If you have, like, a letter or a legal divorce, then it's more than enough to know; it doesn't have to say [on some paper that it is a] Sharia council divorce.

I'll be honest with you as a Muslim, someone who believes in the purity of this faith, I don't like Sharia councils, I don't think they should exist, they are for men, that's it. It's predominantly men on those councils, so four or five men are going to sit around a table and decide whether I can file for this or not when God has already given me the permission to do it.

Often women sought a religious divorce because they wished to remarry in order to avoid the hardships they would face as single parents or because they were under considerable pressure from their families to remarry. Some felt that remarrying was the only way they could start life again without fear of ostracization and discrimination as female divorcees:

It would be bad; they would say bad things like she's married without getting divorced—you know, [like] those people who are considered untouchable, who wash dishes and no one even talks to them.

I mean, if I didn't apply for a divorce and started living with a man, then the community would be up in arms and my family [would] be shamed, saying that I'd come here and look at what I was doing, that I'm doing wrong things.

Marriage for some was also a means of asserting sexual autonomy, albeit heavily circumscribed by the patriarchal framework of marriage:

I thought I would get married. . . . Unless you've had an Islamic divorce, no one wants to marry you without a divorce and no one gives you permission to get married.

Many of the women who sought the help of Sharia councils or religious authorities to obtain a divorce recounted negative experiences of not being heard and of being forced into mediation. They were told to be tolerant of abuse and to allow their abusive partner access to their children even if this contravened formal court protection orders and orders forbidding perpetrators' access to children:

To be honest with you, the experiences I'd had with these *maulanas* and *masjids* telling me to be patient with abuse and violence, and I was saying . . . these Sharia councils are set up by men for men, that's how I see it and as for mediation, I said it's past mediation, I don't want mediation or anything to do with him or his family and . . . he has no right to his children. The courts have already decided that he has no access to the children, and my daughter's turned eighteen and she took out an injunction against him, and my other children can when they turn eighteen as adults; they'll do it to protect themselves because they've seen what kind of monster we lived with and they were on the receiving end of it.

One pregnant woman was told that she could not obtain a divorce because under Islam it was forbidden for a pregnant woman to do so. Another woman was granted a divorce only after it became clear that she was willing to waive her entitlement to maintenance and property:

> I mean, he and I had been separated for many years by that point, he wasn't giving me any maintenance. . . . And he didn't do anything for me, so you see this way it's easy to get a divorce, and so they didn't ask me too many questions because there were no impediments. It wasn't as if he was giving me, he didn't give me any maintenance, nor did I ever take anything from him, the house . . .

Women often experienced undue delays and obstructions in obtaining a religious divorce. For example, Sharia councils would allow unresponsive husbands considerable time before finally approving a divorce, thus keeping distressed women in a state of uncertainty and anxiety and sometimes even at risk of further violence.

By far, the majority of women who approached Sharia councils for divorce were destitute or facing financial hardships as single parents and benefit claimants, yet most were made to pay considerable amounts of money to obtain a divorce. This led one woman to declare that Sharia councils were operating purely for financial gain:

> I approached Birmingham and they wanted 200 pounds plus [about US$300]; it was purely financial. . . . I did write in and say I don't agree with the money, why are you asking me to say, you're just going to sit around and look at my evidence, why do you need paying admin cost, for what? A stamp to Pakistan and Rotherham,

what's your admin? [The administrative costs of such a process would be minimal and at most would amount to nothing more than the cost of a postage stamp; hence the high fees incurred are not warranted.] Because nobody ever spoke to me on the phone.

The majority of women who sought a religious divorce labored under the misapprehension that such divorces were legally valid elsewhere, a myth that Sharia councils were only too willing to perpetuate since it consolidated their pivotal role in the community as interpreters and custodians of religious values. There is in fact no single codified "Sharia" legal framework, and even among the four main schools of Sunni Islamic jurisprudence there are numerous interpretations and applications of Muslim laws, which vary according to ethnic, national, and cultural diversity. There is consensus, on the other hand, on the death penalty for apostasy, homosexuality, and adultery (One Law for All 2010).

Moreover, in many Muslim-majority countries, Muslim family laws have undergone progressive reforms in family matters that have created legal precedents, yet none of this is reflected in the decision-making processes of the religious arbitration forums in this country. The point here is not only that the decisions of Sharia councils and the MAT are arbitrary and inconsistent among the different forums within the United Kingdom, but that even across the Muslim world, a decision by one religious tribunal may not be recognized as valid by another religious tribunal or even by a Muslim-majority state. In Pakistan and Bangladesh, for instance, religious divorces obtained in the United Kingdom are not recognized by the formal courts applying Muslim family laws, whereas civil divorces are accepted as valid divorces between Muslims (Akbar and Balchin 2006).

Do Minority Women Want Religious Arbitration in Family Matters?

In another SBS study conducted in 2009–10 to map the impact of shifts in government policies on integration and multi-faithism, the findings showed that although the majority of the twenty-one South Asian women interviewed were believers and often turned to religion for spiritual sustenance, none expressed any sense of belonging to a faith-based community (P. Patel and Sen 2011). The majority saw religion differently and were acutely critical of aspects of their tradition, culture, and religion for perpetuating gender inequality and discrimination. Their responses challenged the fallacious assumption that those who have no access to or interaction with broader society identify with their particular faith communities or view religion as a counter-hegemonic voice. Far from inspiring confidence and trust, the growing power of religious authority evoked a range of fears about the control that it would have over their lives:

> I would never go to a temple or *gurdwara* for help. I wouldn't feel happy about talking about myself. I feel they would judge me. . . . I couldn't trust them to keep things confidential. . . . I come to SBS to share my innermost feelings. I have never been anywhere else. I couldn't go to a *gurdwara* or temple or *masjid*. I would rather die than go there.

> There is no need for religious laws. Because if you look at the Hindu religion, we had things like sati [immolation of widows]. Everyone has the right to live. Hindu religion will never treat women equally. Hinduism says that a husband is like a god and not to answer back. . . . Not right. Everyone should be treated equally in law.

Most women regarded religion as a continuation of the community collusion that they experienced when seeking to escape violence and oppression. They also recognized religious institutions not just as places of religious worship but as profoundly gendered, elitist, and corrupt spaces in which rival factions often bid for power and authority and/or seek financial or political gain:

> Doesn't make a difference if there are men or women trustees— they feel superior to devotees. . . . I don't know why they have to feel so superior. It is the public that gives them their status. The politics of these places is very dirty. Very corrupt—that's the word— corruption. If anyone rebels against their ideas they would be against that person; they never encourage women to divorce until it happens to their own daughter.

Women were adamant that if religious leaders or institutions took control and became arbitrators of justice, this would close down the rich, syncretic, and dynamic expression of identity that women had struggled to create. Far from religious governance, what they valued most were the everyday forms of secularism that characterized their lived reality:

> There is an increase of women in *hijab* and burkas. Islam doesn't say that you have to show off your religion. Once my daughter was in a *salwar kameez*. One lady in a full burka asked if she was Muslim and asked why she was wearing a *salwar kameez*. My daughter got very angry and said that this was not forbidden. I do not like people telling me what to do.

> Tomorrow I go to celebrate Valentine's Day. Islam says we shouldn't dance. . . . I used to get awards for dancing. I love celebrating Valentine's Day. I will wear red clothes and red lipstick and get a red rose from my husband. I wear lots of make-up and perfume. I also love celebrating Christmas and Easter. These are small pieces of happiness.

Many also cherished the secular spaces provided by organizations like SBS, which they experienced as empowering, giving them access to other ideas, traditions, and cultures. Significantly, many regarded secular state laws as their best hope for obtaining justice:

> Islam does not force anything on anyone, so why should those who live within it force others? I want my children to know what it says in Islam. The main principle is to live by humanity. They should not look at color. The poet Iqbal—our greatest poet—said, whether black or white, poor or rich, old or young, we should all obey Allah. If there is no difference for Allah, why do we bring about difference? I like his [Iqbal's] idea of unity for all human beings.

> First of all, I am a human being. Every other identity comes from being within this community. It is not important to me what religion. I am a Hindu Punjabi but for my own peace of mind, I go to the *gurdwara* and the temples.

> Sikhism is in the heart. I have a clean heart. I'm not hurting anybody. That's what religions is . . . not hurting anybody. It's humanity. At the end of the day it's a human right you are looking at.

Contrary to the view, therefore, that turning away from the cultural and religious life of a community is not an option for most women (Phillips and Dustin 2004), our experience shows that minority women are exercising their right to abandon aspects of their culture and religion that they find oppressive on a daily basis, and in large numbers, even though they remain conflicted and distressed by their ensuing experiences of vilification and isolation. This is precisely why the loss of legal aid, which restricts their access to the formal legal system and therefore to rights and justice, is so devastating.

To Regulate or Not to Regulate?

Advocates of the accommodation of non-state legal orders cite the idea of *joint governance* or various types of reform or regulation of the parallel legal system as a means of overcoming the problem of the lack of protection for the rights of minority women and others (Sachar 2008). But it is difficult to see how a state that has taken a slash and burn approach to legal aid and to the welfare state will be persuaded to provide the resources, training, judicial oversight, licensing, and monitoring that are necessary to regulate what is in effect a second-rate system of justice so that it complies with acceptable ethical and human rights standards. The economic and ideological factors that drive the state to privatize justice are the very factors that explain its tendency to stay out of religion. "Joint governance" also presupposes willingness by those in charge of religious arbitration forums to bring about internal reform and to give up their power to apply religious norms that they regard as superior to secular laws.

The sole aim of Sharia councils and the MAT is to mediate and adjudicate on family matters according to "divine law" and to reject what they consider to be Western secular laws or norms of democratic governance, including the rule of law. They are, in fact, highly political institutions that justify their own existence with reference to regressive religious identity.

Malik, on the other hand, advocates the notion of *cultural voluntarism* as a means of regulation. This is based on the assumption that minorities such as Muslims should have the freedom and autonomy to live according to their preferred social norms, legal rules, and religious law, *except* that at all times judges and legislators have the right to intervene where there is incompatibility with an important principle of English law or, most crucially, a conflict with constitutional or human rights norms.

She argues that cultural voluntarism provides opportunities for the voluntary dynamic transformation of the norms of Islamic law that are being followed by Muslims in this country. It also provides the potential for a constructive dialogue between mainstream state institutions and Muslim minorities (Malik 2013).

Malik maintains that under cultural voluntarism there is nothing to stop the courts from applying what she calls the "principle of severance" to those parts of Islamic law or Islamic religious practice that are incompatible with UK family law, and cites by way of example the English judicial approach to the cases of *KC and NCC v. City of Westminster* and *EM Lebanon*.[33]

KC and NCC v. City of Westminster involved attempts by parents to force a marriage on a young, extremely vulnerable man whose mental age was that of a three-year-old and who did not have the mental capacity to consent to marriage that was contracted over the phone to a woman in Bangladesh. The question before the court was whether or not to recognize the marriage as valid. Expert reports produced for the court on behalf of the young man's parents stated that the marriage was perfectly legitimate according to "Sharia" and civil laws of Bangladesh. Ultimately, the court refused to recognize the marriage on the ground that the young man did not have the mental capacity to consent to a marriage and therefore the marriage could not be recognized in English law.

EM Lebanon was a case involving an abused Muslim woman who sought asylum in the United Kingdom, having fled highly discriminatory Muslim family laws in Lebanon that would have deprived her of custody of her young daughter, for whom she was the sole caregiver. The case wound its way to the Supreme Court, which decided the right to family life for the child and the mother would be violated if they were returned to Lebanon.

In both cases, Malik applauds the courts for showing judicial restraint in not condemning Islamic laws or Islamic religious practice outright and instead providing what she perceives to be a more nuanced judicial examination of the public interest concerns raised by the cases (Malik 2013). In reality, however, what was on display in both cases was not so much cultural voluntarism as unequivocal judicial denunciation of abhorrent family practices legitimated by religion and supported by "Muslim experts" that were deemed to be incompatible with human rights principles, namely the rights of Muslim women and mentally ill adults to protection and to private and family life. The central feature of both cases is that the judicial oversight necessitated not partial severance but wholesale severance of discriminatory religious values that govern the family in ways that are antithetical to fundamental human rights. It is arguable that in rejecting such practices the judiciary (acting out of what seemed to be political sensitivity) did not go far enough in engaging with the cases explicitly on gender-discrimination grounds. With respect to *EM Lebanon*, for example, feminist and legal commentators have argued that the case should have been explicitly decided on gender-equality principles. Freedom from gender discrimination and the right to gender equality per se must be recognized as a universal and fundamental human right and therefore accorded the same higher status that is currently enjoyed by race discrimination in international human rights law (Monaghan 2010). There is considerable force to this argument, which in my view must extend to an examination of gender discrimination that is inherent in formal and informal customary and religious laws and practices throughout the world, including the imposition of dress codes and the denial of women's rights in areas such as marriage, property, and children. But the cases also raise two additional points. First, even though they were decided on public interest grounds, public interest and human rights and ethical concerns cannot be easily divorced from each other, particularly as growing societal awareness of exploitation, abuse, and harm committed in private spaces by non-state actors enhances our understanding of what constitutes human rights abuses and therefore public interest concerns. Second, there can be no state accommodation of religion in family matters since it is precisely family matters that lend themselves to harm and discriminatory gender practices; the family is the only sphere that is readily amenable to culturally relativist processes and therefore to violations of women's human rights and democratic values.

Although the law intervened in its protective capacity in these cases, a considerable cause for concern is that in the majority of cases involving religious arbitration, any decisions on matters relating to women and children may be unlawful or incompatible with domestic and international human rights norms but will not be scrutinized by the courts because complaints will rarely be made by the complainant women. For example, the decisions of the MAT are intended to have a legal effect, since they use the framework of the Arbitration Act 1996 to make a legally binding agreement, as long as the agreement entered into is voluntary and in all respects complies with the rules.[34] But the point here is that the social forces of compulsion that lead women to religious arbitration forums are the very same as those that prevent them from bringing complaints. Sharia councils, on the other hand, are not constituted in the context of the Arbitration Act 1996, so their judgments are not legally binding within English civil and criminal law, but they are nevertheless widely used by the state, for example, through the work of social services and other local authority departments as "experts," and therefore they have an indirect influence on individual legal cases.

Thus, whether direct or indirect, state backing for the work of religious forums will, in effect, mean state backing for the most patriarchal, discriminatory, and often repugnant practices and will actually enforce a lack of choice on the most vulnerable within minority communities. This can and will lead to uncertainty, confusion, and more injustice in a sphere where rights violations already arise. Moreover, in a context where there is considerable deference to multi-faithism, the endorsement of differential norms of justice will also encourage relevant legal and public bodies to defer decision making to the religious authorities for the sake of economic and political expediency and out of fear of being labeled racist or Islamophobic.

Ultimately, the aim of religious fundamentalists and conservatives alike is to use religion to govern family and private matters in ways that ensure that the human rights laws of the secular authorities never enter their sphere. If successful, efforts to embed religious codes in civil law and/or set up parallel legal systems that lie outside of the formal legal system will create a lethal space for the resurrection and perpetuation of harm and patriarchal control over women, vulnerable adults, and children. Indeed, profound questions arise as to female agency for women of minority religious backgrounds in contexts where it is reconfigured within an overarching fundamentalist ideology and politics underpinned by a forceful patriarchal framework that is dependent on a return to so-called authentic religious values. This is why the view that religious norms in relation to the family can be regulated so that they are compatible with human rights standards is both misleading and dangerous.

───────────────

The accommodation of non-state legal orders within state institutions has blurred the critical line between religion and the law in ways that further institutionalize the inequality and marginalization of minority women and other subgroups. If we apply a rule of law analysis to religious-based systems of arbitration and mediation, we can see that many minority women are denied due process at every step of the way. There is no evidence of any meaningful commitment to key principles of the rule of law: accessibility, transparency, impartiality, confidentiality, certainty, procedural fairness, the absence of discretion, and compliance with international human rights obligations. There is no evidence to suggest that the state's duty to exercise due diligence, necessary to examine the harm done and to guarantee human rights, will be readily applied to separate non-state legal systems, given that the state consistently fails to apply due diligence to cases involving the violation of human rights committed by non-state actors.[35]

The growing alignment of the law and religion must therefore be treated with great caution since it contributes ultimately to the privatization of justice, which excludes the application of the principles of the rule of law and legitimizes the fallacious view that the formal legal system and secular human rights values are Western and alien constructs to which minorities have contributed nothing. In our day-to-day work at SBS, we have found little evidence that the most marginalized groups of women within minority communities want engagement with the "marketplace of Islamic ideals" (Malik 2012) or indeed other religious ideals in family matters since they readily recognize that religion is itself implicated in violence, community power, and state structures that militate against their rights and seeks to exert influence over their lives. Indeed, any such engagement would make a mockery of the many struggles for equality and accountability that have been waged by minority women within and outside of the formal legal system. It must be remembered that it is the political struggles by black and minority feminists, not "internal dialogue" with fundamentalist and "moderate" patriarchs with vested interests, that has led to important normative shifts in key areas, including violence against women and child sexual abuse in minority communities.

Those who argue for the formal recognition of non-state personal laws suggest that having recourse to religious forums does not mean that minority women are seeking to opt out of the wider political community, only that they are seeking the right to be governed by their own norms (Malik 2012). But this misses the point entirely: women are not choosing to opt out at all—they are being opted out by religious fundamentalist and conservative forces. Women are denied access to the tools they need to withstand pressures to conform to custom or to invoke a broader set of citizenship and human rights. In the process, they are denied the right to participate in the wider political community as citizens rather than subjects. Ultimately, we need to ask the question that has been posed by human rights commentators in these debates: Why has it come to be accepted, even in human rights circles, that family law may be culturally particular rather than subject to universal human rights norms? (International Council on Human Rights Policy 2009).

The demand for the accommodation of non-state legal orders within the formal legal system is inextricably connected to the rise of religious fundamentalism and neoliberalism, both of which seek to privatize justice for their own ends. What we are witness to is the mobilization of law, religion, and culture in support of political power without accountability. That is why our struggle to keep the law and religion separate, as part of our wider struggle for access to justice, has become the defining struggle of our times.

Notes

1. Southall Black Sisters (SBS) is one of the United Kingdom's leading anti-racist and feminist organizations. It was set up in 1979 to meet the needs of black (Asian, Afro-Caribbean, and other minority) women to counter the multiple and overlapping forms of discrimination, including racism and sexism, that are faced by such women and to give them a voice in the public sphere. SBS operates a specialist center for women who experience violence and abuse within the family. Its work includes campaigning on behalf of black and minority women, providing casework, information and advice, counseling, and other practical support to women who have fled gender-based violence.

2. See http://www.southallblacksisters.org.uk/tag/legal-aid/.

3. See "The Islamic Right: Key Tendencies," *Awaaz—South Asia Watch*, June 2006; http://freethoughtblogs.com/maryamnamazie/files/2013/03/Islamic-Right-Key-Tendencies.pdf, accessed 16 June 2016.

4. See also, e.g., Women's Link and the Maryam Centre projects established and operated by the East London Mosque and the London Muslim Council. Women's Link makes clear that its aim is to offer advice and counseling services to women from within a faith-based perspective, while the Maryam Centre, organized through the Muslim Women's Collective and linked to the East London

Mosque, claims to offer Islamic counseling and domestic violence services to Muslim women in East London and other parts of London. It positions itself as the only women's network in the area. Both projects clearly operate within a faith-based perspective rather than a feminist or rights-based framework. http://www.eastlondonmosque.org.uk/news/maryam-centre-%E2%80%93-first-anniversary-opening, accessed 14 June 2016.

5. See Legal Advice and Assistance Act 1949.

6. Lord Woolf introduced far-reaching reforms of the civil justice system, which included alternative dispute resolution and led to the Civil Procedure Act 1997 and the Civil Procedure Rules in 1998.

7. See, e.g., K & H (Children: Unrepresented Father: Cross-Examination of Child) [2015] EWFC 1.

8. This was achieved after much campaigning by SBS and other women's groups in the United Kingdom. See Southall Black Sisters for further details on their policy submissions and legal challenges on this issue.

9. See "Modernising Justice," 1998 Cm 4155, 1998. HMSO, London (1998).

10. See 10 (1) of the Children and Families Act 2014 and also Practice Direction 3A: Family Mediation Information and Assessment Meetings (MIAMs), Ministry of Justice.

11. See Code of Practice, Family Mediation Council; http://www.familymediationcouncil.org.uk/us/code-practice, accessed 14 June 2016.

12. In Bangladesh, for instance, the use of "in-court" mediation in family matters as a part of the court process is commonplace. It is presided over largely by judges who act as in-court mediators. It is clear that mediation operates very closely with the law, since mediators use legal discourses to protect women's rights in mediation and not to undermine them. The law is seen to embody equality and is therefore regarded as the touchstone for standards in mediation. This acknowledgment is of vital importance, since the view is that the law is more likely to uphold women's rights and women's equality than is recourse to community values that involve built-in discrimination against women. This form of "evaluative mediation" with its aim of reducing power disparity and enhancing fair outcomes, however, is viable in contexts where recourse to litigation by women is itself very problematic for various socioeconomic reasons in Bangladesh. But even those who advocate the advantages of mediation in the Bangladeshi context acknowledge that evaluative mediation must be informed by laws that are gender equalizing and progressive and give women their legal rights. See Choudury (2012).

13. The Muslim Brotherhood ideologue Yusuf al-Qaradawi, who is the chair of the influential European Council for Fatwa and Research, has advocated governance by Sharia laws for European Muslims for some time. In an interview in the *Guardian* he defended wife beating, although of the "only lightly" sort,

and expressed his extreme intolerance for homosexuality. See Bunting (2005). Elsewhere he has also advocated punishment for female rape victims who dress "immodestly." See http://www.telegraph.co.uk/news/uknews/1466715/For-her-to -be-absolved-from-guilt-a-raped-woman-must-have-shown-good-conduct.html, accessed 14 June 2016.

14. There are signs that with growing state acceptance of so-called Muslim family laws, Hindu and Sikh groups will also make similar demands for the formalization of their own forms of religious-based dispute resolution systems. Hindu Council UK and Hindu Forum of Great Britain, influenced by right-wing Hindu nationalism in India, for instance, seeks communal hegemony over Hindu Indians in the United Kingdom by attempting to create a singular "Hindu" identity and to turn Hinduism into a belief rather than a diverse set of practices. The aim is to make the task of political representation as well as internal control and discipline easier.

15. R (Begum) v. Governors of Denbigh High School [2006] UKHL 15.

16. A *jilbab* is a full ankle-length dress.

17. For a full discussion see P. Patel (2013).

18. The guidance declared that gender segregation was permitted for "genuinely held religious beliefs." See also https://www.opendemocracy.net/5050 /radha-bhatt/university-challenge-secular-neutrality-or-religious-privilege, accessed 14 June 2016.

19. "Equality and Human Rights Commission Rules That Gender Segregation Is Unlawful." One Law For All, 23 July 2014; http://www.onelawforall.org.uk /equality-and-human-rights-commission-rules-that-gender-segregation-is -unlawful/, accessed 14 June 2016. See also "Gender Segregation at Events and Meetings," Equality and Human Rights Commission; https://www.equality humanrights.com/en/publication-download/gender-segregation-events-and -meetings-guidance-universities-and-students, accessed 14 June 2016.

20. Following legal action and campaigning by SBS and others, in 2014 the Law Society withdrew the practice note. See http://www.southallblacksisters.org .uk/law-society-withdraws-sharia-wills-practice-note/, accessed 14 June 2016.

21. For example, the Law Society guidance cites as one of its main references a text on Islamic wills and testaments by Muhammad Al Jibaly, a fundamentalist who has publicly defended practices such as public lashings and death by stoning. See https://www.islamweb.net/emerath/index.php?page=articles&id =14830, accessed 14 June 2016.

22. SBS argued that the Law Society was in breach of Section 149 of the Equality Act 2010 and Articles 8 and 14 of the Human Rights Act 1998. See also "Law Society Withdraws Sharia Wills Practice Note." Southall Black Sisters. http://www.southallblacksisters.org.uk/law-society-withdraws-sharia-wills -practice-note/, accessed 14 June 2016.

23. See "Civil and Religious Law in England: A Religious Perspective." Lecture delivered by the Archbishop of Canterbury at the Royal Courts of Justice in February 2008; http://rowanwilliams.archbishopofcanterbury.org/articles.php /1137/archbishops-lecture-civil-and-religious-law-in-england-a-religious-perspe ctive#sthash.mcNqfM98.dpuf, accessed 14 June 2016.

24. See speech given by Lord Phillips at the East London Muslim Centre on 3 July 2008 endorsing the use of Sharia laws in martial disputes; http://news .bbc.co.uk/1/hi/uk/7488790.stm, accessed 14 June 2016. The previous minister of justice, Lord Hunt, also supported the role of the MAT in tackling family matters like forced marriage.

25. Haitham al Haddad, for example, is a well-known fundamentalists who also sits as a "judge" at the Islamic Sharia Council. Other fundamentalists such as Suhaib Hassan also sit as "judges" on Sharia councils. See Council of Ex-Muslims of Britain (2014).

26. A BBC Panorama report in 2013 showed that a number of Sharia councils in England and Wales, including the Leytonstone Sharia Council, were "putting women at risk" and clearly displaying gender bias in areas such as family and divorce matters. Jane Corbin, "Are Sharia Councils Failing Vulnerable Women?" *BBC Panorama*; http://www.bbc.co.uk/news/uk-22044724, accessed 14 June 2016.

27. See Muslim Arbitration Tribunal; http://www.matribunal.com/.

28. See http://www.matribunal.com/family-dispute-cases.php, accessed 14 June 2016.

29. See "Liberation from Forced Marriages." MAT. http://www.matribunal .com/MAT_Forced_%20Marriage_%20Report, accessed 14 June 2016.

30. "Liberation from Forced Marriage," MAT (n.d.); http://www.matribunal .com/MAT_Forced_%20Marriage_%20Report, accessed 14 June 2016.

31. See also evidence of gender discrimination uncovered by a BBC report on the operation of Sharia councils and Jewish *batei din* in the United Kingdom. "Sharia Laws in Britain." 16 April 2015; http://www.bbc.co.uk/podcasts/series /r4report, accessed 14 June 2016. See also Canadian Council of Muslim Women (2007).

32. Forthcoming report by Southall Black Sisters on the use of religious arbitration authorities by black and minority women in the United Kingdom.

33. KC & Anor v. City of Westminster Social and Community Services Department & Anor [2008] EWCA Civ 198; EM (Lebanon) v. SSHD [2008] UKHL 64.

34. The Arbitration Act 1996 provides for recourse to any form of arbitration on civil matters, including religious arbitration, and depends on the written consent of both parties. It was historically set up to address contractual disputes, and the idea was that people could access these avenues voluntarily if they

desired. The act provides the space for any community to establish its own forms of religious dispute resolution, and as a result religious leaders are making use of the act to gain state sanction for retaining religious and cultural autonomy in family matters. This is most clearly evidenced by the establishment of the Muslim Arbitration Tribunal. The concern is that the decisions made under the Arbitration Act are legally binding and can be enforced by county and high courts, provided that both parties have agreed to be bound by the outcome of the religious arbitration.

35. See, e.g., the 2014 report by Her Majesty's Inspectorate of Constabulary (HMIC), which documented the continuing widespread police failures in handling domestic violence. https://www.justiceinspectorates.gov.uk/hmic/wp-content/uploads/2014/04/improving-the-police-response-to-domestic-abuse.pdf, accessed 14 June 2016.

Bibliography

Akbar, S. and Balchin, C. (2006). *Recognising the Un-Recognised*. Women Living Under Muslim Laws Publications.

Anwar, Z. (2004). "Islamisation and Its Impact on Laws and the Law Making Process in Malaysia." In A. Imam, J. Morgan, and N. Yuval-Davies (eds.), *Warning Signs of Fundamentalisms*. Women Living Under Muslim Laws Publications.

Bano, S. (2012). *Muslim Women and Sharia Councils*. London: Palgrave Macmillan.

Bhatt, Chetan (2006). "The Fetish of the Margins: Religious Absolutism, Anti-Racism and Postcolonial Silence." *New Formations*, special issue: "Postcolonial Studies after Iraq," no. 59, Autumn.

Bingham, Lord (2006). "The Rule of Law." Sixth Sir David Williams Lecture. http://www.cpl.law.cam.ac.uk/sites/www.law.cam.ac.uk/files/images/www.cpl.law.cam.ac.uk/legacy/Media/THE%20RULE%20OF%20LAW%202006.pdf, accessed 14 June 2016.

Bunting, M. (2005). "Friendly Fire." *Guardian*, 29 October. http://www.theguardian.com/world/2005/oct/29/religion.uk1, accessed on 14 June 2016.

Canadian Council of Muslim Women (2007). *Canadian Muslim Women at the Crossroads: From Integration to Segregation*. Gananoque, ON: Canadian Council of Muslim Women.

Chowdhury, J. (2012). *Gender, Power, and Mediation*. Cambridge: Cambridge Scholars.

Council of Ex-Muslims of Britain (2014). "Evangelising Hate." Report by the Islamic Education and Research Academy, May. London.

Davies, James (2014). "UK Government Tried to Hide the Chaos Caused by Legal Aid Cuts." *openDemocracy*. https://www.opendemocracy.net/ourkingdom

/james-davies/uk-government-tries-to-hide-chaos-caused-by-legal-aid-cuts, accessed 14 June 2016.

Eade, John and Garbin, David (2002). *Changing Narratives of Violence, Struggle and Resistance: Bangladeshis and the Competition for Resources in the Global City.* Oxford Development Studies, 30(2).

Hélie, A. (2012). "Problematising 'Autonomy' and 'Tradition' with Regard to Veiling: A Response to Seval Yildrim." Symposium on Religion in International Law. *Santa Clara Journal of International Law* 10(1): 93–105.

HMIC (2014). *Everyone's Business: Improving Police Response to Domestic Violence.* London: Her Majesty's Inspectorate of Constabulary.

Hyde, J. (2015). "Munby: Legal Aid System 'Neither Compassionate nor Humane.'" *Law Society Gazette*, 7 January. http://www.lawgazette.co.uk/law/munby-legal-aid-system-not-humane/5045849.fullarticle, accessed 14 June 2016.

International Council on Human Rights Policy (2009). *When Legal Worlds Overlap: Human Rights, State and Non-State Law.* Versoix: International Council on Human Rights Policy.

Malik, M. (2012). *Minority Legal Orders in the UK.* London: British Academy.

Malik, M. (2013). "Islam and English Law." *Prospect Magazine*, July. http://www.prospectmagazine.co.uk/magazine/islam-english-law-courts, accessed 14 June 2015.

Mansfield, M. (2011). "Unequal Before the Law? The Future of Legal Aid." *Solicitors Journal.* http://www.younglegalaidlawyers.org/sites/default/files/Unequal_before_the_law_legal_aid_report_june_2011.pdf, accessed 14 June 2016.

Modood, T. (2008). "Multicultural Citizenship and the Anti-Sharia Storm." *openDemocracy*, 14 February. https://www.opendemocracy.net/article/faith_ideas/europe_islam/anti_sharia_storm, accessed 14 June 2016.

Monaghan, K. (2010). "*EM (Lebanon) v Secretary of State for the Home Department (AF (A Child) and others intervening).*" In R. Hunter, C. McGlynn, and E. Rackley (eds.), *Feminist Judgments: From Theory to Practice*, 449–58. Oxford: Hart.

Muslim Arbitration Tribunal (n.d.). "Liberation from Forced Marriage." http://www.matribunal.com/MAT_Forced_%20Marriage_%20Report, accessed 14 June 2016.

One Law for All (2010). "Sharia Law in Britain: A Threat to One Law for All and Equal Rights." http://www.onelawforall.org.uk/wp-content/uploads/New-Report-Sharia-Law-in-Britain_fixed.pdf, accessed 14 June 2016.

Patel, M. and Siddiqui, H. (2003). "Sad, Mad, or Angry? Mental Illness and Domestic Violence" In R. Gupta (ed.), *Homebreakers to Jailbreakers*, 109–31. London: Zed Books.

Patel, P. (2003). "Shifting Terrains: Old Struggles for New?" In R. Gupta (ed.), *Homebreakers to Jailbreakers*, 234–60. London: Zed Books.

Patel, P. (2013). "Multifaithism and the Gender Question: Implications of Government Policy on the Struggle for Equality and Rights for Minority Women in the UK." In Y. Rehman, L. Kelly, and H. Siddiqui (eds.), *Moving in the Shadows*, 41–58. Farnham: Ashgate.

Patel, P. and Sen, U. (2010). "Cohesion, Faith and Gender: A Report on the Impact of the Cohesion and Faith-Based Approach on Black and Minority Women in Ealing." Southall Black Sisters and Oxfam. http://www.southallblacksisters .org.uk/reports/cohesion-faith-and-gender-report/.

Patel, P., and Siddiqui, H. (2010). "Shrinking Secular Spaces." In R. Thiara and K. Gill (eds.), *Violence Against Women in South Asian Communities*, 102–27. London: Jessica Kingsley.

Penny, L. (2013). "This Isn't 'Feminism': It Is Islamophobia." *Guardian*, 22 September. http://www.theguardian.com/commentisfree/2013/dec/22/this-isnt -feminism-its-islamophobia, accessed 14 June 2016.

Phillips, A. and Dustin, M. (2004). "UK Initiatives on Forced Marriage: Regulation, Dialogue and Exit." *Political Studies* 52(3): 531–51.

Sachar, A. (2008). "Privatising Diversity: A Cautionary Tale from Religious Arbitration in family Law." *Social Science Research Network*. http://ssrn.com /abstract=1151234, accessed 14 June 2016.

Sahgal, G. (2004). "Two Cheers for Multiculturalism." In A. Imam, J. Morgan, and N. Yuval-Davies (eds.), *Warning Signs of Fundamentalisms*. Women Living Under Muslim Laws Publications.

Shahrzad, M. and El-Kassem, N. (2007). "Cultural Relativism: Theoretical, Political and Ideological Debates." In *Canadian Muslim Women at the Crossroads: From Integration to Segregation*. Gananoque, ON: Canadian Council of Muslim Women.

Siddiqui, H. (2005). "There Is No 'Honour' in Domestic Violence Only Shame! Women's Struggles Against 'Honour' Crimes in the UK." In L. Wlechman and S. Hossain (eds.), *"Honour" Crimes, Paradigms, and Violence Against Women*, 263–81. London: Zed Books.

Yurdakul, G. (2007). "Islam and Decision Making: The Effects of Religion and Family in Muslim Women's Lives." In *Canadian Muslim Women at the Crossroads: From Integration to Segregation*. Gananoque, ON: Canadian Council of Muslim Women.

Yuval-Davies, N. and Sahgal, G., eds. (1992). *Refusing Holy Orders*. Women Living Under Muslim Laws Publications.

Zainah, A. (2004). "Islamisation and Its Impact on Laws and the Law Making Process in Malaysia." In A. Imam, J. Morgan, and N. Yuval-Davies (eds.), *Warning Signs of Fundamentalisms.'* Women Living Under Muslim Laws Publications.

4

Family Law and Mediation in Practice in England and Wales

Sarah Beskine

AS A SPECIALIST FAMILY LAWYER and family mediator I work in a number of fields of family law, including divorce, financial issues following matrimonial and relationship breakdown, disputes regarding arrangements for children, domestic abuse, and international child abduction. This chapter reflects my experience of more than twenty-five years of case work in law and fifteen years in mediation in Hopkin Murray Beskine, a specialist London lawyers' practice I jointly manage. We are experts in family law as well as human rights, public law, and landlord and tenant issues. London is a diverse community, and our clients come to us from a variety of backgrounds and with very different resources at their disposal, from clients with very high value financial divorce matters to the very poor. One feature of London is the high price of housing and the scarcity of affordable social housing. Divorce clients might have very substantial assets if they own a house in London but not always a high income.

This work focuses on the interrelationship between the fields of family law and mediation. I explore the use of family mediation and the prerequisites to ensuring effective and positive mediation that protects participants from reaching an unfair resolution, either as a result of a lack of knowledge of the legal context of their dispute or because their individual circumstances might suggest that mediation is not suitable.

Like many practices, ours comprises energetic and enthusiastic lawyers who love their work and feel privileged to be able to offer services to both private and legally aided clients. If a client's income is low enough and the case falls within the work authorized under the current rules, the client can instruct us and be funded by legal aid. This is either free to the client, or with a monthly or one-off contribution. It is no mean feat to be able to say we still offer legal aid work alongside privately funded work. This is because over the years, cuts and complexities added to the system have left it hard to access, overburdened, and vulnerable to minor technical errors; it is not easy to practice and provide legally aided advice.

The legal aid scheme underwent fundamental changes in April 2013 (Legal Aid, Sentencing and Punishment of Offenders Act 2012), which resulted in a reduction of provisions available. However, despite widespread belief to the contrary, legal aid is still available for a wide range of family law advice. Too few agencies and user groups realize that there is still a great deal that is funded but it is hard to access. Domestic violence is a priority, but it is also used as a "gatekeeper," leading to a full range of legal aid available for virtually all types of family disputes. For any case involving domestic violence, legal aid may be available not only for advice about the violence itself, but also for the work relating to almost any kind of family dispute, including disputes about children and money. Legal aid is also still available for family mediation. Mediation as a form of dispute resolution process is used for other disputes too—for example, some local authorities have neighbor mediation schemes—but these are not funded under legal aid and are outside the scope of this chapter.

Mediation

Since the implementation of the Legal Aid, Sentencing and Punishment of Offenders Act 2012, family mediation financed by legal aid provision has fallen by more than one-third. Some years back, mediation was promoted as cheaper, quicker, less stressful, and providing better solutions than courts and the legal process. The National Audit Office had found that family breakdown problems resolved through professional family mediation were cheaper and quicker to settle, and secured better outcomes, particularly for children, because they were less acrimonious.[1] Legal aid was made available to couples to encourage them to mediate in an attempt to resolve their differences, rather than go to law or court.[2]

It was obvious to most practitioners that the argument that mediation was always the best and cheapest form of dispute resolution was flawed.

Those cases that were settled in mediation were inherently more likely to be settled in any form of dispute resolution processes. They would be the cases that were settled quickly and easily in the legal process too. It is undoubtedly better for those cases to be settled in mediation. However, it would be wrong to assume from the experience of that group of cases that mediation is therefore the best forum for settling all disputes.[3] Intractable problematic cases, where issues of safety and inequality were prevalent, were never the types of disputes that would be settled easily in mediation and should not be pushed into mediation.

Making legal aid available to mediate family disputes in the early 1990s encouraged a number of lawyers to train in the field. This is how I came to mediation. Lawyers saw a way in which we could enhance our practices and use our existing Legal Aid systems to fund a new alternative approach and to expand the services we could offer our clients. Mediation can also directly involve children. They can come to a meeting with a mediator to talk about their own hopes in the situation. For this to take place, their parents must both agree and must also be able to agree on how to manage the possible outcomes of such a meeting.

There are many other forms of alternative dispute resolution, including informal arrangements between friends to help each other resolve differences and more formal systems within different communities, including religious communities. What differentiates mediation in the context of family law, or the shadow of it, is that it involves the availability and consideration of independent legal advice.

Essentials for Mediation

For mediation to be a service recommended to a couple, several prerequisites are essential in my opinion. It can be carried out appropriately only when both parties are aware of their legal rights and responsibilities and when the mediator has a role above and beyond her work as a mediator face-to-face with clients. This role is to consider with clients whether mediation is the appropriate service, taking into account issues of power differences, the need for safety and protection, and a range of other criteria.

We do not usher all clients into mediation. For some it is entirely inappropriate and harmful; for others, it just does not suit them. We consider the suitability of mediation for and with each of the clients, either separately or, if they both wish, together. They take part in the decision as to whether to proceed or not into mediation. This process is often referred to as "screening."

Screening

Both clients and the mediator need to agree that mediation is a suitable service for the clients to use to settle their dispute. The first and essential question is: Is mediation the correct process for this dispute and these people? To answer that question, we refer to our knowledge of the dispute and the law and listen carefully to the issues the clients want to resolve. Recognized family mediators are trained to consider these issues in the first meeting. Mediators should identify when to refer clients out of the mediation process if they need the support or the strength of the law instead, or to another service, such as counseling, if they are trying to reconcile. The mediator will consider facts such as the following:

· Can both clients freely speak their minds?

· Is there a power difference that, as a mediator, I cannot bridge for the weaker participant?

· Is one party so intimidated by fear of repercussions that mediation just could not work?

· Is there a need for the power or authority of the courts?

Sometimes the answers to these questions may be obvious—for example, where there is abuse or domestic violence or a threat of child abduction or removal of assets. In such cases, mediation is not suitable, because the clients, or at least one of them, need a more direct form of assistance and help from the law itself. One not untypical example is that of a client who returned home from visiting family abroad to find that her husband had changed the locks on the family home and had put another of his properties on the market to sell. That property was in his sole name and also represented most of the assets available between them. He proposed to pay her a very small sum sufficient only to help her put down a deposit on a one-bedroom flat for her and their child. The only way to protect the assets so as to keep them available for reasonable negotiation or a court adjudication as to how to distribute them was by the court's power. A court has power to make an immediate order to prohibit the sale of a property. This in turn allows an entry on the registered records of ownership that will prevent a sale by ensuring that no purchase would be registered without a court order. The client was also able to use the law to obtain an order to require the husband to let both her and the child back into the family home to live and to provide her with a key.

Sometimes there are more subtle reasons why mediation would not be the best forum—for example, anxieties about the manipulation of children. Maybe years of undermining emotional and psychological abuse have gradually eroded one party's ability to hold her own in negotiations, or one party may be vulnerable as a result of a mental health difficulty. If there is such a level of inequality, mediation is almost never suitable. In situations like this, mediation is likely to reflect the imbalance already existing between the couple.

Legal Advice and Mediation

In addition to the screening process, to make mediation effective and suitable, participants also need access to good-quality legal advice. It is crucial to ensure that participants in mediation are resourced with a broad knowledge of their legal rights.

This is because, to reach an agreement in mediation, to negotiate successfully, participants need to know more than simply what they want to achieve from the negotiation. They need to know what alternative methods may be available for achieving their desired outcome and becoming informed about the strengths and weaknesses of the other party's positions. This puts the negotiation in a wider framework. It makes it possible for the conflict to be considered and hopefully resolved, by taking into account factors existing beyond the limit of the disagreement that emerged within the relationship, such as legal rights and responsibilities of which the couple may have been unaware.

Ideas and proposals about how to resolve conflict are shaped to a degree by the environment within which the conflict emerges. As a lawyer I often find people are shocked and surprised when they are properly advised about the rights they have. They are surprised that a family law judge will recognize their position even if it is not apparently a clear or strong one. This is perhaps the most important insight that the lawyer brings to discussions about the value and risks of alternative dispute resolution. It indicates that ill-informed or relatively less powerful parties to the dispute may be ill served by mediation without safeguards.

Understanding the relevance of family law is essential to anybody who has a family dispute. There is a wide range of dispute resolution mechanisms on offer, and it is important that people use them with the benefit of informed choice. This means choice about which dispute resolution process is best for them, as well as choice about the compromise to reach, if any.

If you were bidding for something at an auction, either you would already know the value of the item you were bidding for, or you would have researched it in advance. In the same way, before entering negotiation or mediation in relation to what are often the most important decisions and disputes in your life—managing your primary relationships, marriage, children, assets—it is important to know objectively how reasonable or strong the parties' respective positions are.

You also need to address as a preliminary point what you want to achieve. In this you are severely limited if you have no idea of the strength or weakness of your position.

You need the law in a number of places. You need it to help you decide if it is appropriate to use mediation in the first place, and you need it again to help you weigh the strengths and weaknesses of your position as mediation progresses. In my experience the first step is obtaining advice about your legal rights. After that you can think about practical steps, such as which process to use—for example, mediation informed by family law, other forms of mediation, including those within families or extended families or provided specifically within one religious community, inter-cultural mediation services, collaborative law, arbitration, or law. Choosing the process comes second to an understanding of your rights, responsibilities, strengths, and weaknesses.

Legal Issues in Family Breakdown

A typical example of not recognizing rights occurs when a relationship breaks down and the ex-couple are thinking about how to achieve living apart. Many people, especially women, are under the impression that they have no rights to continue to live in the family or matrimonial home. It may be in the sole name of her partner or husband. He may be demanding she leave. Yet since the 1970s the law has recognized her rights to live there and be protected along with her children.[4] This information appears in my experience not to have been widely assimilated.

A surprisingly small number of people are aware of their rights to remain living in the family home even if the other party, who owns it, wants them to leave. In fact, in certain situations, such as when one party is the main caregiver of children and the other's behavior is damaging or harmful, the non-owner can require the *owner* to leave until a court looks at the longer-term issues of who owns what, often in months to come. Need of the home is far more significant than whose name is on the ownership deeds or tenancy contract. If you do not know this, any mediation not only is severely limited, but will almost inevitably lead to an outcome very different from the outcome of a dispute where both parties are properly informed about the legal context.

Conversely, another example is the idea of the "common-law wife," which is still popular. This has no basis in law. Either you are married or you are not. Civil marriage and civil partnership are vehicles that provide the greatest legal protection on breakup, as well as a public commitment of togetherness. If you are not married, you do not have that protection. The marriage has to be a civil marriage. A marriage that is not recognized by the state administration is not the same. I have clients who have had a religious marriage but not a civil marriage. While they still need to go through the appropriate steps within the religion to obtain a divorce, and while they may be seen as married within the religion, they are not treated as spouses by the civil courts. It is essential that if a client has a religious marriage she ensures that the ceremony is recognized in civil administration of marriages. If not, she will not have the full protection that civil marriage affords.

Couples still have rights outside marriage, but they are not as comprehensive and certainly not as clear. Also they are not always as "strong." In particular, in terms of finance and property, the right to a financial share has to be carefully and skillfully established, and it is not always possible to do this. Same-sex couples who wanted to marry before civil partnership existed are in a complex legal position. They can try to establish that the intention to marry had existed, even if they were not able to in fact marry. This is less open to cohabiting couples who could have married. These are complex technical arguments, and clients need advice to understand their position in these cases. Similarly, if a couple had a religious marriage but not a recognized civil marriage, they need legal advice as to their legal position vis-à-vis assets and property of the relationship. The legal status of men in relation to children depends on whether they are married to the mother and whether their names appear on the birth certificate. These are key issues and require legal advice as they lead to parties having drastically more or drastically fewer rights and opportunities to share the assets of the relationship.

So for mediation to be safe and effective it has to be combined with good-quality legal advice. What are the key elements of good legal advice? Lawyers have to be able to understand what their client wants. This is the starting point of the client–lawyer relationship. A lawyer needs to listen in order to understand the client's concerns, which will underpin choices and goals. Priorities might include the importance of a particular school, a need to live close to extended family here or abroad, or the fear a child will be abducted or her mind "poisoned" against one parent. Other issues of great concern include the importance of a *get*, or marriage contract, in Jewish marriages, an understanding of mechanisms of *mehrieh* to negotiate divorce agreements or financial settlements.[5] It is important to note whether any such sum is engulfed by the value of a share of a London home, as can easily or usually be the case. It is essential that lawyers be alert to the dangers in the client's situation, protecting property especially if it is only in one person's name. Religious differences and different practices in relation to the disciplining and guidance of children can create difficulties while parents are together, but these can become insurmountable if they split up. Some of these issues fall squarely within a court's jurisdiction and some cannot be pursued effectively within most family law courts.

Legal advice has to be three-dimensional. It has to help a client understand the priorities of the court, how much room there might be to maneuver, and what impact the law and its decision will have in practice, in real life, and on the family and extended family. The best way to put this knowledge into effect is to identify a plan of action. There is a need to be clear and to explain why a certain goal is not realizable and help the client search for and decide on the best alternatives.

It can take clients several meetings to understand their legal position, and this might involve communication between different advisers. The aim is to identify the best plan, and this can be done as long as the pros and cons of every option are explored and explained and the different ways of achieving the plan considered.

It is very important to recognize the impact of change on the other areas of dispute. Moving out of a family home will mean that the arrangements for payment of the mortgage or the rent have to be reviewed. What welfare benefits will a family be entitled to? How will the accommodation and food be paid for if the main earner refuses to offer financial support—for example, when the wife and mother leaves with the children?

Will there be an impact on immigration status? This will depend on the client's status in the United Kingdom and whether it might be linked to the partner's status. Are all these surmountable problems? Are there solutions available with specialist immigration advice? How will a father establish contact with a child if he cannot remain in the United Kingdom?

Deciding to leave an impossible family situation is the hardest step, followed very quickly by the practical problems of achieving this. Contemplation of the practical difficulties can be so overwhelming as to prevent change. Practical issues can include finding an alternative accommodation, paying for it, dealing with the children's distress, the partner's anger, the disapproval of family and others, and the danger of violent repercussions or emotionally damaging fear of repercussions. Withstanding the complexities of a wave of emotional and practical problems at a time when the children in the relationship will be at their most needy is very difficult. Clear legal advice can be a starting point for understanding a way through the maze. With knowledge, clients can decide how to achieve the end result they are aiming for. Do they need to access the court's power to protect a child or assets? Can the issues be resolved by discussion and compromise in mediation?

Legal Guidelines

In family law a court can consider the best arrangements for children, and in such a case it considers a range of issues. These include the ascertainable wishes of the children in light of their age or understanding, their physical, emotional, and educational needs, the likely effect on them of any change in their circumstances, their age, sex, background, and any other characteristics that the court thinks are relevant, any harm the children have suffered or are at risk of suffering, how capable each parent or any other person the court thinks is relevant is of meeting need, and the powers that the court has available.

How should an ex-husband or ex-wife divide their assets? Most would say "fairly," but that is a very broad term and relative to what each person or wider community thinks is fair or reasonable. The court also says assets should be divided fairly. As a basic approach, the court would split things equally if an equal split would cover the needs of the children and the parties. If it did not, which is often the case, then needs come first and there would be an unequal split. Therefore, often the spouse looking after the children needs more and thus gets more if there are not enough assets to make an equal split possible. Sometimes a party gets a deferred share, for example, when the children are older and the house can be sold.

The court has a checklist that must be taken into account. The priority is to consider how to ensure adequate maintenance and housing for the children until they leave full-time education. After this the court looks at how long the parties have been married, the assets each party has and how they got them, their earning capacity, standard of living in the marriage, ages and health, contributions made, and, only very rarely, conduct.

Long ago the court separated behavior from the division of assets. That is why the conduct of each spouse is rarely relevant. It comes into play only if it is inequitable to disregard it—and usually it is linked to financial conduct. Conduct that might be taken into account includes running up legal fees by refusing to obey rules about showing financial papers to the other party, hiding money deliberately, or dissipating assets extravagantly or in an attempt to prevent the other spouse from having a share.

The Practice of Family Mediation

Mediation is often seen in opposition to the use of law to resolve a family problem. However, as I hope I have described, it is not appropriate to use mediation without a broad understanding of the legal issues and a clear grasp of how a family court would view the dispute. This means that when you choose one path, you have a good sense of where you would get to if you took another. For this reason most alternative dispute resolution systems insist on advising users to get legal advice as well. It means that all participants can make informed choices.

It is nonetheless important to recognize that the work of mediation is very different from the work of a lawyer. Lawyers represent the interests of one client. We put the client's interests first, and only the client's interests. The lawyer's job is to offer knowledge and explain choices, to advise on the likely outcome and the consequences of each choice. The lawyer's job is not to judge a decision that clients might want to make or make the decision for them, but to advise them on what is achievable and the likely outcome and then to follow the instructions.

The role of a mediator is in complete contrast to this. It is to represent neither party, but to take, as far as possible, a neutral position to assist the parties in reaching a real, lasting agreement. Mediators can give *information* about the law, but they cannot *advise*. Their job is to help the couple reach an agreement that might already be in the air—an agreement a mediator will try to capture, crystallize, and then draft so that it can become legally binding or lasting, for example being referred to court through the parties' legal advisers.

Mediators, like lawyers, have to try to understand as much of the full agenda that is in front of them as they can. For example, mediators might be trying to mediate arrangements for children. The mother may be apparently reluctant to let the children see the father. The mediators might find on further discussion that the real issue underlying all of this is that the husband will not give the wife a religious divorce if it is solely in his power to give one, or the wife cannot tolerate the husband letting the children meet his new partner or a change in religious practices.

Mediation can provide the time and attention to issues that parents think are important. The courts do not always operate like this. Time is very limited in court, so opportunities to provide a delicate, sensitive plan can be varied. Mediation can offer the opportunity to explore things in more detail. We might find that a difficulty is not, for instance, about the arrangements for the children at all, but it is a preexisting parental conflict that has developed or anger over failure to make financial provisions. All these issues can easily spill over into current arrangements for the children once the parents have split up. Mediation is not counseling or reconciliation. It is a way of agreeing on arrangements as parties separate, looking toward the future.

Disputes about children arouse the deepest and most passionate feelings in my experience, especially as they often arise as the relationship is breaking down, when emotions are the most heightened anyway.

Disputes about children can be the battleground for the couple's own deep dispute. These differences have probably existed for years and were managed within the relationship, including things like different parenting approaches or accepting that one parent holds all the power or controls the assets. While these could be tolerated more or less in the relationship, as soon as the relationship ends the toleration abruptly ends too and disputes that have been around for a long time come to the surface.

Mediation can help put these disputes into context and help the couple decide on which ones are to be ignored and which matter. Court processes can tend to make people become embedded in positions and to polarize early on, sometimes making negotiations difficult.

Religious differences and change can lead to great conflict, particularly for any children once the parents separate. These can be effectively dealt with in mediation as long as the mediator and both parties understand the differences in the parents' situations and discuss them openly. For example, one parent leaving a religious community such as the Scientologists or a strictly observant group brings up numerous difficulties and details that need to be dealt with in terms of observance of the group behavior, food choices, and educational issues. Everybody has to be aware of the critical nature of these issues. A court can deal with these issues, but can be a blunt instrument. If parents can develop a dialogue together and manage to tolerate discussing the changes, they will be able to fine-tune the changes much more effectively.

Issues Unsuitable for the Mediation Process

Some situations are totally unsuitable for mediation—for example, if a parent thinks a child is about to be removed to another country. This is especially serious if the intended country has no international agreements in place regarding the return of the removed child. The power and speed of the High Court are needed to prevent a removal or, for example, to trace a child brought to the United Kingdom from a foreign country without the knowledge or agreement of the foreign parent. Situations like this require immediate access to the courts, to the police, and to the systems set up to locate and prevent abduction or to locate a child already removed. It is essential that decisive, effective action be taken at once to protect children in such circumstances.

Another situation might be one in which there is a significant disparity between the two parties' knowledge about finances. It is not unusual to find that one party understands finances better than the other. If all the assets or the main ones are in the name of one party, it is important to make sure that property and finances are secured. Otherwise when property is owned by one party and that party has control over and knowledge of the finances, it is very easy for the party to sell the property and try to hide the money in order to frustrate any financial claim that might be brought later. This kind of situation cannot possibly be dealt with in mediation or in arbitration. It needs direct and immediate access to the considerable power of the family court. Injunctions can be made, bank accounts frozen, property sales prevented, and assets secured.

Other important family issues can arise that lead to the family feeling misunderstood by the state, represented in the form of social workers. For example, the practice of exorcisms on children believed to be witches is an issue of huge concern in some areas. Parents need to understand how this is seen by social services and social services needs to recognize the danger in the situation, despite its cultural background. In this situation, mediation may need to involve more participants than just the parents. The parents might instead find that their children are at the center of a care case or a formal case conference held by social services.

A financial distribution after a relationship breaks down can be dealt with effectively in mediation, but only if certain things are in place—in particular, if there is no likelihood of dishonesty, fraud, or a deliberate attempt to remove assets. If all assets are in the name of one person, it is important to obtain legal advice in order to protect the position of the nonearning spouse and to think about this carefully *before* any mediation can go ahead.

Similarly, mediation cannot work if one party simply does not accept the concept of *fairness* or *need* in distributing assets. Parties need to be in the same ballpark to mediate. Mediation should not be undertaken regarding financial assets if both parties are not completely confident that they understand or can understand the financial assets of the other party, and both must have a clear understanding of what the court would order. This is so that if they choose to give up what is seen as their rights in family law, they understand what they have given up.

The breakup of a relationship is a volatile situation, and people sometimes are under pressure to make decisions that are not in their long-term interests. Decisions may be made out of guilt by the person who is seen as having caused the end of the relationship or through pressure to adhere to other people's ideas of what is reasonable and fair.

Importance of Independence

Independence is central to the roles of lawyers and mediators. A lawyer can take instructions only from the client—not their friends, referral agencies, family members, or religious leaders. The lawyer is safeguarding and representing only the best interests of that one client. The independent role of a mediator means that one is mediating only with the people in the room. The aim is to help clients reach agreement armed with as much knowledge as possible about their rights in every arena, including legal knowledge or advice as to the options and consequences of their proposals.

This is the heart of negotiation whether it entails family law or family mediation. The role of a lawyer is to make sure every client has access to the UK family legal system, to understand what clients want and how to achieve this if possible, to help them fund their case through legal aid, loans, or private fees, and to pursue their interests and advise them about consequences. If clients choose to settle on terms that the lawyer thinks are not beneficial, the lawyer's job is to make sure that they understand what they have given up, to help them see the pitfalls and possible problems along the way, and then to respect their choice. The lawyer's job is not to tell clients what to do, but to advise them about the consequences and make sure they know the full range of options.

As a lawyer I always think about whether a client would benefit from mediation. There are numerous benefits of an agreement that is reached this way. There are also situations where that is completely out of the question, such as where there is a threat of violence, where parties are simply not able to negotiate equally, where there is a need to protect people, children, or property, or where the honesty of the other party just cannot be trusted.

***

In my opinion, family mediation should take place only in the context of participants having the opportunity to access the wider legal framework. Participants should have a real opportunity to be resourced with knowledge about their dispute and their legal rights, responsibilities, weaknesses, and strengths. They need to have an idea of how a family court would view their position. This facilitates the reaching of a settlement, and it aids the process by correcting a lack of knowledge that one party, often the weaker party, might have as to her legal position. With no understanding of her rights to the family home, for example, a person participating in mediation has little chance of securing an outcome for herself and her children that is consistent with the outcomes available to her through the law. The family court has considerable powers. It can provide security to enable one party to occupy the family home even if that party does not own it, and it can offer protection from violence. The court can issue orders that prevent children from being removed from the home country or that give a party a share of the wealth of the relationship and prevent assets from being removed. When people understand that these powers exist, they recognize that they have the opportunity to ask for them to be exercised in their favor.

Once aware of the power and opportunity that family law courts can offer, a person can make an informed choice as to how to resolve a family dispute. The choice to use mediation then becomes a real choice, selected because of the special quality that settling in mediation can offer. Mediation should be considered a possibility for every dispute, but it has to be excluded if the circumstances are not right. Mediation can be a very effective process and can result in a sustainable good-quality agreement that both parties follow because they participated in the making of the agreement. It is therefore a voluntary decision rather than one imposed on them by a court. Neither party feels there has been a winner or a loser. Both parties are likely to end up compromising. Mediated agreements ideally leave the parties feeling that the agreement is a result of joint discussions—not imposed on them from the outside and resented, usually by one party. It is important that mediation be an opportunity to enhance the knowledge of the participants and to offer them the opportunity to settle in the full knowledge of their rights and of the steps that they can take to protect and enforce those rights if need be.

Notes

1. Legal Services Commission, "Legal Aid and Mediation, for People Involved in Family Breakdown," Report by the Comptroller and Auditor General Legal

Services Commission HC 256 Session, 2006–2007, 2 March 2007; http://www.nao.org.uk/report/legal-aid-and-mediation-for-people-involved-in-family-break down/.

2. "Mediation—The Best Option for Children," press release, 26 November 2014, Ministry of Justice and the Rt Hon Lord McNally; https://www.gov.uk/government/news/family-mediation-an-alternative-to-courts; http://webarchive.nationalarchives.gov.uk/20121015000000/http://www.direct.gov.uk/.

3. Ministry of Justice Report of the Mediation Task Force, June 2014, p. 10; http://www.justice.gov.uk/downloads/family-mediation-task-force-report.pdf.

4. Domestic Violence and Matrimonial Proceedings Act 1976, Domestic Proceedings and Magistrates Courts Act 1978, Guardianship of Minors Act 1971, Family Law Act 1996 part IV.

5. Payment by a groom or his family to the bride, available to her at various times on demand, including the dissolution of the marriage.

Muslim Mediation and Arbitration

INSIGHTS FROM COMMUNITY AND LEGAL PRACTICE

Saher Tariq

THIS CHAPTER SEEKS TO HIGHLIGHT Islamic thought about and practice of religious arbitration in matters of divorce among Muslims. Specifically, it draws from a reading of the Holy Quran as well as my practices as a solicitor at my law firm, YHM Solicitors in Leeds, United Kingdom. This is a high street law firm based in a multiethnic area of Leeds. In light of the experiences of my clients and colleagues in the legal field, I have set up a new service called Islamic Divorce & Khula to assist women in the United Kingdom in obtaining a *khula* professionally and efficiently.

Prior to working as a lawyer I worked in various women's organizations in Nottingham and dealt with the difficulties faced by women. The background of many of these women was South Asian, and the backgrounds of my clients at the law firm are predominantly South Asian and African.

The examples and cases in this chapter are drawn from my own experience in working with women. I acknowledge that they are not representative in the academic sense of the term: the results I describe here are based on my work with clients who have approached me and on discussions I have had with other solicitors, barristers, and community workers involved with Muslim couples going through a divorce or attempting to resolve other family matters. Nonetheless, I consider them illustrative of the problems other women encounter, and I hope they provide insight into this area. It is important to note that I have no experience in dealing with Sharia councils, although research on these councils has been done, as reported, for example, by Samia Bano in *Muslim Women and Shari'ah Councils.*

Importance of Mediation and Arbitration in Islam

To understand Muslim mediation and arbitration and how it is used and implemented in Western society, it is important to understand its origins. It is given immense importance in Islam, as it originates from the Holy Quran, which Muslims believe to be the most authentic source of knowledge. It is stated: "The believers are brothers, so reconcile between your brothers, and remain conscious of God, so that you may receive mercy."[1] A clear duty has been placed on Muslims to arbitrate and make all attempts to resolve disputes. This is backed by the Hadith, sayings of the Prophet Muhammad (Peace be upon him), which is considered a source of knowledge secondary only to the Quran. One of the sayings relating to mediation is that "there is a reward of a *sadaqa* [charitable gift] for the one who establishes justice among people."[2] The importance of mediation in the context of family law is emphasized in the Quran: "If you fear a breach between the two, appoint an arbitrator from his family and an arbitrator from her family."[3] It is clear that Islam has been encouraging the settlement of disputes by amicable means and resorting to forms of alternative dispute resolution for the past fourteen hundred years. Not only has a duty been placed on Muslims to participate in and encourage mediation, but a reward has been prescribed for those who "establish justice."

Many organizations, such as Relate and the Family Mediation Council, have been set up in the United Kingdom to encourage mediation in family matters. However, my clients often tell me that they feel more comfortable going to a Muslim for mediation. When asked to file a divorce petition for a client, lawyers are required to complete a form to confirm that they have provided clients with details about mediation organizations. This is sent to the court with the divorce petition. Such is the emphasis placed on mediation in the courts of England and Wales. As my practice is focused on family law and immigration law, my experiences as a practitioner are restricted to those areas.

Muslim Marriages and Divorce

It is possible for a woman who has married in a Muslim country, in a ceremony that is legal in that country, and who fulfills the residence requirements in the United Kingdom to apply for a divorce in the UK civil courts. Ironically, this puts persons who have entered the United Kingdom as a spouse after a marriage abroad in a stronger position than those who have entered into a religious marriage in the United Kingdom.

It is surprising to note that many marriages are still conducted in the United Kingdom without being recognized under the laws of this country. A *nikah*, an Islamic religious ceremony, can be conducted by an institution that has been registered, and it would be recognized by UK laws. However, a number of nikahs still take place in the United Kingdom that are unregistered. There are so far no reliable statistics on what proportion of Muslims who get married in Britain have both a civil marriage (e.g., in a registry) and a nikah, or just a civil marriage or just a nikah.[4]

In my discussions with clients who have had only a religious marriage, I encourage them to have their marriage registered in the United Kingdom; many men, however, state that having an unregistered marriage leaves them with the option of having more than one wife. Some couples have also stated that it is then easier to get out of the marriage, as they would not have to resort to the English civil courts. The man can end the marriage by pronouncing a *talaq*,[5] but it is the woman who is left in an extremely difficult position should she wish to end the marriage. As the marriage is not recognized in the United Kingdom, she cannot apply to the civil courts for a divorce and has no choice but to turn to a Sharia council or panel to obtain a declaration that the marriage has ended. This is very often referred to as a khula.

The right of the khula has been given to women, and it can be argued that this is an absolute right. The wife of Thabit bin Qais came to the Prophet Muhammad (Peace be upon him) during his lifetime and stated, "I do not blame Thabit for defects in his character or his religion,"[6] but she asked for an end to her marriage. Her husband was asked to divorce her and he did. The lady had asked for a divorce despite having made it clear that she had no complaints against her husband but perhaps conveying that there was no understanding, love, or bond between them. Her desire was granted. This example from the very early days of Islam provides insight into how Islam allows a woman to obtain a divorce.

It is interesting that no further details were asked for, again evidence that supports the woman's right to ask for a divorce without giving any substantive reason. It can be argued that the omission by the Prophet Muhammad (Peace be upon him) furthers the right of a woman to ask for an end to her marriage—a notion similar to that in English civil law that the marriage has "irretrievably broken down." Clearly this is irrefutable evidence that a woman can ask for a divorce for personal reasons, and her wishes should be upheld. Islam does not force a couple to stay in a marriage against the will of either party. The wife of Thabit bin Qais made it very clear that she did not have any complaints against her husband but expressed her desire for a divorce and was permitted to get a divorce.

In the preceding example, the husband was asked to grant a divorce and he agreed, but in my experience the most complex situations are those in which the husband refuses to grant a divorce or refuses to reply to any papers sent to him asking his views in relation to the wife's request for a khula.

Difficulties Faced by Women Seeking a Khula

It has to be remembered that the khula, a declaration that the marriage has ended, is a purely religious doctrine. A woman needs to obtain a khula so that she knows her marriage has ended. The khula is not recognized in the United Kingdom, but without a valid khula any subsequent marriage entered into by a woman will be invalid in Islam, and any children born as a result of such a marriage will be considered to be illegitimate and will not be entitled to a share in their father's inheritance. It is evident that a valid khula is of utmost importance for a Muslim woman.

Unfortunately, this also means that a Muslim woman is then at the mercy of the panels who can grant her the khula. There are many such panels and councils in the United Kingdom, such as the Islamic Sharia Council, Sharee Council Dewsbury, and the Muslim Law Sharia Council UK, to name but a few.

From comments made by my clients, it seems that the panels follow culture rather than Islam, and in many cases, as stated by my clients, a "journey of horror, embarrassment and humiliation begins." Any woman who chooses to apply for a khula has to decide which panel to go to. Sadly, as the panels are not regulated, there is no way of determining how these panels operate in the United Kingdom. But it has been suggested that there could be as many as eighty-five Islamic Sharia law courts in the Britain.[7]

Over the years Muslims have come to the United Kingdom from many regions, and culture has seeped into what should be a matter of Islamic law. There are number of considerations that then confront a woman and the practitioners of this area, some of which are outlined as follows to illustrate why what should be a simple religious procedure becomes confusing tangle cultural and social dilemmas.

If a Muslim woman wants to apply for a khula, should she turn to a panel operated by members of the same ethnic background as her own—for example, South Asian? What if she does so and then chooses to marry someone of African descent and her future in-laws do not accept the khula she has? Should, but most importantly can, she then apply to another panel for a khula where the members are of African descent when she believes that the khula she has obtained is valid and she is no longer married?

Would a subsequent panel give her the khula based on the certificate she has been granted, or would the panel members consider it their duty to conduct their own investigations and inquiries to assure themselves that the marriage has been dissolved?

Should the Muslim woman apply to a panel where she knows that she will not be asked to go in person or to a panel from whom the khula will gain widespread acceptance?

As there are different schools of thought in Islam, should that be a consideration for the women when choosing a panel?

In my experience, however, there are informal methods that can be used before the woman resorts to appearing before a panel. These generally consist of the elders of the family getting together and attempting to resolve the issue. My clients tell me that, unfortunately, it is mostly the men who are included in these discussions. There is a stigma attached to divorce, and many South Asians are of the mentality that a woman should leave her husband's house only in a coffin. Again this a cultural saying that not only have I heard from a young age but is also confirmed by many of my clients, and they are often led to believe that asking for an end to marriage would result in a black mark not only on her but also on the family.

As I deal with many women from South Asian communities living in the United Kingdom, my experience is that a woman asking for a khula will meet the most resistance from her brothers, their wives, and her uncles, as they fear that after the divorce she will become reliant on them for financial support. Although in the United Kingdom a divorced woman will be able to rely on the state in a situation where she is unable to support herself, the mind-set of brothers and uncles seems to have been imported to Britain.

The "elders" who gather together to try to reach a reconciliation seem to have the view that the marriage should be preserved at all costs and often ask the women to make compromises ranging from tolerating abuse, to accepting an adulterous husband, to allowing the husband to have a second wife. These are all examples of what my clients have been asked to accept so as to preserve the marriage.

Another important issue raised by my clients regarding reconciliation attempts by family members is that generally only the male members of the family attend these meetings. The women are excluded, and this creates a barrier for any woman who struggles to be open about marital issues with men.

As one client said, "All my life I was told that I had to respect my grandfather and uncles and that I should only talk to them when necessary; when I had marital issues I had to explain my reasons to these people. They were all gathered in a room before I returned from work, and I felt like they had already decided that they could not let themselves be dishonored by letting me get a divorce. After a number of negotiations I was advised that I did not have to maintain any relationship with my husband but I could not get divorced as his visa still needed to be sorted." Clearly, these informal attempts at mediation are biased toward men, take no account of the feelings of the women, and contravene religious principles.

As stated by the commissioner for women's affairs of the Central Council of Muslims in Germany in an interview, "Islam is not in need of a commissioner for women's affairs. It is not Islam [that] suppresses women, but men. And therefore Muslim women are in need of a commissioner for women's affairs."[8] In my experience, many women are pressured into staying in a marriage to allow their husband time to get his permanent residency. There are many cases in which women were openly told that they did not have to establish any relations with their husband but would need to stay in the marriage until their husband had obtained his permanent residency.

In one matter I had the impression that the young woman was not happy with her marriage, and although I was able to speak to her in a separate room, explaining that she did not have to support her husband's application and did not have to stay in the marriage, she informed me that it was not worth the backlash she would get from her own family; she added that like other wives she had difficulties but she wanted to proceed in sponsoring her husband to help him get his permanent residency. She said that she would continue to work on the marriage for two years, and if things did not work out she was aware of her right to get a divorce. I noticed that after two years her husband would get his permanent residency and would not need her to sponsor his stay in the United Kingdom.

In one case, the father had openly said to his daughter that he had always given her whatever she had asked for, and just this once he wanted three years of her life. He wanted her to marry his nephew, who was abroad, and apply for him to come to the United Kingdom as her spouse. Under the immigration rules at the time, her husband would get permanent residency after three years and she would then be free to do what she wanted. She told me that she felt lucky, as she had been reassured that she would not have to have any marital relations with him. She subsequently got divorced by consent. Both the husband and wife have remarried.

These cases go unreported, as many women have thought that by doing a paper marriage they would retain the support of their family, but if they tried to refuse or end the marriage any sooner they would be disowned by the family. There is no way of documenting these cases, but my work in this area of law and comments made by my clients have provided insight into such practices.

However, the problems for a woman can continue. If after an unregistered marriage the husband refuses to divorce his spouse, she has to go through the elders, mediators, civil courts, and the Sharia councils as well. In many instances the family who had initially assured the woman that she would be married only on paper pushes for her not to take any formal steps to end the marriage, as she might as well stay married to the same person if that's what he wants. Clearly there is no consideration of the desires of the woman in such matters. The changes in immigration laws have reduced the incidence of such cases, but we will never truly be aware of how many such marriages have taken place and what the outcomes have later been.

If a woman is strong enough to continue to ask for a divorce, in many cases she will break her family ties and often the mothers who are willing to support their daughters are then threatened with a divorce by their husbands. This is a sad outcome imposed by the very men who are the first port of call for women using informal mediation. A woman who was initially willing to fight and end her marriage then faces the possibility that her actions will lead to her mother being divorced as well—again, a strong deterrent that often means that the cycle will continue.

There have been instances of women having to move to a different city due to the hostility they face. Losing the support of one's mother and sisters and an entire network of friends and family at a time when support is much needed understandably serves as a strong disincentive to continue with the demand for divorce. A barrister the writer met at a seminar said she had been told by her female client "that she would end the cycle and would not let her daughters have to go through what she had to tolerate." This resulted in her moving to a different city, and she was forced to sever contact with all her friends, as her new location had to be kept a secret due to threats from her own family, ranging the threat of physical harm to that of death.

Another barrister from Leeds who is also a mediator gave the following account of a female mediator who was a volunteer from a mosque-based marriage mediation service. The incident took place in the West Yorkshire area, and it involved the mediator accepting in oral evidence the wife's complaint that she had been nearly strangled by the husband, to the point where she feared she would lose consciousness (among other, regular incidents of domestic violence) but that she had been given no advice regarding the risks to herself and/or her children and was never informed of domestic violence organizations, because the aim of the mediation was to preserve the marriage. Indeed, she said that the service always worked toward this goal, which was based on religious imperatives, regardless of domestic violence.

As stated earlier, in a civil divorce in the English courts, there is a requirement for family law practitioners to confirm to the court that reconciliation has been discussed and that the names and addresses of persons qualified to help have been provided.[9] It is to be noted that the requirement is only that such contact details have been provided, not that they have been utilized. A similar procedure is followed by the Muslim community in the United Kingdom to ensure that if matrimonial issues can be dealt with by arbitration and mediation, then the marriage may not need to come to an end.

The usual community practice, in my experience, is that after the option of the elders has been exercised, the women turn to their local mosques for mediators. The local imam is often the person who will play the role of the mediator. Again from a woman's point of view, there is now another man with whom she has to discuss her marital issues. Due to lack of support from her family, it is very often the case that she is not accompanied by any female relative or friend, which causes further gender imbalance.

If the imam, who in many cases will have had no formal training in mediation and arbitration, is unable to resolve the issue, the woman has to turn to a Sharia council or panel with the power to grant her the khula. This opens up a plethora of other issues. For example, who can pronounce a khula? Common sense states that any person who has knowledge of the laws and principles relating to a khula can pronounce a khula, but who is to assess the level of knowledge? The woman who is applying for a khula may not have been aware of her right to get a khula, let alone have known who could grant the khula. This is a common issue faced by practitioners in this area, as there is no centralized system of assessing the level of education and also because it is very likely that different scholars have studied in a variety of institutions around the world. There cannot be a standard grade or type of exam that can be set as the minimum level of knowledge required to enable a person to grant a khula.

Once a decision has been made as to which panel to use, the woman files a completed application form with a Sharia council, and this is where religion and culture start conflicting. Religion, as illustrated earlier, states that some efforts at mediation should be made. If such efforts are unsuccessful, the marriage should be dissolved, as in the case of the marriage of Thabit bin Qais. Custom and culture seem to dictate that the wife be asked to meet the husband and attempt to mediate regardless of what mediation efforts have been made in the past. Religion states that a woman's wishes should be a vital consideration.

Discussions with imams and scholars have made it evident that they consider most woman who apply for a khula to be very liberal and influenced by the West. This thinking seeps, perhaps unconsciously, into their approach to the matter.

The home page of the Sharee Council Dewsbury has the following statement: "The scholars have recommended the establishment of Sharee Councils presided by Islamically qualified Qadhis to consider the fate of unhappy marriages in which the couple can't agree to an Islamic divorce, and to declare them annulled if necessary after careful consideration in the light of Islamic Shariah." It is stipulated that as a man can end a Muslim marriage by pronouncing a talaq three times, the Dewsbury council statement is for women. The use of the phrases "consider the fate of unhappy marriages" and "declare them annulled if necessary" shows that they do not guarantee a khula.

As has been pointed out, in my opinion this is not in line with the teachings of Islam but rather is the result of a convoluted set of values that have no basis in Islam but have been instilled in people during their upbringing, when they are led to believe that any woman who demands any rights is liberal and every effort is made to deny all her rights.

It is difficult ever to be sure how many women who apply for a khula are unsuccessful, but it is important to note that in many instances the conduct of family members and other community figures, including imams, prevents a woman from even getting to the stage of formally applying for a khula. She may agree to compromise or just decide to separate and not apply for a khula.

This also complicates efforts to obtain and analyze data, as no record is kept when informal mediation is carried out by imams. This was confirmed by various imams who were consulted in the Leeds and Nottingham area but who did not want to be named. The accounts given in this chapter are snapshots of what actually happens. This is not to say that all women who try to resolve their marital issues meet with resistance, but sadly a large proportion do. This is my personal view based on my own legal practice and community work.

It has to be remembered that at the time of the marriage it is advisable either for the nikah to be conducted in such a manner that it is registered or for the couple to take part in a civil ceremony. Despite the advice they receive, there is a reluctance by many men and their families to have a registered marriage. One man who agreed to a marriage at the local registry office, in addition to his nikah, was told by his friends that this was the first of many demands that he would have to give in to, as he had chosen to marry a British-educated woman. He was also told by his friends that his future wife clearly did not trust him.

In conservative Muslim families in the United Kingdom, typically the bride's family would not want to rock the boat and risk offending the family of the groom-to-be, and very often the topic of a registered marriage is not touched upon. Sadly, in many Muslim families the groom's family is still given immense importance, and the bride's family is always cautious in its approach to dealing with the groom and his family. In many instances a woman is forbidden by her family to touch on many topics with the groom. Female clients have stated that they were expressly forbidden to ask for a marriage that was recognized in the United Kingdom, as it would be thought that she was not serious about the relationship.

On the basis of my experiences as a lawyer, it is reasonable to conclude that the women who are unable to enter into a registered marriage due to family pressure are the women who are unable to go through with the tiring and exhausting process of obtaining a khula. The discrimination and attitudes of the elders and local mediators are strong factors in deterring them from formally applying to a Sharia council or panel.

Many female clients have confirmed that they were never given a copy of their nikah nama, the Islamic marriage certificate, and despite the fact that they knew that members of the family had the document, it was withheld from them in the hope that this would lead to difficulties and possibly even make obtaining a khula an impossibility.

In light of all these issues, I have, as mentioned at the start of this essay, set up a new service, Islamic Divorce & Khula. This service works on the underlying principle that if a woman wants a khula then she is entitled to get a khula. Difficulties such as the lack of a nikah nama, non-cooperation of family members, and the sensitivities surrounding the issues discussed in this chapter are all taken into consideration.

Setting Up a New Initiative: Islamic Divorce & Khula

As Islamic Divorce & Khula has been set up by myself, a female lawyer who practices family law and has had experience working in community-based organizations and also has worked with women of different ethnic minorities including Muslim women, I have a lot of firsthand experience of dealing with women who are in a disadvantaged situation due to their gender and have also heard many firsthand accounts of how women have been treated by the informal alternative dispute resolution (ADR) providers and Sharia councils.

The service recognizes the importance of trying to preserve a marriage where it is evident that this can be done, but at the very outset the view is taken that if a woman has stated that she does not want to mediate then she is entitled to take that approach and no pressure is put on her to meet with her husband or his family members. It is understood that a woman who wants to use the service has thought the process through and has possibly already used informal methods such as ADR. If it is felt that she has not exhausted these options, Islamic Divorce & Khula offers a free mediation service. But no pressure is applied, as the woman's right to choose for herself is paramount. If there is evidence of severe domestic violence, clearly the woman will not be asked to mediate and all efforts will be made to ensure that her address is not disclosed to the husband.

The woman can go through the whole procedure without the need for a male guardian to grant his permission, and if the husband refuses to reply to letters sent by the panel, the panel members are of the view that the khula can be granted. The approach, very similar to that taken by the English civil courts, is that as long as it can be shown that the husband has been served with the papers asking for a khula and he still fails to reply, a khula can be granted. As is the case with the English courts, if it cannot be proved that the husband has received the papers because he has changed his address or even changed his country of residence, provisions have been made to allow the panel to grant a khula, although in such cases the procedure will take longer.

The khula is usually granted after the woman has returned her *mehr*, the amount that was paid to her by the husband at the time of the marriage; this could also include gold and other gifts that were given by the husband and his family. However, this may lead to a situation where the husband asks for more than what he had given. The mehr should be documented in the nikah nama, but in the case of gold and other gifts it is often one party's word against the other's. Obviously, if the woman does not have a copy of her nikah nama, she will not know what the amount of the mehr is. Again the panel has decided that a khula will be granted in such matters.

There have been reports of a husband demanding much more money than what he initially gave to the woman and, knowing that she has no means of returning the sum demanded, refusing to consent to his wife's request; the Sharia council then takes the view that it cannot grant a khula. For example, a husband, living in Pakistan, had initially asked for £15,000 (about US$22,000), but upon learning that his wife, who was living in the United Kingdom, had received her inheritance he demanded £50,000 (about US$73,300) for his cooperation. It was only because a member of the Sharia council at the time personally knew the Pakistani president, and warned the husband that if he continued to be unreasonable he would ask the president to intercede, that the matter was settled for £5,000 (about US$7,300).[10]

This is an example of the difficulties faced by both women and the panels who issue the khula. Sadly, judging from my experiences in dealing with women living in the United Kingdom over the past twenty years, this is not an isolated incident, but a compromise was reached due to the connection between the member of the Sharia council and the president of Pakistan. Clearly, there will be many cases where such connections do not exist, and in such matters the councils and panels are left in an extremely difficult position due to the strict approach they choose to adopt.

The cases in which a husband lies about the size of the gifts that have been given should not be forgotten. When there is a dispute as to the amount of mehr or gifts, Islamic Divorce & Khula has taken the approach that, given all the circumstances, a decision may be made to grant a khula and the husband will then be free to proceed via the civil courts to obtain any amount he says is due to him.

As seeking a khula is a purely Islamic step taken by the woman, both she and her husband will be advised of their rights and duties in Islam. Again, the view is that any woman who is trying to obtain a khula is doing so to fulfill her religious obligations and will therefore be willing to follow other rules of Islam. A husband who is trying to keep his wife in a marriage against her will is acting against Islam and therefore should not be able to choose which aspects of the religion he wishes to follow and which aspects he does not want to follow.

Islamic Divorce & Khula has also taken the approach that a divorce granted in the civil courts can lead to a khula being granted immediately. There is a huge difference of opinion on this topic. There are many who are of the opinion that a civil divorce granted by the courts that had been initiated by a woman cannot be a valid dissolution of a nikah.[11] However, at Islamic Divorce & Khula the view is taken that as the civil divorce fulfills all the requirements of a khula, then if a civil divorce is granted a khula will follow. This approach ensures that the woman does not have to go through the whole experience twice.

Islamic Divorce & Khula has also taken the approach that a khula can be granted without the woman ever having to meet with the panel, although in some cases the panel may need to meet the woman. Again, this approach is used successfully by the English civil courts. Islamic Divorce & Khula has a team of women who are the first point of contact with the applicant to make the process as comfortable as possible for her.

As I asked one scholar who opposed this view on the grounds that a nikah cannot be dissolved by a non-Muslim, what if this harsh approach led a woman to decide that she was not going to put up with the hassle and humiliation of the process of getting a khula after obtaining a civil divorce and would just not apply for a khula? If it was then to be said that her subsequent marriage was wrong and that her children were illegitimate, would some blame not fall on the scholars who were interpreting the rules so harshly and forcing women to stop approaching them? It is ironic that to avoid these issues, some Muslims living in non-Muslim societies have to conduct two marriages and then go through two divorces.

In the interests of socio-legal cohesion it is vital that a middle way be established and followed to make it easier for women who decide to follow Islamic principles in order to get the desired result. Clearly from a Muslim's point of view it is important not to compromise the teachings of Islam, but it is claimed that a responsibility lies with the scholars to make it easier to abide by Islam rather than create unnecessary hardships. As is stated in the Holy Quran, "Allah intends for you ease, and does not intend for you hardship."[12]

Islamic Divorce & Khula has also taken the view that matters such as child custody and financial arrangements will be left to the civil courts. This approach has been adopted because if the panel were to make any order regarding the custody and financial arrangements, then if either party defaulted in following the order issued by the panel there would be no means of enforcing or ensuring compliance. Leaving such matters to the English courts also ensures that Islamic Divorce & Khula does not act contrary to the English law. This is vital to for integration without segregation for Muslims living in a non-Muslim society.

As stated by Chief Rabbi Dr. Jonathan Sacks in his Reith Lectures in 1990, "And that is to think of a plural society not as one in which there is a Babel of conflicting languages, but rather as one in which we each have to be bilingual."[13]

In conclusion, the relevant issue here is that women wish to follow the principles of Islam but want to do so in such a way that the laws of their country of residence are not infringed. It goes without saying that women applying for a khula or utilizing other methods of ADR want to preserve their dignity during this process. They want to be treated with respect and want the process to be handled professionally and efficiently. I suggest that the best way forward toward religious freedom without contravention of local laws is the approach taken by Islamic Divorce & Khula. Only time will tell how effective this service is, but it is hoped that it will be a platform where women will be able to take advantage of ADR and fulfill their religious obligations without causing any friction with the English civil courts.

Clearly, the easiest way to achieve this will be to encourage all nikahs to be registered in the United Kingdom or for couples to have a registered marriage as per the UK laws. Clearly if the Sharia councils were able to agree on a set of rules that they would all follow, this would assist the service users greatly; however, in the United Kingdom, sadly, Muslims cannot even agree on one day to celebrate Eid. It may be wishful thinking to hope that all schools of thought and all ethnic minorities will collaborate in compiling a set of rules for khula.

Notes

1. Quran 49:10.
2. *Sahih Al-Bukhari*, vol. 3, book 49, hadith no. 870.
3. Quran 4:35.
4. http://muslimmarriagecontract.org/about.html, last modified 2010, accessed 11 April 2015.
5. Quran 2:230.
6. *Sahih Al-Bukhari*, vol. 7, book 63, hadith no. 197.
7. http://www.gatestoneinstitute.org/3682/uk-sharia-courts, last modified 23 April 2013, accessed 11 April 2015.

8. "Verschleiret, aber Selbstbewubt," *Frankfurter Allgemeine Zeitung,* 27 February 2001.

9. Statement of reconciliation form D6 available from HMCTS website, http://hmctsformfinder.justice.gov.uk/courtfinder/forms/d006-eng.pdf, accessed April 2015.

10. Mohamed M. Keshavjee, *Islam, Sharia and Alternative Dispute Resolution* (London: I. B. Tauris, 2013), 1–2.

11. http://www.islam21c.com/fataawa/912-fatwa-a-civil-divorce-is-not-a-valid -islamic-divorce/, last modified 21 July 2010, accessed 11 April 2015.

12. Quran 2:185.

13. http://www.rabbisacks.org/wp-content/uploads/1990/11/1990_reith4 .pdf, accessed April 2015.

6

Do Sharia Councils Meet the Needs of Muslim Women?

Rehana Parveen

> The believing men and believing women are allies of one another. They enjoin what is right and forbid what is wrong and establish prayer and give *zakah* and obey Allah and His Messenger. Those—Allah will have mercy upon them. Indeed Allah is exalted in Might and Wise.
>
> —*Quran 9:71 (translation Sahih International)*

MY AIM IN THE RESEARCH described in this chapter has been to study the workings of a specific Sharia council in order to understand how it works, the types of cases that it deals with, how it treats its female users, and more generally how it fits into the framework of English law. I shall argue that, when Muslim women decide to terminate their marriages, it is absolutely essential to them that this be done in a manner that conforms to their religious beliefs. Irrespective of whether civil courts grant Muslim women civil divorces, Muslim women need a religious ruling regarding the status of their marriage. The primary function that a Sharia council performs is to adjudicate and give an authoritative *religious* ruling to a Muslim woman in such cases. Muslim men do not have the same need of a Sharia council. Thus Muslim women are the primary service users of Sharia councils.

There is a perception that Sharia councils generally are shrouded in mystery, closed off to outsiders, and unwilling to engage with wider society.[1] They have been criticized inter alia for being unfair to women and for operating a parallel system of law for which they have no jurisdiction (MacEoin and Green 2009, 69–73). There have been calls to introduce laws that would effectively criminalize them.[2] Although there is a growing body of academic research on Sharia councils (Shah-Kazemi 2001; Bano 2012; Keshavjee 2013; Douglas et al. 2013), more is needed. Most of the published research, to date, has centered on the experience of Muslim women whose cultural background is that of the Indian/Pakistani subcontinent. There has been no published research on the views of Muslim men regarding Sharia councils.

In my research I analyzed one hundred closed files of one Sharia council, sat in on sixteen interviews/meetings, observed a board meeting of the Sharia council where eleven cases were decided, and interviewed twenty Muslim women who had had an experience with either a Sharia council, an English civil court, or both. A variety of women were selected for an interview: some were personal contacts, some were recommended, and some were women whom I had observed in my attendance at the Sharia council and who were willing to be interviewed by me once their cases had concluded.

In my study I compare the work of the Sharia council with that of the English civil courts. As important as religion is, Muslim women living in the United Kingdom do not experience the breakdown of their relationship in a purely "Islamic" or religious context. They navigate that breakdown within the context of English civil law, their own understanding of Islamic law, their social and familial ties, and the customary practices of the cultural heritage to which they belong. These multiple social fields cannot be isolated from one another.[3] Sometimes they operate in harmony, sometimes they clash, and many times they are simply independent of one another.

I remember from my own childhood as a Muslim girl attending a mixed comprehensive school in Birmingham that I tried to keep my English school life separate from my Muslim home life and became very uneasy when they overlapped. In adulthood I realized this compartmentalization was neither realistic nor appropriate. In the same manner the Sharia council process cannot be understood independently of all the other contexts in which the breakdown is taking place. As a practicing Muslim woman and former family law solicitor, I am familiar with the complex nature of the interactions and negotiations that take place during the breakdown of a Muslim woman's marital relationship. I have been particularly interested in using women's experiences to compare the relationship between English law and Islamic law. In recent years questions have been asked about the compatibility of Muslims with Western societies. Muslims are seen as problematic because they do some things differently than non-Muslims living in the West.[4] The simplistic implication is that the manner in which Western societies order their lives is unproblematic. In judging whether Sharia councils meet the needs of Muslim women, it is important not only to identify the place of Sharia councils within English law but to also compare Muslim women's experiences of Sharia councils with their experience of civil law.

Before I discuss my research, it may be helpful to provide some background information about myself and my approach to this subject. After having practiced law for around nine years (my first two years were as a trainee and then seven subsequent years as a solicitor), I left private practice and began teaching law at a postgraduate level. I taught vocational courses, namely the Graduate Diploma in Law, the Legal Practice Course, and the Bar Professional Training Course, to budding solicitors and barristers for more than ten years. I then decided to return to academia, and the research described here forms part of my PhD thesis. However, as I have continued to teach law, I suppose I would describe myself as a former solicitor who is now a tutor with a desire to become a legal scholar. As a Muslim woman, I write within an Islamic framework. Any investigation into the history of Islamic scholarship will demonstrate how hugely pluralistic Islam is. While fully supporting the range of pluralistic opinions, I am not attempting to reform Islam, nor do I call for any reinterpretation of Islam through the prism of feminism or liberalism. I do, however, note that classical Muslim scholarship, on the whole, has been dedicated to addressing the needs of Muslims living in Muslim-majority lands. The status of Muslims living as minorities in non-Muslim lands is barely mentioned. This topic is one that in recent years has begun to attract the attention of Muslims themselves, and rightly so. There are many debates taking place within Islam among scholars, theologians, and lay Muslims as to how Muslims should practice their Islam and live in harmony with the non-Muslim majority. Sharia councils are just one dimension of this continuing evolution whereby Muslims are attempting to find a way to fit their normative practice of Islam into British society.

My research was carried out with the Islamic Judiciary Board (IJB), whose offices are based in Green Lane Masjid and Community Centre

(GLM), one of the biggest mosques in Birmingham. According to the 2011 census, 4.8 percent of the residents of England and Wales identified themselves as Muslims. This amounts to a little more than 2.7 million people. Birmingham is home to around 234, 400 of those Muslims, accounting for 21.8 percent of the population of Birmingham as a whole. This means that almost a quarter of Birmingham's population is Muslim. By far Muslims are the largest religious minority group in Birmingham.[5] Aside from Christians, who at 46.1 percent of Birmingham's population, are more numerous than Muslims, all the other religious groups are smaller than those who identify themselves as having no religion. When compared nationally, Birmingham ranks ninth in its proportion of Muslims. However, in actual figures the number of Muslims living in Birmingham is far greater than in any other local authority district and is almost double the number of Muslims living in Bradford (a little more than 129,000) (Birmingham Local Authority 2013, 18). GLM is situated in the Small Heath of Birmingham. Small Heath is not classified as a ward of Birmingham. It is split between the Bordesley Green, South Yardley, and Sparkbrook wards. Bordesley Green and Sparkbrook are two of the three areas of Birmingham where more than 70 percent of the residents identify themselves as Muslims (Birmingham Local Authority 2013, 19). It is clear, therefore, that GLM is situated in an area where the proportion of Muslims is far beyond the national average and the average for Birmingham.

GLM is part of a larger affiliation of mosques located throughout England under the banner of "Markaz Jamiat Ahle Hadith UK" (MJAH), of which it is the head office. GLM provides a range of services delivered in different languages, although the predominant language is English. It aligns itself with Salafi Islam, which is regarded as more conservative and pure in that its adherents consider themselves free from cultural distortions of Islam, or at least if they do follow any particular cultural practices, they try to minimize their impact. Whereas GLM seems to be staffed by younger men whose first language is English, the IJB has older men, mainly of a Pakistani background and whose first language is not English. I approached GLM/IJB staff by writing to them, explaining my research and asking if they would be willing to assist me. I had expected them to say no; I thought they might be suspicious of my intentions. Indeed, GLM has been the subject of a covert investigation in the past by a Channel 4 *Dispatches* program (15 January 2007) named "Undercover Mosque."

Despite my apprehensions, they were very willing to engage with me and have welcomed the opportunity for their services to be examined.

This mosque is particularly attractive to second- and third-generation British Muslims for a number of reasons, including the fact that English is the main language used, it follows a version of Islam that is not linked to any particular culture, and it caters to women. Younger Muslims may not have strong ties to their parents' cultural heritage; they may wish to distance themselves from any specific ethnic heritage and, as such, will more readily identify themselves with the Muslim *ummah* as a whole (Kundani 2014, 53). At a time when Muslims feel threatened, turning to the guidance of what is perceived to be an authentic version of Islam is particularly appealing to young Muslims (Gilliat-Ray 2010, 72–73).[6] It has been noted that relatively few mosques identify themselves as Salafi. GLM is key among them and the rise of young British Muslims who also identify themselves as Salafi Muslims is a topic that is receiving increasing attention (Hamid 2009, 384–403).

Muslims are not one homogeneous group, so a diverse range of Muslims are likely to use the services of the IJB. The diversity of Muslims is a complex issue. Diversity here not only includes ethnicity, socioeconomic background, class, and whether a person is British born or an immigrant; when it comes to religion, diversity also includes the type of Islam that is practiced and the extent of practice or religiosity. My research revealed that the IJB receives applications from throughout England and Wales, and in my interviews with the women, they spanned the range of these diversity factors. What I found particularly interesting is that although GLM/IJB identify themselves as Salafi, many of the women I interviewed who used their services did not identify their Islam in the same way. The women who applied to the IJB generally did so because they thought the IJB would grant them an Islamic divorce rather than because they specifically ascribe to the same type of Islam.

The IJB is a separate entity from GLM, with its own office space, staff, and telephone line, but it remains affiliated with GLM. It became apparent in some of my interviews with the women that they made no distinction between the IJB and GLM. The IJB was set up around twenty years ago and consists of an administrator (who was my main point of contact), one other employee, and a chairman of the board. The board itself has another nine members, all of whom serve as members of affiliated mosques of MJAH and so come from different parts of the United Kingdom.

As each Sharia council operates independently, the conclusions I have drawn from my observations of the IJB are not necessarily representative of all Sharia councils. Although I have sought to provide insight into how one particular Sharia council operates, the recommendations that I advance on the basis of my study are of significance to Sharia councils throughout the United Kingdom.

In my analysis of the one hundred closed files from the IJB, I found that, although the majority of applicants categorize themselves as having a Pakistani background (64 percent), the IJB also deals with a very diverse range of other Muslim ethnicities, including Bangladeshi (7 percent), Yemeni (6 percent), Somalian (6 percent European/English converts (3 percent), Afghan (2 percent), Kenyan (2 percent), Iranian (2 percent), Palestinian (2 percent), as well as Moroccan, Indian, Malaysian, Malawi, Zambian, and Arab (1 percent each). I observed that the IJB recognizes and takes account of many of the different cultural practices followed in the different communities. In addition, the IJB has created links with members of local Yemeni and Somalian mosques in order to take advice or assistance when a particular cultural context is important in a case.

What Are the Needs of Muslim Women?

All of the applicants in the closed files that I analyzed were women. All had entered a Muslim marriage (*nikaah*) contract and were applying for a divorce. Men generally do not "apply" to a Sharia council for a divorce.[7] I have investigated only applications for divorce, and the IJB confirmed that such cases constituted the overwhelming majority of its work. These Muslim women want to terminate their marriages in a manner that conforms with their religious beliefs—that is, through a divorce acceptable to Allah. It has always been accepted within orthodox Islam that a man has the right to pronounce a unilateral divorce, a *talaq*, upon his wife, but there is no reciprocal right for a woman, although even classical scholars agree that a man can delegate this right of divorce to his wife (Tucker 2008, 86–92). Among the Muslim women I interviewed, there was very little, if any, support for the view that women should have the same unilateral right as men to pronounce a talaq.[8] However, they did show a desire for their Islamic rights to a termination of the marriage to be recognized and applied in an efficient manner.

A Muslim wife who wants her marriage terminated has two main routes open to her.[9] If her husband consents to her request, the marriage is terminated. This is known as a *khul*.[10] If he refuses, she needs to apply to an authority that can issue an order terminating the marriage, known as a *faskh*. In the United Kingdom that authority is a Sharia council. A civil court will have jurisdiction under the law of the state only if a civil marriage has been entered into and, more important, it will determine any application for divorce on the basis of English civil law, not Islamic law. If a Muslim woman is expected to accept a civil divorce, then as one interviewee put it, "What is the point of having a nikaah?"

The issue here is not whether these rules on divorce are fair between the genders. Nor is it whether Muslims should accept the rulings of an English civil court in relation to the religious status of their marriages. The argument is that if a Muslim woman follows the normative Islamic opinion that Allah has not given her a unilateral right to a divorce and her only method of divorcing a husband who is refusing to consent is to apply to an authority that will terminate it in accordance with Islamic law, a belief that she is entitled to hold, the Sharia council is essential for her. Without an authority that can pronounce a faskh, a Muslim woman will be left in the unhappy situation of being tied to a marriage from which she has no means to free herself.[11] For Muslim women, a Sharia council intervenes only when the husband has not pronounced a talaq or there is some issue regarding the talaq. It is entirely possible that many religious divorces will take place among Muslims without any record or intervention by any authority.

One may conclude that every woman who applies to a Sharia council for a termination of her marriage has a husband who at least initially is unwilling to release her by a talaq. Of the one hundred files examined, 56 percent were terminated by a faskh pronounced by the board and 39 percent were terminated by a khul with the husband's consent. In only one file did the husband give a talaq during the course of the proceedings. In the other 4 percent the IJB issued a confirmation (known as a *fatwa*) declaring that the husband's actions amounted to a talaq, even though he might not have appreciated this. Cases in which a faskh was pronounced included those where the husband failed to engage with the process at all (16 percent) and where he initially engaged and then for some reason refused to consent to a khul. Even in those cases where a khul has been agreed to, this has usually required meetings, negotiations, and some persuasive pressure by the IJB on the husband. In the majority of cases, whether the matter ended with a faskh or a khul, and where husbands engaged, the process came to an end only after a number of letters had been written and a variety of methods had been employed to ensure that the husbands were given an opportunity to put forward their versions of events.

All the files inspected indicated that the marriages were terminated. It does not necessarily follow that there were no cases in which the board refused to terminate the marriage, since I examined only closed files. A file is closed if the marriage is terminated. If the marriage does not end (whether because the board has refused to terminate it or because the parties have chosen to reconcile), the file remains open. The board may decide that further information is needed or may require that a particular step be undertaken. A file may therefore be presented to the board on more than one occasion. In at least one case that I examined, the file had been referred to the board on two occasions, and it was only on the second that the board terminated the marriage. It is therefore difficult to determine the rate at which the board refuses applications or what course of action women decide to take in such cases. However, there is no evidence that I could find of applications being refused outright.

The IJB Process in Outline

The process consists of completing a standardized application form and paying a fee of £150 (approximately US $215). The IJB generally carries out some identity checks and then writes to the husband informing him of the wife's application. At this stage, little information is given to the husband about the reasons for the application, and he is encouraged to contact the IJB. If he does not respond, the IJB writes at least two more letters over a period of two months and may use alternative methods of communication such as a telephone call, an email, hand delivery of letters, or even placement of a notice in an Asian-language newspaper. If the husband fails to respond, a detailed account of the circumstances is taken from the wife (normally in a face-to-face meeting), and thereafter the file is referred to a board meeting for a final decision.

When the husband does respond, the IJB considers the prospects of saving the marriage and, if it cannot be saved, considers whether the husband will consent to the divorce. If the parties agree to a divorce, a certificate confirming the same is issued by the IJB. If the parties cannot agree on a divorce, the file is referred to a board meeting for a final decision. The board meets about every six to eight weeks at the IJB offices to consider the files in these cases. No applicant, respondent, or any other family member is present during this meeting. Once the board has made a decision, the parties are notified of the outcome. This may be appear to be a simple, straightforward process, but many complexities may arise in individual cases.

General Observations of the IJB

No women are employed at the IJB in any capacity. This is in keeping with the majority of Sharia councils in the United Kingdom. This makes it a somewhat intimidating environment for a woman to walk into. As you step into the offices, the GLM staff members sit behind a counter that is directly ahead, and to the right is the main office of the IJB. There is a small waiting area and other office rooms. There is no clear demarcation between the GLM offices and the IJB offices and no signs to indicate any distinction. As a woman, I felt intimidated walking into an all-male environment and, in my observations and interviews, I noticed that women were conscious of how they were dressed, partly because they felt they might be judged by the men working there and partly because they understood the IJB to be part of the mosque itself. During one of my observations, the female applicant apologized for attending in her work clothes, although she was immediately told not to worry and that it did not matter. It may also be remarked that concern for how one might appear is not limited to parties attending a Sharia council. One interviewee who is employed as a nurse informed me that she wore her nurse's uniform to her civil court hearing, as she felt she would be taken more seriously if she presented herself to the court as a professional.

Whereas the layout of the offices is inevitably limited by the space available, simple improvements can be made by better signage and separate waiting areas for men and women, particularly when women come for joint meetings. More important, since the primary users of its services are women, I think that the IJB should assign a female support worker to whom the women can speak and who can accompany them to meetings or hearings. Support from a female staff member is not only a need expressed by those I interviewed but one that is apparent from my own observations, a point I will return to later.

Analysis of the Divorce Process

In every application for termination of a marriage, two themes emerge. First, the IJB explores the prospects of saving the marriage, and second, if the marriage cannot be saved, it considers the likelihood of the husband's consenting to a khul. The manner and extent to which each question is explored depend largely on the extent to which the husband engages with the process. The fact that in more than half of the files examined (56 percent) the marriage was terminated by a faskh is a strong indicator that most husbands were not agreeable to the granting of a divorce, requiring the board to make the decision. About one-third of these husbands never responded at all.

The length of the discussions in the cases in which a khul divorce was agreed to varied considerably. In most cases in which the husband made some attempt to engage with the process, the parties were asked about the prospects of saving the marriage. Consequently, many of the case files state that the faskh was granted only after the board had decided there was no hope of saving the marriage. Sometimes this element of no hope was obvious. For example, in one case where the husband was in prison for sexual offenses against his wife, the issue of reconciliation was only given a cursory nod. In other cases the point of no hope was reached only after both parties had had an opportunity to put forward their version of events. In those cases where the husband engaged, he was expected to explain why he was not consenting to a khul.

Thus there were shifts in pressure placed on the applicant and respondent respectively. On the one hand, when the IJB explored whether there was any hope of saving the marriage, the spotlight was on the wife to articulate why she did not wish to remain. On the other hand, pressure was placed on the husband to explain why he was not willing to consent to a divorce. Both of these questions would be explored at the same time, usually in a joint meeting before the chairman of the board. This can be confusing. These are two entirely different questions, and they need to be addressed separately. There should be an initial screening process in which the wife is asked whether she will consider a reconciliation. If her answer is no, then there is little point in exploring the issue further, and the proceedings can move on to a consideration of whether the husband will consent to a khul. This confusion in meetings is addressed in more detail later.

A brief oral explanation of the overall process is normally provided to women when they complete the application and pay the fee. However, they receive no written explanation, nor is there any reference to the process on the GLM website. Nowhere is it made clear exactly what each stage of the process involves, or how long it is likely to take. In my view this reluctance to provide a timetable arises from fear that the IJB might not be able to keep to it and would thus risk complaints. This matter was raised in the board meeting that I observed, and board members expressed concern over complaints they had received from women who felt their applications were taking too long. I also heard this complaint from the women I interviewed who stated that they had to keep "chasing" the IJB. It is interesting that those women who had been through both a civil court process and the IJB process did not have similar complaints regarding delays about the civil system even when the civil case took longer.

The key reason women were more satisfied with the civil system was that they had the support of legal advisers. They all had a solicitor who had clearly provided them with very good support, ensuring they were kept informed, particularly when delays occurred. The women were not, however, suggesting that they needed lawyers to be involved in the Sharia council process. I raised this issue with the IJB, since I had noted in some case files communications from lawyers acting for the husbands or wives. However, the IJB took the view that introducing lawyers into their process would make it unnecessarily complex and more costly for the parties. I agree with this. I would argue that the provision of one or more female support workers to keep the women updated and generally offer support might well provide a suitable solution. The overwhelming majority of women felt that female support was particularly important.

Observations of Meetings and Views as to Their Appropriateness

One of the complaints from the women concerned meetings and the confusion as to the objectives of the meetings. I observed sixteen meetings with the chairman of the board. Some were with an applicant or a respondent alone; others were joint meetings with a husband and wife.

The meetings were normally held in a conference room with a large, round table, the chairman sitting on one side. I sat a few chairs away on the same side. The parties sat opposite, normally with a couple of empty chairs between them. The table was large enough to accommodate at least twelve people. The room seemed entirely appropriate to me.

My impression of the chairman is that he is skilled, experienced, and very knowledgeable about Islamic law of marriage and divorce and that he has a good understanding of the civil divorce process. He has a soft demeanor and spoke to the parties in a gentle, although sometimes firm manner. The parties responded to him respectfully, referring to him as "Sheikh," "Mufti," "Sir," or even "Uncle." It is entirely possible that the chairman was on his best behavior when I observed him, but he appeared quite natural during my observations both at the meetings with the parties and in the board meeting.

Meetings with one party only are convened largely for the purposes of gathering information about background, children, civil proceedings, court orders, and reasons for the divorce application. The chairman also explored the possibility of a reconciliation and of a khul-type divorce, but these two issues were addressed in greater detail in the joint meetings. In the joint meetings that I observed, the chairman treated both parties fairly and allowed both an opportunity to speak and to present their version of events. There was absolutely no indication that the evidence of the women was given any less weight than that of the men. The chairman made it clear to the parties that he had no authority to force a reconciliation if both did not agree, but he would ask them questions to try to elicit some good memories that they might have of their marriage or each other, with various degrees of success. Notwithstanding this, in none of the meetings that I observed did the parties agree to reconcile.

The chairman also explored the issue of the khul, asking the husband if he would consent to one and pointing out to him that there was little benefit in refusing to consent to the divorce when his wife did not wish to remain in the marriage. In all the joint meetings the chairman offered the parties the opportunity to think about what had been discussed (the period ranging from three to seven days) before making a final decision. All of this takes place within an Islamic framework, so the chairman and parties make reference to what they believe Islam says on any given issue.[12]

The main criticism of the meetings by the women I interviewed was that the objectives of the meetings were never entirely clear, and I share this view. The parties did not seem to be aware at the beginning of the meeting what its purpose was, nor were they sure at the end what was likely to happen next. Some of the women said that they had expected a final decision at the end of the meeting and had not been aware that the matter would need to go before the board. I suggest that the purpose of each meeting should be stated in writing prior to the meeting and repeated verbally at the start of the meeting. The issue of reconciliation should be separated from the issue of an agreed-upon divorce. One of the goals of the Sharia is the preservation of the family, and within an Islamic framework it is fair to explore the issue of reconciliation. However, there are better ways of exploring this issue, and there should be a more systematic process for identifying cases where a joint meeting may or may not be appropriate.

My suggestion is that once an application is submitted the case should be assigned to a female support worker. She should take a detailed account from the wife and address the issue of reconciliation with her. Many of the women interviewed explained that they would have felt more comfortable speaking to a woman about the personal and sometimes intimate issues regarding their marriages. Indeed, some of them gave me details about their marital breakdown that they had never mentioned in the Sharia council process. A female support worker could also provide a screening process to discuss with the wife if she were willing to consider a reconciliation and whether she would be willing to attend a joint meeting to explore this issue. Even if she were not willing to reconcile, the support worker could also address with the wife any concerns that she may might have about attending joint meetings or hearings for the purposes of the divorce, the most obvious concerns being allegations of abuse, violence, or any other threats to her safety. In this way additional support that the wife might need could be identified prior to any joint meetings or hearings. I noted in my observations that the IJB allowed women to wait in a separate office when they came for a joint meeting. I saw one of the administrative workers who went out of his way to wait for a female applicant, and as soon as she walked into the building he took her into the office so that she did not have to sit in the waiting area with her husband. She later informed me in her interview that she had told the administrative worker she felt very distressed at the thought of facing her husband alone, and she had been informed that as soon as she came the IJB would ensure she sat separately from him. The staff also suggested to the women who did not wish to come into contact with their husbands outside the mosque area that they sit in the women's part of the mosque and wait for their husbands to leave before leaving themselves. The women's section of the mosque has an entirely separate means of entry and exit, which is clearly identified. Daily activities for women take place in this section, so it would be very unlikely that a man would be able to walk into the area unnoticed and without someone asking him to leave. The mosque also has security cameras throughout. I observed the staff speaking to the women in a reassuring manner when they appeared nervous or anxious.

The IJB staff informed me that there were occasions where they considered it inappropriate to hold a joint meeting—for example, when the husband is subject to a non-molestation order or bail conditions or the staff have been advised by social services that such a meeting is inappropriate. Also they have sometimes allowed women to attend joint meetings with a family member, a police officer, or social worker for support. The chairman informed me that having a family member present requires careful consideration in each case, as family members are not always helpful and indeed sometimes their presence puts pressure on the wife to take a particular course of action. In many of the meetings that I observed the women were asked by the chairman if anyone was pressuring them in any way.

While individually these are all good practices, there seems to be no systematic approach to identifying and addressing women's vulnerabilities or concerns. I would suggest that this is an area in which IJB staff members would benefit from some training. A support worker could identify when a joint meeting is inappropriate, or even when appropriate, and could recommend measures to protect against vulnerabilities, including her own attendance at a joint meeting to support the wife. In my observations I noted that the women would sometimes direct their responses to me or look to me for support. Some of them even commented that they found my presence helpful to them even though I was simply observing and did not participate in the meeting itself.

If the wife is unwilling to reconcile with the husband, the Sharia council can move on to the next stage to adjudicate on the status of the marriage. In the interests of open and fair justice this may well require both parties to attend the session, but it will be clear that the purpose of the session is adjudication on the marriage and that it is more akin to a hearing than a meeting. At this hearing the chairman of the board may ask the husband to consider consenting to the divorce, and if he will not consent then the chairman may wish to hear from both parties regarding any allegations, consider any evidence they bring with them, and hear from any witnesses. This in my view is entirely legitimate provided there has been a prior consideration of any vulnerabilities and the purpose of this hearing is explained to the parties beforehand and at the hearing. If the husband is not willing to agree to the khul, the chairman should, at the conclusion of this meeting, inform the parties that the matter will be put before the board and a date given to the parties by which they will receive a final decision. That final decision should be provided in writing. I have noted that the faskh certificates issued by the IJB often state the basis on which the faskh has been determined. It would be good practice to provide a short written determination, similar to a judgment, for each case.

In considering the evidence, if the chairman has concerns regarding the credibility of any evidence, he explores the matter further with the parties. As mentioned earlier, in my experience there was no indication that the evidence of the women was considered any less credible than that of the men. There is no formal procedure for giving evidence, such as swearing an oath or a requirement for written statements. This allows for flexibility. If the process was more formal, the parties might find it difficult to meet strict evidential requirements.

A specific type of oath may be used as an evidential tool if the chairman is unable to decide who is telling the truth. The oath is based on Islamic evidence rules and can apply to any disputed issue of fact. The chairman can employ an oath to bring a disputed issue to a conclusion when there is no other way. The burden of proof in Islam is on the one who makes the allegation, so if, for example, the husband alleges he paid the *mahr*,[13] he puts forward his evidence. If the wife denies the allegation, she may be asked to take an oath to confirm she is telling the truth. Once she has taken this oath, there is no further debate and the matter is settled. The taking of an oath in this manner is very serious and is not offered lightly. As Muslims who believe that there will be a day when they will be judged by Allah, parties will be reminded of the serious repercussions of lying on oath. The only occasions on which I noted the use of this oath involved instances of missing gold jewelry or mahr.

Observations of the Board Meeting

Eleven files were considered at the board meeting, which took place over one full day. Many of the issues raised at the meeting have already been mentioned. Overall I found that the board members gave careful consideration to each of the files. There appeared to be genuine concern for the people involved in the cases, particularly the women. The board members were concerned about delays and at times interrogated the administrative staff regarding procedural delays that were evident in some of the files. Matters were discussed within an Islamic framework, but there was considerable flexibility and the board members did not appear to be following any one school of Islamic thought. Their discussions were wide ranging, taking into account matters such as the effect of the divorce on other family members, the position in civil law, the cultural background of the parties, the level of engagement by the husband, and any demands being made. The primary concern always remained the needs of the parties themselves, particularly the needs of the wife.

The board had to address some complex international jurisdictional issues and issues concerning the overlap with English civil law. In my view, the board members would benefit from training on these matters, as mentioned earlier, as well as from the help of someone with legal qualifications and experience who could act as an adviser, much like a clerk who assists lay magistrates. Training would equip the board members with a deeper understanding of the civil process (sometimes I noted that members were asking one another about the civil process). More important, if board members who already have detailed knowledge of Islamic law have a more detailed understanding of the civil process too, they can continue to develop the evolution of Islam for minorities living in the West. Sharia councils by themselves have decided to make use of a husband's consent to a civil divorce as a basis for the pronouncement of an Islamic divorce. They have remained faithful to orthodox Islamic principles while making use of civil law. It is important that Muslims who have authority and credibility within Muslim communities remain part of this evolving relationship between Islamic law and English law. The only way this will occur is if the board members have sufficient knowledge of the civil process. This all feeds into the development and accommodation of Muslims as minorities within the West.

While there were disagreements over some issues, the board reached a general consensus regarding each file. In all the cases observed, the key issue was the status of the marriage. Consideration was given to how many attempts had been made to contact the husband and, in cases where the husband had responded, to his views. There were no outright refusals of a divorce, although in some cases the board imposed conditions such as requiring a woman to apply for a civil divorce before she would be provided with a faskh certificate. This issue of applying for a civil divorce was discussed in some detail, as the board members were concerned that Muslims were not being sufficiently encouraged to obtain a civil divorce in conjunction with their religious one.

In the discussion of each case, the board was informed of any disputes regarding children or finances, but the members appeared to be fully aware that they had no jurisdiction to adjudicate on these matters and were not seeking to adjudicate.

One final issue is whether it would be helpful if the board had female members. I am not of the view that gender alone should be a basis for board membership, but equally I do not think that suitably qualified women should be precluded. The point of the board meeting is to obtain the advice of all members and to come to an agreed-upon decision. I see no reason why suitably qualified women cannot participate in this process. Having said that, I believe it is of greater importance to the women going through the process that female support workers be present at board meetings to provide necessary information, as is the case for all other members of the staff.

Some Further Comparisons with English Law

It is not my intention in this chapter to compare every aspect of the Sharia council process with English civil law, but some comparisons are useful to note. There is only one ground for divorce in English law, namely that the marriage has irretrievably broken down (Matrimonial Causes Act 1973 s1(1) (MCA 1973), which can be satisfied by any one of the five facts set out in the MCA 1973 s1(2)(a)–(e). The process of obtaining a divorce is by no means simple or easy, but it is the same irrespective of whether it is the husband or wife applying.

The parties are not entitled to commence divorce proceedings within the first year of marriage (MCA 1973 s3). Even after the expiry of this one-year period, civil law allows parties to commence proceedings for divorce immediately only if the petitioner can show that the respondent has behaved unreasonably or has committed adultery. In all other cases there must be a period of at least two years of separation immediately preceding the presentation of the divorce petition. In cases where the petitioner is unable to establish the respondent's unreasonable behavior or adultery, or where the respondent is unwilling to consent to a divorce following a two-year period of separation, there must be a period of five years' separation before the petitioner can commence proceedings. I would argue that although reconciliation is not necessarily directly discussed with the parties, the civil legal system itself has processes that effectively force a couple to remain married long after one or both may have decided they no longer wish to be married.

Islamic law has no specific agreed-upon legal criteria that have to be met in order for a Muslim wife to be granted a faskh. Although there is ample room for flexibility in this area, it was evident that most cases at the ɪᴊʙ were decided on the basis of the wife's allegations of some fault on the part of her husband (similar to unreasonable behavior in English law). These faults included the failure to fulfill orthodox Islamic obligations by the husband, such as not financially providing for the family. It also included allegations that the husband was not abiding by general Islamic obligations such as not praying, or drinking alcohol. In one file, there was evidence of a faskh being granted when parties simply "had a lack of understanding." As a Sharia council is not bound by rigid criteria, in theory they should be much more flexible in deciding on the termination of a marriage.

A respondent in a civil divorce is also encouraged to allow the divorce to proceed uncontested, even if the respondent disputes the allegations being made. There are similarities here to the IJB's encouraging a husband to agree to a divorce by khul, regardless of whether he accepts his wife's version of events. The ɪᴊʙ does, however, make an interesting use of civil law. Where the husband has commenced proceedings for a civil divorce or has signed the acknowledgment of service confirming that he will not contest the divorce, the ɪᴊʙ takes this to mean he has agreed to an Islamic divorce too. This is the case even if the husband informs the ɪᴊʙ that he wanted only a civil divorce and that he is specifically *not* consenting to a religious divorce. This is an example of what has sometimes been termed "British Sharia,"[14] a hybridization where English law is being used to apply aspects of Islamic law. The right to pronounce a talaq is seen as such a powerful right in the hands of the husband that he is not permitted to joke about it or say it without meaning it. The IJB takes the view that if the husband has agreed to a civil divorce, then that is sufficient to issue a fatwa that this couple are now religiously divorced too. In one of the joint meetings that I observed, the husband had commenced civil proceedings and had been issued a decree nisi but was still refusing to agree to a religious divorce. The chairman explained to the husband that his petition was sufficient for an Islamic divorce, although the meeting continued for another hour as the parties debated various allegations that each was making.

A surprising difficulty with making use of civil divorce in this way is that wives do not seem to accept this as a proper religious divorce. One of the women whom I interviewed had been informed that her husband's petition for a civil divorce was sufficient for her religious divorce, but she refused to accept this and insisted that the Sharia council either obtain a khul from her husband or grant her a faskh. In one respect it is understandable why both the IJB and the women would prefer the khul or faskh rather than a fatwa confirming a talaq. As the talaq is given by the husband, it is something that he can rescind provided he does so within the period of *iddah* (normally counted as three menstrual cycles or three months) and that he has given no more than one talaq previously. In many cases it will be in the interests of the wife to obtain a khul or faskh so that she is not left open to the possibility that her husband will revoke his talaq.

An issue that has arisen in recent years is the growing number of Muslims who do not choose to enter into a civil marriage but rather take part in a nikaah-only marriage. Although my research is not directly concerned with this issue, sixty-eight couples had entered into marriages that were valid for civil law purposes and thus required a civil divorce to terminate them. Twenty-nine couples had entered into nikaah-only marriages. Another three couples had married abroad, but the IJB questioned whether the marriage was recognized in the United Kingdom and as such it was treated as a nikaah-only marriage. Thus most Muslim couples had entered into marriages valid for civil law purposes. On closer examination, however, I found that fifty-four of the sixty-eight couples mentioned above had conducted their nikaah outside of Europe. These nikaahs were automatically recognized by English law, normally because one of the parties was entering the United Kingdom as a spouse. Such couples required a civil divorce as well as a religious ruling. It is evident that a significant proportion of Muslims who entered into a nikaah in the United Kingdom had not entered into a civil marriage. No indication is given in the case files as to the reason for this. One may argue that British Muslims are simply doing what a significant proportion of the rest of British society is doing, namely cohabiting rather than entering into a legally recognized marriage.[15] Those who enter into a nikaah-only marriage are not married as far as civil law is concerned; they are cohabitees and there is no civil divorce to adjudicate upon. In effect, this is the Muslim *halal* (permissible in Islam) way of cohabiting. As stated, this is not a topic that I have explored in any detail in this chapter, but whatever the reasons for this trend, it highlights that the work of Sharia councils is unlikely to diminish. To the contrary, for many Muslim women Sharia councils will be the only authority that can decide on the termination of their relationship. In some respects one could argue it makes no difference to the volume of a Sharia council's work because even those who go through a civil marriage will still want a religious termination of that marriage.

The role and place of Sharia councils is reaching a pivotal point in English legal history. They are no longer simply responding to a community need. They have a growing body of users, and they are now attracting a significant, indeed an increasing, amount of media and government attention.[16] In my view Sharia councils have remained reactive for far too long. They need to think carefully about the direction that they wish to head in and put in place processes that will enable them to deliver a professional service within an Islamic framework. I suggest that there are two primary functions that they can fulfill. First, they can adjudicate on a religious divorce. The need for this could be met in a much better manner, with the inclusion of at least female support workers, a more structured timetable, the provision of clearer information to their users, a screening process with suitable measures to address issues of vulnerability, the keeping of users up to date throughout, and written reasons for any final determination.

Second, they can provide mediation services to address disputes regarding children and finances within an Islamic framework. I have not addressed this in this chapter. It seems clear that the issue of the status of the marriage must be separated from the ancillary issues concerning children and finances, although I do accept that a financial element comes into the khul divorce if a husband asks for the mahr in return for his consent to the khul.

Neither the IJB nor the women I interviewed were asking for Sharia councils to be given a legal status equivalent to that of civil courts. What many of the women did ask for was that civil courts and Sharia councils make a greater effort to cooperate with each other. At the moment Sharia councils seem to be making some use of civil law, while civil law for the most part ignores the religious status of a Muslim woman's marriage. The IJB board members and scholars of Sharia councils generally need to have more than a superficial understanding of English civil law, not only so that they can make more informed, specific decisions on individual cases, but more important, so that they can establish a long-term strategy whereby they continue to develop the jurisprudential rules for British Muslims living as a minority in the United Kingdom, at least in the sphere of personal family law. They have the legitimacy on the ground to enable such developments to take place.

For its part, if English law wishes to see the needs of Muslim women being met, the answer is neither to ban Sharia councils nor to ignore them. Rather it is to recognize that Sharia councils provide an essential service for British Muslim women and to assist them in providing that service while remaining faithful to normative Islam.[17] In my observations of the IJB it is clear that although this may not be an easy task, it is certainly achievable.[18]

Notes

1. This perception is often created by the media in its discussions of Sharia councils. For example, media refer to Sharia councils as "courts" that operate in "secret" or suggest that I have gained "rare" or "exclusive" access to them, or it subjects them to undercover investigations such as that undertaken by the BBC Panorama program "Secrets of Britain's Sharia Councils" in 2013. This type of language and reporting has created a perception that secret networks of courts are operating in the United Kingdom.

2. Arbitration and Mediation Services (Equality) Bill [HL] 2014–15, a private member's bill introduced by Baroness Caroline Cox. There is some debate on

the extent of impact this piece of legislation will have on Sharia councils. It has been launched three times, and having received its third reading from the House of Lords it is now awaiting its first reading in the House of Commons. http://services.parliament.uk/bills/2015-16/arbitrationandmediationservicesequality/stages.html, accessed 17 June 2016.

3. In using these terms, I draw on the work of Merry (1988), where she discusses legal pluralism as a situation in which two or more legal systems coexist in the same social field.

4. Ralph Grillo (2015) notes in the preface to *Muslim Families, Politics and the Law* that for Muslims "what I eat, what I wear, how I pray" are all aspects of what is seen as contentious across Europe.

5. http://www.birmingham.gov.uk/cs/Satellite?c=Page&childpagename=Planning-and-Regeneration%2FPageLayout&cid=1223408087932&pagename=BCC%2FCommon%2FWrapper%2FWrapper, accessed 17 June 2016. All figures have been obtained from the Birmingham City Council's website page containing breakdowns of information obtained from the 2011 Census, which took place on 27 March 2011.

6. The rise of Salafism, particularly in Western nations, has been explored in more detail elsewhere (Hamid 2009, 384–402; Commins 2006).

7. The IJB maintains individual files only when a formal application is completed, which triggers the opening of a manual file. For any other queries, some paperwork may be maintained but no individual case file is created. This means that, when any other service user inquires about a matter, it is unlikely that a file will be opened. The record keeping for matters other than an application for a divorce is an issue that is currently under review by the IJB, and it seems likely a more rigid file management system will be introduced for all matters.

8. It is interesting to note that some Muslim feminist scholars such as Aysha A. Hidayatullah (2014, 147) are asking what it would mean if Muslim feminists found that the Quran does sanction gender hierarchy.

9. I acknowledge there are other methods of Islamic divorce but I have concentrated on the most widely accepted and widely used methods.

10. There is some disagreement as to whether, strictly speaking, the husband's consent is required or if he can be ordered to give his consent. The IJB issues a khul certificate only when the husband consents.

11. Where parties have entered into a civil marriage this issue has been referred to as a "limping marriage" in that a civil divorce has been obtained but the wife is still unable to free herself from the religious marriage.

12. One husband brought with him what appeared to be a booklet that he had printed from the Internet about the marital relationship in Islam and how spouses should behave toward one another. Parties frequently referred to what they considered one another's Islamic obligations within the marriage.

13. *Mahr* is the gift to the bride from the groom. It is an essential part of the Islamic marriage contract and can be given either at the time of the marriage or later. Normally it is a sum of money or jewelry but can be anything of value.

14. David Pearl and Werner Menski (1998) originally referred to this hybridization as "angrezi shariat."

15. According to the report of the Office of National Statistics "Families and Households 2014" during the period 2004–14, the proportion of cohabiting couples grew by 29.7 percent, the fastest-growing type of family in the United Kingdom. http://www.ons.gov.uk/ons/dcp171778_393133.pdf, accessed 17 June 2016.

16. The government has announced a review of Sharia councils and has also announced the panel members who will carry out the review. It is unfortunate that this review forms part of the government's Counter-Extremism Strategy. The government website states that the review will examine the workings of Sharia councils, and its terms of reference will also include exploring whether, and to what extent, the application of Sharia law may be incompatible with the law in England and Wales. The panel is expected to complete its review in 2017. https://www.gov.uk/government/news/independent-review-into-sharia-law-launched, accessed 17 June 2016.

17. Grillo (2015, 279) refers to a comment that I made to him, namely that Muslims are allowed to call themselves Muslim as long as they don't actually do those things that make them Muslim. An example of this would be the desire by Muslim women to follow normative, orthodox Islam in obtaining a religious ruling on the status of their marriage.

18. As in all matters I end by stating that I pray what I have written is pleasing to Allah azwajal, that any mistakes are wholly mine, and that if there is any benefit in what I have written it comes entirely from the blessings of Allah. And Allah knows best.

Bibliography

Bano, Samia (2012). *Muslim Women and Shari'ah Councils: Transcending the Boundaries of Community and Law*. London: Palgrave Macmillan.

Birmingham Local Authority (2013). "2011 Census: Population and Migration Topic Report." Census report, Birmingham Local Authority.

Commins, David (2006). *The Wahhabi Mission and Saudi Arabia*. London: I. B. Tauris.

Douglas, Gillian, Sandberg, Norman, Doe, Russell, Gilliat-Ray, Sophie, and Khan, Asma (2013). "Accomodating Religious Divorce in the Secular State: A Case Study Analysis." In Maclean Mavis and Eeklaar John (eds.), *Managing Family Justice in Diverse Societies*, 185–201. Oxford: Hart.

Gilliat-Ray, Sophie (2010). *Muslims in Britain: An Introduction.* Cambridge: Cambridge Univeristy Press.

Grillo, Ralph (2105). *Muslim Families, Politics and the Law: A Legal Industry in Multicultural Britain.* Farnham: Ashgate.

Hamid, Sadek (2009). "The Attraction of 'Authentic' Islam Salafism and British Muslim Youth." In Roel Meijer (ed.), *Global Salafism Islam's New Religious Movement*, 384–403. London: C. Hurst.

Hidayatullah, Aysha A. (2014). *Feminist Edges of the Quran.* Oxford: Oxford University Press.

Keshavjee, M. Mohammed (2013). *Islam, Sharia & Alternative Dispute Resolution: Mechanisms for Legal Redress in the Muslim Community.* London: I. B. Tauris.

Kundani, Arun (2014). *The Muslims Are Coming! Islamophobia, Extremism and the Domestic War on Terror.* London: Verso Books.

MacEoin, Dennis and Green, David (2009). *Shariah Law or "One Law for All?"* Trowbridge: Cromwell Press Group, for Civitas: Institute for the Study of Civil Society.

Merry, Sally Engle (1988). "Legal Pluralism." *Law and Society Review* 22: 5.

Pearl, David and Menski, Werner (1998). *Muslim Family Law.* London: Sweet & Maxwell.

Shah-Kazemi, Sonia Nurin (2001). *Untying the Knot: Muslim Women, Divorce and the Shariah.* Nuffield Foundation. http://www.nuffieldfoundation.org/untying-knot-muslim-women-divorce-and-shariah, accessed 17 June 2016.

Tucker, Judith E. (2008). *Women, Family, and Gender in Islamic Law.* Cambridge: Cambridge University Press.

7

British Muslim Women and Barriers to Obtaining a Religious Divorce

Shaista Gohir and Nazmin Akthar-Sheikh

NO FAITH OR CULTURE can, or should ever be able to, compel a woman to remain in a marriage she does not wish to continue. In the Muslim-majority country of Pakistan, its Supreme Court declared as far back as 1967 that a woman's right to a divorce, or *khullah* (a divorce initiated by the woman rather than *talaq*, which is a divorce initiated by the man), is indeed established (*Bibi v. Amin*, 1967). A woman in Pakistan is not required to provide any cause, whether good or bad, to exercise her right and obtain this divorce. The religion of Islam makes clear that a woman cannot be compelled to remain in a marriage she does not wish to be in, and while state and cultural practices may differ in how this right of choice is exercised, the right in itself is very much confirmed.

The Convention on the Elimination of All Forms of Discrimination Against Women (CEDAW) places an obligation on the United Kingdom to prevent discrimination against women in marriage and divorce. In 2013 the CEDAW committee issued a recommendation to all member states that legislation be adopted to eliminate discriminatory aspects of the family law regime, whether civil, religious, ethnic custom, or any combination of such laws and practices that regulate women. In the United Kingdom, however, the story appears to be different when one considers the qualitative evidence available to the Muslim Women's Network UK (MWNUK) in the form of lived experiences of Muslim women in the United Kingdom who try to obtain an Islamic divorce.

166

MWNUK is a charity operating nationally and working toward the promotion of equality, diversity, and social inclusion of Muslim women in the United Kingdom. This includes working at a grassroots level with Muslim women, providing them support and guidance, as well as engaging with governmental bodies and other key stakeholder organizations to effect positive change. MWNUK has more than six hundred members, among which are a diverse range of individuals and organizations with a collective reach of tens of thousands of women. Muslim women are highly diverse in terms of their ethnicity, culture, socioeconomic status, education, and religiosity; this diversity is important to bear in mind throughout the course of this chapter and in particular with respect to the various case studies that will be presented. Although MWNUK is focused on highlighting the experiences of Muslim women, in each case there will be a natural overlap with other cultural and socioeconomic factors, as well as individual characteristics and circumstances involved in each case. Thus, while some Muslim women have faced difficulties in trying to obtain an Islamic divorce, others have recounted positive experiences to MWNUK despite various similarities among them. Moreover, not all Muslim women approach MWNUK or indeed need to. In a similar vein not all Muslim women need to approach a Sharia council or utilize any other mechanism to finalize their Islamic divorce; the issues that will be discussed in this chapter are not reflective of the total female Muslim population of the United Kingdom. However, while not all Muslim women in the United Kingdom face problems, MWNUK's work highlights that there are a large group of women who do, and the hurdles they face require addressing. This chapter is aimed at highlighting the experiences of Muslim women in the United Kingdom when they attempt to obtain an Islamic divorce, as uncovered through MWNUK case studies, workshops, round tables, and other events in the hope that the issues such women face can be addressed. MWNUK regularly deals with inquiries and calls for help related to Islamic divorce, and it is vital that these Muslim women not be restricted in living their lives.

It is also simplistic to assume that Muslim women are a homogeneous group with the same problems or that one solution could be sufficient for all in respect of a particular problem. Unfortunately, it appears from the vast number of cases that come to MWNUK that there are Muslim women in the United Kingdom who, irrespective of their various backgrounds, hold many misunderstandings in respect of their rights within the realm of Islamic marriages and divorce. MWNUK is regularly contacted by Muslim women, both through its membership and outside, for support and guidance as to how to overcome their difficulties. Some Muslim women call MWNUK to discuss the problems they face in attempting to obtain an Islamic divorce. However, others contact MWNUK in respect of other problems, such as domestic violence, and issues related to marriage and divorce are uncovered during the investigation of the matter.

MWNUK has consistently been approached by Muslim women seeking support and guidance, and in January 2015 the Muslim Women's Network Helpline was launched to formalize the process and provide a dedicated service for those in need of assistance. It is interesting to note that although MWNUK works on a broad range of issues, including mental health matters, discrimination, and Islamophobia, a recent helpline evaluation of calls and inquiries received showed that out of thirty-nine issues, Islamic divorce was one of the top five, and was an issue even when the initial call was related to homelessness and the need for shelter. As well as the qualitative evidence obtained from such calls and service, MWNUK is informed by the experiences recounted by Muslim women at workshops, events, and round tables across the country. It is important to note that it is the real voices of Muslim women that form the basis of MWNUK's evidence and campaigns for change. This chapter focuses on certain case studies to highlight key issues Muslim women face in the United Kingdom; these, however, are not isolated cases or unique examples.

Whether or not a civil divorce is obtained (and in some cases it cannot be, as there was no legally recognized marriage to begin with), generally a Muslim woman will also want to ensure that she is divorced in accordance with her faith. In Muslim countries the religious authority would be the court system itself. In the United Kingdom, however, aside from having to deal with the stigma of divorce and the pressure to remain in a marriage even if suffering from abuse, Muslim women find themselves at the mercy of others—husbands, community members, and Sharia councils.

Alternative Dispute Resolution for Muslim Women?

Recent times have seen a great push toward the promotion of alternative dispute resolution (ADR) in all legal spheres, and the arena of family law has been no different. In April 2014, the Family and Children Act 2013 made attending an initial mediation information assessment meeting mandatory; the idea is, of course, to come to a resolution in a conciliatory manner while also limiting the costs of litigation. This also saves court time and resources, in turn shortening the process for all.

From experiences recounted to MWNUK through its network, it appears that the aims of ADR are not always achieved, even when Muslim women are within the UK court process itself. The use of conventional forms of ADR is almost always restricted to circumstances involving a legally recognized marriage—that is, where a registered civil marriage was entered into along with a religious marriage in the United Kingdom or in the case of a religious marriage conducted abroad and registered in accordance with the laws of that country with the appropriate authority. Although mediation services can be utilized by anyone involved in a dispute, analysis of case studies and in particular personal statements suggests that Muslim women not involved in litigation are less likely to pursue such an avenue, especially as such a service will not provide them with the solutions (or, more specifically, the Islamic divorce) they seek.

It appears from some of the experiences recounted to MWNUK that due to a lack of understanding of religious and cultural factors at play, key questions are not asked, important issues are overlooked, or their significance is not properly assessed. One experience narrated to MWNUK was that of a couple fighting over the custody of their three-year-old son. The mother proposed that the father take the child after he finished work on Fridays and drop the child off to her on Sunday evenings. The father insisted that the child be dropped off on Thursday evenings or Friday mornings at the latest. The natural question to consider was why the father was so insistent given that he worked full time and would be at work all Friday anyway, but this was not delved into in as great a depth as perhaps required. It was when eventually a family friend questioned his intentions that the significance of Friday was uncovered. The father wanted to be able to take his son to the Friday Jummah prayers while the child was still out of school and able to do so without any disruption to his studies. His workplace was located near a mosque, and he was hoping that his father, the child's grandfather, could bring the child to him on Fridays and they would all go to the mosque together. This would also mean the child would have time to spend with his grandparents as well. Once his true intentions were relayed to the mother, she not only agreed to allow the child to be dropped off at the father's house on Friday mornings but also agreed that should the grandparents be unwell at any point she would herself bring the child to the mosque. Perhaps had the matter been investigated in greater detail earlier by other agencies involved and in contact with the father, such as the respective lawyers, valuable court time could have been saved and the emotional well-being of the parents and child ensured. In this matter no mediators were involved who might have assisted in bringing to light the crux of the issue sooner. It must be borne in mind that individual characteristics also need to be considered; it is not always the case that if a question is asked the correct answer will be provided, and in this case the father did not volunteer much information to his lawyer. However, this matter does highlight the need for greater awareness of faith and culture, and MWNUK has access to many other case studies where a lack of understanding has led to key issues remaining unexplored by various agencies, including social workers, even when the matter was within the court system.

In another matter brought to MWNUK's attention, the father insisted on sole custody of his children on the basis of his belief that Islam ordains that children remain with their father. The parents agreed to mediation after family members advised that it would be more beneficial to discuss and strive for a mutual agreement than to become involved in a prolonged court case. In this instance, the mediator was also Muslim (although other details about the mediator were not disclosed to MWNUK; the case was recounted during a focus group). He discussed, first, the fact that according to Islamic principles the mother is given custody if the children are young and, second, that it is important to ensure a positive upbringing for the children. The parents agreed to joint custody. They were satisfied that their mutual decision was for the betterment of everyone involved and in line with their faith, which was reassuring, especially for the mother, who would have faced her family's question as to why the father had not been given custody.

This is not to say that the significance of Friday or Islamic principles relating to the presumption of custody would have been obvious only to a Muslim lawyer or mediator, nor does it mean that the same situation would apply to another Muslim couple. Indeed, a number of MWNUK case studies show Muslim couples having requested that their mediator be of a different faith or ethnicity so as to allow a fair playing field devoid of bias or conflict of interest. British Muslims are of various backgrounds, and it is unwise to assume that one rule would apply to all. This case does, however, highlight the importance of being aware of religious and cultural factors as well as the need to provide a service appropriate for the couple and the circumstances. Unfortunately, not everyone will have such awareness.

A solution in this regard is to ensure that detailed training in and awareness of cultural and faith matters are included in initial accreditation and also continuing professional development (CPD) training of mediators. Indeed, such training and awareness would be beneficial for all agents involved, including lawyers, judges, and even social workers. The inclusion of female Muslim mediators would also assist in promoting inclusivity and diversity within the process as well as empower Muslim women, both as service providers and as service users, and MWNUK hopes to be able to encourage more Muslim women to enter the profession of mediation. It is appreciated that it is not always possible to know immediately which form or the extent of mediation required—that is, general or specialist—but it is important to be able to first gain an understanding of the situation. After that it can be decided which form of mediation, or even co-mediation, is needed.

The Judgment of the "Wise" Elders

It is interesting that Islam itself directs Muslims to seek conciliatory redress in the form of mediation and arbitration. "If you fear a breach between them, appoint [two] arbitrators, one from his family, and the other one from hers; if they wish for peace God will cause their reconciliation" (Quran 4:35). As an example of how this principle is being misused to the detriment of some Muslim women in the United Kingdom, the practice of *bisar* (generally translated as "justice" or "charge"),[1] which is utilized by some individuals in the British Bangladeshi Muslim community, will be considered. It must first be noted that although the practice of bisar is being considered because of the qualitative evidence available to MWNUK in this respect, this practice is not utilized by all individuals within the British Bangladeshi Muslim community. Nor is it limited to the Bangladeshi Muslim community; MWNUK is aware of examples of the same practice or very similar variants being used within the

Pakistani Muslim, Indian Muslim, and Indian Sikh communities. Second, in such a discussion there is an undeniable overlap between faith, culture, socioeconomic factors, and individual circumstances. By discussing the concept of bisar, MWNUK wishes to highlight the issues faced by some Muslim women in the United Kingdom who become involved in this form of mediation.

In respect of bisar, where a dispute has arisen among a couple or even between other family members, elders are called to assess the situation and come to a decision. Usually male, these elders may or may not be related to the couple but are regarded as wise, respected, and trusted members of the community. Members and service users of MWNUK who have undergone such a process have stated that the elders in reality become involved due to familial links (such as a link with the grandfather of a spouse) or due to a hierarchical system linked to Bangladesh, which is then replicated within the community in the United Kingdom. For example, the forefathers of this individual may have been in positions of authority in the village from which the family members in dispute hail; it is likely that their offspring in the United Kingdom will in turn hold positions on the mosque committee or community center, which adds to the respect with which they are held. Members and service users who are not of the British Bangladeshi Muslim community but have been a part of a similar process have mentioned similar experiences. Irrespective of how they are chosen, the fact is they are not trained mediators or arbitrators and possess neither the knowledge nor the skills to act as such. With their patriarchal beliefs and cultural bias, their decisions offend both Islamic principles and UK law.

For example, in the MWNUK case study of Rahima, who initially approached us for guidance in respect of her financial debt, her complaints against her husband and in-laws included their being abusive, curtailing her freedom, and placing her under great financial stress by frivolously spending her wages.[2] Her husband's complaint was that Rahima was not performing the household chores and was "too modern" and argumentative; it was his complaints that were given attention. Questions were asked as to why Rahima was still working when she should be fulfilling her household duties, despite Rahima's father's assertions that it had been made clear before the marriage that Rahima wanted to further her career. The fact that her husband was spending the wages Rahima earned at the very same job he was complaining of, and the domestic abuse she had suffered, were ignored. The result of the mediation by the community elders was that Rahima was considered to be at fault and told to leave her job and return to her husband's home to try again. She was told that divorce should be only a last resort in Islam, and by wanting to end the marriage without giving her husband another chance she was going against her religion. It is common for various *hadiths* (accounts of the sayings of Prophet Muhammad [pbuh], which were recorded after his death) to be manipulated to support such claims and emotionally blackmail Muslim women, who want to ensure that their actions do not offend their religion. In reality the *hadiths* either are used selectively or are regarded as weak and potentially fabricated.

When after various attempts it was clear that the marriage had irretrievably broken down, the families called a final meeting at Rahima's maternal home; the fathers of the spouses, Rahima's grandfather, her husband's eldest uncle, and a number of mutual family friends were invited and between them decided on the terms of the separation. Rahima was in a separate room upstairs throughout these discussions and called later to sign an agreement handwritten onto a piece of paper in which she agreed to withdraw her claims to *mahr* (a marriage gift that the groom gives to the bride, an essential part of the marriage contract) and return the jewelry she received at the time of the wedding, and in return the husband would pay the monthly installments of the loan he made her take out in her name during their marriage while his business was failing. The unfairness of the decision is clear. Rahima's husband stopped making loan payments a few months after the divorce was finalized; the family community elders who had made the decision for Rahima could do nothing.

Sharia Councils

A further option is to seek the assistance of a Sharia council operating in the United Kingdom, a body that is said to provide assistance in Islamic divorce matters. This is especially the case for Muslim women, who have entered into an Islamic marriage only and are therefore not deemed to be married under UK law. It is noteworthy that services tend to be sought by Muslim women who are finding it difficult to acquire an Islamic divorce from their husbands (Kennett 2011, 9), rather than for dispute resolution.

Before proceeding, we wish to make it clear that not all Muslim women face difficulties in obtaining an Islamic divorce, and there are indeed women who have had positive experiences with Sharia councils. MWNUK, however, is regularly approached by Muslim women complaining of negative experiences that need to be addressed. Certain complaints regularly appear in MWNUK case studies, including those of Muslim women who say that they are not listened to, that their grievances are not taken seriously or given due consideration, and that they are questioned in accusatory tones and made to feel guilty about pursuing a divorce, while the grievances of their husbands are given disproportionate attention.

Ameera's situation is a composite of MWNUK case studies that highlights key issues faced by Muslim women approaching Sharia councils.[3] Ameera's husband had married again; it was an Islamic marriage, which is not recognized as a legal marriage under UK law, and as such bigamy charges could not be pursued. He would regularly watch pornography and rape her; he had also given Ameera sexually transmitted infections. Her husband would not consent to an Islamic divorce. When she contacted the Sharia council for a divorce, the members pressured her into mediation. As the council was in another city, she was instructed to visit a local religious adviser for the mediation; this man worked in association with the council, and she was expected to visit this man alone. Intrusive questions were asked about her sex life. Despite her testimonies of rape and abuse, she was told that polygyny was allowed in Islam and was asked to "be patient; you have lasted twenty-two years, why do you want a divorce now?" This was the extent of her mediation, for which she had to pay a fee. The abuse she had suffered was not taken into account and *hadith*s condemning divorce were quoted in an attempt to dissuade Ameera from pursuing the divorce. Ameera's experiences offend Islamic principles relating to domestic violence and polygamy (Quran 4:129), the Human Rights Act 1998 and Equality Act 2010, as well as Article 16 of the Convention on the Elimination of All Forms of Discrimination Against Women (CEDAW). It is interesting to note that the mediation that the Sharia council in Ameera's case insisted on was not provided by a reputable and accredited mediation service; it was provided by an individual connected to such a service. Surely if the council believed mediation was necessary, it should not have mattered who Ameera chose for such a service.

Dalia came to MWNUK after two years of attempting to obtain an Islamic divorce from three different Sharia councils.[4] Two of the councils did not pick up on the fact that her husband, who was raising objections to the Islamic divorce, had been the one to instigate the civil divorce. They in turn insisted that the Islamic divorce process be deemed as having been commenced by her and that she pay her husband £25,000 (about US$ 36,000) before they would grant an Islamic divorce; there was no evidence that this sum was owed to her husband and the two Sharia councils based their decision solely on the husband stating that it was. A third Sharia council recognized that as her husband initiated the civil divorce this should also be interpreted as his having initiated the Islamic divorce, which would negate any potential financial claims he could make against her. The council, however, insisted that the husband attend the hearing, which he hadn't planned to do given that he was purposely creating barriers to his wife's obtaining an Islamic divorce. MWNUK was able to help her finally obtain an Islamic divorce elsewhere.

In a further MWNUK case study, a victim of forced marriage ran away from home and was hiding in a refuge. She approached a Sharia council for her divorce, and the council arranged for her to attend a meeting with them on the same day that they arranged for her family to attend a separate meeting. Although the appointment times were different, there were, of course, still concerns for her safety, as the family would be able to monitor her entering and leaving the building and potentially could uncover the refuge where she was hiding. MWNUK intervened: the appointment day was changed and an MWNUK caseworker was sent with her; however, the meeting itself was far from constructive, as the victim's account of forced marriage was questioned in an accusatory manner, and she had to be provided with counseling and emotional support to recover from the ordeal.

Such processes are tantamount to arbitration (in the procedural sense), and in reality Sharia councils should be deemed to operate under the Arbitration Act 1996. MWNUK has been informed by Muslim women that some of these organizations claim they provide neither mediation nor arbitration and merely facilitate requests for Islamic divorces, thus asserting that the Arbitration Act does not apply. However (keeping the principles of equality and justice aside for the moment and concentrating solely on procedure), when a Muslim woman requests a divorce and has to prove her case against her husband, await assessment by the Sharia council as to whether an Islamic divorce will be granted, which includes awaiting evidence from her husband, and then accept the final decision, how is this not arbitration? When a Muslim woman who has suffered domestic abuse has to return to the Sharia council again and again to put forward her request for divorce and wait for its acceptance of her request, is it not acting as an arbitrator? It is especially so as members and service users have informed MWNUK of some Sharia councils that give the impression their decisions hold legal weight and are binding; admittedly, however, this is not directly stated, and women's lack of knowledge and understanding about legal matters is a contributing factor in building such impressions. In turn, it should follow that all Sharia councils be made to abide by the requirements of the Arbitration Act to act fairly and impartially with respect to the parties, and Muslim women should be able to challenge their decisions when duties are breached.

If we now consider the Muslim Arbitration Tribunal (MAT), which does profess to operate under the Arbitration Act, we can see that questions of transparency and fairness remain of concern. For example, the MAT is said to have dealt with domestic violence cases where husbands were allegedly instructed to take anger management classes and receive community mentoring in return for the women's withdrawal of police complaints (Bano 2012a, 241). Thus operation under the Arbitration Act does not in itself suffice as protection for Muslim women in the United Kingdom.

MWNUK case studies and experiences recounted by Muslim women at various workshops and events suggest that some Sharia councils follow a hardline view that custody is the right of the father only, thus pressuring British Muslim women to abandon their request for a divorce in order to keep their children with them or to agree to unfair terms in respect of child custody, visitation rights, or even maintenance. Yet countries such as Iran and Bangladesh that place great importance on the identity of the father, to the point that even admission into schools is dependent on this information, at least on a legislative basis appear to provide better protective measures to Muslim women who wish to divorce their husbands than does the United Kingdom. The Islamic Republic of Iran follows Sharia law from a Shia perspective. Under Article 1169 of the Iranian Civil Code, the mother has priority in the custody of children until the age of seven, after which custody reverts to the father. However, even after the child has reached this age, the court is still able to decide that it is better for the child to remain with the mother rather than to be in the custody of the father; this may be the case when the father is known to be abusive or an alcoholic and the child's physical and moral upbringing would be in jeopardy.[5] A similar case is provided for by the Family Court Ordinances of 1985 and Article 17 of the Guardian and Wards Act in Bangladesh, where a majority of Muslims are of the Sunni sect and follow the Hanafi school of thought.

It must also be noted that, as with the situation involving the community elders, there is no evidence to suggest that Sharia council members, mediators, and caseworkers have had any adequate training in mediation, arbitration, or even general counseling. They, therefore, have neither the skills nor the knowledge to deal with family and divorce matters, whether from an Islamic or UK perspective. It is also of concern that panelists can interchangeably act as mediators with no separation of role or procedure. The lack of training, lack of transparency, and lack of accountability and discriminatory processes make it essential that the issues surrounding certain Sharia councils be addressed as soon as possible.

Benchmarking

Would benchmarking Sharia councils when they agree to adhere to good practice standards improve the situation? It is estimated that approximately eighty-five Sharia council operate in the United Kingdom, although the exact number is not known (BBC News 2012). The practices of Sharia councils will vary in accordance with the different schools of thought and individual understandings of Islamic principles (Sardar Ali 2013, 13). The first problem with the proposed solution is the inability to identify all Sharia councils operating in the United Kingdom; research performed by the University of Reading as recently as 2012 identified only thirty Sharia councils that issued Islamic divorces, and of these only twenty-two cooperated with the researchers (Bano 2012b, 14). This would mean that some Sharia councils follow good practice standards while others continue in the same fashion. We would then need to undertake a campaign in order to inform Muslim women as to which councils have agreed to implement good practice standards and, in turn, which councils they should approach for assistance. The second problem is that benchmarking relies on voluntary agreement and therefore does not compel Sharia councils to go along with such an agreement. Where they do, they would not necessarily be required to do more than pay lip-service to the agreement while maintaining the status quo, and instances of Muslim women being told that their husbands' polygamy is not a ground for Islamic divorce would continue to occur. Bearing in mind, as suggested, that the actions and processes of the councils should be regulated by the Arbitration Act 1996 even though the mere statement that they do not provide mediation or arbitration creates a sufficient loophole for not following the Arbitration Act, it is unlikely that benchmarking without mechanisms in place to ensure accountability will make any difference.

It has already been suggested that one means to address the gap between religious mediation and arbitration is to provide better training and greater inclusion of women mediators and arbitrators, so as to offer specialized services where necessary, especially for Muslim women. MUNUK is currently exploring the possibility of a model divorce service, which includes participation by women, even if it is not entirely women-led, and applies Islamic principles on a gender-equitable basis as well as adhering to principles of fairness and best interests as required by the family and equality laws of the United Kingdom. Round table meetings have been arranged to explore the possibilities. The aim is to replace Sharia councils with this alternative service; this would, of course, require a strategic campaign to raise awareness as well as ensure national reach. With the availability of such a service, receiving an Islamic divorce would become a mere formality. That is, where it was clear that the marriage had irretrievably broken down, Muslim women would not have to continue putting their case forward as to why they should be granted a divorce. It is noted, however, that such a service would take time to develop and establish itself, and MWNUK is conscious of the fact that it might still result in British Muslim women choosing between the services available. It is important, therefore, that the current situation, which limits the rights of British Muslim women, be addressed as quickly as possible and that additional legislative measures be suggested.

Facilitating Islamic Divorces via English Law

According to the Divorce (Religious Marriages) Act 2002, the court may order that a decree of divorce not be made absolute without a declaration by both parties that they have taken such steps as required to dissolve any religious marriage. These provisions have been used successfully by the Jewish community, and this process can also apply to Muslims if an order is granted by the Lord Chancellor to include the Muslim community as other "prescribed" usages under the act. Thus where the couple have entered into both a civil and Islamic marriage, the courts can ensure that the husband grants the Islamic divorce by withholding the decree absolute. Without this decree absolute the husband would be unable to move on and remarry, which would act as an incentive for him to agree to an Islamic divorce. MWNUK will formally apply for an order, which makes the Divorce (Religious Marriages) Act applicable to Muslim marriages. MWNUK notes the difference in the circumstances of Jewish and Muslim women in that the consent of the husband is mandatory in Jewish law, which is not the case for Islamic divorces; however, this does not change the reality, as highlighted by case studies, that in actual fact Muslim women are prevented from obtaining an Islamic divorce due to hurdles imposed by their husbands.

It must be highlighted that the Divorce (Religious Marriages) Act requires only a declaration that the necessary steps have been taken to obtain an Islamic divorce; this does not mean that the husband or the Sharia council cannot continue to create obstacles after the decree absolute has been granted. It may be necessary, therefore, to ask for the Islamic divorce certificate to be produced at court before matters are finalized. In turn it is necessary for judges and lawyers to be made aware of such considerations. Lawyers in particular should be aware of the potential implications of an Islamic divorce so that they may properly assist their client; if a Sharia council pressured the wife to accept a lesser settlement in the civil courts in return for an Islamic divorce, it would be inexcusable for her representative lawyer or the judge to accept her consent in the civil court proceedings when they had the chance to question her and ensure there was no undue coercion or pressure. Issues remain with this solution, however. What of the situation where the husband is happy to delay the granting of the decree absolute or the wife wants the civil divorce finalized as soon as possible? The increasing costs of litigation aside, a decree absolute can be viewed as amounting to an Islamic divorce, as it fulfills the criteria for divorce, although most Sharia councils in the United Kingdom will insist that an Islamic divorce must be obtained from them and will take advantage of the differing forms of religiosity among Muslim women. Some Muslim women will be content that a civil divorce is sufficient for them to obtain an Islamic divorce, while others will want confirmation from a religious figure or authority to provide them with the peace of mind that comes from knowing they have indeed divorced in accordance with their faith. Despite their insistence that an Islamic divorce is necessary, Sharia councils feel compelled to grant an Islamic divorce when a decree absolute has been granted; obtaining an Islamic divorce from them therefore becomes a mere formality that serves more to maintain the authority and importance of Sharia councils (and financial gain) than to empower women. It is interesting to note that, in principle at least, the Kingdom of Saudi Arabia is able to enforce judgments made by non-Saudi courts, such as that of the United Kingdom, should the Grievances Board of Saudi Arabia decide to allow enforcement.[6] Indeed, Pakistan will recognize a civil divorce obtained in a British court as legally valid according to Islamic law (Balchin 2009, 4). It is appreciated that the reality may be far from the principle, but it highlights the inconsistencies for British Muslim women whereby the UK courts seem unable to provide justice for its own citizens.

It has also come to MWNUK's attention that some solicitors in the United Kingdom have been taking advantage of this policy in operation within some Sharia councils. Some solicitors offer to deal with the Islamic divorce in addition to the civil divorce for additional legal fees, even though in reality their clients could obtain the Islamic divorce certificate on their own. Bearing in mind that the Sharia council's fees are paid for separately as disbursements and the granting of an Islamic divorce is automatic once the decree absolute has been issued, what then do these additional legal fees cover? The plea for an Islamic divorce in such a situation would simply consist of mentioning that a decree absolute has been granted; we do not see how the drafting of such a plea can justify the legal fees that are being sought. Are the Sharia councils really fulfilling their duty to provide advice in an informed and impartial manner?

Difficulties arise, however, as it is will not always be clear which scenario an individual's circumstances may fall within and what would be the most appropriate procedure—that is, whether it will be necessary to invoke the Divorce (Religious Marriages) Act or whether a decree absolute should be granted immediately for the Sharia council to grant an Islamic divorce. This legislative change will therefore not be sufficient to address the issues on its own, and it is for this reason that the model divorce service is being explored as part of an overall package. It would also be useful to explore avenues by which additional conditions may be imposed by courts to ensure that the Islamic divorce is granted. For example, on granting the decree absolute the court may order that the Islamic divorce be finalized within a certain time frame and parties re-called where this has not taken place. If it has, the wife can confirm this in writing with a copy of the Islamic divorce certificate for the court records. This would, however, mean an increase in wasted time and costs for the parties involved as well as for the court. Further, the usefulness of attaching such conditions is limited; just as Islamic marriages are not recognized in the United Kingdom, neither are Islamic divorces.

This lack of recognition is also a likely barrier to placing any compensatory burdens on the husband that could act as an incentive for him to agree to an Islamic divorce; the principle *damnum absque injuria* (Latin for "loss without injury") acknowledges that a person may sustain loss or damage without an interference in legal rights (Halsburys Laws of England 2010, 412), but this does not go so far as to allow compensation in this respect. As Islamic marriages and in turn Islamic divorces are not recognized in UK law, and therefore do not recognize the need for the latter in order for an individual to continue with his or her life, it is unlikely that the law of torts can be used to demand compensation for the injury caused by the refusal to grant such a divorce. In the Netherlands, on the other hand, in Shireen Musa's case (Radio 1 Netherlands 2011) the Dutch civil court ruled that her husband's refusal to grant an Islamic divorce despite having obtained a civil divorce amounted to an unlawful act incurring injury as per tort law principles. On the other hand, although the laws of tort in the United Kingdom are limited in this respect and generally require that a claimant have a recognized psychiatric condition rather than the harm being limited to anxiety and distress (*Wong v. Parkside Health NHS Trust*), allowing a claim for anxiety and distress caused may convey a strong message, and in the appropriate extenuating circumstances it may still be possible to allow for a claim in tort as trespass to the person where a husband inflicts harm on his wife by not granting a divorce and essentially keeping her hostage in a relationship she no longer wishes to be a part of.

On a related note, it may be useful to consider potentially utilizing the Equalities Act 2010 in respect of the discriminatory procedures in place within certain Sharia councils, and in particular those that profess to be service providers of Islamic divorce, rather than working within the realm of dispute resolution. Merely comparing the fee structure whereby women are expected to pay higher application fees than men in some Sharia councils would be an immediate indication of gender inequality, and the disparity would be worth pursuing as a claim; if these Sharia councils profess to be providing a service to members of the public, then discrimination in such a service cannot and should not be tolerated. However, due to the practicalities involved, the possibility of pursuing such a claim appears to be limited; MWNUK has been researching, where available, the websites of Sharia councils and has noted the very limited information provided. The burden is therefore high in proving that the services provided should fall within the Equality Act.

Alternatively, the issuance of an Islamic divorce could be brought within the UK court system itself. On the basis that adequate mediation has been provided within the process with all ancillary matters finalized and the decree absolute granted, a referral could be forwarded to an accredited body, which would issue the Islamic divorce. Such a body could indeed be placed within all family courts to expedite the process.

Where an Islamic marriage is followed by a civil marriage, a further solution may be to provide for the annexation of the Islamic marriage into the civil marriage. That is, it could be confirmed that the parties participated in an Islamic marriage on said date and that the civil marriage now being entered into includes but supersedes the first. In turn, when the civil marriage ends, this would automatically end the Islamic marriage.

Legislative measures could also be designed to regulate Islamic marriages at inception so as to avoid the issues that arise when the parties are trying to obtain an Islamic divorce, such as regulating imams, recognizing Islamic marriages, or alternatively making the performance of a religious wedding illegal if carried out before a civil wedding, akin to the laws in France. Such considerations fall outside the scope of this chapter, however.

British Muslim women are in serious need of a legal system that recognizes their plight and provides them with appropriate legal remedies; indeed, it is obligatory for the UK government to implement such a system, and steps must be taken immediately. Muslim Women's Network UK has long been aware of the various hurdles Muslim women face in the United Kingdom and has discussed them on a range of platforms, including government meetings and consultations. It is of concern that no concrete steps have been taken to address and rectify the barriers in place. It has been noted that Baroness Cox is hoping to turn into law the Arbitration and Mediation Services (Equality) Bill; however, her concerns seem focused on Sharia councils that may be acting on matters outside their legal remit. In reality, these issues can be covered by various legislative measures already in existence. Additionally, despite suggesting that the root issue is the unequal treatment of women, this is not in fact adequately addressed by the bill.

What is needed is a commitment to providing remedies and placing gender equality and the needs of British Muslim women at the heart of discussions. Ample legislative and grassroots solutions have been put forward that would provide a legal system that is fit for purpose and would in turn eliminate the need for Sharia councils. Better-trained mediators and panelists, with women at the forefront, campaigns raising awareness, as well as legislative action and pragmatic case decisions can collectively pave the way to equality, justice, and empowerment of Muslim women in the United Kingdom. It will also uphold the supremacy of UK law over Islamic law and overcome concerns of a parallel legal system.

It is vital to remember that marriage and divorce are personal matters, just as is faith. The United Kingdom allows a difference of opinions, and indeed that is a mark of a society that holds principles of equality and justice to be of paramount importance. Where a Muslim woman feels unable to move on with her life because she believes she is still married according to her religion, irrespective of whether another Muslim woman would disagree, the laws of the United Kingdom should be able to assist rather than keep her entrapped. This does not diminish the importance of the rule of law or allow the transplantation of laws; rather it caters to a diverse and multicultural society by making it fit for purpose.

Notes

1. Author's translation.
2. Rahima is a pseudonym.
3. Ameera is a pseudonym.
4. Dalia is a pseudonym.
5. If the mother remarries, custody reverts to the father.

6. Article 8(1)(g) of Royal Decree No. M/51 dated 17/7/1402 H / 11 May 1982 (the Grievances Board Law) grants the Grievances Board the authority to accept applications for the enforcement in Saudi Arabia of foreign judgments. Article 6 of the Rules of Pleadings and Procedures of the Grievances Board, as issued by Council of Ministers Resolution No. 190 dated 16/11/1409 H / 20 June 1989 (the Rules), provides that an application to enforce a foreign judgment in Saudi Arabia will be assessed on two bases. First, the applicant must show that the jurisdiction that issued the foreign judgment will reciprocally enforce judgments of the courts of Saudi Arabia. Second, the applicant must show that the terms of the foreign judgment are consistent with Islamic law as enforced in Saudi Arabia. In practice these requirements are difficult to meet.

Bibliography

Balchin, Cassandra (2009). "Divorce in Classical Muslim Jurisprudence and the Differences between Jewish and Muslim Divorce." http://muslimmarriage contract.org/documents/Divorce%20in%20classical%20Muslim%20jurispru dence%20and%20the%20Differences%20between%20Jewish%20and%20 Muslim%20divorce.pdf, accessed 15 April 2015.

Balchin, Cassandra (2011). "Having Our Cake and Eating It: British Muslim Women." https://www.opendemocracy.net/5050/cassandra-balchin/having-our -cake-and-eating-it-british-muslim-women, accessed 15 April 2015.

Bano, Samia (2012a). *Muslim Women and Shari'ah Councils: Transcending the Boundaries of Community and Law.* London: Palgrave Macmillan.

Bano, Samia (2012b). *An Exploratory Study of Shariah Councils in England with Respect to Family Law.* Reading: University of Reading.

BBC News (2012). "Growing Use of Sharia by UK Muslims." http://www.bbc .co.uk/news/uk-16522447, accessed 15 April 2015.

Gohir, Shaista (2013). *Unheard Voices.* Birmingham: Muslim Women's Network UK.

Gohir, Shaista (2016). *Information and Guidance on Muslim Marriage and Divorce in Britain.* Birmingham: Muslim Women's Network UK.

H v. H (Talaq Divorce) [2007] EWHC 2945 (Fam), [2008] 2 F.L.R 857, [2008] Fam. Law 404.

Halsburys Laws of England (2010). *Tort,* vol. 97.

Kennett, Wendy (2011). "Women Living under Shariah Law, Part One: Distinct Legal Worlds?" *Women in Society Journal* 2 (Autumn): 1–20.

Khurshid Bibi v. Babu Mohammed Amin PLD [1967] SC 97.

Radio 1 Netherlands (2011). "Shirin Musa Strijdt voor Gelijkwaardigheid Religieuze Vrouwen." http://www.radio1.nl/items/30507-shirin-musa-strijdt-voor-geli jkwaardigheid-religieuze-vrouwen, accessed 15 April 2015.

Sardar Ali, Shahin (2013). "Authority and Authenticity: Shariah Councils, Muslim Women's Rights and the English Courts." *Child & Family Law Quarterly* 25(2): 113–37.

Wong v. Parkside Health NHS Trust [2001] EWCA Civ 1721, [2003] 3All ER 932, CA.

PART TWO

Mediation
and
Religious Arbitration
in
Different National Contexts

8

Religious Arbitration in North America

Wendy Kennett

ARBITRATION OF FAMILY LAW DISPUTES is a recent innovation for most of the legal systems that currently offer such a possibility. It is consequently little known and used as a method of alternative dispute resolution. Nevertheless, in some US states arbitration has been recognized as a method of family dispute resolution for decades.[1] This is notably true in New York, where court cases confirming the arbitrability of family disputes can be found dating back to 1945.[2] Moreover, the arbitral awards enforced in family cases include awards in Jewish *beth din* proceedings.[3]

The Ontario "Sharia Debate"

Family arbitration has also been recognized in Ontario, Canada, for several decades (Wolfson 2010), but the decisions of religious tribunals are not enforceable arbitral awards. The 1991 Arbitration Act (henceforth, the 1991 Act) did not require the law of Ontario or Canada to be applied in an arbitration and so facilitated the setting up of religious dispute resolution panels. Some Jewish and Christian groups took advantage of this opportunity without awakening public concern; but when, in 2003, Syed Mumtaz Ali, spokesperson for the Islamic Institute of Civil Justice (IICJ), announced that the IICJ intended to offer arbitration services in accordance with Islamic law in family disputes under the 1991 Act (Selby and Korteweg 2012), this caused a political storm—reflecting an assumption that awards would be oppressive and patriarchal in accordance with public perceptions of "Sharia law."

Former attorney general Marion Boyd was appointed to conduct a formal review of the use of arbitration in family and inheritance law in Ontario (Boyd 2004). She concluded that religious arbitration in accordance with Islamic principles was permissible under the 1991 Act, but made recommendations for amendments to the act to ensure better guarantees of gender equality and of the reality of consent to an arbitration agreement. Her concern was to ensure an appropriate balance between respect for minority groups and protection of individual rights.

Boyd's report was not, however, in tune with public opinion. Muslim groups that supported religious arbitration were slow to mobilize, whereas their opponents were numerous and vociferous, and benefited from more favorable media coverage (Selby and Korteweg 2012; Bullock 2012). Although it seemed initially that the government would adopt Boyd's recommendations, "the debate moved towards linking shared civic secularism and women's rights against accommodation of religions in the public sphere" (Selby and Korteweg 2012). The premier, Dalton McGuinty, concluded that he could not allow his province to become the first Western government to allow the use of Islamic law to settle family disputes. To ensure that the law was nondiscriminatory, the 1991 Act was amended to exclude from the scope of recognized family arbitration a process "not conducted exclusively in accordance with the law of Ontario or of another Canadian jurisdiction,"[4] thus also excluding Jewish and Christian arbitration from recognition and rendering awards resulting from such arbitration unenforceable.

The success of the Jewish *batei din*, and particularly the Beth Din of America (BDA), has been cited as a model that could be followed by Muslim arbitration tribunals in order to achieve greater acceptance and recognition (Broyde 2012–13; Rafeeq 2010; Bambach 2009). In the following pages I shall explore two issues arising out of this comparison. The first is the extent to which the Jewish and Muslim experiences are comparable as they relate to the application of religious laws. This breaks down into two parts: (1) the factors that have promoted *beth din* arbitration in North America and (2) some contrasts between Jewish and Muslim demographics and legal culture in the North American context, which have an impact on the use of arbitration to resolve disputes. The second issue is the extent to which there is a demand for application of religious laws. This again breaks down into two parts: (1) the level of interest in arbitration as a method of dispute resolution and (2) the problems associated with religious divorces. The chapter will conclude with some comments on the extent to which the amendments to the 1991 Act have achieved their desired objective.

Comparison of the Jewish and Muslim Immigration Experience as It Relates to the Application of Religious Laws

FACTORS PROMOTING JEWISH ARBITRATION IN NORTH AMERICA

The Immigration Context The first Jewish immigrants in North America were pioneers—drawn from Jewish populations in Europe, notably from England and Germany, where there was already a high level of assimilation.[5] Mass immigration to the United States occurred in two waves: the first as a result of persecution in Eastern Europe and Russia from the 1880s, the second as a result of Nazi persecution and in the immediate aftermath of World War II. In particular, the number of Jews in New York City rose rapidly from the 1880s following persecution in Eastern Europe. In the 1950s, the city's Jewish population peaked at around 2.1 million (UJA–Federation of New York et al. 2012). In 2011, some areas of New York are still more than 20 percent Jewish (UJA–Federation of New York et al. 2012).

Given this population size and density, it does not seem surprising that specifically Jewish dispute resolution institutions were established, but in fact during the first few decades of mass immigration they failed to flourish. Many of the Jewish immigrants to America at the turn of the twentieth century were seeking the opportunity to relinquish the religious ties by which they were bound in their settlements in Eastern Europe and Russia (Gurock 2009), and conversely devout Jews—forewarned as to the level of secularism—rarely ventured to the New World (Sachar 1992). In the late nineteenth century fewer than 10 percent of American Jews were affiliated with a synagogue or reform temple congregation (Sachar 1992). Nevertheless, eventually small bastions of Orthodoxy emerged (Gurock 2009), which helped to ease the settlement of the next major influx of Jewish immigrants at the time of World War II. It was only with this new wave of immigrants that large halakhically observant Jewish communities began to appear (Gurock 2009; Sachar 1992). The Holocaust gave rise to the flight from Eastern Europe of Jewish populations that had previously resisted the lure of the New World. These communities migrated en masse, bringing with them their rabbis and religious practices, creating enclaves immune to Americanization.

While the numbers are less striking, a similar pattern of immigration and institution building can be found in Canada.[6] Toronto, in particular, has a significant Jewish population and thriving Jewish institutions (Shahar, Rosenbaum, and United Jewish Federation of Greater Toronto 2006).

Halakhic Obligation Arbitral bodies were initially established by local, largely assimilated elites to facilitate the integration of the new arrivals (Zelcer 2007; Sachar 1992). But the post–World War II wave of Jewish immigration brought to New York Jews who sought to reestablish their familiar communities in their new land. While the newcomers were greatly aided by the established Jewish community in America, they were also "fired with a level of commitment and enthusiasm for Old World ways not seen previously in [America]" (Gurock 2009). They respected the halakhic rule requiring Jews to resolve their disputes in a *beth din* rather than in a secular court,[7] and so they set up local *batei din* and continued to resolve disputes through that mechanism (Feit 2012; Fried 2003; Bambach 2009).

A similar pattern can be observed in Canada. Early dispute resolution institutions, established under the leadership and patronage of wealthy Jews who were among the local elite, later gave way to local *batei din.*

Accommodation to the Requirements of Secular Law The *batei din* established by Jewish immigrants to North America after World War II were many and varied. Many decisions made by such institutions were implemented by the parties on the basis of a mixture of religious obligation and community pressure. But they were vulnerable to challenge in the secular courts by a disgruntled litigant. An arbitration award may be challenged on various procedural grounds, including notably bias and absence of due process. Many *batei din* are run on a voluntary and part-time basis and lack professionalism. If they serve a small community, it is hard to guarantee impartiality. Nor are rabbis necessarily aware of civil procedural rules concerning due process (Fried 2003).

The Beth Din of America (BDA)—the national rabbinic court of the Orthodox community—based in New York, was originally established by the Rabbinical Council of America in 1960, but it was reestablished as an independent entity in 1996. In light of the growth and visibility of arbitration as a method of dispute resolution, in recent years "an independent board of directors has worked with the BDA's rabbinic leaders to craft an arbitration process that secular courts would feel comfortable upholding" (Broyde 2012–13). This means, in particular, that the BDA has published detailed and transparent procedures comparable with those of secular arbitration institutions, it applies secular laws and commercial practices—where relevant—to the extent permitted by Jewish law, and it employs as arbitrators lawyers and other professionals who can provide expertise in secular law and commercial practice as well as Jewish law (Broyde 2012–13, 2015). It also has an internal appellate procedure to reduce the risk of error. In the interests of further transparency, it has begun to publish some of its decisions, with the consent of the parties.[8] Nevertheless, for all its success it has a limited reach: "There are too many diverse groups who will never give up their right to run their own bet din" (Zelcer 2007, 110).

Orthodox Jews have also had resort to *beth din* arbitration in Toronto. In her report *Dispute Resolution in Family Law*, Marion Boyd (2004, 41) commented that "in about thirty cases a year the *Beis Din* deals with all issues of marriage breakdown, such as support, property division, custody and access. The Toronto *Beis Din* has nevertheless received criticism of its arrangements—as involving part-time, voluntary, unpaid staff who lack a secular legal education—and the BDA has been recommended as a model for reform."

Substantive Jewish law has also reacted to changes in the legal environment. A good example here is the resolution of disputes relating to child residence and contact (Kaplan 2008). Although early Jewish law emphasized the authority of the father, from the medieval period there was a recognition in principle that child welfare should be the prime consideration—an approach that has more recently lent itself to integration with the "best interests of the child" standard applied in the secular courts.

COMPARISON WITH MUSLIM COMMUNITIES
IN NORTH AMERICA

Demographics Since there is no official collection of statistics on religious affiliation in the United States, data on population size are highly variable. A 2011 publication by the Pew Research Center suggests a figure of 2.6 million Muslims in the United States in 2010 (Pew Research Center 2011a). On the other hand, a publication by the Council on American–Islamic Relations (CAIR) in the same year suggests a 2.6 million figure for those connected to a mosque and estimates that the total figure will be significantly higher—perhaps in the region of 7 million (Bagby 2011).

The number of Muslims in the United States thus may be smaller than or similar to the number of Jews. But the population is nevertheless distinctly different. First of all, it contains a very large proportion of first-generation immigrants (63 percent). According to the Pew Research Center, 45 percent of Muslims arrived in the United States after 1990. Only 12 percent arrived before 1980 (2011b, 8, 13–14). The great waves of Jewish immigration ended fifty years ago, and a substantial proportion of immigrant families arrived in America more than a century ago.

Second, there is a more general spread across the country. CAIR's studies of mosques from 1994 to 2011 indicate an expanding geographical range (Bagby 2011), which may be compared with the closely knit Jewish Orthodox communities that are geographically concentrated in areas such as Brooklyn, Manhattan, New Jersey, and Miami.

Third, there is a much larger degree of ethnic diversity in the Muslim population. About a third of American Muslims are African American converts. The remainder come from Muslim populations from at least seventy-seven countries across the world (Pew Research Center 2011b). As Bagby notes:

> The US Muslim community is arguably the most diverse religious community in America. The main groups that comprise the American Muslim community are South Asians (Pakistanis, Indians, Bangladeshis, and Afghanis), Arab (prominent groups include Egyptians, Palestinians, Lebanese, Yemenis; 22 Arab countries are represented), and African Americans. . . . Other significant groups include Iranians who came in large numbers since 1979

and many recent arrivals such as West Africans, Somalis and Bosnians. (2011, 13)

Like the US data, the data concerning the Muslim population of Canada are incomplete.[9] The majority of Muslims (in common with other immigrant communities) live in the Toronto area, with a significant number also in Quebec and British Columbia (Selby 2010). In 2001, there were nearly 600,000 Muslims in Canada. By 2011, the number had nearly doubled. As in the United States, the large majority of the Muslim population has immigrated to Canada since 1990 and shows similar ethnic diversity (Selby 2010).

Motives for Immigration As noted earlier, the first Jewish immigrants in North America were to a large degree already assimilated into British and European culture, and the first large wave of immigrants from the 1880s was not significantly composed of religiously observant Jews. Among these populations there was little demand for institutions applying religious laws. It was the Jewish immigrants to North America fleeing Nazi persecution who re-created supportive communities in their new homeland.

Like the early Jewish immigrants, in most cases Muslims have come seeking study and work opportunities. Community support is not their first consideration. In the context of Muslim immigration in Canada, five main factors are thought to have drawn Muslim immigrants: economic advantages; educational opportunities; political alienation from native countries; family sponsorship; and notions of a freedom of faith and expression guaranteed in Canadian law (Yousif 2008). Muslim immigrants to the United States typically have a high educational standard and occupy professional positions, often in the engineering and IT sectors. They are "largely assimilated, happy with their lives, and moderate with respect to many of the issues that have divided Muslims and Westerners around the world" (Pew Research Center 2007).

Legalism There is no space in this chapter to trace the development and implementation of the legal and ethical principles of Islam and Judaism[10] or to explore the range of attitudes toward religious law in both Muslim and Jewish communities. Both have an extensive body of legal literature dealing with principles, case law, argument, and hermeneutics. Both have spawned different schools of thought but have until the modern era maintained an overarching unity despite dissent. Nevertheless, from the perspective of its ability to flourish in North America, Jewish law benefits from the fact that it was for centuries the cement that held together a people without a homeland: "Israel is a people only in virtue of its religious laws" (Sa'adia Gaon, Emunot vedeot 3:7, cited from Sacks 1993).

Three other factors in particular contribute to a certain unity in the development of Jewish law. First, the historical fact of its application to a single "nation," whose principal scholars were for more than a millennium based in Jerusalem and Babylon (Libson 1996, 197–98). Second, the fact that the communities that continue to be halakhically observant are overwhelmingly of East European origin and therefore have a degree of cultural similarity. And finally, the existence of Israel as a state in which the *halakhah* is a part of the law of the land has an inevitable influence on the development of the law within the Orthodox diasporic communities.

No such unified tradition exists for a Muslim diaspora. The rapid spread of Islam was necessarily followed by centuries of consolidation. Different schools of thought appeared and coexisted. It took time for the "inchoate" principles (Hughes 2013) derived from the Quran to be refined and built upon to create a legal and ethical system that covered all areas of life. Moreover, that system was being used to blend together people from communities and cultures extending from North Africa to China and from the banks of the Danube and the Volga Rivers to Madagascar, across different empires and independent states. It is clear that despite the existence of a body of detailed principles developed by Islamic scholars, local customs and practices also remained strong, aided by the existence of both Sharia and non-Sharia laws and courts (Vikør 2005; Gerber 1994; Barkey 2009). Foreign colonization of Islamic lands and, later, the creation of independent nation-states have each in turn contributed to the absence of a clear distinction between the laws of individual nation-states and universally applicable principles of Islamic law (Vikør 2005; Emon 2012). As Clarke points out, "The systems and rules of law now operating in various Muslim-majority states are actually very different from the old law and from each other; but as long as they are regarded by the population as religiously legitimate—as 'Islamic' . . . —they effectively function . . . as Muslim law" (2012, 163).

Furthermore, the application of Islamic law to a Muslim minority is problematic (Hassan 2013; Alalwānī 2010). Muslims were not encouraged to live in non-Muslim countries, and so the relationship between Islamic law and a non-Islamic local law, and the potential for a "European" or "Western" Islam, have only relatively recently become a focus of discussion (Hassan 2013; El Fadl 1994; Ramadan 2004). Given this limited experience, "Muslims in the West with ties to Muslim-majority countries often believe that the rules familiar to them from home are the 'correct' ones" (Clarke 2012, 163).

On the other hand, the notion of Islamic law in the West as "idealized" or "negotiable" (An-Naʿīm 2008) has become a common theme. Furthermore, in the United States many Muslims approach the Quran and the Sunna as legal texts that they should explore and interpret for themselves, rather than accept traditional interpretations (Curtis 2009, 77–78), and this independence is facilitated by the existence of a large indigenous body of Muslims, who have developed a highly Americanized Islam (2009, 78–79).[11]

The Time Factor As occurred earlier in the case of Jewish communities, in recent decades a range of Muslim institutions has begun to emerge in North America, defining themselves in harmony with or in contradistinction to the surrounding secular culture. Indeed, in the United States the term *Islam* "has gained political currency and come to incorporate ethnicity, nationality, religiosity, and community as one construct in American society" (Bakalian and Bozorgmehr 2005, 9). Muslims may thus, like Jews, manifest as secular or religious and may demonstrate a range of perspectives, from those that emphasize personal autonomy to those that attribute significance to community traditions, with religious arbitration being primarily of significance to this latter group.[12] Furthermore, the focus on institution building has intensified since 9/11 with the political mobilization of the Muslim community (Bakalian and Bozorgmehr 2005). According to Chishti et al., "The notion of a distinct 'American Muslim' identity has gained new currency. It is an identity that seeks to assert its independence from forces abroad, one that combines the essential elements of Islam and the values of American constitutional democracy" (2003, 7).

Nevertheless, Jewish communities in North America who desire *beth din* dispute resolution have consolidated their practices over several decades and have drawn on centuries of relatively homogeneous practice. By comparison, Muslim communities have had only a short time to establish institutions and links. Since they are spread more thinly, and—because of the diversity of their ethnic and national origins—come from widely differing legal and dispute resolution traditions—it is to be anticipated that any common practices and interpretations of Islamic law will take a long while to emerge.

Jewish law in the West represents a system that, for those who accept its yoke,[13] offers a significant degree of objectivity and certainty. There may be dissent. There may be intractable problems of articulation between religious and secular law. But the substantive and institutional framework is clear. Islamic law in the West remains a work in progress. Individuals or particular communities may have clear understandings of the obligations that it imposes, but those understandings remain largely personalized and/or localized. The strongest community pressures to conform to specific Islamic doctrines arise in the context of ethno-religious communities that retain strong links with their state of origin (e.g., on the relationship between the Canadian IICJ and the All-India Personal Law Board, see Clarke 2012).

The Demand for the Application of Religious Laws

Two distinct issues arise in this context. On the one hand, observant Jews and Muslims may seek to resolve their disputes in a forum that recognizes their religious commitments—whether through arbitration or mediation. On the other hand, even those who are not religiously observant may desire a divorce in accordance with Jewish or Islamic law for reasons that relate to identity, culture, and community. Macfarlane refers to Islamic divorce as a "social-psychological phenomenon" (2012a, 147). Jewish divorce raises rather different issues. While the "social-psychological" element is important, the legal issues are also clearly more starkly defined.

ABSENCE OF DEMAND FOR FORMAL DISPUTE RESOLUTION PROCEDURES

The Ontario Sharia debate presupposed that a significant number of Muslims desired a forum for dispute resolution in harmony with religious principles, one that would hand down decisions enforceable in the state courts. But ethnographic research suggests that in reality there is little demand for such a formal dispute resolution body for family matters.[14] According to Selby and Korteweg, "Religiously based family law arbitration was not something that Canadian Muslims engaged in or that Muslim Arbitration Boards conducted" (2012, 13). As Cutting notes, "Very few in the Muslim community, leaders or adherents, were or are interested in formal faith-based arbitration as such" (2012, 78). Finally, Macfarlane states: "I quickly discovered Muslim men and women had little interest in their religious outcomes being recognized by Ontario law" (2012a, 16).

On the other hand, such research highlights the fact that although Muslim family arbitration is not desired, negotiation and mediation in the shadow of Islamic law occur regularly (Macfarlane 2012a, 155ff.; Cutting 2012, 66). Imams, whether individually or through organizations such as the Darul Iftaa (Canada) (Cutting 2012, 70–74), assist Muslims through faith-based mediation to form separation agreements, wills, and prenuptial agreements. "All of these contracts are enforceable by provincial law . . . in so far as advice is given and women are encouraged to accept property and child arrangements that are less advantageous than those that would be offered by the law of Ontario, the 2006 amendments to the 1991 Act provide no assistance" (Cutting 2012, 76; see also Macklin 2012, 92; Kutty 2012, 129).

Macklin highlights the way in which Ontario law, in common with all Western laws, facilitates this, as part of a wider critique of privatized decision making:

> The "one law for all" governing family law in Ontario was a law that lets parties make their own law. It sets out default rules . . . and then authorizes consenting parties to opt out of the process and substance of the public legal regime. . . . Domestic contracts do not generally set out the normative framework that guides the parties. They usually contain only the outcome of the application of those norms, namely the terms of the settlement. If the agreement does not signal its religious provenance . . . the religious predicates of the agreement may be undetectable anyway. (2012, 100, 115)

While in part this reflects a concern that, in the wake of the arbitration debate, women continue to be subject to precisely the same pressures as before—whether they are considered to be cultural or religious—Macklin also points out the double standards adopted by secular commentators. If, in the secular context, a woman agrees to a financial arrangement that is not in her best interests, that can be ascribed to free choice. If the same thing occurs in a religious context, it is labeled oppression (Macklin 2012,103ff.). Macklin views Muslim dispute resolution as just a part of a much broader concern about the vulnerable legal position of women in intimate relationships.

The claimed advantage of a recognized place for Muslim arbitration is that it would lead to transparency and thus assist in the development of a law for Western Muslim minorities—a reformed law reflecting the North American legal and social environment (Kutty 2012; 135ff., Emon 2012, 210ff.). Clarke notes that this claim would be difficult to put into operation because of the current lack of agreement on what such a law would include (2012, 178). Additionally, transparency would be limited. Arbitration awards are not usually published—indeed, confidentiality concerning the dispute is usually claimed as one of the great advantages of arbitration. The recognition of Muslim family arbitration might therefore—by legitimating such a development—contribute to a protected space in which a North American Islamic family law could be elaborated, but it would not in itself contribute significantly to the transparent development of specific rules in the absence of a single, unified arbitral tribunal. Even if there were a demand for Muslim family arbitration, a single tribunal would be unachievable in the light of the diversity of Islamic perspectives among immigrants.[15]

By contrast, *beth din* dispute resolution, leading to awards enforceable in the civil courts, has long been established in US and Canadian laws. *Batei din* resolve the full range of disputes, from commercial to family law issues. And their decisions may also have some transnational effect in family as well as commercial cases.[16] The amendments to the 1991 Act thus interrupted what had previously seemed to be a settled and uncontroversial practice. However, although the act prevents recognition of religious arbitration, it does not prohibit it from taking place. Orthodox Jews can therefore continue to use *beth din* arbitration in a family context, as before relying on personal commitment and community pressure for compliance with an award. Formal mechanisms for exerting community pressure are anyway a significant method of enforcing decisions.

Furthermore, since one of the advantages of arbitration is the possibility of selecting arbitrators with specific expertise, disputants may select an arbitrator with knowledge of the *halakhah*—or simply with an awareness of Jewish culture and practices—without this formally constituting "religious" arbitration. It is clear from recent case law that this is continuing without any problem under the amended 1991 Act. Indeed, it is worth drawing a comparison here between the situation in Ontario and that in New York. Family arbitration in Ontario can extend to child support and child arrangements, although the award will be open to review to ensure that it meets the "best interests of the child" standard. There are cases in Ontario since the 2006 amendments to the 1991 Act that concern or refer to the arbitration of disputes with respect to child arrangements in the context of the divorce of a Jewish couple.[17] The arbitrators are well-established family lawyers who also happen to be Jewish. By contrast, under New York law, as a safeguard to ensure that the "best interests" standard is observed, although spousal support, property division, and child support may be the subject of arbitration, child custody arrangements may not.[18] Prenuptial agreements conferring jurisdiction on the BDA to deal with all issues arising on divorce may thus lead to an award that is unenforceable.[19]

Social services agencies are also of increasing significance in the area of family dispute resolution. Such agencies can provide mediation services that respect religious principles and can provide a wider range of religiously and culturally sensitive support in situations of family conflict and breakdown. In Toronto, the Jewish Child and Family Services is well established, having been founded in 1943 as a merger between associations originally established in the nineteenth century. Its (nonsectarian) service provision is wide ranging, but it includes specifically Jewish services, such as kosher emergency shelters for victims of abuse. The Muslim communities have had a much shorter period of time in which to establish this form of support, but some agencies do exist, such as the Islamic Social Services Association (ISSA) in Canada and the United States. The ISSA has limited resources and so plays a supporting role, providing training and advice to local communities so that they can provide a better service, while at the same time training secular service providers to have a greater awareness of Muslim concerns. It also campaigns on family and welfare issues, such as combating domestic violence.

While arbitration is not desired and comparisons with the BDA are misplaced for a variety of reasons, efforts are being made to ensure better provision of women-centered advice and support in many Muslim communities and to work toward the professionalization of mediation and counseling services.

THE RELIGIOUS DIVORCE PROBLEM

Islamic Divorce One of the most significant facts that emerged from research in the aftermath of the Ontario Sharia debate was that Islamic dispute resolution was sought almost solely by women, and in one single context: in order to obtain a divorce.

Julie Macfarlane's monograph, *Islamic Divorce in North America*, demonstrates that North American Muslims are fully aware of their rights under US and Canadian law. They regularly use the courts to obtain a civil divorce, deal with financial matters, and, especially, regulate child arrangements (Macfarlane 2012a, 16; see also Cutting 2012, 66). As noted previously, there is no demand for a resolution of these issues in accordance with religious law. But many feel the need for a religious divorce.

This can be for a variety of reasons. Macfarlane identifies five: religious obligation; Islamic identity (as a "tradition of social and community living rather than a formal set of religious obligations"); finding closure, especially in relation to the freedom to remarry within a Muslim community; and practical considerations such as the relative speed and cost of an Islamic divorce compared with a secular one (Macfarlane 2012b). But in line with the earlier comments about the nature of Sharia in North America, "There is no given or universal procedure for obtaining an Islamic divorce in North America, nor any universally recognized outcomes. Each imam follows his own process. . . . Islamic divorce in North America manifests no consistent formal process, but lives instead in the beliefs and imaginations of those Muslim men and women for whom it is psychologically and spiritually important" (Selby and Korteweg 2012, 41–42; see also Macfarlane 2012a, 147).

As in England (Bano 2012), imams in North America have responded to a demand from women unhappy in their marriages and have sought to persuade a husband to provide a *talaq* divorce or negotiate a *khula*. Some have been willing to issue a *faskh* (Macfarlane 2012a, 168, 176).[20] They are not community leaders, but occupy an ambiguous space and have to operate within the margin for maneuver permitted them by mosque leaders and their community (for the more institutional role carved out by Sharia councils in England, see Bano 2012, 86–91). Some are more acculturated than others, and in this respect the range of responses seems to be wider than in England. In the United States in particular, some of Macfarlane's interviewees "imam shopped" to find a sympathetic response (2012a, 160–61). Most obtained a religious divorce eventually. A few were unable to do so. Most imams had no training in counseling or mediation, but did their best to find an acceptable solution. They recognized that in a state in which Islamic law was applied by the courts, relief would be available in many of the cases presented to them, which involved adultery, abandonment, or domestic violence (2012a, 168).

The imams interviewed by Macfarlane usually limited their intervention to the Islamic divorce itself—not child or financial consequences. Nevertheless, sometimes financial or child-related issues were used as bargaining chips (2012a, 171).

Macfarlane traces the problems faced by her interviewees—who were mainly women—in obtaining a religious divorce. Her conclusion is that many of those difficulties stem from the women's personal desire to be true to their marriage vows, and from family pressures, rather than from specifically *religious* or *legal* issues. Moreover, this is recognized by the women themselves: "This is not religion, this is culture" (Macfarlane 2012b, 43).

In order to ameliorate this problem, the same approach is being advocated in North America as in the United Kingdom—the inclusion of a delegation of a right of divorce to the wife (*talaq-i-tafwid*) in the marriage contract, giving women as well as men the possibility of ending their marriage. This solution is being promoted in Canada by the ISSA in its *Professional Guide* for imams, being derived from the Muslim Council of Britain initiative. Insofar as the problems arising from divorce are cultural and family based rather than religious, however, finding a legal mechanism to restore equality to spouses in relation to access to divorce is only one part of the solution, and it remains to be seen whether the marriage contract "solution" will be widely used.

Jewish Divorce: The Agunah *Problem* It is arguable that religious divorce is a greater problem in Jewish than in Muslim communities. The community cohesion that provides a degree of legal certainty and has facilitated the development of religious law arbitration makes any unilateral change by one sector of the community highly problematic, and Jews who would not go to a *beth din* for arbitration may want a religious divorce for reasons similar to those applying in the case of Muslim men and women.

According to Jewish law, only a husband can grant a divorce (a *get*).[21] Attendance at a *beth din* is necessary in order to certify the *get*—and uniform standards mean that the *get* should have a transnational effect, in contrast with the purely local and psychological effect of an Islamic divorce issued by an imam or Sharia council. But if a man refuses to grant his wife a divorce, it is difficult for her to move on from the relationship: she is a "chained" wife—an *agunah*. Orthodox Judaism is matrilineal. She can obtain a civil divorce, but if she remarries any children of that relationship will be considered illegitimate and not Jewish (Vogelstein 2012, 1002). This is a serious consideration even for less observant Jews, with the possible implications for a right of Israeli citizenship.

In past centuries, when movement was restricted and Jewish communities were more closely connected than they are today, the problem was far less acute (Miller 1997, 3). The rabbi would be responsible for marriage and divorce, and so a husband could not remarry until he had granted a divorce. Furthermore, Jewish law does permit sanctions to be used against a recalcitrant husband, but only after a *beth din* has deliberated on the issue and concluded that the circumstances justify it—which involves a finding of fault (Broyde 2001; Schwartz 1997). Community pressure may then be brought to bear on the husband. He may be shunned, or his business may be boycotted until he complies. But in our modern, liquid times a husband can disappear and leave his wife with no means of recourse (Vogelstein 2012, 1002). In addition, in a way that is reminiscent of what occurs in the Muslim community, husbands have used their right to grant a *get* as a way of extorting money from their wives. It is also argued that an all-male rabbinate has been too reluctant to impose sanctions on husbands.

Jewish women, bound by tradition, have been slow to mobilize to seek a solution to this problem. Miller (1997) traces the history of efforts to provide relief, but a further feature of Jewish law has proved a substantial obstacle: the husband's grant of a *get* must be voluntary and not forced. This has meant that a variety of initiatives—such as the imposition of financial penalties for refusal to grant a *get*—have been found unacceptable by rabbis.[22]

As in the case of Muslim divorces, the best solution is considered to be found in the undertakings included in a prenuptial agreement (*ketubah*). But Jewish law will not permit the right to grant a divorce simply to be transferred to the wife. Instead, rabbis have sought to find a formula that creates incentives for the husband to grant a *get* without such incentives being regarded in Jewish law as undue pressure.

A first attempt to design a suitable undertaking came from the Conservative rabbi Louis Epstein in the 1930s. Under his proposal, every bridegroom would be required to sign a marriage document authorizing the Rabbinical Assembly to grant his wife a divorce in his absence and appointing the necessary witnesses and agents for that purpose. This proposal was vigorously opposed, and the views of fifteen hundred rabbis worldwide were cited in support of maintaining the traditional approach.

A more successful proposal was drafted by Saul Lieberman, a Conservative rabbi, in 1954. His clause authorized the *beth din* of the Conservative Rabbinical Assembly of America to "summon either party at the request of the other, in order to enable the party so requesting to live in accordance with the standards of the Jewish Law of Marriage throughout his or her lifetime." The hope was that if a husband could be required to appear before a *beth din* he could be encouraged to grant a *get*. The "Lieberman provision" had some success and has been enforced by civil courts in New York as an arbitration clause.[23] In Canada, on the other hand, a *ketubah* is not enforceable in the civil courts.[24] In fact, the Conservative movement eventually progressed to a more definitive solution to the *agunah* problem. In 1968, the Rabbinical Assembly introduced the rule that if a husband does not provide a *get* to his wife within six months, the Rabbinical Assembly will nullify the marriage.

Only Orthodox Jewish women are thus at risk of becoming *agunot*. Even so, pressure to find a solution has continued to mount because of increasing divorce rates within the Orthodox community. In some instances, appeal has been made to civil courts for assistance. Thus in 1973 a husband who had agreed as part of his civil divorce that he would grant his wife a *get*, but who later refused to do so, was fined by a New York court for contempt of court,[25] and in 1976 the New York Supreme Court ordered specific performance of an agreement between husband

and wife under which the husband was to grant a *get*.[26] An alternative civil law device used to mitigate the *agunah* problem is a damages award to the injured wife on the basis of a tort of intentional infliction of emotional distress (Vogelstein 2012, 1018).

Given the size of the Orthodox Jewish lobby in New York, the legislature there has also introduced measures to combat the problem. Section 253 of the New York Domestic Relations Act provides that an applicant cannot obtain a final judgment of civil divorce until "he or she has . . . taken all steps solely within his or her power to remove all barriers to the defendant's remarriage."[27] This circumlocution was used to avoid the measure being found unconstitutional on First Amendment grounds (Zornberg 1995, 706–707), and so far it has survived challenge, but it has been of limited utility since it bites only where the husband is seeking a civil divorce. Moreover, wives in strictly observant communities may be reluctant to use the civil courts out of either personal conviction or fear of being shunned by the community. A more widely drafted Canadian provision—s.21.1 of the Divorce Act 1990—which allows either party to bring to the attention of the court a barrier to religious remarriage, has also been little utilized in practice (Fournier 2012, 175–77).

In the light of community attitudes toward the *agunah* problem, the main route to a solution is still perceived as being through prenuptial agreements. The Rabbinical Council of America jointly with the BDA introduced a model agreement in 1992, which "received approval from significant Torah authorities, and has resulted in the efficient resolution of scores of divorce cases in the years since its introduction" (Willig 2012, 12). As currently drafted, the BDA prenup contains a clause conferring jurisdiction on the BDA along with an undertaking to "abide by the decision of the Beth Din with respect to the get" (Beth Din of America 2010). In addition, it provides that if the couple separates, the Jewish law obligation of the husband to support his wife is formalized, so that he is obligated to pay $150 per day (indexed to inflation), from the date he receives notice from her of her intention to collect that sum, until the date a Jewish divorce is obtained. This support obligation ends if the wife fails to appear at the Beth Din of America or to abide by a decision of the Beth Din of America.

To reinforce comments made earlier in this chapter about the relative harmony of interpretation of Jewish law across Orthodox communities, a similar approach is now also being pursued in Israel. Agreement on the form of a prenup negotiated by Tzohar, a Religious Zionist rabbinic organization and the Israeli Bar Association—requiring six years and sixteen drafts to achieve—was announced in March 2015 (Jewish Telegraphic Agency 2015). Like the BDA prenup, it relies on the formalization of the obligation of spousal support and puts payments at a high level as an incentive to grant the *get*. The "spousal support" characterization avoids the problem of the payment being seen as a penalty forcing the husband to grant the *get*. Members of Tzohar are among the principal "marriage facilitators" in Israel and therefore are well positioned to ensure that the prenup is widely used.

Full Circle

Returning to the Sharia debate in Ontario, we see an example of the law of unintended consequences. A change in the law that was intended to protect Muslim women from oppressive religious arbitration has had little or no impact on dispute resolution within the Muslim communities, since such dispute resolution takes the form of informal negotiation or mediation anyway. On the other hand, it may have damaged the position of Jewish women. The BDA and Tzohar prenups rely on the ability of *batei din* to arbitrate any dispute between husband and wife concerning the amount due for failure to grant a *get*, as specified in the prenup. Involving the civil courts in such a dispute, should it be possible as a matter of civil law, would not be halakhically permissible. But any award made by a *beth din* will not be enforceable in Ontario (or indeed elsewhere in Canada) because of the stance adopted toward religious arbitration. Nor will the arbitration clause in the prenup be enforced. A measure designed to protect one group of women has arguably disadvantaged a different group.

Jewish and Muslim communities both exhibit a huge range of attitudes toward religious observance. As noted in this chapter, many of the Jews who came to North America rapidly assimilated into American society. Among those who have retained a desire to practice Judaism, the Reform movement is by far the largest, but there remains a critical mass of Orthodox and ultra-Orthodox Jews who live in accordance with religious laws.

Assimilation is also rapidly taking place in Muslim communities—speeding up as a result of intermarriage and the weaker hold of traditional cultures on new generations. But current developments also point toward an increase in religious observance: a polarization between extremes. Jewish and Islamic family laws will undoubtedly remain significant in North America in the immediate future.

Unequal treatment of the spouses in relation to the availability of divorce is a feature of both Jewish and Islamic law, but Islamic law seems to have greater potential in this respect to develop solutions that can ameliorate the situation of the wife, through the inclusion of a *talaq-al-tafwid* in the marriage contract. It remains to be seen how far this solution can be implemented in practice, since implementation is dependent on the dissemination of information and on the acceptability of the solution within particular cultural and family contexts. In North America, feminist reinterpretations of Islam also exist, but these remain outside the mainstream.

The design of a solution to the *agunah* problem has been more problematic—at least for the Orthodox community. Initiatives, such as those of the BDA and the Tzohar / Israel Bar Association, have the potential to ameliorate the situation of *agunot* in Israel, North America, and elsewhere, but the prenup solution can be effective only if it leads to financial penalties that can be enforced through the civil courts as a result of the recognition of *beth din* adjudication.

Notes

1. The picture in the United States is quite varied, in particular where the dispute relates to child support and child arrangements. Arbitration over the division of property and spousal support is more widely recognized.

2. Matter of Luttinger, Court of Appeals of New York, 294 N.Y. 855; 62 N.E.2d 487 (1945); Matter of Robinson, Court of Appeals of New York, 296 N.Y. 778; 71 N.E.2d 214 (1947).

3. For a recent example see, e.g., Berg v. Berg, 85 A.D.3d 952; 927 N.Y.S.2d 83 (N.Y. App. Div. 2d Dep't, June 21, 2011). For a decision enforcing an agreement to arbitration in a *beth din* see Friedman v. Friedman, 34 A.D.3d 418; 824 N.Y.S.2d 357 (N.Y. App.Div.2d Dep't, Nov. 8, 2006).

4. 1991 Act s.2.2(1); Family Law Act 1990, ss.51, 59.2(1).

5. To the extent that they were religiously observant, a high proportion of the immigrants adhered to Reform Judaism, a German movement viewing Jewish

law as providing general guidelines, adaptable to modern life, rather than as immutable, divine rules. German Jewish families in the nineteenth century created fortunes as merchants, manufacturers, and investment bankers (including such families as Schiff, Goldman, Sachs, Lehman, Guggenheim, and Seligman).

6. The Jewish population of Canada rose from 6,501 in 1891 to 74,564 in 1911 (Tulchinsky 2008) and approximately 150,000 by 1930 (Robinson 2013). Further waves of immigration came after World War II.

7. Shulchan Aruch, Choshen Mishpat 26:1. *Beth din* authorization may be obtained to litigate where, for example, the other party refuses to submit to *beth din* arbitration or where the case is deemed by a competent halakchic authority to be of a type that the *beth din* is incapable of handling (Reiss 1999). For the mixture of reasons that Jews may use a *beth din*, going beyond the prohibition on access to secular courts, see Fried (2003).

8. In the *Journal of the Beth Din of America*; http://www.bethdin.org/journal, accessed 14 March 2015.

9. Although census data up until 2001 provided details of religious affiliation, this category was abandoned for the 2011 census, and information was instead captured through a less reliable National Household Survey.

10. For a comparative approach see Neusner and Sonn (1999).

11. An additional factor contributing to the fluid nature of Islam in North America is its character as a missionary religion and the ease of conversion. No formal process or ratification is required, and thus no knowledge of Islamic laws and practices. By contrast, Judaism does not actively seek converts. Conversion to Judaism (and particularly Orthodox Judaism) is a long and arduous process that may include gaining some knowledge of Hebrew and of Jewish history and culture, observance of Jewish holidays, and familiarity with other rituals, keeping kosher, and observing Shabbat and other halakhic rules. Conversion is prepared for with the assistance of a rabbi, but must be certified by a *beth din*. The importance of the process is evident from the fact that the Israeli "Law of Return" grants all Jews the right to immigrate to Israel, and this in turn gives rise to almost automatic Israeli citizenship. Reform and Conservative conversions are not, however, recognized by the Israeli Chief Rabbinate. In recent years, the politics of conversion has become fraught as a result of the control of the Chief Rabbinate by ultra-Orthodox Jews and the refusal to recognize many overseas Orthodox conversions. Only a small number of overseas *batei din* are officially recognized in Israel as competent to certify conversion.

12. These perspectives can be found across Reform, Reconstructionist, Conservative, and varieties of Orthodox Judaism.

13. Whether willingly or through community pressure.

14. Compare the growth of Sharia arbitration in commercial and banking matters, which does not raise the same public policy issues.

15. But there is the potential for a degree of systematization in local areas, as in the case of Cutting's discussion of the work of the Darul Iftaa in Toronto, which serves a Muslim population of South Asian origin (2102, 170–74).

16. For instances of transnational family dispute resolution see, e.g., Canada: (1991), 32 R.F.L.(3d) (Ont. Ct. Gen. Div.); England: *AI v MT* [2013] EWHC 100 (Fam).

17. Ronen v. Ronen, 2012 ONSC 4950; Rosenberg v. Minster, 2014 ONSC 845.

18. Glauber v. Glauber, 600 N.Y.S.2d 740, 743 (N.Y. 1993).

19. Rakoszynski v. Rakoszynski, 663 N.Y.S.2d 957, 958 (Sup. Ct. 1997); Cohen v. Cohen, 600 N.Y.S.2d 996 (App. Div. 1993); Lieberman v. Lieberman, 566 N.Y.S.2d 490, 490 (Sup. Ct. 1991); Stein v. Stein, 707 N.Y.S.2d 754, 754 (Sup. Ct. 1999).

20. A *talaq* is a divorce granted unilaterally by the husband. (The power to grant a divorce can, however, be transferred to the wife, and this is sometimes done in a marriage contract; this is referred to as *tafweedh-e-talaq*.) In the common case, where the power to grant a divorce is not transferred to the wife, separation may be by way of consent between the parties (*khula*), but this is disadvantageous to the wife since she will usually be required to return her dower (*mahr*). A *faskh* divorce is granted where a competent authority dissolves the marriage because of fault on the part of the husband. See, for a brief outline, Bano (2012, 93f., 186 ff.); see also Patel (2014).

21. Deuteronomy 24:1–2, as interpreted in Babylonian Talmud, Gittin 24b; Babylonian Talmud, Baba Batra 168a (Isidore Epstein, ed., 1960).

22. But Reform Judaism accepted a civil divorce as ending a Jewish marriage as long ago as 1869 (Miller 1997).

23. Avitzur v. Avitzur, 446 N.E.2d 136, 138 (N.Y. 1983), cert. denied, 464 U.S. 817 (1983).

24. Morris v. Morris, 1974 42 D.L.R. (3d) 550 (Manitoba Court of Appeal). See also Fournier (2012, 173).

25. Marguiles v. Marguiles, 344 N.Y.S.2d 482, 484 (App. Div.), appeal dismissed, 307 N.E.2d 562 (N.Y. 1973).

26. Waxstein v. Waxstein, 395 N.Y.S.2d 877, 879–80 (Sup. Ct. 1976), aff'd, 394 N.Y.S.2d 253 (App. Div. 1977.

27. Compare in the United Kingdom the Divorce (Religious Marriages) Act 2002. See also §§ 236B(5)(h), 6(d) of the New York Domestic Relations Law.

Bibliography

Alalwānī, Ṭāhā Jābir Fayyāḍ (2010). *Towards a Fiqh for Minorities: Some Basic Reflections*, rev. ed. Occasional Papers Series. London: International Institute of Islamic Thought.

An-Naʿīm, ʿAbd Allāh Aḥmad (2008). *Islam and the Secular State: Negotiating the Future of Shariʿa*. Cambridge, MA: Harvard University Press.

Bagby, Ihsan (2011). *Basic Characteristics of the American Mosque: Attitudes of Mosque Leaders*. Washington, DC: Council on American–Islamic Relations.

Bakalian, Anny, and Mehdi Bozorgmehr (2005). "Muslim American Mobilization." *Diaspora: A Journal of Transnational Studies* 14(1): 7–43.

Bambach, Lee Ann (2009). "The Enforceability of Arbitration Decisions Made by Muslim Religious Tribunals: Examining the Beth Din Precedent." *Journal of Law and Religion* 25(2): 379–414. doi: 10.2307/20789488.

Bano, Samia (2012). *Muslim Women and Shari'ah Councils: Transcending the Boundaries of Community and Law*. Basingstoke: Palgrave Macmillan.

Barkey, Karen (2009). *Empire of Difference: The Ottomans in Comparative Perspective*. Cambridge: Cambridge University Press.

Beth Din of America (2010). http://theprenup.org/explainingtheprenup .html, accessed 13 April 2015.

Boyd, Marion (2004). *Dispute Resolution in Family Law: Protecting Choice, Promoting Inclusion*. Toronto: Ministry of the Attorney General, Ontario.

Broyde, Michael J. (2001). *Marriage, Divorce, and the Abandoned Wife in Jewish Law: A Conceptual Understanding of the Agunah Problems in America*. Hoboken, NJ: KTAV.

Broyde, Michael J. (2012–13). "Jewish Law Courts in America: Lessons Offered to Sharia Courts by the Beth Din of America Precedent." *New York Law School Law Review* 57(2): 287–311.

Broyde, Michael J. (2015). "Faith-Based Private Arbitration as a Model for Preserving Rights and Values in a Pluralistic Society Symposium: Shari'a and Halakha in North America." *Chicago-Kent Law Review* 90: 111–40.

Bullock, Katherine (2012). " 'The Muslims Have Ruined Our Party': A Case Study of Ontario Media Portrayals of Supporters of Faith-Based Arbitration." In Anna C. Korteweg and Jennifer A. Selby (eds.), *Debating Sharia: Islam, Gender Politics, and Family Law Arbitration*, 257–76. Toronto: University of Toronto Press.

Chishti, Muzaffar, Meissner, Doris, Papademetriou, Demetrios G., Wishnie, Michael J., Yale-Loehr, Stephen W., and Peterzell, Jay. (2003). *America's Challenge: Domestic Security, Civil Liberties, and National Unity after September 11*. Washington, DC: Migration Policy Institute.

Clarke, L. (2012). "Asking Questions about Sharia: Lessons from Ontario." In Anna C. Korteweg and Jennifer A. Selby (eds.), *Debating Sharia: Islam, Gender Politics, and Family Law Arbitration*, 153–91. Toronto: University of Toronto Press.

Curtis, Edward E. (2009). *Muslims in America: A Short History*. New York: Oxford University Press.

Cutting, Christopher (2012). "Faith-Based Arbitration or Religious Divorce: What Was the Issue?" In Anna C. Korteweg and Jennifer A. Selby (eds.), *Debating*

Sharia: Islam, Gender Politics, and Family Law Arbitration, 66–87. Toronto: University of Toronto Press.

El Fadl, Khaled Abou (1994). "Islamic Law and Muslim Minorities: The Juristic Discourse on Muslim Minorities from the Second/Eighth to the Eleventh/Seventeenth Centuries." *Islamic Law and Society* 1(2): 141–87. doi: 10.2307/3399332.

Emon, Anver (2012). "Islamic Law and the Canadian Mosaic: Politics, Jurisprudence, and Multicultural Accommodation." In Anna C. Korteweg and Jennifer A. Selby (eds.), *Debating Sharia: Islam, Gender Politics, and Family Law Arbitration*, 192–227. Toronto: University of Toronto Press.

Feit, Rabbi Yaacov (2012). "The Prohibition Against Going to Secular Courts." *Journal of the Beth Din of America* 1(1): 30–47.

Fournier, Pascale (2012). "Halacha, The 'Jewish State' and the Canadian Agunah: Comparative Law at the Intersection of Religious and Secular Orders." *Journal of Legal Pluralism and Unofficial Law* 44(65): 165–204. doi: 10.1080/07329113.2012.10756685.

Fried, Ginnine (2003). "Collision of Church and State: A Primer to Beth Din Arbitration and the New York Secular Courts, the Comment." *Fordham Urban Law Journal* 31: 633–56.

Gerber, Haim (1994). *State, Society, and Law in Islam: Ottoman Law in Comparative Perspective*. Albany: State University of New York Press.

Gurock, Jeffrey S. (2009). *Orthodox Jews in America: The Modern Jewish Experience*. Bloomington: Indiana University Press.

Hassan, Said Fares (2013). *Fiqh al-Aqalliyyāt: History, Development, and Progress*. Palgrave Series in Islamic Theology, Law, and History. New York: Palgrave Macmillan.

Hughes, Aaron W. (2013). *Muslim Identities: An Introduction to Islam*. New York: Columbia University Press.

Jewish Telegraphic Agency (2015). "Rabbinic and Legal Groups Partner to Prevent Agunot." *Jewish Daily Forward*, 3 May 2015. http://forward.com/articles/215849/rabbinic-and-legal-groups-partner-to-prevent-aguno/#ixzz3UUdpoZbv, accessed 15 June 2016.

Kaplan, Yehiel S. (2008). "Child Custody in Jewish Law: From Authority of the Father to the Best Interest of the Child." *Journal of Law and Religion* 24(1): 89–122. doi: 10.2307/27639133.

Kutty, Faisal (2012). " 'Sharia' Courts in Canada: A Delayed Opportunity for the Indigenization of Islamic Legal Rulings." In Anna C. Korteweg and Jennifer A. Selby (eds.), *Debating Sharia: Islam, Gender Politics, and Family Law Arbitration*, 123–49. Toronto: University of Toronto Press.

Libson, Gideon (1996). "Halakhah and Law in the Period of the Geonim." In Neil S. Hecht, S. M. Passamaneck, Daniella Piattelli, Alfredo Rabello, and

Bernard S. Jackson (eds.), *An Introduction to the History and Sources of Jewish Law*, xvii. Oxford: Clarendon Press.

Macfarlane, Julie (2012a). *Islamic Divorce in North America: A Shari'a Path in a Secular Society*. New York: Oxford University Press.

Macfarlane, Julie (2012b). "Practising an 'Islamic Imagination': Islamic Divorce in North America." In Anna C. Korteweg and Jennifer A. Selby (eds.), *Debating Sharia: Islam, Gender Politics, and Family Law Arbitration*, 35–65. Toronto: University of Toronto Press.

Macklin, Audrey (2012). "Regulating Faith-Based Arbitration." In Anna C. Korteweg and Jennifer A. Selby (eds.), *Debating Sharia: Islam, Gender Politics, and Family Law Arbitration*, 91–122. Toronto: University of Toronto Press.

Miller, Jessica Davidson (1997). "The History of the Agunah in America: A Clash of Religious Law and Social Progress." *Women's Rights Law Reporter* 19: 1–16.

Neusner, Jacob, and Tamara Sonn (1999). *Comparing Religions through Law: Judaism and Islam*. London: Routledge.

Siddique Patel, "Talaq, Khula, Faskh and Tafweedh: The Different Methods of Islamic Separation—Part 1." 10 November 2014. http://www.familylaw.co.uk /news_and_comment/talaq-khula-faskh-tafweedh-the-different-methods-of -islamic-separation-part-1#, accessed 19 July 2016.

Pew Research Center (2007). *Muslim Americans: Middle Class and Mostly Mainstream*. Religion and Public Life. Washington, DC: Pew Research Center.

Pew Research Center (2011a). *The Future of the Global Muslim Population*. Religion and Public Life. Washington, DC: Pew Research Center.

Pew Research Center (2011b). *Muslim Americans: No Sign of Growth in Alienation or Support for Extremism*. Religion and Public Life. Washington, DC: Pew Research Center.

Rafeeq, Mona (2010). "Rethinking Islamic Law Arbitration Tribunals: Are They Compatible with Traditional American Notions of Justice Comment?" *Wisconsin International Law Journal* 28: 108–39.

Ramadan, Tariq (2004). *Western Muslims and the Future of Islam*: Oxford: Oxford University Press.

Reiss, Rabbi Jonathan (1999). "Jewish Divorce and the Role of Beit Din." http://www.jlaw.com/Articles/divorcebeit.html, accessed 10 April 2015.

Robinson, Ira (2013). *Canada's Jews: In Time, Space and Spirit*. Brighton, MA: Academic Studies.

Sachar, Howard Morley (1992). *A History of the Jews in America*. New York: Knopf.

Sacks, Jonathan (1993). *One People? Tradition, Modernity, and Jewish Unity*. London: Littman Library of Jewish Civilization.

Schwartz, Rabbi Gedalia Dov (1997). "Comments on the New York State 'Get Law.'" http://www.jlaw.com/Articles/get_law1.html, accessed 10 April 2015.

Selby, Jennifer (2010). "Islam in Canada." *Euro-Islam: News and Analysis on Islam in Europe and North America*. http://www.euro-islam.info/country-profiles /canada/, accessed 10 April 2015.

Selby, Jennifer A., and Anna C. Korteweg (2012). "Introduction: Situating the Sharia Debate in Ontario." In Anna C. Korteweg and Jennifer A. Selby (eds.), *Debating Sharia: Islam, Gender Politics, and Family Law Arbitration*, 12–31. Toronto: University of Toronto Press.

Shahar, Charles, Rosenbaum, Tina, and United Jewish Federation of Greater Toronto (2006). *Jewish Life in Greater Toronto: Trends and Attitudes of the Greater Toronto Jewish Community*. [Toronto]: UJA Federation of Greater Toronto.

Tulchinsky, Gerald (2008). *Canada's Jews: A People's Journey*. Toronto: University of Toronto Press.

UJA–Federation of New York, Cohen, Steven M., Ukeles, Jacob B., and Miller, Ron (2012). *Jewish Community Study of New York: 2011*. New York: UJA–Federation of New York.

Vikør, Knut S. (2005). *Between God and the Sultan: A History of Islamic Law*. London: Hurst & Co.

Vogelstein, Aviva (2012). "Is ADR the Solution? How ADR Gets around the Get Controversy in Jewish Divorce Note." *Cardozo Journal of Conflict Resolution* 14: 999–1026.

Willig, Rabbi Mordechai (2012). "The Prenuptial Agreement: Recent Developments." *Journal of the Beth Din of America* 1(1): 12–16.

Wolfson, Lorne F. (2010). "Family Law Arbitration in Canada." Federation of Law Societies' National Family Law Program, Victoria, British Columbia, 12 July.

Yousif, Ahmad F. (2008). *Muslims in Canada: A Question of Identity*, 2d ed. Ottawa: Legas.

Zelcer, Heshey (2007). "Two Models of Alternative Dispute Resolution." *Ḥakirah, the Flatbush Journal of Jewish Law and Thought* 4: 69–113.

Zornberg, Lisa (1995). "Beyond the Constitution: Is the New York Get Legislation Good Law?" *Pace Law Review* 15(3): 703–86.

9

A Court of Her Own

AUTONOMY, GENDER, AND WOMEN'S COURTS
IN INDIA

Gopika Solanki

FEMINISTS DEBATE THE QUESTIONS of whether women constitute culturally undifferentiated selves, whether women's autonomy can flourish under oppressive societal and familial conditions, and whether autonomy can undermine equality (Benson 1991; Fineman 2004; Kristinsson 2000; Meyers 1987; Nelson 2001; Oshana 2006). These questions are echoed in the body of literature on religious arbitration in the context of family laws; scholars stress how these religio-customary forums potentially restrict women's liberty (Okin 1999) and point to the clash between women's self-determination and community values that could arise in some instances. Studies of religious arbitration in Islamic law suggest that bargaining in the shadow of state and religious laws can yield contradictory and unpredictable outcomes but deny systemic asymmetry against the woman in the process (Bano 2012; Fournier 2012). Others suggest that religious arbitration can enhance women's autonomy (Ahmed and Luk 2012) and equality (Solanki 2011), and challenge patriarchy. Merging these bodies of literature and expanding the scope of the inquiry to include women-centered dispute resolution bodies, this chapter investigates modes of intervention in a women's court in western India and asks: How do informal dispute resolution processes impact women's capacity for autonomy? The chapter demonstrates that the ideological orientation of these courts, along with their ability to synthesize feminist collective action with individual intervention in family law disputes, comprises necessary conditions to facilitate women's autonomy through intervention in disputes related to religious family laws. Drawing on debates in political theory and feminist studies, for the purpose of this chapter I define autonomy as the ability to critically self-reflect on one's desires, actions, and social circumstances and to author one's projects, often in communication with significant others, as part of a continuous, partial, and often contradictory process, impinged upon by social contexts but not entirely shaped by them.

Multireligious and culturally plural states have debated whether to enact common laws or to opt for legal pluralism in the governance of the family. India is one such example. Following decolonization, India has not enacted a uniform civil code, and it recognizes religious laws of majority Hindu and minority Christian, Muslim, and Parsi religious communities.[1] The Indian state has also adopted the "shared adjudication model," in which the state splits its adjudicative authority with ethnoreligious groups in the governance of marriage and divorce (Solanki 2011). As a result, state courts, caste, and sect councils, doorstep courts, and religious clergy and civil society actors adjudicate in the matters of marriage and divorce. The Indian state's failure to enact a uniform code has been debated widely in India since 1947. Liberals and a section of the Indian women's movements,[2] as the proponents of uniform laws, saw it as a tool of modernization, secularism, and gender equality. A section of religious minorities, as opponents, believed that it would undermine diversity and entrench majoritarian values in law. The Hindu Right in India supported the uniform civil code, as they saw it as a tool to craft a homogeneous nation and assimilate minorities by erasing the markers of their religious identities. These debates became sharper in the 1980s with the Shah Bano case. Shah Bano, a divorced Muslim woman, had filed for maintenance under Section 125, CrPC.[3] Her husband argued that he was not liable to pay maintenance beyond *iddat* under Muslim Personal Law.[4] The Supreme Court awarded her the maintenance, but also observed that the state should enact a uniform civil code. This statement led to protests from conservative sections of Muslims, led by the All India Muslim Personal Law Board, and the Congress Party, which was in power at the federal level, passed the Muslim Women's (Protection of Rights on Divorce) Act, 1986, to govern post-divorce rights of divorced Muslim women and exempt them from the purview of uniformly applicable Section 125, Criminal Procedure Code.

Hindu nationalists took this opportunity to excoriate the Muslim minority as anti-modern and backward, unwilling to become part of the political community. In 1992, the Hindu Right led the destruction of the Babri Mosque,[5] and nationwide communal riots followed, marking a crucial setback for secularism and minority rights in India; in 2002 the violence against Muslims in the state of Gujarat in western India, ruled by the Bharatiya Janata Party, reinforced this sense. In the aftermath of these events, secular forces joined hands to challenge Hindu nationalism; these contestations continue in contemporary India, and feminist groups remain important actors in the struggle against Hindu nationalism. In the context of these political developments, Indian feminists have begun to realize that the uniform civil code was central to the Hindu Right's ideology of a common family as a foundation of a unified Hindu nation. As a result, a majority of women's groups have dropped their demand for the uniform civil code (Menon 1998) and shelved efforts to introduce legislative reforms in individual personal laws until internal consensus develops within communities. Women's groups have also pushed for reforms in uniformly applied civil and criminal laws that impact the family and have experimented with informal dispute resolution, developing women's courts to deliver piecemeal reforms for women (Solanki 2013). These women's courts intervene in cases, offering counseling, informal arbitration, and legal aid in cases of domestic violence or family disputes, and may serve as adjudicating bodies in cases of religious family laws. In family law, arbitration is understood to be a voluntary consensual agreement of the parties to resolve dispute through third-party mediation, often supported by state laws, such as the Arbitration Act (Bisset-Johnson 1984), and adjudication is defined as an authoritative decision given by a third party, possibly involving coercion (Gulliver 1969). In legally plural postcolonial societies, arbitration could also be an informal process in which two parties approach societal legal forums to resolve the dispute and arrive at mutually agreeable solutions, which are not always seen as legitimate and binding and are at times unrecognized by the state, but often socially validated by religio-customary norms and practices. Besides, there is often considerable overlap between these different modes of dispute resolution.

The body of literature regarding women's courts in India is more explicitly focused around their effectiveness in enhancing individual women's autonomy or, more tacitly, on their ability to bring about structural change, and the evidence is mixed. My work (Solanki 2013) on Nari Adalats (women's courts) in Gujarat suggests that these courts often arrive at ethically particular and context-sensitive solutions that privilege women's autonomy and subvert the content of ethno-religious patriarchal norms. Occupying a nonliberal conceptual ground, and based on her study of an NGO-based women's court, Hong Tschalaer (2010) suggests that the women's court in question offers solutions that are different from formal legal solutions that liberal feminists might advocate, but could be read as a conflict of "entangled plural modernities" (Hong Tschalaer 2010, 41). Others suggest, however, that while these forums offer congenial spaces for women to air their grievances, in many cases social constraints shape individual women's lives and a patriarchal script is imposed by women's court members on individual women who appeal to them. They note that the outcome in many such cases is reconciliation, when women agree to reside with the man, adhering to patrilineal kinship norms in exchange for a reduction in domestic violence (Basu 2015; Grover 2011; Lemons 2010). Women lack viable survival options, and reconciliation is women's submission to patriarchal and patrilineal kinship norms in exchange for economic security and social stability—a patriarchal bargain (Vatuk 2013). Reviewing these different bodies of literature brings forth the following question: Do these women's courts provide a context that is conducive to the development of women's agency?

Women's courts vary in terms of their ideologies, composition, procedures for resolving disputes, funding sources, and autonomy, and they are not exhaustively classified, studied, and mapped. Vatuk (2013) and Basu (2015) classify these courts as offshoots of state-led, decentralized dispute resolution systems or peer-led all-women's courts affiliated with NGOs with middle-class leadership. This chapter expands this typology and includes the women's courts affiliated with the Mumbai-based secular Muslim women's feminist collective Awaaz-e-Niswaan (AEN). In contrast to dispute resolution forums in hierarchical NGO settings, this study focuses on the AEN, an organization established and run by Muslim women from different castes, regional and linguistic backgrounds, residing in low-income neighborhoods in Mumbai. The group strives to employ egalitarian ideology, uses a relatively horizontal workplace hierarchy, and runs a women's court staffed by volunteers and former litigants who had once approached the AEN for help; new women join in the process, as it is an open group. The AEN intervenes in religious family laws and negotiates with religious clergy, but it does not define its activism as lying outside a secular liberal context and provides a platform to investigate the question of women's agency within the context of the dispute resolution process. This chapter is based on my ongoing engagement with the group since 1993. I conducted extensive fieldwork with the group in 2002–2003 for my dissertation, shared my findings with them in 2008 and 2011, and discussed new developments and cases with them in the summers of 2010, 2011, and 2012. Since December 2014, I am again conducting fieldwork with the group for my new research project on inter-religious marriage in Mumbai. In terms of methods, I have combined nonparticipant observation with interviews and used the longitudinal case study method to construct cases that capture some aspects of politics and practice of feminist intervention at the AEN.

The Context: The Women's Movements in Mumbai

Since its emergence in 1970s, the autonomous feminist movements in India have spanned many geographical locations, evolved diverse organizational strategies, and built alliances with other peasant movements, environmental movements, and movements for communal harmony.

Arguing that women's activism is embedded in a political culture of states in a federal system, Ray's (1999) comparative analysis of women's movements in Calcutta (now Kolkata) and Mumbai notes that, historically, women's groups in Calcutta have prioritized women's practical gender concerns and have privileged organizing for women's economic rights, and their activism has been shaped by the influence of the politics of the Communist Party of India (Marxist). Feminists in Mumbai, functioning in a more politically heterogeneous environment, on the other hand, have prioritized women's strategic gender interests, shaped the politics of protest, and built their activism around issues of violence within the family, sexual division of labor, law reforms, women's health, body, and sexuality, consciousness-building, and religious fundamentalism and have been critical of state co-optation. The Mumbai feminist organizations have engaged with law, initiating legal campaigns that challenge custodial rape, pornography, the practice of female feticide, and reforms in religious family laws, and build formal and informal institutional links with the police, the judiciary, and lawyers, evolving different models of women's courts to adjudicate in family laws. An array of organizations, feminists, other NGOs, and cause lawyers in Mumbai offer legal services to the vulnerable sections of society (Solanki 2011).

Consciousness-raising has been an intrinsic element of autonomous feminist groups, and the AEN, an outgrowth of feminist history, was initiated in 1985 by Shahnaaz Shaikh, a Muslim feminist who was part of the nonfunded, nonregistered feminist collective Forum Against the Oppression of Women in Mumbai, to highlight issues, concerns, and interests of Muslim women who faced sociopolitical and economic discrimination, communal violence, and gender inequality in religious family laws. She filed a case in the Supreme Court suggesting that India's provision of religious family laws violated Muslim women's right to equality within the family under Article 15 of the Indian Constitution.[6] Her struggles, however, were co-opted by the Hindu communal forces, which used her case to bolster their demand for a uniform civil code that assimilates minorities into the Indian Union, and she was attacked by religious patriarchies within the minorities for maligning the faith (Gangoli 2007). In 1987, she started the organization AEN with some volunteers in central Mumbai in a low-income neighborhood with a high concentration of Muslims. In December 1992, the Hindu Right destroyed the Babri Mosque in North India, and riots followed in the country. The AEN volunteers participated actively and extensively in post-riot relief and rehabilitation activities in Mumbai. The group was registered as an NGO in 1997, and since 2003 it has two locations, an office in the eastern suburb of Mumbai (Kurla) and a feminist shelter cum office in Mumbra, a neighborhood on the outer edge of Mumbai that emerged after the relocation of Muslims from the riot-torn areas of Mumbai.

Intersectional Politics of the AEN

The AEN recognizes the simultaneous and interacting axes of Muslim women's positioning at cleavages of age, class, caste, religion, and nation. From its inception, it has been a secular feminist collective run by Muslim women that highlights the issues and concerns of Muslim women but offers its services to women across religious boundaries and focuses on Muslim women's rights within the framework of feminist solidarity. It combines individual intervention in the informal dispute resolution process with social action.

One dimension of political agency that the AEN exercises as a secular Muslim women's organization is working in the context of rising Hindu nationalism. The turning point in the AEN during the period of communal violence in Mumbai, in 1992–93, when its volunteers and, more important, women who had been helped by the organization galvanized into action and participated extensively in working with riot-affected families. They also networked with other organizations to help local youths who had been illegally detained in cases related to communal violence and terrorism and to provide legal aid. Since 1992, the AEN has been an important voice in anti-communalism movements and has highlighted the specific issues that Muslim women face in the family and community, and as citizens marked by gender and minority status. In 2002, the AEN worked extensively in Gujarat in the aftermath of communal violence against Muslims; it became an important voice in the Mumbai-based Citizens for Justice and Peace, a network that emerged to confront Hindu majoritarianism. This was part of a coordinated effort by feminists to highlight violence against Muslim women during the Gujarat violence, along with feminist activists from nine countries who had worked on cases of genocide and violence against women in conflict. The report titled "Threatened Existence: A Feminist Analysis of the Genocide in Gujarat" by the International Initiative for Justice in Gujarat resulted from this coordination.[7]

Hindu communalism and riots also fueled internal patriarchy within the Muslim community given that women are seen to be repositories of a community's honor. In the early years of AEN's activism, a *maulavi* (clergy) told local women that riots happen because Muslim women do not wear the veil and they watch too much television. In response, the AEN was one of the organizations that demonstrated outside the clergy's office.[8] At the same time, the AEN cooperates with voices among Muslims that are open to dialogue with secular Muslim women's organizations. The AEN has initiated efforts to introduce reforms in Muslim personal law through a dialogue between Muslim religious bodies and Muslim women's networks. The group was part of a nationwide dialogue between women's groups in India regarding reforms in personal laws from 1993 on, and in 1999 the AEN organized a conference titled "Muslim Personal Law and Women" in which Muslim women shared their experiences of living under Muslim personal law.[9] This conference initiated the Muslim Women's Rights Network, a coalition of twenty-four Muslim women's organizations that seek legal reforms in religious family laws. The network initiated discussions with women in their respective groups in which they were encouraged to imagine a gender-just family law for Muslim women and suggest reforms in the legal system. After conversations with women who had approached these twenty-four organizations for help in different parts of India, the network gathered their findings and identified two issues: an end to triple *talaq* and maintenance during separation and after divorce.[10] They organized a dialogue with members of thirteen Muslim religious organizations, prominent lawyers, feminist activists, and citizens' groups in an effort to build a consensus within the community toward a bottom-up process of reform.

Their status as minority women working on family violence and conflict led to different challenges in their practice as women's courts. As one of the founders of the group shared:

> In the aftermath of the riots and the bomb blast, the police had detained many young Muslim men; their families were also harassed. The standard practice was that the police would pick up young men and torture them and their family, especially wives, sisters; mothers would be made to come to the local police station and made to wait for hours on end, to place a psychological pressure on men.[11]

This complicated the AEN's handling of cases of domestic or sexual harassment. Approaching the police for help or to register cases of domestic violence was criticized as an act of in-group betrayal. However, as the following excerpt suggests, the AEN did not change its practice:

> We were against domestic violence and continued to approach the police when women complained of domestic violence. At the same time, we questioned the communal bias of the police in illegal detention of Muslim youth, we criticized the police for failing to respond sensitively to address domestic violence, and yet approached them for help and ensured that Muslim women received a hearing.[12]

The AEN is one of the few Muslim women's groups working on religious family laws that has openly supported lesbian, gay, bisexual, and transgender (LGBT) movements in India. Some members of the AEN have dual membership in the Stree Sangam, a lesbian women's collective in Mumbai. Its library offers women access to feminist literature on sexuality and the body. Campaign meetings are hosted in the AEN office, and the organization is often actively involved in organizing protests, exhibitions, and marches on LGBT issues and in legal campaigns.

Bridging Individual Interventions and Collective Action

The AEN offers a three-tiered model of intervention that integrates feminist concerns of individual agency of women with the challenge of patriarchal structures. First, the AEN seeks to provide safe, woman-centered spaces within which women can share, rename, and reclaim their experiences and stories of kinship, procreation, cohabitation, family, sexual relations, love, religion, and laws. The group uses a pro-women approach in its intervention and prioritizes women's autonomy during counseling. Second, recognizing that an intervention that privileges women's agency can challenge and possibly disrupt socially oppressive relationships, it aims to provide a counterculture to society by attempting to build a group as a microcosm of a supportive network of women, many of whom are survivors of violence and oppression within the family and society. Third, it recognizes that women's agency/autonomy can flourish under unequal societal conditions, and therefore offers women an opportunity for political engagement with broader social movements, especially feminist movements, the anti-communalism movement, and the LGBT movement.

Individual Intervention

A group of about eight to ten women, three full-time workers, five or more volunteers, and former litigants who had sought and received support from the AEN meet as a team twice a week in a partitioned area of the large hall that is the AEN's office. They provide informal dispute resolution in cases of marital conflict, domestic violence, and sexual violence, and also adjudicate in religious family laws. In its intervention, the AEN relies on religious family laws, state laws, customary laws and religious precepts, and judicial precedents. Women from different religious groups approach the AEN for help. It aligns with the clergy, doorstep courts, *jamaats* (informal community groups), caste and sect councils, police, lawyers, family court counselors, and other NGOs or women's groups.

Against Neutrality and Impartiality: *Aap Ke Liye to Pura Samaj Hai*

Two core principles undergird the AEN's intervention and differentiate it from other informal forums. The AEN is explicitly pro-women, it is not neutral, and it privileges women's autonomy in its approach to dispute resolution. The AEN believes that dispute resolution is a moral, political project and that it should not be value-neutral. It believes that claims of objectivity and neutrality during intervention often insulate patriarchy and render invisible the ways in which sexist values are deployed during the process, which consolidates gender inequality in the family. In contrast, it begins the arbitration process with the feminist presupposition that women are oppressed in societal institutions of marriage and family and that the subordination of women is unjust. Furthermore, the AEN privileges women's voices and experiences during counseling and arbitration and works toward ends identified by individual women. Its opponents argue that its pro-women bias subverts the meaning of the counseling, leads to the breakdown of the family, and adversely affects social harmony. Some excerpts from interviews with AEN team members, who respond to these and other related issues, follow.

> We [AEN team members] are often accused of being home-breakers, and I tell them it is not us, it's you. It is injustice and male violence that breaks homes. We hold a mirror to society, showing the sheer brutality of violence, and [in doing so], we are showing them what they don't want to see or hear.[13]

> We are often accused of being biased toward women. During counseling, agitated men and their relatives, at times clergy, and other male social workers tell us, "You only listen to women, you only take their side." We tell them that you have the whole society to turn

to (*Aap ke liye to pura samaj hai*), why grudge women just one corner of their own?[14]

A woman had approached us for help; she was married in the nearby village and had returned to her natal family in Mumbai. She wanted divorce and wanted us to go to her husband's village to negotiate her divorce and to recover her *mahr* and dowry. We went to the village and met the local clergy and the religious *jamaat*. Everyone was surprised to see the contingent (*kafila*) of women, and the first puzzle was where should we all sit as negotiators? In that village men decided all the disputes sitting in the mosque, and women were not allowed in. Now they had to accommodate us as equal adjudicators. We ultimately decided to have the meeting on the grounds of the village school. The fact that there is not even a place for women to sit during these processes is seen as normal and we are accused of being biased![15]

The AEN's opponents suggest that this approach challenges the group's claim to impartiality and makes them close-minded, rejecting any reasoning or evidence during counseling that does not lead to a foregone conclusion that matches the group's political preferences. The AEN counters that its position does not hamper its ability to consider all sides of conflicting stories and worldviews during intervention. Indeed, the AEN's presupposition that women are oppressed by the family, and its belief in gender-just families, in fact increase its awareness about injustices meted out to women. The group see its intervention process as a means to refute the patriarchal values undergirding the family, sometimes religion, and society. Their bias increases their effectiveness in meeting the AEN's transformative goals and uncovers women's subjectivities in significant ways. In answer to the question of whether they would discount stories that do not fit their political certitudes, activists suggest that dispute resolution is a process whereby new facts come to light, ends are revised, and presuppositions are challenged or, at times, reconfirmed.

Both Lemons (2010) and Grover (2011) suggest that women's courts impose on litigants predetermined frames of "reconciliation" as a solution to a marital dispute in an attempt to "mend homes rather than break them" (Grover 2011, 169), thus depriving women of their autonomy. Hong

Tschalaer's (2010) work on women's courts in rural western India offers a different interpretation, by noting the disjuncture between action taken by women's courts and their justificatory narratives. She suggests that women's courts strategically use the language of reconciliation to obtain pragmatic solutions for women in a patriarchal rural setting where women have even fewer options than urban women, and she argues that aphorisms such as "We cannot clap with only one hand" and "A cart cannot move with one wheel, it needs two" as used by her informants, seemingly apportioning blame for disputes equally on both parties to the dispute, reflect the necessity of cooperation between men and women in order to secure social legitimacy for the committee's decisions and its authority as an institution (Hong Tschalaer 2010, 54). Hence, at times the language of reconciliation is an elaborate performance, a feminist subversion to secure a pragmatic bargain for the woman. However, the AEN, working in a more pluralized and heterogeneous setting where more legal options remain available, is able to take a more confrontational approach. In addition, working within a liberal and rights-oriented framework that values women's autonomy and equality, the AEN team remains alert about slipping into paternalism during counseling and does not impose its own conceptual frames or solutions on women. The AEN provides a space for women to arrive at choices and works toward providing enabling conditions so that women might realize their choices. The next section elaborates on this theme.

Grover (2011) also suggests that given that members of women's courts live in the same locales as their litigants, they are also personally subject to social opprobrium in ways that middle-class women who are associated with women's courts are not, as they do not have to confront irate male litigants or their families in their private lives. In contrast, the women members of the AEN persist in their approach despite tremendous social pressure, often from their own families and neighborhoods. As Yasmin Sheikh, a core member of the AEN, shared with me, "I was walking through the lane leading to my house and someone shouted, 'There goes women's judiciary.'"[16] The AEN women often speak of the constant blurring of work and family life, of women from their locality knocking at their doors in the night, of their meals being interrupted so that they can address an urgent dispute or a case of domestic violence, of pressure from their own immediate and extended family members, and of efforts of local leaders to influence the outcome and challenge their pro-women stance. However, these experiences do not affect their feminist practice in the same way that Grover's study (2011) suggests.

Individual Interventions and Privileging Women's Autonomy

In individual cases, the AEN acknowledges that women's choices are constrained and shaped by the wider sociocultural politics and relations of power, but the group also holds that individual women and organizations can resist these forces. It believes that women are able to arrive at a decision about their lives and that feminists should work toward providing enabling conditions and respect women's choices. The AEN realizes that any critical intervention is an open-ended process during which individual women engage in critical reflection, discover a language for understanding and interpreting their experiences, and deliberate on their lives and circumstances. Furthermore, women reflect on the dilemmas confronting them in intersubjective exchange and dialogue with others (Rossler 2002), and the team at the AEN becomes their interlocutors. The AEN members recognize that dispute resolution is also a process involving dialogue with different actors, and it can shift the subjectivity of women (Merry 2006) and provide the opportunity for diverse actors to resist gender inequality within the family, religion, and society and construct new norms of "doing family" (Solanki 2011). The following excerpts illustrate these points and make a case for developing a more expansive notion of autonomy, as discussed in the concluding section of this chapter. They are taken from my case notes during a counseling session with the AEN team members in Mumbai and subsequent incidents involving the same case as events unfolded during an intervention.

Farhat, a frail woman in her thirties and the mother of three children, has complained that her husband, Arif, doesn't provide enough money to run the house, and insults and belittles her.

Arif: She is just inefficient; her mother has not taught her anything—she doesn't know how to cook and run the house; my children are neglected.

Farhat: He wants me to cook meat every day—how can I manage that with the amount of money he gives me? We have three children—I run after them the whole time.

Arif: You are just lazy; you sleep the whole day. She falls sick at the drop of a hat.

Team member: Men have no idea how women work from morning to night to put food on the table and to raise three young children. This kind of lack of respect and appreciation takes a toll on women.

Team member: She looks weak—have you taken her to a doctor? She could be anemic.

Arif: She is just lazy and all this is drama. My employer would fire me if I sat around the whole day.

Team member: You earn well, and your boss is happy with you; why don't you give her money?

Team member: You are efficient. Why not start by shouldering some domestic work? You can see that she is run down.

Arif (outraged): I am a man—have you seen how men are treated in other families? I work outside the whole day and now you want me to work in the house as well?

Team member: You work outside because your family educated you; if she was also allowed to study, she would also have worked as well.

Team member: That is marriage—you help each other and run a house. You men don't understand the amount of work women do to run a house.

Farhat (slowly): I used to be very good in studies; my father forced me to marry early.

The outcome of the case was reconciliation. Farhat chose not to end the marriage but wanted some relief from daily conflict. One of the team members, who followed up on the case, said that the harassment had not lessened for Farhat but that her husband was rattled (*hil gaya tha*). Farhat said that she would let the team know if she urgently needed help, and she was assured that the AEN's doors would always be open to her.

Two months later Farhat comes to the AEN again, this time with another young woman, and narrates the story of how they met: "I was walking down the street and Salma [the young woman] just came out of nowhere and held my hand and said 'Apa, sister, help me. My husband has left me and I have a small son and no one to turn to.'" So Farhat had brought the young woman to the AEN. The AEN team listens to Salma, and Farhat joins in. The team asks what Salma thinks her next step should be. Farhat advises her: "Leave him, now; you have only one child. Once I, too, stood at the same crossroads of life (*mein bhi isi mod pe khadi thi*) . . . but I didn't have the courage and now I have three children. It gets harder to leave."

A month later, Farhat drops by the office, sharing that she has decided "to bear the harassment," as her children are small but that she plans to give private coaching to the neighborhood children so that they have a modicum of financial autonomy.

A few months later, there is a crisis in the AEN. A woman has called from her home, stating that her husband has beaten her and that she wants to go to the police station, but she doesn't know where it is, as she is new to Mumbai. The neighborhood is far from the AEN office, and it would take an AEN team a long time to reach her. Someone realizes that the caller lives in Farhat's neighborhood, so the team asks Farhat if she would be comfortable going to the woman's home and taking her to the police. Farhat agrees to do so. A couple of hours later, Farhat calls. She is excited and speaks with a newfound confidence. She reports on her experience: She had helped the woman lodge a complaint. The police had initially refused to respond, but she insisted on their help and threatened to call some women's groups; in the end, the police complied.

Reflecting on the change in Farhat, it is clear that autonomy is often a matter of degree: a woman's decision to reconcile with her oppressive husband does not transform her into a nonautonomous person in every respect; autonomy is often acquired gradually (Anderson 2003; Rossler 2002). Catherine MacKinnon (1984, 226) has argued that "participating in community and political life as active agents [is] important to women's well-being[;] acting in the world makes one feel more competent and gives one a sense of positive control over one's life." By offering options, information, a glimpse of new ways of life, and exposure to different worldviews and experiences, feminist courts provide mechanisms for critically altering the preferences and choices of women.

The problem of acquiring autonomy under oppressive social conditions has been discussed widely in feminist literature (see, e.g., Benjamin 1988; Benson 1991); many feminists question the idea of the deontological self and conceptualize relational autonomy, where autonomy is acquired in connectedness with significant others (Nedelsky 2011). However, Joseph (1999) shows that while both women and men in Lebanon are constituted by connected selves that are embedded in family, kin, and communities, patriarchal power favors men and elders in the social context, limiting women's options. In contrast, Seyla Benhabib (1992) argues on the basis of Habermas's theory of procedural autonomy that while social relations are important for the construction of self, after all the "I" becomes an "I" only in a community of speech and action; the social embeddedness of individuals does not translate into an uncritical acceptance of social structures, and through their participation in politics, socially embedded women can reflexively distance themselves from social relations and arrive at a critical vantage point to evaluate their lives and gain a sense of personhood.

The AEN does not see its politics as informed by piety, nor are its members extensively trained in theology; their interventions do not quite resemble the discursive politics of hermeneutical communities of Catholic women activists, who form study groups, participate in conferences, and write extensively, reinterpreting the meanings of church, of ritual, and of theological treatises, and challenge the heterosexist and anti-women bias of the Catholic Church (Katzenstein 1998). The AEN team does not identify with Islamic feminist politics (Rinaldo 2013) and does not rely only on textual reading or reinterpretation of Islamic law as an intervention strategy. As skilled negotiators, its members shift between religious and state laws, translate marital conflict in religio-legal categories, address individual dilemmas, consider cases from various angles and deploy suitable socio-legal strategies, use persuasion and rational deliberation, question, interpret and contest social meanings, and invent new rhetorical tools. For instance, in India, corruption is a big issue in the public sphere, and these discourses become part of the rhetorical tools used by the AEN to challenge inegalitarian relationships in society and hold religious clergy morally accountable.

The incident recounted in the following paragraphs is one that I observed firsthand. A woman has been given a fatwa of triple talaq, unilateral, unarbitrated repudiation by the husband. The wife, Mohsina, refuses to accept the talaq and has approached the AEN for help. The AEN team accompanies the woman to the office of the *qazi* (Islamic judge). They tell him that the woman refuses to accept the talaq. The qazi insists that the talaq is valid under Islamic law. A team member asks: "How can you just give the talaq like that? You should also reflect on these requests by men to grant talaq in the name of humanity (*insaniyat*). This woman has three small children. She has only studied till middle school. Where will they go?"

The qazi stands his ground. The discourse gets heated, and a team member comments that the corruption rampant in politics has spread to religion as well. Even the qazis are affected. They have forgotten their religious duty and have begun to earn money by giving fatwas that favor men, and this *talaqnama* is one such example. The team tells the qazi that this matter is not over yet and that it will go to another qazi and get a fatwa challenging the divorce, even though that will "besmirch the name of religion."

The AEN group debates Mohsina's options and tells her that one can always look for alternative clergy and challenge the fatwa, or it can be challenged in court, since the divorce was granted without arbitration. Another option is to file for a case of maintenance under the Protection of Women upon Domestic Violence Act (DVA), 2005.[17] Mohsina later decides not to challenge the triple talaq, but files for a case under the DVA, 2005.

The AEN team acknowledges that women's groups do not have magic wands. There are times when their interventions remain ineffective or can create a backlash for women for having approached a women's group to report a dispute. At the same time, other interventions may increase women's discretion and power in household affairs or bring domestic violence to a halt. Some women leave violent homes, while others may not. The processes in each case might be similar, but outcomes can vary. The AEN also believes that adverse situations limit the options of many women; minority women are further hampered by religious fundamentalism and violence. However, while these circumstances might not be conducive to women's autonomy, they do not entirely shape women's subjectivities and choices. The following case study builds on these issues.

When I arrived at the AEN one morning, a sense of urgency prevailed. The AEN activists were clustered around Naseem and her five children, aged three to fifteen, scared, disheveled, and crying. Naseem lived with her husband in Rajasthan; he had thrown her out of the house with the children and told her to leave the premises, not letting her enter the house even to pack their bags. She was forced to borrow money from relatives and had come to Mumbai, to the house of her only brother, Ashraf, traveling by train in a cramped compartment with the children for a day and a half. They arrived in Mumbai in the early morning, but when they reached Ashraf's small room in a Mumbai slum, he and his wife said that they could not give Naseem and her children shelter and asked them to leave. Distraught, she sat on the road, crying, when a neighbor gave her the address of the AEN.

At the AEN, they were given tea and snacks, someone talked to the children, and the group sat with Naseem, listening to her story, debating options with her. The room that her brother lived in with his family belonged to her father, who had passed away a few months ago. Naseem and her sister, both married, lived in other cities. The counseling team and Naseem discuss her options. There are two. The first is that the AEN can send her to an NGO-funded shelter with her children and write a letter to her husband asking him to come and discuss the marital conflict. However, this has some disadvantages. Her husband may take a long time to respond, or not respond at all, and she would not be able to work in the meantime, as the shelter does not allow women residents to work. (Later, reflecting on this case, the AEN team would reiterate the need for a feminist shelter in Mumbai, and a few years later, in 2002, they would build one and manage it themselves.)

Naseem, however, is not comfortable with this idea—the conflict is serious; Naseem does not wish to reconcile with her husband and, in any case, she feels that he may not take her back and is anxious to find some work to support herself and the children. Besides, there is the matter of the children's schooling. What she needs is a place to stay, and staying with her brother is her only option; no extended family could support a large family.

The second option is a legal one. As mentioned previously, the room in which Ashraf and his family live belonged to their father. Under the Muslim Personal Law (Shariat) Act, 1937, the Islamic law of inheritance, a sister is considered a primary heir of the deceased father, and while she does not have the same share in the property as a brother, her share gives her the right to secure an injunction against the sale of that property. The AEN can help Naseem with legal aid. Naseem is clearly relieved, but she adds: "Apa, my brother is not a bad man. He is under pressure, it is difficult for him to manage with all these mouths to feed. I want to reassure him that I won't be a burden . . . I can't fight with him and stay in that house day in and out. Besides, what will society (*log kya kahenge*) say? Let him know about the law only after all else fails." The team confers with Naseem and they discuss which elders in the family and which neighborhood leaders can mediate the dispute. The organization contacts a number of elders in the community and the locality, and a joint meeting is organized.

The brother, prompted by local leaders, comes up with an answer: he is willing to take Naseem in, but on the condition that she send her children back to her husband. Under the Sharia, the father has the right to elder children. The brother's reference to Sharia is a curveball, for he knows full well that Naseem won't allow the children to go, out of fear that her husband will abuse them. Seizing this opportunity, the AEN team reiterates that Naseem has a right to her share in the property under Sharia, and there is no reason why some tenets of the Sharia should be upheld and others sidelined. The team adds that Naseem can approach the court but that as of now she has not resorted to law, because she has not wanted to drag her brother to court. It is a veiled comment. Ashraf is left in no doubt that this road is open to Naseem.

The brother, startled, says, "This is my house, I live there and my sisters do not have the right according to the Sharia." A team member states, "It is your father's house and according to the Sharia, she has the right to it as well, and as long as she has that, you cannot deny her entrance. Would you prefer a legal option?" At this juncture, the community leaders are divided. They point out that the sister has a right to the property but not an equal right under Sharia, and customary practice overrides the Sharia, but her right cannot be denied under the Sharia. Temporarily, it is decided that Naseem and the children will stay with her brother, and arrangements are made for the children's school admission.

From that point on begins a long process of negotiation and bargaining and, for Naseem, of rebuilding her life as she steels herself against the enormous odds of living as a single woman with little training and support and fending for herself and five children. A letter from the AEN is dispatched to Naseem's husband, asking him to come to Mumbai to discuss the case, efforts are made to find work for Naseem, and a case is filed for maintenance on her behalf. Women's groups in Rajasthan are contacted so that they can persuade her husband and his family to come to

Mumbai and provide maintenance. To survive, the older children begin to find work alongside their studies, and Naseem returns again and again to the AEN, as her brother has begun using violence to make her and the children unwelcome. The AEN team begins to discuss the possibility of her brother giving her a share of the money so that she and the children can move to a room in a low-income neighborhood.

Reflecting on the enormity of the challenge that she has faced and continues to confront, Naseem, who has dropped by at the AEN, shakes her head. Though the case of maintenance is filed, her husband does not pay maintenance regularly; she has to go to court time and again. At times he pays up, and then stops for six months, and she has to file a petition once again to recover the arrears. The legal process is exhausting; she reflects that the children's education has suffered: her elder children, a son and a daughter, have had to take on additional chores and work to support the family, and her daughter, an especially good student, has been lagging behind in school. The harassment and emotional violence from her brother continues; she faces social pressure from extended family, neighbors, and society to go back to her husband. She is chastised for being a burden on her brother, for asking for her share of the property, for not being strategic enough regarding her marital family, and for depriving her children, especially her sons, of their maintenance and, more important, rights of inheritance of their father's property. "Out of sight is out of mind, especially for fathers," she is told. She finds that she has lost social status and the protection of her father—"Since my father's death, I feel that my children and I are standing in the rain, day in and day out, without an umbrella." How has coming to the AEN helped her? She couldn't have rebuilt her life without the AEN; however hard it is, it is her own for the first time, but, most of all, she says, "No matter how hard one's life is, what one needs is a place to unburden oneself, a corner to cry in. I get solace only at the AEN (*sukun sifr yahan milta hai*)."

What we find here is that the politics of the AEN disrupted previously accepted and relatively unquestioned religious and customary assumptions; they also challenged religious and customary norms, selectively prioritizing Islamic law over gender-unequal customs, and encouraged and supported Naseem in the struggle to exercise control over her life and to negotiate better terms in her relationship with others. Each of these changes is important in itself, but it is through their mutual interactions that the empowerment of individual women is most likely to translate into broader struggles for gender justice and social transformation.

What are the reasons for religious bodies, organizations, and clergy to cooperate with the AEN despite their ideological differences? Mumbai's socio-legal and legal sphere is plural and heterogeneous, and the AEN's linkages with other feminist organizations, lawyers, citizens' groups, and courts increase the group's effectiveness in dealing with the police and the judiciary in working with women; many local grassroots organizations run by religious groups among Muslims benefit from collaborating with them. In addition, the AEN's work during times of communal violence and their public stand on secular initiatives along with many other organizations has brought it respect from other organizations and local groups. Its efforts at engaging with religious organizations in order to deliberate over the content of religious family laws have been positively acknowledged by religious actors as an example of an effort to engage in a constructive, bottom-up dialogue with them, and while not all religious organizations respond to the AEN's stand that women should be granted substantive equality through citizenship reforms and uniform laws, many others continue to work with the AEN at the individual level through cooperation in the handling of women's cases despite ideological and political differences. These constructive efforts have resulted in the AEN's ability to successfully resist, cooperate with, and confront socio-religious conservatives within the Muslim community.

Women who have approached the AEN also meet in informal spaces—they participate in photography workshops, theater workshops, literacy classes, and English lessons, and libraries are in great demand. Young women also perform street plays or play rugby. Local women, litigants, and their families often drop by the office and talk about various matters with group members, visitors, other feminists, or NGO workers who might be involved with the organization. They often share life experiences in informal, small groups of twos and threes, giving voice to their private experiences. Group interaction provides the members with new ideas about the injustices of gender and support for instigating change. It also provides them with information and other worldviews, which broadens their horizons (Chambers 2005).

A joint meeting was planned at the AEN office in Mumbra—Seema had accompanied her sister Zubeida, who had approached the AEN for help. Before the meeting, Seema was browsing through books in the library and came across a Hindi booklet, inspired by *Our Bodies, Ourselves*, by the Boston Women's Health Book Collective. She hesitantly asked if she could come to the library to read, and began to drop by. As her sister's case progressed, Seema joined in the discussions and at times lingered behind to talk to the AEN team. On a Wednesday, she walked into the office. It was not a day that the women's court met, but two volunteers were there. She talked to them informally and shared that she was married and had children, but she was also in a relationship with another woman, a neighbor. Both were married, and she didn't really understand the relationship, but it gave her happiness. After reading the book in the library she had begun to understand and make peace with herself and her sexuality, and this was the first time she had voiced it to anyone else. While Seema did not come out, Naseem, the activist with whom she shared the story, told me that she comes for all gay pride marches, and she was there when the AEN joined other LGBT groups to celebrate the Delhi High Court verdict that decriminalized private same-sex relations between consenting adults;[18] she was again there to protest against the Indian Supreme Court's verdict that reversed the order of the Delhi High Court.[19] The opportunity to participate in collective action offers new cultural alternatives, feminist solidarity, and a sense of belonging.

Taking Stock

There is mixed evidence regarding the women's courts and their impact on women's liberty. Hong Tschalaer (2010) has discussed a women-led judicial body, the Social Reform Community, among the Meena (an indigenous group in Rajasthan, western India) that is supported by an NGO, the Astha Sansthan, as a space of resistance that offers an opportunity to renegotiate gender and power. In its operation, it is different from other state and non-state legal forums, establishing its legitimacy in society by eschewing bribery, cooperating with the police and judiciary (especially in cases involving violence), evincing a balanced approach to cases, and seeming to appear neutral while pushing a pro-women agenda. She suggests that such forums do not view women as undifferentiated atomistic individuals but as socially embedded members of their family, village, and caste communities. The Social Reform Community, therefore, balances negotiations for women's rights and their well-being, and it recognizes their need for social recognition and respect from their communities while acknowledging social constraints, yet challenging patriarchy.

Katherine Lemons's (2010) work on women's courts run by Action India, a feminist organization led by middle-class women but run by peer-led women's courts in low-income, Muslim-dominated neighborhoods in Delhi, and Shalini Grover's (2011) study in a Hindu-majority locality in Delhi conclude that while these courts listen to women's stories, the counselors in such places often persuade or coerce women to staying within the marriage by effecting reconciliation in exchange for economic security and social stability. Offering a nuanced explanation of the trend reported by these scholars, Vatuk (2013) states that women who approach these courts are in positions of extreme vulnerability due to low literacy levels, limited access to employment opportunities, lack of access to and control over property rights, and low confidence in negotiating with the judiciary and other state institutions. Given that they have to rely on the precarious support of their natal families to survive, options such as divorce and criminal charges appear neither desirable nor feasible from an economic or socio-legal perspective. Given the lack of survival options, these women's courts find that the only solution they can offer these women is to bargain during counseling in ways that ease their immediate concerns (such as domestic violence) in exchange for agreeing to adhere to strong patriarchal and patrilineal norms within the marriage—a modest, pragmatic solution. Vatuk also suggests that while women counselors in peer-led courts have the same socioeconomic backgrounds as women they work with, they often come to embrace the middle-class ideology of the man as the breadwinner and the woman as the housewife, and reinforce this through informal dispute resolution even if it diverges from their own and local women's actual experiences. However, she neglects to explain the mechanisms of this shift. Thus Vatuk argues that in the case of India, structures have to change before individuals can reasonably resist domination. In other words, she suggests that a context of institutionalized rights, economic opportunities, and social egalitarianism is constitutive of liberty. This claim is both normatively and empirically questionable.

While Vatuk's (2013) caution is an important reminder that acts of will alone cannot bring about change, her conclusion also challenges feminist insight and the practice of consciousness-raising and political engagement with structures of oppression. As we see, the AEN team resists individual discrimination in the family, religion, society, and the state, but it also simultaneously advocates politics of social and economic transformation. It recognizes that the dispute resolution process addressing domestic violence and women's rights in the family must be bolstered by a coordinated, proactively normative program of change in the family, in legal institutions, and in wider social norms. And we see the AEN linking individualized and local action with conceptualizing, organizing, and joining in regional, national, and transnational action and movements. While one agrees with Grover (2011) and Lemons (2010) that group interaction may not always be transformative and that traditional women's groups foster conformity, they are unable to explain the reasons for the gap between the collective politics of feminist groups that women's courts espouse and their reaffirmation of patriarchal familial model through their counseling and intervention.

Vatuk's (2013) observations that women's courts re-traditionalize gender norms lead to several questions for the feminist theory of agency and social change. The above-mentioned discussions of women's courts have stayed within the ambit of understanding of what Isaiah Berlin calls negative liberty,[20] or absence of constraints; it suggests that the woman should be able to make the choice to stay in a relationship or leave, and that feminists should respect that choice. This approach suggests that it is possible that women accept or compromise with subordination given community pressure, economic dependence, prejudice against divorce, lack of employment opportunity, and property rights. Its logical conclusion is that such micro-decisions and actions of women further consolidate patriarchy. However, overt reliance on negative liberty as a framework to situate women's autonomy is problematic because it relies on an overly individualistic concept of choice, leading one to question how women arrive at choices (Hirschmann 1995). Vatuk hypothesizes that patriarchies constitute women, and this leads her to conclude that there is not much potential for change. Her approach, however, fails to explain why some women dissent despite oppressive social conditions. It also fails to take into account the link between social action and individual intervention that we find in the AEN. As a result, this does not, nor can it, explain why the outcomes of cases might differ in various instances and why different women's courts vary in their processes of intervention and their differentiated impact on social change. Vatuk also puts forth a claim that agency is constitutive of conditions, what Mariana Oshana (2006) calls a system of conditions of absolute civil liberties, political freedoms, and economic prosperity. Such accounts do not, however, help us understand how women's subjectivity that we find in the data from the activities of women's court in the AEN leads to autonomy.

In her study of the women's mosque movement in Cairo, Mahmood (2005) identifies a paradox for feminist conceptions of agency: although women participants in mosque movement are asserting themselves in various social institutions, their ultimate aim is to discover, adhere to, and submit to the doctrines of religious scriptures, which may contradict feminist ideals of equality. In order to recognize the agency of women participants in the mosque movement, Mahmood argues that we need to decouple agency from freedom and to expand the notion of agency, not merely as norm-resistance, but as norm-inhabitation. This approach does not account for faithful women's ability to critically reflect on some aspects of their religion, nor does it explain how women can use religion instrumentally (MacLeod 1992). The mosque movement does not claim to be a feminist movement, and it differs from the AEN's focus on social change through concerted action. In the mosque movement, social change occurs—women resist the authority of husbands, infusing their presence into religio-social worlds, and these actions, as Mahmood suggests, are political actions, but they remain incidental by-products of their efforts at arriving at substantive religious ends. In addition, the mode of agency that privileges norm-inhabitation does not answer the question that is central to the AEN's work: Can actions that do not privilege individual rights leave one open to societal oppression (Weir 2013, 336)? However, through her articulation of feminist reconceptualization of freedom as connectivity, or belonging, Alison Weir offers an expansive interpretation of the pietists' agency, not only as norm-inhabitation, but as practices of "reworking and renegotiating connections" to themselves, their families, the mosque, the piety movement, to Islam, to actualize the ideal of "being in relations that support and sustain their relation to God" (336). Weir's rereading of Mahmood helps us to challenge the emptiness of "choice" and the idea of unencumbered deontological self, but one can also draw from her work the reassertion of the notion of freedom as belonging and to retrieve and locate agency in the AEN's efforts as building networks of litigant women and counterculture.

In a similar vein, Pamela Sue Anderson's (2003) essay, "Autonomy, Vulnerability and Gender," discusses a gendered conception of autonomy, one located in an understanding of the way in which the self is both written and read. Using the metaphor of the narratable self, Anderson rejects the Kantian accounts that focus exclusively on the subject as self-governing, an author. In its place, she proposes an understanding of the self that recognizes that the subject is relentlessly involved, not only in writing her own story "but also in reading the stories in which she finds herself" (Anderson 2003, 149). She also stresses the temporal aspect of agency, for she finds that the interplay between the future and the past affects the way in which autonomy is conceived. She suggests that if we weave the possibilities of the contingency, our vulnerability, and our embodiment into the manner in which these form parts of us, the author, what we can conceptualize is not the self-sufficient ahistorical subject, but an ambiguous one, a fractured, vulnerable, indeterminate, and embodied one that is still scripted.

Similarly, expanding on the more capacious notion of agency rather than a more limited notion of autonomy, Carisa Showden (2011) develops theoretical tools that capture the messy complexity and imperfection of women's lives. She argues that we need to separate the understanding of autonomy (the individual's capacity to act) from freedom (conditions that facilitate action) (ix). She theorizes the tension and interaction between the two as integral to an understanding of subjectivity. She suggests that agency is "both a process and capacity that is shaped by subjects' temporal and relational circumstances" (ix) and argues against evaluating a subject's agency on the basis of outcome alone. Locating her theoretical approach within the context of domestic violence in the United States, she shows how women do leave abusive relationships and gradually develop internal capacities of autonomy over time, often taking an average of six to eight years to leave. She, like the women of the AEN, is cognizant of the structural constraints, and highlights that it might not be the failure to resist but structural failures that affect the outcome in many instances. She suggests that rather than focusing on the outcome, we should look at the web of conflicting demands, relations, circumstances, and constraints that determine women's choices (77). Indeed, Showden develops the argument that agency is always "partial and constrained" (40). How do we conceptualize change through this conception of agency? For Showden, it is not merely modes of acting that make one's life "livable and endurable on [a] day to day basis," for these may not affect change unless "there is an effort to disturb or interrupt or corrupt the material weight of determinism through a creative, generative challenge" (xv). The women litigants' experiences at the AEN demonstrate the subtle complexity of barriers to agency, and the potential for agency, allowing us to capture the dynamic processes of agency in face of new challenges, demonstrating that the path to dignity and self-worth is a long one, and as Naseem's case shows, the cessation of violence from one source may not end violence that women face. However, feminist women's courts provide a platform to insert one's will in the world, different interpretive grounds, an opportunity to arrive at choices through intersubjective dialogue, a sense of belonging in women's networks, and the scope to participate in a political movement. It is in the integration of individual and collective action by the AEN that we find these possibilities that allow us to see the combination of active promotion of a new set of norms for "doing" gender, family, sexuality, and religion along with efforts to bring about structural change.

Notes

1. All other civil and criminal laws fall under the domain of the state. Indigenous peoples are governed by their customary family laws.

2. For the purpose of this chapter, Indian women's movements include autonomous women's groups, women's groups and wings affiliated with the radical left and the left-of-the-center parties, mass organizations of women, NGOs working exclusively on women's rights and issues as well as NGOs running projects related to women, and women's organizations affiliated with other organizations working for civil liberties, democratic unions, and social work groups/organizations. The typology excludes right-wing women and organizations.

3. This section, meant to protect indigent wives, was applied uniformly across religions under Indian criminal laws. Although the amount then under this law was Rs. 500 ($10) a month, this section was popular with women—under the law, the recovery rate of arrears was higher because failure to pay invited criminal liability.

4. Under Islamic laws, the term *iddat* refers to a period of roughly three months and ten days post-divorce.

5. The Babri Mosque is a sixteenth-century structure. The Hindu Right claims that it was built on the ruins of the temple of the Hindu god Ram, though the archaeological evidence is disputed. The site was used for religious purposes

by both Hindus and Muslims, but after several suits from opposing religious groups claiming the site were filed in the immediate aftermath of the partition of India, its gates were locked in 1949. The gates were reopened to allow Hindus to offer prayers in 1986, and Rajiv Gandhi, the Congress Party leader, allowed a Hindu ceremony near the site in order to gain Hindu conservatives' votes. To counterbalance this move and to revive its support among Muslims, the Congress Party enacted the Muslim Women's Act, 1986. In the late 1980s, the Hindu Right mobilized to destroy the mosque; this culminated in the demolition of the mosque by groups of Hindu fundamentalists on 6 December 1992.

6. *Shahnaaz Shaikh v. Union of India and Abdul Rab Kavish*, 1983 (Gangoli 2007, 28).

7. See "Threatened Existence: A Feminist Analysis of the Genocide in Gujarat," Report by the International Initiative for Justice in Gujarat, Mumbai, 2003. The international activists and scholars included Sunila Abeysekara, director of Inform, Colombo, Sri Lanka; Rhonda Copelon, professor of law, City University of New York; Anissa Helie of Women Living Under Muslim Laws Algeria/France; Gabriela Mischkowski, historian and cofounder of Medica Mondiale, Germany; Nira Yuval-Davis, professor of gender and ethnic studies at the University of Greenwich, UK; and several other prominent feminists. The initiative was organized by the Citizens' Initiative, People's Union for Civil Liberties (PUCL), Shanti Abhiyan, Communalism Combat, Awaaz-E-Niswaan, Forum Against Oppression of Women, Stree Sangam, Saheli, Jagori, Sama, and Nirantar, Organized Lesbian Alliance for Visibility and Action, and other women's organizations in India.

8. Interview with Hasina Khan, 17 January 2003.

9. Interview with Saira Bano Arab, 3 January 2003.

10. The *talaq e bidaat* consists of three pronouncements (of divorce) made during a single *tuhr* (menstrual cycle) in one sentence or a single pronouncement made during a *tuhr* clearly indicating an intention to dissolve a marriage irrevocably (Mulla 1955, 267).

11. Interview with Hasina Khan, 17 January 2003.

12. Interview with Hasina Khan, 17 January 2003.

13. Interview with Naseem Sheikh, 31 July 2008.

14. Interview with Aisha Pathan, 13 June 2008.

15. Interview with Hasina Khan, 17 January 2003.

16. Interview with Yasmin Sheikh, 20 February 2003.

17. The act provides emergency relief to the woman by restraining the abuser, gives her the right to live in the matrimonial home, and gives her access to all the privileges she had prior to making the complaint; it has provisions for maintenance and monetary relief and for interim custody of children to married women as well as women in domestic relationships.

18. Naz Foundation v. Govt. of NCT of Delhi, WP(C) No.7455/2001 (Del. H.C.) (2009) (India).

19. Suresh Kumar Koushal and another v. Naz Foundation and Ors. Civil appeal 10974 of 2013.

20. See Berlin (1971, 123).

Bibliography

Ahmed, Farrah and Luk, Senwung (2012). "How Religious Arbitration Could Enhance Personal Autonomy." *Oxford Journal of Law and Religion* 1(2): 424–45.

Anderson, Pamela Sue (2003). "Autonomy, Vulnerability and Gender." *Feminist Theory* 4(2): 149–64.

Bano, Samia (2012). *Muslim Women and Sharia'h Councils: Transcending the Boundaries of Community and Law.* New York: Palgrave Macmillan.

Benhabib, Seyla (1992). *Situating the Self: Gender, Community, and Postmodernism in Contemporary Ethics.* New York: Routledge.

Benjamin, Jessica (1988). *The Bonds of Love: Psychoanalysis, Feminism, and the Problem of Domination.* New York: Pantheon Books.

Benson, Paul (1991). "Autonomy and Oppressive Socialization." *Social Theory and Practice* 17(3): 385–408.

Berlin, Isaiah (1971). *Four Essays on Liberty.* New York: Oxford University Press.

Bisset-Johnson, Alastair (1984). "Arbitration and Mediation of Disputes Involving Children and Matrimonial Property in Canada." In John Eekelaar and Sanford N. Katz (eds.), *The Resolution of Family Conflict: Comparative Legal Perspectives,* 233–47. Toronto: Butterworths.

Chambers, Clare (2005). "Masculine Domination, Radical Feminism and Change." *Feminist Theory* 6(3): 325–46.

Fineman, Martha (2004). *The Autonomy Myth: A Theory of Dependency.* New York: New Press.

Fournier, Pascale (2012). "Calculating Claims: Jewish and Muslim Women Navigating Religion, Economics and Law in Canada." *International Journal of Law in Context* 8(1): 47–72.

Gangoli, Geetanjali (2007). *Indian Feminisms: Law, Patriarchy and Violence in India.* Aldershot: Ashgate.

Grover, Shalini (2011). *Marriage, Love, Caste, and Kinship Support: Lived Experiences of the Urban Poor in India.* New Delhi: Social Science Press.

Gulliver, P. H. (1969). "Case Studies of Law in Non-Western Societies." In Laura Nader (ed.), *Law in Culture and Society,* 11–23. Berkeley: University of California Press.

Hirschmann, Nancy (1996). "Domestic Violence and the Theoretical Discourse of Freedom." *Frontiers: Journal of Women's Studies* 16(1): 126–51.

Hong Tschalaer, Mengia (2010). "Women Entering the Legal Landscape: Negotiating Legal Gender Reforms in a 'Tribal' Women's Forum in South Rajasthan, India." *Journal of Legal Pluralism and Unofficial Laws* 42(60): 41–72.

Joseph, Suad (1999). "Theories and Dynamics of Gender Self and Identity in Arab Families." In Suad Joseph (ed.), *Intimate Selving in Arab Families: Gender, Self, and Identity*, 1–20. Syracuse, NY: Syracuse University Press.

Katzenstein, Mary Fainsod (1998). *Faithful and Fearless: Moving Feminist Protest inside the Church and Military*. Princeton, NJ: Princeton University Press.

Kristinsson, Sigurdur (2000). "The Limits of Neutrality: Toward a Weakly Substantive Account of Autonomy. *Canadian Journal of Philosophy* 30: 257–86.

Lemons, Katherine (2010). "At the Margins of Law: Adjudicating Muslim Families in Contemporary Delhi." PhD diss., University of California–Berkeley.

MacLeod, Arlene Elowe (1992). "Hegemonic Relations and Gender Resistance: The New Veiling as Accommodating Protest in Cairo. *Signs* 17(3): 533–57.

Mahmood, Saba (2005). *Politics of Piety: The Islamic Revival and the Feminist Subject*. Princeton, NJ: Princeton University Press.

McNay, Lois (2004). "Agency and Experience: Gender as Lived Relation. *Sociological Review* 52(2): 173–90.

Menon, Nivedita (1998). "Women and Citizenship." In Partha Chatterjee (ed.), *Wages of Freedom: Fifty Years of the Indian Nation-State*, 241–266. Delhi: Oxford University Press.

Merry, Sally (2006). "Transnational Human Rights and Local Activism: Mapping the Middle." *American Anthropologist* 108(1): 38–51.

Meyers, Diana T. (1987). "Personal Autonomy and the Paradox of Feminine Socialization." *Journal of Philosophy* 84: 619–28.

Mulla, Dinshaw F. (1955). *Principles of Mahomedan Law*. Calcutta: Eastern Law House.

Nedelsky, Jennifer (2011). *Law's Relations: A Relational Theory of Self, Autonomy, and Law*. New York: Oxford University Press.

Nelson, Hilde Lindemann (2001). *Damaged Identities, Narrative Repair*. Ithaca, NY: Cornell University Press.

Okin, Susan (1999). "Is Multiculturalism Bad for Women? In Joshua Cohen, Mathew Howard, and Martha Nussbaum (eds.), *Is Multiculturalism Bad for Women?* 7–26. Princeton, NJ: Princeton University Press.

Oshana, Mariana (2006). *Personal Autonomy in Society*. Aldershott: Ashgate.

Ray, Raka (1999). *Fields of Protest: Women's Movements in India*. Minneapolis: University of Minnesota Press.

Rinaldo, Rachel (2013). *Mobilizing Piety: Islam and Feminism in Indonesia*. London: Oxford University Press.

Rossler, Beate (2002). "Problems with Autonomy." *Hypatia* 17(4): 143–62.

Showden, Carisa (2011). *Choices Women Make: Agency in Domestic Violence, Assisted Reproduction, and Sex Work*. Minneapolis: University of Minnesota Press.

Solanki, Gopika (2011). *Adjudication in Religious Family Laws: Cultural Accommodation, Legal Pluralism and Gender Equality in India*. Cambridge: Cambridge University Press.

Solanki, Gopika (2013). "Beyond the Limitations of an Impasse: Feminism, Multiculturalism, and Legal Reforms in Religious Family Laws." *Politikon* 40(1): 83–111.

Vatuk, Sylvia (2013). "The 'Women's Court' in India: An Alternative Dispute Resolution Body for Women in Distress." *Journal of Legal Pluralism and Unofficial Law* 45(1): 76–103.

Weir, Alison (2013). "Freedom and the Islamic Revival: Freedom as a Practice of Belonging." *Hypatia* 28(2): 323–40.

10

Islamic Community Processes in Australia

AN INTRODUCTION

Ghena Krayem and Farrah Ahmed

THE MUSLIM COMMUNITY IN AUSTRALIA has a variety of community-based dispute resolution processes for dealing with family conflict (Black and Sadiq 2011; Black 2010; Hussain 2006). Often these practices are informal and unenforceable, with little interaction with the formal legal system (Armstrong 2010). We refer to such processes where family disputes are resolved using Sharia as well as other cultural nonlegal norms as "Islamic community processes." In recent years some in the Muslim community have called for the legal recognition of decisions and settlements reached in these community forums (Berkovic 2012). For instance, the submission by the Australian Federation of Islamic Councils to the Parliamentary Joint Standing Committee on Migration asks for "legal pluralism," possibly suggesting greater recognition of Islamic decision makers (Australian Federation of Islamic Councils 2011). At the same time, Australia has seen the emergence of government initiatives to enhance access to the legal system's services for people of culturally and linguistically diverse backgrounds (Family Law Council 2012; Urbis 2007; Victoria Legal Aid 2011), including the development of culturally responsive models of dispute resolution for families from migrant background communities (e.g., Armstrong 2010; Family Law Council 2012).

Despite this growing recognition of the importance of an inclusive approach to family law service delivery, calls for the recognition of Islamic community processes have been deeply controversial. In 2006, Peter Costello (then the treasurer of Australia) gave a speech in response to media reports that Australian Muslims were seeking recognition of aspects of Islamic family law. In this, he stated:

> There is not a separate stream of law derived from religious sources that competes with or supplants Australian law in governing our civil society. The source of our law is the democratically elected legislature. There are countries that apply religious or sharia law— Saudi Arabia and Iran come to mind. If a person wants to live under sharia law these are countries where they might feel at ease. But not Australia.

In 2011, the federal attorney general at the time, Robert McClelland, said, "There is no place for sharia law in Australian society and the government strongly rejects any proposal for its introduction" (Hole 2011), and "As our citizenship pledge makes clear, coming to Australia means obeying Australian laws and upholding Australia's values. . . . Indeed all applicants for citizenship swear a collective allegiance to the people of Australia and undertake to respect our customs and abide by our laws" (Karvelas 2011). The Joint Standing Committee on Migration does not think that the "legal recognition of Islamic practices is necessary or desirable" (2013; see also Karvelas 2013).

This rejection of Islamic community processes is accompanied by more extreme denunciations of "Sharia law" and those who support it. For instance, the Australian senator Jacqui Lambie, describing supporters of Sharia law in a recent speech to Parliament, said, "These maniacs and depraved humans will not stop committing their cold blooded butchery and rapes until every woman in Australia wears a burka and is subservient to men" (Jennett 2014).

Despite these public reactions to Islamic community processes, little is presently known about the experiences of Muslim women who use community processes to resolve family disputes[1] or about how the Australian family law system might go about responding to these processes in a way that supports Muslim women. As a recent literature review conducted for the Australian Human Rights Commission found, "The research required to identify and analyse the patterns and dynamics of alternative dispute resolution related to family law matters in Islamic communities in Australia does not yet exist" (Schofield King Lawyers 2011). Following this report, one of the authors of this chapter, Ghena Krayem, conducted the only relevant empirical research on Islamic community processes in Australia to date, which documents how Australian Muslims deal with family disputes (see Krayem 2014).

Using empirical research methods that included interviewing sixty-five members of the Australian Muslim community, including imams, community leaders, and community workers, as well as community members who had been through the experience of marriage, divorce, or both in the Australian context, this chapter offers an introduction to how Islamic community processes operate as revealed by this groundbreaking research. Drawing on the research, the next section describes the operation of Islamic community processes, including the role of community organizations, Muslim women's organizations, the role of imams, and concerns raised by participants about the role imams play in Islamic community processes. The second section addresses the way in which Islamic community processes interact with Australian law.

The Operation of Islamic Community Processes

The Australian Muslim community is a diverse community, so much so that some commentators write about communities rather than community. This diversity is not limited to cultural backgrounds and languages spoken, but also extends to the general makeup of the community, which ranges from newly arrived migrants such as recent refugees to more established groups that have generations of Australian-born Muslims (Krayem 2014, 58). According to the 2011 census figures, the Muslim population in Australia is 2.2 percent of the total population, or 476,000 people, with 61.5 percent of that population born overseas (Krayem 2014, 58). The most frequently cited country of birth for Australian Muslims is Australia at 38 percent. In terms of cultural background, 42 percent of the Muslim community claims Lebanese heritage, 28 percent claims Turkish ancestry, and a growing number claims African ancestry, including 5 percent Somali, with the rest of the community being drawn from all over the world (Krayem 2014, 58). This cultural diversity was reflected in the interviewees who participated in the study, as their backgrounds were Lebanese, Egyptian, Syrian, Fijian, Indian, Palestinian, South African, Bosnian, Turkish, Jordanian, Iraqi, Iranian, Bangladeshi, Pakistani, and Algerian (Krayem 2014, xii).

The imams, community leaders, and community members interviewed were of the view that significant numbers of Muslims in Australia rely on Islamic community processes to resolve their family law matters (Krayem 2014, 86). But Islamic community processes in Australia do not center around bodies that work like "Sharia councils" in the United Kingdom (Krayem 2014, 29). Instead informal, nonpermanent groupings of imams work together toward dispute settlement in particular cases, even though they may sometimes call themselves Sharia councils or imam boards (Krayem 2014, 85).

Family members often play an important role in Islamic community processes, at least initially. Several interviewees discussed the role that family members, particularly older family members, played in resolving conflicts (Krayem 2014, 94–95). One interviewee said:

> When we first started having problems, I sought advice from my parents, and of course they attempted to help us to resolve our problems. Actually come to think of it, they did this many times, before we went to see an imam. (Community member, quoted in Krayem 2014, 187)

Because of the vital role played by family members, for Muslims with no extended family in Australia, dealing with marital problems can be particularly difficult (Krayem 2014, 95). For many in the community, community leaders or community organizations were the next port of call when the conflict could not be addressed satisfactorily by the family. One interviewee suggests that the community leader was a more effective counselor than the couple's family would have been:

> My husband and I sought some counselling for our problems; we would go to meet up with a respected community leader. We truly appreciated the time she spent with us and the space she created for us to talk. I don't think we would still be together if we had sought help from our families. (Community member, quoted in Krayem 2014, 187)

One imam explains the community's response to requests for help with family conflicts:

> We have two parts to the way the community deals with these issues. . . . There are those that are qualified in Islamic law that deal with issues of marriage and divorce. Then there are those that are not necessarily qualified in Islamic law, like the community organisations like the Muslim Women's Association; they deal with such issues at a community level. Of the former there are many individual Shaykhs who do this work; there is no one body. As to the latter there are numerous organisations that deal with social issues. (Religious leader, quoted in Krayem 2014, 95)

ROLE OF COMMUNITY ORGANIZATIONS

After families, community organizations play a very important role. The services they provide are evident from these remarks from a participant in such an organization:

> They come into our office and ask to speak to an imam; we try to help them first by speaking to them and if possible reconcile the relationship, get them to understand what their rights and responsibilities are. If we can't resolve it then we refer them to the imam. (Community worker, quoted in Krayem 2014, 96)

One of the key roles played by these organizations is their referral role; that is, even if they themselves cannot help the person who comes to them, they can certainly advise them where to go. This is particularly important, as these organizations usually have close links with the religious leaders.

> The community organisations play an important part of the whole process . . . [as] our staff refer the couple to the appropriate people. Most assessments are done at this level. If mediation needs to take place, then it is planned and set out for the couple with a specific religious leader agreed to by the couple and their family. When the mediation takes place the leader and our staff are there to help sort it out. When the decision to divorce is made, the religious leader

handles it from then on because it becomes an Islamic law issue—the community workers will then help if there is fallout. (Community leader, quoted in Krayem 2014, 96–97)

The process allows time for people to think about their actions, and we have a case-by-case approach; we have case plans to work with each couple. I think this reduces the demand on the formal court system. But not all cases can be dealt with in such a way. But overall the amicable mediation process takes more time, effort, counselling and support but the outcome is much better for the whole family unit. Our mediation process reduces the pain and agony, because we do case planning for the children and provide support for the children. (Community worker, quoted in Krayem 2014, 96–97)

All the organizations interviewed indicated that unless there were exceptional circumstances such as violence, they offered avenues to support reconciliation. They did this mainly by attempting to mediate between the parties, seeking the intervention and advice of religious leaders where necessary, and referring couples to services that could meet their needs. They also indicated that if the couple or at least one party chose to divorce, then the matter would be referred to an imam.

Mediation from an Islamic perspective is not dissimilar to other types of mediation processes, but there is a religious element to it—we rely on Islamic principles to remind both parties that you are under a religious obligation to resolve these issues with mercy. (Community worker, quoted in Krayem 2014, 189)

Thus it can be seen that families, respected community members, leaders, and community organizations all play an important role in helping couples to resolve their dispute. However, if matters cannot be resolved, one of the parties will seek the intervention of an imam, a religious figure who is respected by both parties.

THE ROLE OF MUSLIM WOMEN'S ORGANIZATIONS

Women's organizations such as the Muslim Women's Association (MWA) in New South Wales play a particularly important role in Islamic community processes in Australia (Krayem 2014, 97). When a woman with family difficulties walks into an organization like the MWA, she is interviewed and a case plan is made for her; depending on her individual circumstances, this can involve counseling, as well as dealing with social security issues, immigration issues, housing (particularly when women may be escaping situations of domestic violence), and separation and divorce processes. The MWA in particular manages the only Muslim women's refuge in Australia, and has been doing so for more than twenty-five years. It provides emergency accommodation and assistance to women, many of whom are fleeing because of domestic violence or marital discord. It also plays a pivotal role in supporting many Muslim women through the resolution of family law issues (Krayem 2014, 97). As one of its staff members remarked:

> We provide much-needed support for women going through the process of divorce. We would advocate on her behalf, guide her to a lawyer or to access legal assistance and give her valid religious reasons she can present, and also try to reason with the imam. . . . We talk to the imam, debate with him about the rights and wrongs of the situation. (Community worker, quoted in Krayem 2014, 97)

While some organizations, such as the MWA, are able to offer assistance directly to the community members, others refer them to other services. The importance of their work can be seen from the responses of some of their clients, who commented that they rely entirely on the women from the Support Centre and the MWA for help and advice about what to do and where to go (Krayem 2014, 97):

> I had nowhere to go. . . . I contacted the MWA and I was very afraid but when I spoke to them I felt at ease and once I saw them I was even more comfortable, and when I arrived at the centre I felt even better. (Community member, quoted in Krayem 2014, 98)

> They [social workers] asked me what I wanted to do, what my demands were, and whether there was any chance of reconciliation— they appeared to genuinely be able to help. . . . I told them I wanted to proceed with the divorce process, both under Islamic law and

under Australian law. (Community member, quoted in Krayem 2014, 98)

These statements illustrate the pivotal role that women's organizations play in the community, a role that quite often is not recognized (Krayem 2014, 98). There is a strong emphasis on encouraging women to make decisions for themselves. Some community workers from the MWA commented on the criticism that such organizations face because of their support for women's choices:

Sometimes we are accused of being home breakers . . . but we do no such thing. . . . In fact we do the exact opposite; we go to great lengths to facilitate reconciliation between a wife and her husband— sometimes we succeed and sometimes we don't. Ultimately it is up to the woman to make the decision as to whether she wants to reconcile with her husband; our role is to support her in her decision. Once she makes that decision, then we guide her through the divorce process, seeking the intervention of a religious leader and encouraging her to seek appropriate legal advice. (Community worker, quoted in Krayem 2014, 188)

Educating women about their rights—many women are now beginning to question that if Islam gives me these rights then how can I ensure that I enjoy them and what is the process that I can go through to seek those rights without having to feel guilty about it. (Community leader, quoted in Krayem 2014, 188)

ROLE OF IMAMS

As the previous interview excerpts indicate, community leaders and community organizations often refer family conflicts to imams or sheikhs when a divorce has been decided on or they are unable to resolve the conflict. Each imam sought by couples is usually associated with a particular mosque (Krayem 2014, 98). What, then, do these religious leaders do when faced with a couple with family law issues? One imam noted, "I have a procedure . . . people will come to me and I will write their story and after that I will send the letter to the other party to invite them to come and present their side of the story" (quoted in Krayem 2014, 99).

Another imam said that he helped a couple reach an agreement, then advised them to go to a solicitor to make the agreement legal (quoted in Krayem 2014, 99). Others drew on specific religious texts and Islamic principles:

> We have a whole chapter in the Qur'an to instruct us on the importance of giving people a fair hearing . . . where Allah (SWT) responds to a complaint by a woman who had been telling the Prophet how she had been treated, and the response comes from God and treats the issue in a really profound way and shows . . . the importance of listening attentively. It is a good story and what it says to me is that if God had responded to this woman who felt she had been dealt with wrongly . . . it speaks volumes to me that if someone comes to talk to you about a problem, the importance of listening to them in a non-judgemental way and listen to their grievances and pay attention—you have a duty of care to such a person. (Community leader, quoted in Krayem 2014, 99)

> Once we hear both sides of the story, then we use Islamic legal principles to help the parties come to an agreement. Of course when it comes to matters of divorce, that is determined according to Islamic Law, but then once we have determined whether or not a divorce has taken place we aim to facilitate negotiation between the parties on other matters, such as property or financial issues. (Religious leader, quoted in Krayem 2014, 99–100)

While imams play an important role in family disputes in general, they play a particularly important role in the facilitation of divorces and the settlement of property disputes. We focus in what follows on property disputes, as this is where imams play an important role in mediating between the parties. Parties to a marriage in Australia can apply to the family court for orders settling their property, and according to section 79(1) of the Family Law Act 1975 (Cth), wide discretion is granted to the court, which "may make such order as it considers appropriate and thereby alter the interests of parties in the property." In exercising its discretion, the court must take into account a list of factors set out in section 79(4) of the act. The court identifies and values the parties' property and financial resources, then assesses their contribution to the property and to the welfare of the family (ss 79(4)(a)–(c)). This assessment is a retrospective exercise, which takes into account both the financial (s 79(4)(a)) and nonfinancial (s 79(4)(b)) contributions of both parties to their property. This assessment also takes into account contributions to the welfare of the family (s 79(4)(c)), which the court often finds difficult to value and assess (Fehlberg and Behrens 2008, 510). Ultimately, the court must ensure that any orders that are made are just and equitable in all the circumstances (s 79(2)).

When it comes to property settlements under Islamic community processes, although principles of Islamic law are strictly followed in regard to the divorce process, imams indicated that they were far more flexible in negotiating agreements between the parties about matters to do with property. They indicated that this was largely because they were aware of the existence and availability of the court system (Haisam Farache, solicitor and imam, interviewed 14 April 2011). So, in a rather ad hoc way, imams are taking on the role of helping couples reach a negotiated agreement concerning their financial affairs. In fact, this is seen as a desirable approach because of the emphasis in Islam on resolving disputes (particularly family disputes) in an amicable way and on the general principle that husbands should be generous to their wives upon divorce.

> We need to be realistic that when we advise the couples about their financial entitlements under Islamic law, they will indeed weigh this up with what they think they would get according to Australian law, and then choose how they want to proceed. (Religious leader, quoted in Krayem 2014, 205)

> The best outcome is one that works for both parties. . . . I believe there is sufficient flexibility in Islam to allow a couple to come to any agreement that they want, and I also think that this works under Australian law as well. (Religious leader, quoted in Krayem 2014, 205)

The imams are guided by the principles of property settlement according to Islamic law, with all advising the couple that when the husband has initiated the divorce, the wife is entitled, first, to any outstanding *mahr*, or dowry amount. They go to great lengths to encourage the husband to pay this amount, knowing that this is unenforceable in Australia:

> A majority of people abide by the requirement of paying the *mahr* at the time of divorce . . . even though it is not enforceable . . . but we tell them what is *halal* [permissible] and what is *harām* [forbidden], and then it is up to them. (Religious leader, quoted in Krayem 2014, 206)

> The *mahr* is very important, especially when there is not much property, so the woman knows there is no point in going to court because there is nothing to give her, but Islamically this is still a debt that a husband owes his wife and should be paid. (Religious leader, quoted in Krayem 2014, 206)

CONCERNS ABOUT IMAMS' ROLE AND PROCESSES

Several of the interviewees questioned whether the imams currently had all the skills required to resolve family law disputes and if the mosque committees were reviewing the qualifications of the imams they appoint carefully enough. While many acknowledged the imams' extensive religious knowledge, they also said that this was not enough and that there was a need for dispute resolution skills as well. Many went further to say that there was a need for additional training for imams who dealt with these issues in particular, stating that the imams should undertake specific training prior to becoming marriage celebrants, as well as training in family law procedures and on how family law operates in Australia. They also said imams need specific training in divorce issues so that they understand the rules and regulations of family law processes and can educate the community about these matters. Some questioned whether imams should devote so much time to resolving family law issues, as they felt that imams were overworked in this area. There was a suggestion that perhaps imams should be part of the process of resolving family law issues but that qualified professionals should undertake the actual dispute resolution role. Many of those interviewed expressed a desire to see change in this area from within the community, particularly in having the imams work more closely together and in a more consistent way. A common response was the expressed need for the imams to be more professional, including the need for the legitimacy, qualifications, and length of service of imams to be examined (Krayem 2014, 101). These observations raise concerns about the way some of the current community dispute resolution processes are conducted. As can be seen, there is no uniformity among the practices of the imams, and clearly some adhere to procedural rules more closely than others. It is often this ad hoc nature that frustrates women participants most.

The gender issue in the divorce and dispute resolution processes is one that many interviewees highlighted and appears to generate the most concern and perceived need for improvement. Many commentators argue that these processes are not in the best interests of women, who are framed as being vulnerable to community pressure that forces them to be part of these processes. There is no doubt that there are aspects of these community processes that need to be addressed in order to benefit women, particularly in ensuring that there is due process. Some women appeared to be frustrated by the feeling that they were not heard in these male-dominated processes:

> In the negotiations, one of the men I took along, my brother-in-law, was in a different religious group to the men on the panel, as if I understand or care, but I was in the middle and needed my affairs sorted out, and the men were fighting about the different sects—can you believe that—why were they there? I didn't even understand or care about what they were fighting about. It was very heated—men's egos! (Community member, quoted in Krayem 2014, 102)

Yet it appears that in most cases it is the men who are called before an imam, as it is the women who are more likely to go to the imam first. As one imam said, "Each day I have more than ten calls from women asking about their rights [and] I push and support them all the way" (quoted in Krayem 2014, 103). And another said, "We find that it is the women who come to us first and then we proceed to contact the husband to get him to come to a meeting" (quoted in Krayem 2014, 103). It is clear that the impact of these community processes on women is a crucial consideration in any evaluation of their effectiveness.

To return to the question of property settlement post-divorce, some imams could be criticized for their approach to what a wife is entitled to after the divorce. While the imams interviewed all made an effort to secure a women her *mahr* or dowry, for many imams in Australia, the concept of *mutat-a-talāq*, or post-divorce financial entitlement for women is not one that they rely on when advising couples. Some imams, when questioned about the financial entitlements of a wife upon divorce, quickly replied that it is the *mahr* and no more. For example:

> The wife is entitled to her *mahr*. If there are children then she is entitled to the child support. If there are no children then she is not entitled to any more than the *mahr*. . . . Extra money that is provided is for the children and is not hers. (Religious leader, quoted in Krayem 2014, 206)

> The matter is rather simple; if the husband divorces the wife then she is entitled to her *mahr*. There is nothing else, as ordinarily if the woman is no longer married, the responsibility of her maintenance goes back to her father, her brother, etc. (Religious leader, quoted in Krayem 2014, 206

These statements reflect the criticism made earlier that there has been a lack of attention given to the way Muslims live their lives and the applicability of Islamic law to the current context that Muslims find themselves in. The reality is that Muslim women are financial contributors to the household, and some imams are not considering the applicability of Islamic legal principles to meet the changing needs of couples who come before them.

> Many of our imams are traditionally minded and not really mindful of many of the circumstances concerning women in our community . . . particularly when it comes to financial settlement and taking into account the wife's contribution. (Community leader, quoted in Krayem 2014, 207)

When these imams were asked what they would do if a woman had been working and financially contributing to the home, the response by some was similar to the following:

> If she voluntarily spent her money then she forgoes it, but if she was forced to spend the money and the husband has a lot of wealth then

the judge could intervene to award her a sum of money, but within reason, because the general principle is that no one can take from the wealth of others. (Religious leader, quoted in Krayem 2014, 207)

According to this approach, a wife needed to make it very clear that any amount she spent was a loan to her husband and she expected it to be paid back. However, as many women community leaders and social workers that supported women through the divorce process were quick to point out, such a view was flawed because "What woman is going to make a grand statement that the money I pay towards the mortgage or the car or the school fees is a loan? I mean, that would probably cause relationship problems" (community leader, quoted in Krayem 2014, 207).

Other imams took a very different approach. They considered the circumstances of each case and were very conscious of the fact that women needed to be duly compensated upon divorce:

If she is working and putting money into the house she has a right to be compensated because a man should support his wife financially. . . . I will not shy away from a man in such circumstances. (Religious leader, quoted in Krayem 2014, 207)

It all depends on the individual circumstances. If the wife was working and she contributed to the household expenses, then she owns with her husband and it is her right to take joint ownership of any assets. (Religious leader, quoted in Krayem 2014, 207–208)

It is wrong and unjust to claim that a wife is not to be compensated for her financial contributions. (Religious leader, quoted in Krayem 2014, 208)

While the preceding comments by the interviewees demonstrate that there can be a significant difference in how imams approach the issue of the financial entitlement of women, several prominent women community leaders expressed the view that there was greater awareness of this issue, and more and more respected and experienced imams are becoming aware of its importance:

I feel that we have come a long way in the twenty years that I have been working in the community. . . . I don't think that we are all the way there, but I think that most of the imams that deal with the majority of divorce cases are aware of the need to do justice to women. (Community leader, quoted in Krayem 2014, 208)

With the women that come to seek our assistance we try and get the involvement of an imam that understands the needs of women, and we have a relationship of trust with these imams, and we tell them that sometimes they need to reconsider their decision when it is unfair. (Community worker, quoted in Krayem 2014, 208)

The reality is that a woman has a choice. If the community processes do not safeguard her financial interests then she has the option of going to see a lawyer, and more and more imams are realising this. (Community worker, quoted in Krayem 2014, 208–209)

The imams are realising that applying Islamic law in Australia is not like applying it in Lebanon or Egypt or Pakistan; here we do not have a society where women are maintained by men. I mean, after divorce a woman will need to set up home again; she generally does not just fall back onto the responsibility of her father or brother—that is just not how we live as Muslims in Australia. (Community member, quoted in Krayem 2014, 209)

It should also be mentioned that some imams interviewed recognized the need to compensate the wife for her nonfinancial contributions to the marriage as well:

If the husband divorces her she is entitled to her *mahr*, and we look to compensating her financially for her services in the house—we may estimate it to be 20, 30, 40 per cent . . . this is *halal* for her. (Religious leader, quoted in Krayem 2014, 209)

The issue is social justice and the need in today's society for something to sustain the wife after divorce. When she has lived with him for a long time, it does not matter if she worked or not because she was looking after the house and kids—that in itself is owed a salary—because in Islam a wife is not compelled to do housework, although it depends on the financial situation of the husband. (Religious leader, quoted in Krayem 2014, 209)

More generally, all of the community leaders interviewed accepted that while there were these difficulties with the current processes, they played a very important and valuable role in how Muslims resolved their family law affairs. For example:

> The process is not perfect, and certainly there have been criticisms of how we do things, but I think that we need to be careful to acknowledge the good and be honest about the bad; there is no doubt that we need the imams to do what they are doing. (Community leader, quoted in Krayem 2014, 214)

> Let's not throw the baby out with the bath water . . . we need to remember that these processes are actually very much needed; it does not mean that we can't improve them. (Community leader, quoted in Krayem 2014, 214)

These same leaders spoke of the need to evaluate these community processes and to accept that if these processes are to be accommodated or recognized by the official legal system, they will have to change. This willingness to seek ways to improve current practice goes against the mistaken assumption that Islamic principles are incapable of adapting to the modern-day needs of Muslims. Rather, these sentiments indicate that Islamic community processes are dynamic and based on an appreciation of the time and place in which they are to be applied. This means that community leaders are willing to consider ways of improving the current processes to address some of the concerns raised by this research.

Several community leaders spoke about the need for a proper evaluation of the existing community processes and structures, and in particular the need to be reflective and self-critical. One noted that "if we identify our weaknesses then we can improve" (quoted in Krayem 2014, 102), while another commented that "the Shariah is flexible . . . you can't apply a law from the desert thousands of years ago to a city life now without contextualising it" (quoted in Krayem 2014, 102). In addition, two interviewees made the following comments:

> It is sometimes hard to criticise our own process because immediately you think that someone out there will pick it up and publicise it and before you know it we are tomorrow's headlines. . . . Really

I am not exaggerating. . . . We can only look inwards as a community when we are in a safe space, not when we are already daily dodging crisis after crisis. (Community leader, quoted in Krayem 2014, 214)

We are already as a community changing our processes. I mean in the twenty years that I have been in the community, much has changed and I have no doubt that this will continue to happen. (Community leader, quoted in Krayem 2014, 214–15)

These comments show a willingness to respond to concerns, but it seems that the public spotlight on the Muslim community is the very thing that makes it difficult to identify these concerns.

Interaction between Islamic Community Processes and Australian Law

POTENTIAL FOR ISLAMIC COMMUNITY PROCESSES TO BE RECOGNIZED AS FAMILY DISPUTE RESOLUTION

The fact that Islamic community processes might constitute a form of alternative dispute settlement recognized by the Family Law Act is one point of contact between Islamic community processes and Australian law. Recent changes in the Family Law Act, particularly with the introduction of family relationship centers (FRCS) across Australia, have reflected the preference for keeping family disputes out of the court system. This means that there is greater encouragement than ever before to facilitate some sort of agreement between the parties through various forms of family dispute resolution, commonly known as FDR. Section 60I of the Family Law Act provides that the parties must "make a genuine effort to resolve that dispute by family dispute resolution" (s 60I(1)). FDR is defined as

A process (other than a judicial process):
    (a) in which a family dispute resolution practitioner helps people affected, or likely to be affected, by separation or divorce to resolve some or all of their disputes with each other; and
    (b) in which the practitioner is independent of all of the parties involved in the process. (s 10F)

It has been suggested that the term does not specifically refer to any particular form of dispute resolution because "some of the legislative requirements are arguably inconsistent with the traditional mediation model such as the legislative requirement that advisers are to suggest particular outcomes to clients" (Fehlberg and Behrens 2008, 334, quoted in Krayem 2014, 186). However, in principle, Islamic community processes could constitute FDR under the terms of the act, obviously by complying with the requirements of the act and being conducted by a registered family dispute resolution practitioner.

LEGAL ENFORCEMENT OF OUTCOMES OF ISLAMIC COMMUNITY PROCESSES

As indicated previously, when agreement is reached in property settlements, the couple is encouraged to seek legal advice to formalize the agreement and ensure its enforceability. In a small number of cases, the couple will actually do this: if they have already instituted proceedings, they will draft consent orders to be filed with the court to resolve their dispute, although they are still subject to scrutiny by the courts, which must be satisfied that the orders they make are "just and equitable" (Family Law Act s 79(2)). The court usually makes a decision quickly, without any consideration of the factors in sections 79(4) and 79(2) referred to earlier (Fehlberg and Behrens 2008, 559). If proceedings have not commenced, the couple can turn their agreement into a "binding financial agreement," as part VIIIA of the Family Law Act allows couples to enter into a financial agreement before marriage (s 90B), during marriage (s 90C), or after divorce (s 90D). A binding financial agreement may cover property and financial matters, spousal maintenance, and other "incidental and ancillary" matters, a phrase that Fehlberg and Behrens argue is currently untested (2008, 560). Again, this is part of a wider trend in Australian family law toward private agreements and the resolution of disputes away from the court. There are formal requirements that must be satisfied: the agreement must be signed by both parties and must contain a statement that, prior to signing it, each party received independent legal advice on the effect of the agreement on his or her rights and on the advantages and disadvantages to him or her at that time of entering into the agreement (s 90DA(1); Dickey 2007, 655). The emphasis is on financial matters, although such agreements may also cover other matters (ss 90B(3), 90C(3), 90D(3)). Essentially, the agreement is a contract and subject to the laws concerning contracts (Dickey 2007, 658). Most important, if an agreement is binding, the court is prevented from dealing with matters covered by that agreement, except in certain circumstances.

Binding financial agreements are relevant not only at times of divorce, but also at times of marriage. Commonly referred to as "prenuptial agreements," these can be used to formalize the Islamic marriage contract, which all couples currently sign when entering into a marriage. Anecdotal evidence suggests that most Muslims are unaware that they are signing such a document at the time of the Islamic marriage ceremony (Haisam Farache, solicitor and imam, interviewed 14 April 2011), and encouraging a greater understanding and promoting the use of marriage contracts in the form of binding financial agreements or otherwise can assist Muslim women to safeguard many rights and entitlements that they have under Islamic law that are currently unenforceable under the official legal system. Furthermore, as already mentioned, specifying clearly a right to divorce can help women deal with the difficulties that they face in securing a religious divorce in the absence of a religious court authority. In fact, the use of a marriage contract can be an important and legally sanctioned way for Muslim women to exercise agency and protect their interests while simultaneously meeting the requirements of both Islamic and Australian law.

FORUM SHOPPING BETWEEN AUSTRALIAN LAW AND ISLAMIC COMMUNITY PROCESSES

As some of the interviewee comments have so far indicated, many of the women interviewed for this research were aware of their options under Australian family law. Particularly in cases where a substantial amount of property has to be divided, some women, after finalizing their religious divorce, sought a property settlement in the family courts. Some imams saw this as wrong, while other imams and community leaders accepted it as an option for women when they were dissatisfied with the community processes:

> In general people like to follow Shariah, but when they feel they don't get what they want they go to the Australian legal system. (Community leader, quoted in Krayem 2014, 210)

There is a lot of shopping around that happens—people are conve-
niently choosing when and where to go to get what they perceive
as the best deal for them. (Community leader, quoted in Krayem
2014, 210)

Some imams encourage a woman to seek the advice of a lawyer when they
know that the husband is treating her unfairly:

If it means getting what she is owed then I encourage her to go to
court, because it doesn't matter what I say. I cannot enforce anything, but a court can do that for her. (Religious leader, quoted in
Krayem 2014, 210–11)

This raises an important issue concerning the intersection of these informal community processes and the formal legal system; that is, when
one or both parties are dissatisfied with the informal process or when they
simply fail to reach an agreement, they have the option of turning to the
formal legal system for resolution of their dispute. Indeed, as already mentioned, several interviewees indicated that they had chosen to seek the
advice of a lawyer and initiate proceedings in the family courts when the
community processes failed to resolve their dispute. The choice of forum
reflects an often ignored aspect of these processes, namely the agency
that women may exercise as they navigate their way through the legal
and community processes. It is often assumed that the danger of informal community processes is that women are coerced into participating
in these forums. Yet in reality the research demonstrates that "women
were far more likely than men to initiate the informal community processes" (Krayem 2014, 236). This is not to dismiss that there are many
ways in which these processes can be improved to better meet the needs
of Muslim women, particularly in a procedural sense, but it recognizes
the value that many Muslim women place on their faith and the importance of this in family law matters.

Finally, many imams who recognize that they are resolving a couple's
affairs in the shadow of Australian law will encourage the couple to
negotiate to reach a settlement or compromise that they both can live with.
For many this is seen to have Islamic validity, as Islamic law recognizes
the right of the husband and wife to reach an amicable agreement. As
discussed previously, this commitment to reach an amicable settlement

coincides with one of the key objectives of family dispute resolution under the Family Law Act 1975—that is, to resolve family disputes outside of the court system.

Imams also have insight into the difficulties Muslims face in Australia:

> You have families at the moment sitting between two laws. You have an Islamic community that is driven by their specific religious philosophy that is reflected in their everyday behaviour and conduct, and then if a family breaks down, the problem then lies in which laws we are required to abide by. You still have to go through the normal procedures of filing for divorce and then discussing and resolving the maintenance issues and custody and property—which are in some cases quite different to Islamic family law. How to deal with this is a real challenge facing the Muslim community. (Community leader, quoted in Krayem 2014, 86)

Despite these difficulties there is an acceptance of the dual system of law operating in Australia. For example:

> At the end of the day you have to be divorced by both legal systems, under both sets of laws—it is important that you are married and divorced under Australian family law—the recognition is important. (Community leader, quoted in Krayem 2014, 86)

This chapter, based on empirical research, provides an account of how Islamic community processes in Australia often take the form of informal, nonpermanent groupings of imams working together. It highlights the role of family members, community organizations, and Muslim women's organizations in Islamic community processes. Its observations raise some concerns about the way some of the current community dispute resolution processes are conducted. It considers the potential for Islamic community processes to be recognized as family dispute resolution and the potential for legal enforcement of the outcomes of Islamic community processes.

But there is a need for much more empirical work on the question. From 2015 to 2018 a team of researchers from the Universities of

Melbourne and Sydney will carry out research funded by the Australian Research Council to provide a reliable evidence base for evaluating how Australia's family law system might best respond to Islamic dispute resolution processes with a particular focus on the position of Muslim women and propose the best response of a legal system such as Australia's to Islamic community processes based on rigorous empirical and normative research. Using insights from interviews with imams, community leaders, community workers, and service providers, Muslim men and women with experience in community processes, youth leaders, Muslim family law professionals, including psychologists and social workers, as well as representatives from key Muslim women's organizations, the research team will consider how Islamic community processes affect the religious freedom of women, affect the cultural inclusivity of women, benefit or harm women as a result of the decisions made (are they materially better or worse off than if they had used the general Australian family law system?), benefit or harm women in the decision-making process (was the process open, fair, and respectful of the autonomy of these women?), and affect the openness of the Islamic community process (e.g., did they encourage transparency as opposed to drive women underground). It is hoped that this research will represent a step in a much-needed conversation about Islamic community processes in Australia.

Note

1. There has been some work on this in other jurisdictions, e.g., that of Samia Bano (2012).

Bibliography

Armstrong, Susan (2010). "Enhancing Access to Family Dispute Resolution for Families from Culturally and Linguistically Diverse Backgrounds." (Briefing Paper no. 18, Australian Family Relationships Clearinghouse. https://www3 .aifs.gov.au/cfca/publications/enhancing-access-family-dispute-resolution -families-f/terminology, accessed 14 December 2014.

Australian Federation of Islamic Councils (2011). "Multiculturalism and the Muslim Community." Submission no. 431, Joint Standing Committee on Migration, Parliament of Australia, 4 April.

Bano, Samia (2012). *Muslim Women and Shariah Councils: Transcending the Boundaries of Community and Law*. London: Palgrave Macmillan.

Berkovic, Nicola (2012), "Hyder Gulam Calls for Australia to Embrace Legal Pluralism." *Australian*, 28 September. http://www.theaustralian.com.au/busi ness/legal-affairs/hyder-gulam-calls-for-australia-to-embrace-legal-pluralism /story-e6frg97x-1226482919791?nk=60bbcb784dc97ddf9aa2f98871a9bfd3, accessed 14 December 2014.

Black, Ann (2010). "Window into Shariah Family Law." *Family Relationships Quarterly* 15: 3–6. https://www3.aifs.gov.au/cfca/sites/default/files/publication -documents/n15.pdf, accessed 14 December 2014.

Black, Ann, and Kerrie Sadiq (2011). "Good and Bad Sharia: Australia's Mixed Response to Islamic Law." *University of New South Wales Law Journal* 34: 383–412.

Costello, Peter (2006). "Worth Promoting, Worth Defending: Australian Citizenship, What It Means and How to Nurture It." Address to the Sydney Institute, Sydney, Australia, 23 February.

Dickey, Anthony (2007). *Family Law*, 5th ed. Sydney: Law Book Co.

Family Law Council (2012). *Improving the Family Law System for Clients from Culturally and Linguistically Diverse Backgrounds*. Report to the Attorney General.

Fehlberg, Belinda, and Juliet Behrens (2008). *Australian Family Law: The Contemporary Context*. Melbourne: Oxford University Press.

Hole, Jacquelyn (2011). "Muslim Group Wants Sharia Law in Australia." *PM Report* (ABC Radio), 17 May. http://www.abc.net.au/news/2011–05–17/muslim -group-wants-sharia-law-in-australia/2717096, accessed 14 December 2014.

Hussain, Jamila (2006). "The Sharia—Ignore It? Reform It? Or Learn to Live with It?" *UTS Law Review* 8: 87–102.

Jennett, Greg (2014). "Jacqui Lambie Says Sharia Supporters are 'Maniacs' Who Will Rape and Murder 'Until Every Woman in Australia Wears a Burka,'" *ABC News*, 30 October. http://www.abc.net.au/news/2014–09–22/jacqui-lambie -renews-attack-on-sharia-law/5761342, accessed 13 December 2014.

Joint Standing Committee on Migration, Parliament of Australia (2013). *Inquiry into Migration and Multiculturalism in Australia*.

Karvelas, Patricia (2011). "Attorney-General Robert McClelland Says There Is 'No Place' for Sharia Law in Australia." *Australian*, 17 May. http://www.the australian.com.au/national-affairs/muslims-use-multiculturalism-to-push-for -sharia/story-fn59niix-1226057476571?nk=ba3e2076ceffad2237d6734b93bd1fd 3, accessed 12 December 2014.

Karvelas Patricia (2013). "No Room for Sharia Law in Multicultural Society." *Australian*, 3 March. http://www.theaustralian.com.au/national-affairs/immi gration/no-room-for-sharia-law-in-multicultural-society/story-fn9hm1gu-1226 589091260, accessed 14 December 2014.

Krayem, Ghena (2014). *Islamic Family Law in Australia: To Recognise or Not to Recognise*. Carlton: Melbourne University Publishing.

Schofield King Lawyers (2011). *Intersection between the Law, Religion and Human Rights: Literature Review.* https://www.humanrights.gov.au/publications /intersections-between-law-religion-and-human-rights-project-literature-review -prepared, accessed 14 December 2014.

Urbis (2007). *Evaluation of the Family Relationships Services for Humanitarian Entrants Initiative.* Department for Families, Housing, Community Services and Indigenous Affairs.

Victoria Legal Aid (2011). *Family Harmony Sessions for the Newly Arrived Communities.*

11

Faith-Based Family Dispute Resolution in Finnish Mosques

UNFOLDING ROLES AND EVOLVING PRACTICES

Mulki Al-Sharmani, Sanna Mustasaari,
and Abdirashid A. Ismail

THIS CHAPTER EXAMINES MUSLIM faith-based family dispute resolution in Finland. We investigate dispute resolution in mosques, the
norms and goals guiding this work, the ways in which faith-based dispute
resolution processes as well as their benefits and limits are gendered, the
obstacles to this work, and how faith-based dispute resolution functions
in the larger context of the Finnish legal system and institutions. The
analysis draws primarily on interview data collected from five mosques
located in Helsinki and a review of the Finnish legal system and mechanisms of family dispute resolution. We also draw on interview data from
Muslim immigrants of Somali background. Our research suggests that
the mosques we studied favor an integrated system of dispute resolution
that would flexibly combine both mosques and state legal institutions
and in which the mosques' work would be incorporated into the broader
state framework by providing mosques with resources, training, some
forms of legal authority, and mechanisms for coordination with other
relevant institutions. This finding, however, must be further investigated
and corroborated by additional research.

Recent research on secular and religious dispute resolution in family
matters has increased our understanding of the access to justice of

individuals and families with different backgrounds (Bano 2012, 2013; Broyde et al. 2014; Jänterä-Jareborg 2014; Taj 2013a; Wolfe 2006). While this research and its ensuing debates all around Europe as well as in Nordic countries have been extensive, these issues remain understudied in Finland. This chapter addresses this gap by examining the dispute resolution work in five mosques located in the capital city of Helsinki. We situate our analysis, particularly, in the context of recent research and debates in the other three Nordic countries, Sweden, Denmark and Norway, as these countries share much with Finland in terms of societal and political developments. The Nordic countries share, for instance, a similar welfare model that is often referred to as the "Nordic Model" as well as a long history of close cooperation in the field of family law.

Finnish migratory history has characteristics that distinguish it from the migratory history of other Nordic countries. Finland became a receiving country of immigrants rather late, from the late 1980s onward. In 2013, the number of immigrants (first-generation immigrants and their Finland-born children) in Finland was a little more than 300,000, thus constituting approximately 5.5 percent of the population of the country (Official Statistics of Finland 2013a). Most of the immigrants come from Russia and Estonia and from other EU countries (Official Statistics of Finland 2013a). Since the 1990s the number of Muslim immigrants has increased considerably, with the majority arriving in the country as refugees (Shayan 2013). By 2011, the total number of Muslims in the country was estimated at 60,000–65,000, equaling about 1 percent of the country's total population of 5.4 million (Pauha and Martikainen 2014) and about 20 percent of the immigrant population. The number is small compared with that for the other Nordic countries, where the number of Muslims and their percentage of the total population are estimated as follows: Sweden: 350,000–400,000 (4 percent) (Larsson 2014); Norway: 220,000 (4.5 percent) (Leirvik 2014); Denmark: 220,000 (4 percent) (Jacobsen 2014). The Finnish Muslim population consists of ethnically diverse communities. The Somalis, a predominantly refugee diaspora, constitute the largest Muslim immigrant group, with a total population of 15,789 (Official Statistics of Finland 2013a), their arrival in the country dating to the early 1990s when the Somali civil war broke out.

Studies show that Muslim immigrant populations in Finland suffer from a high unemployment rate, fewer opportunities for university and higher-level education, and racism (Shayan 2013; OSF 2013; EU-MIDIS

2009; Kilpi 2010; Peltola 2014). In this challenging context, mosques in Finland, as elsewhere in Europe, play central roles in the lives of Muslim immigrants by meeting their religious and social needs (Borell and Gerdner 2011; Ketola et al. 2014). While in the early 1990s, only a few mosques had been established in Finland, most of them became divided along ethnic lines; by the 2010s the number of mosques reached fifty and included multiethnic ones (Ketola et al. 2014). In addition to conducting religious marriages and divorces, mosques provide religious education to Muslim immigrant families and their children, mediation and arbitration services in family disputes, and religious services such as communal prayers and burial rites. In addition, mosques serve as community spaces for the socialization of immigrants and their families.

Like other Nordic countries, the Finnish state grants registered religious communities licenses to marry, while the jurisdiction to issue divorce is held strictly in the hands of the state. According to the Finnish Act on the Performing of Marriage Ceremonies (2008/571), religious communities, such as churches or mosques that are registered according to the Freedom of Religion Act (2003/453), may upon request obtain a license from the local register office (*maistraatti*) to perform religious marriages. A religious marriage performed by a licensed servant of a religious community is thus immediately legally valid without further acts of registration. The religious community or person performing a marriage ceremony is obliged to inform the local register office of the marriage, as this information has to be included in the population register.

In this chapter, we shed light on the organization of family dispute resolution work in five mosques; the norms and goals that guide their work; the ways in which the benefits and limits of faith-based dispute resolution are gendered; and the obstacles that mosques encounter. We examine, further, how faith-based dispute resolution works in relation to the Finnish legal system and institutions. In particular, we analyze how the obstacles to faith-based dispute resolution—as identified by the mosques—relate to the Finnish legal system and the kinds of relationship and coordination that are lacking or hindered between the two systems. We reflect on the possibilities and the challenges of addressing these obstacles.

We note that conflict theories in general distinguish between conflicts and disputes, the latter referring to the juridical element or dimension in a conflict (Roberts 2008). A family conflict may thus be discerned to include a variable number of disputes as well as other issues, such as communicational problems between family members or even forms of severe oppression. Accordingly, the management of family conflicts would include a variety of procedures. We, however, use the term *dispute resolution* in a general manner, as the people we interviewed for our study were using it, to refer to various dimensions in the mosques' work with family conflicts such as providing counseling for spouses having marital problems and mediating to settle financial claims. By *arbitration*, we mean the divorce process whereby a mosque plays a central role in issuing the religious divorce.

In the first section of the chapter, we describe the field research and the data informing our central arguments. In the second section, we situate our analysis in the context of the literature on faith-based dispute resolution among Muslim immigrants in Europe and North America. In the third section, we describe the organization of dispute resolution and the actors undertaking this work in the five mosques. In the fourth section, we analyze the philosophy and norms guiding processes of dispute resolution and their gendered dimensions and implications, particularly for women. In the fifth section, we examine faith-based dispute resolution work and its challenges in relation to the Finnish legal and welfare systems. We shed light on the Finnish legal and institutional landscape as it pertains to family disputes, and in particular to the needs of Muslim families. We reflect on the possibilities, challenges, and implications of coordination (and perhaps integration) of the state and faith-based systems.

Research and Methodology

This chapter draws on an ongoing study (2013–17) titled "Transnational Somali Families in Finland: Discourses and Lived Realities of Marriage."[1] Our analysis is based primarily on the interview data collected from five mosques undertaking family dispute resolution. Our arguments are also informed by other field data (i.e., individual interviews with immigrants and participant observation of mosque activities) collected in the aforementioned study. All field research was conducted by the first and third authors.[2] Our analysis is also based on a review conducted by the second author of the Finnish legal and welfare system and mechanisms of family dispute resolution as well as comparisons with other Nordic countries.

We chose the five mosques because they serve diverse Muslim populations. Two of the mosques are frequented by Somali immigrants. The third is frequented by immigrants from a South Asian country, whereas the remaining two mosques are multiethnic and serve different Muslim communities, including Finnish converts. The mosques are located in different neighborhoods. Four of them were established in the early 1990s, while the fifth was established five years ago. Structured dispute resolution work in the mosques began five to ten years ago. In two of the mosques, we interviewed the imams, who were exclusively handling the family dispute cases. In the third mosque, we interviewed one member of the dispute resolution committee. In the remaining two, the interviews were conducted with two committee members in each mosque.[3]

Revisiting Binaries: Faith-Based Dispute Resolution and Minority Rights in Nordic Contexts

The literature on Muslim faith-based dispute resolution in Western contexts is extensive, with the key questions centering on the compatibility of faith-based dispute resolution with secular legal systems; the tensions between individual (and specifically gender) rights, on the one hand, and community rights, on the other; the underlying premises and procedures of faith-based dispute resolution work and their implications for the power differentials between the actors taking part in the processes; the ways in which disputants strategically and variedly make use of faith-based dispute resolution; and how the benefits and challenges of faith-dispute resolution are differentiated among disputants depending on intersecting factors (Bano 2012, 2013; Shachar 2009, 2010; Wolfe 2006; Blackstone 2005; Boyd 2004, Broyde et al. 2014; Shah Kazemi 2001).

This chapter addresses two issues in this literature. First, our analysis builds on studies (Bano 2013; Shachar 2009; Malik 2009) that question mutually exclusive binaries of religious versus state law, community rights versus individual rights, and religion versus gender equality. Our analysis will demonstrate that such binaries often prevent us from capturing the dynamic and nuanced ways in which mosques view and conduct their dispute resolution work in relation to the state legal system; it will also show that the goals and the practices of their dispute resolution work are mixed and in flux, with complex implications for the relation between the state and faith-based legal systems, on the one hand, and for gender equality, on the other.

Second, faith-based dispute resolution among Muslim communities has been discussed within the larger question of the rights of immigrants and religious minorities in the West (Mehdi 2013; Grillo et al. 2009; Shachar 2009, 2010; Shah with Foblets and Rohe 2014), and our chapter contributes specifically to the Nordic debates in this area. Several research institutes in Denmark, Norway, and Sweden have produced research reports on Muslim family practices. This research focused primarily on the human rights of Muslim women and children (Ferrari de Carli 2008, 2013; Bredal and Wærstad 2014; Taj 2013a; Jänterä-Jareborg 2014; Mehdi 2013), and the public demand for this research has often emerged in relation to the rise of anti-immigration speech and policies, such as in Denmark in 2011 (Liversage and Jensen 2011). Keskinen (2011) points to the linking of gendered violence to ethnicity and race in Nordic discussions surrounding issues such as honor-related violence, female genital cutting, and forced marriages. In Finland, these debates relating to multiculturalism emerged rather late and here, too, they were linked to the rise of anti-immigration and neo-nationalist political movements (Keskinen 2011). The question of Islamic family law or mediation has not been widely debated in the Finnish context, and the few exceptions are somewhat anecdotal, focusing on the possibility of having Sharia councils in Finland (Muhammed 2011, 2012; Husa 2012). This discussion, however, has not been extensive or based on empirical research.

The aforementioned Nordic research projects have produced nuanced information about the interrelationships between religious communities, civil society, and the state. The organization of the relations between majority religion and the state has proved significant also in the minority context, as it tends to inform the struggles for recognition (Jänterä-Jareborg 2014; Taj 2013b). For these Nordic analyses, gender has been an important focus of research. For example, focusing on the Norwegian Pakistani community, Taj (2013b) notes that the religious interpretations of mosques have on a general level promoted women's human rights, but that in individual cases women and NGOs may prefer engaging with the mosque only selectively. While recognizing that mosques are an influential public voice of the Muslim community, she questions whether the mosques are, in fact, representative of all Muslims. Furthermore, Liversage (2012) notes that the needs of different groups might turn out to be quite different; the Turks in Denmark, for example, mostly considered a secular divorce signed by both spouses to fulfill the *talaq* divorce as well,[4] whereas for some other groups, and specifically their female members, the need to obtain a religious divorce issued by the mosque was much more urgent. This diversity highlights the need for empirically informed research before policies are formulated. Although the basic elements of the family justice systems in Sweden, Denmark, and Norway are similar, the fact that the Muslim population in Finland is new, small, and ethnically diverse signals that the policies adopted in the three other countries cannot be simply transferred to Finland. These observations underscore the need for research on these issues in Finland—hence the contribution of this chapter.

Faith-Based Family Dispute Resolution in Five Finnish Mosques

The organization and volume of the dispute work in the five mosques varied. For example, in one of the smaller mosques frequented by multiethnic Muslims and Finnish converts, the imam undertook all the work. In another small mosque, frequented by Muslim immigrants whose background was South Asian, this work was undertaken by the imam of the same ethnic background, with help from his wife, who had strong ties to the families in the community. In the third mosque, the dispute resolution work was carried out by a committee of three members (two of Somali background and one Lebanese). A male Finnish Muslim, although not a regular member of the committee, assisted the committee with cases involving Finnish converts. In the fourth mosque, frequented mostly by Somalis but also serving Muslim immigrants from North Africa and the Middle East, a committee of five male members carried out the dispute resolution work. Two members were Somali and the other three were of different ethnic backgrounds. In the fifth mosque, which was the largest and served mostly Somali Muslims, a committee of five male members (predominantly Somalis) handled the dispute resolution work. The imam was also an adviser to and the head of the committee.

Some of these interviewees held degrees in Islamic sciences from universities in Saudi Arabia and Malaysia. Others held university degrees from Finnish universities in natural sciences and physical education and acquired their religious education by studying with former imams or family members who were well versed in the religious sciences.

The majority of the disputants were women, and they were often closely connected to the mosque through personal acquaintances. Only one mosque advertised its services through its website and a twenty-four-hour phone helpline.

The issues brought to mosque dispute resolution committees varied, including disputes arising from husbands' negligence to spend enough time with the family and help the wife with childcare and housework; conflicts over sending remittances to extended families of spouses; disputes arising from disagreement among spouses on norms regarding gender relations and roles; husbands' failure to pay *mahr* (dower) to the wife; spousal violence; female disputants seeking Islamic divorce from unwilling or absent husbands; and parents having problems with the socialization of their (teenage) children.

Some types of cases were more prevalent among disputants of a particular profile than others. For example, polygamy disputes were more common among Somali disputants, whereas disputes about gender norms were more common in ethnically mixed marriages. The few cases that were initiated by husbands involved seeking a religious legal opinion (i.e., *fatwa*) on the husbands' hasty pronouncements of divorce. Some husbands also sought advice on the challenges related to raising their children in a non-Muslim secular country.

According to the interviewees, disputants usually had three broad aims for seeking the mosque's services. Some sought a *fatwa* on a particular issue pertaining to a family dispute, while others wanted the mosque to mediate in a family conflict, often with the aim of maintaining the marital relations. And other disputants specifically sought the arbitration of the mosque in order to bring an end to a particular conflict (and often to the marriage) and secure some claims. The latter kinds of cases mostly concerned women seeking Islamic divorce from their unwilling or absent husbands. In some cases, the boundaries between the second and third aims became blurred, as sometimes a case of mediation with the goal of reconciliation developed into one of arbitration. The opposite, however, was rare as divorce arbitration cases hardly ever ended in reconciliation.

The total number of cases that the mosques reported annually varied but remained less than twenty-five for all of them. The largest of the mosques also reported receiving an average of one hundred cases per year in which individuals called the helpline to ask for a *fatwa* or advice on a variety of issues, some of which concerned family disputes. The mosque imams and committee members attributed the relatively small number of cases to the general reluctance to disclose family conflicts to external parties because of a sense of shame and the fear of loss of privacy, as immigrant families of the same ethnic background tended to be congregated in the same neighborhoods and went to the same mosques. The reluctance of couples to resort to the mosque was also corroborated by the interviews with Somali immigrants.

The five mosques, more or less, followed similar steps when conducting dispute resolution sessions. They met with the spouses individually and together, sometimes on several occasions. Once a settlement was reached, it was written down and signed by the two parties. Writing the settlement was a strategy for encouraging disputants to take the agreement seriously, even though the mosques did not have adequate resources for follow-up. The other challenge regarding enforcement had to do with securing the authority of the mosque in divorce cases involving uncooperative husbands.

Guiding Philosophies and Norms

According to all five mosques, the philosophy guiding their work centered on two dimensions. One had to do with goals related to cultivating particular Islamic norms. The other was related to challenges that confronted Muslim immigrant families in the larger Finnish society. We will elaborate on each dimension as follows. First, mosque interviewees identified a number of purposes for their work, which they specifically linked to religious norms. One was to promote Islamic norms of harmonious and just family relations. In their mosque, the goal of the dispute resolution work was reconciliation, and if that was not possible, then the aim was an amicable and just settlement in order to fulfill the religious duty of promoting harmonious family relations. Another interviewee considered such resolution important for the spiritual duty of Muslims to work on themselves and strengthen their piety. Interviewees also described their work as fulfilling the religious obligation of ensuring that no transgression was committed by one disputant against another and that the Islamic rights entitled to both spouses were preserved. But could seeking harmonious family relations lead to pressuring female disputants to stay in unwanted marriages? On the basis of the divorce cases that the mosques described in their interviews as well as the ones studied through interviews with individual immigrants, we infer that although the mosques favored reconciliation in any family dispute case, in divorce cases if the wife refused the initial offer of reconciliation, the mosques focused their efforts on assisting her to secure a divorce.

The second dimension of the mosques' guiding philosophy was related to a larger process of tackling the problems of the marginalization and stigmatization of Muslim communities in the Finnish public discourse. For instance, one interviewee saw that by promoting and striving for harmonious family relations, he could spare disputants the challenges of divorce and broken families, since such families, he believed, were more likely to suffer from economic marginalization and youth-related problems often associated with immigrants. Some interviewees were motivated by the goal of contributing to the safety and stability of families, which in turn would result in a culture of peace and healthy family and community environments where Muslim youth were less likely to feel alienated and were able to take active and empowering roles in the larger society. The overall purpose for these interviewees in regard to this guiding philosophy was to enable Muslim families to be cohesive, harmonious, and thus better equipped to succeed in the larger society.

When adjudicating, mosques applied Islamic law. This application took complex forms, with mixed outcomes for women and men. For example in one of the mosques, the committee adopted the following steps when dealing with divorce cases initiated by women. First, the committee suggested reconciliation to the petitioning disputant. If she refused, the committee attempted to persuade the husband to agree to divorce. If he declined, the committee attempted to negotiate a *khul'* divorce with the husband, after first securing the wife's consent. In this kind of Islamic divorce, a wife relinquished her spousal financial rights such as the *mahr* in exchange for the divorce. If this step failed as well, the committee sought *faskh*, a divorce issued by the religious authority/judge without the husband's consent. The steps for *faskh* entailed the following. First a family relative of each disputing party was brought in, and the two relatives were asked to attest in writing to the fact that the couples could no longer live together. Then the mosque proceeded to issue the divorce. If an agreement on divorce was reached between the two parties, the mosque required the disputants to secure a civil divorce from state courts before the religious divorce was granted, to ensure that the two processes were linked. With this latter practice the mosque wanted to ensure that immigrants linked both systems in their marriage and divorce practices, thereby promoting a life of honesty and piety in which Muslim couples and families were not cheating either the religious or state legal system.

A number of things are noteworthy about the ways the mosques understood and applied Islamic norms and law. First, the use of *khul'* divorce as a negotiating card has complex implications. On the one hand, by agreeing to *khul'*, women seeking religious divorce on fault-based grounds (e.g., spousal violence, husband's failure to provide, or husband's abandonment) were put in a position to forgo their financial rights. In theory, this is unjust to female disputants and blurs the boundaries between fault-based forms of Islamic divorces in which women are entitled to financial dues, on the one hand, and negotiated divorce such as *khul'*, on the other hand, where women give up their financial rights. But one could also argue that the use of *khul'* divorce in the Finnish context would have little negative impact on female disputants because spousal maintenance was not a main concern for women seeking divorce, for they would be able to secure an independent income, either from state welfare provisions or from their own employment. This observation was corroborated both by the small number of cases concerning spousal maintenance and/or *mahr* disputes that were reported to the mosques and by the findings from the interviews with Somali individual informants. We could also add that this particular mosque's linking of the two-tiered process of securing religious and civil divorce would be beneficial for women because it would ensure that they secured both types of divorce (religious and civil). But this practice would also hinder immigrants' flexible use of both legal systems (e.g., opting to be married or divorced in one system but not the other to better suit particular life circumstances of immigrants).

In difficult divorce cases involving belligerent husbands, the authority of mosques to issue a divorce without the husband's consent was contested. Some husbands did not accept the mosques' authority and even threatened committee members, as reported by some of the interviewees. In addition, mosques needed to ensure that their religious authority would not be challenged by other religious scholars or Muslims in the communities. The mosques handled this challenge in a number of ways. They would give closer attention to these divorce cases and involve several committee members in the decision. In some cases, they would also seek the input of other religious scholars or imams from other mosques before reaching a decision. And recently, two of the mosques were applying a new practice of securing the approval of the board of religious scholars in the umbrella organization of Muslim religious associations in the country known as SINE (Suomen Islamilainen Neuvosto, Islamic Council of Finland).

In other cases, a particular understanding and implementation of Islamic law on the part of the imams worked in interesting ways for women. For instance, in one of the mosques, the imam was very keen to educate female disputants, who were Finnish converts, about their rights under Islamic law and to ensure that these disputants did not relinquish their spousal rights wittingly or unwittingly during dispute resolution processes. This imam, for example, worked toward settlements that obligated husbands to fulfill the multiple duties that they had toward their (Finnish) wives according to Islamic law. The imam explained that he saw himself as the guardian (*wali*) of these female Finnish disputants and believed that he had a legal obligation to ensure that their rights were protected. The imam saw himself as obligated to take on the role of the guardian of these disputants, since the women's non-Muslim male relatives were not available or would not be able to take on this responsibility.

In some cases, mosque mediators not only applied Islamic law but also drew on the cultural knowledge they shared with disputants. For example, in two of the mosques, Somali committee members used Somali cultural practices to reach settlements in polygamy cases involving Somalis. Mediators proposed that the husband pay a financial compensation to the grieved wife (usually the first wife). This drew on a Somali practice where husbands would give their wives financial compensation as a form of redress when they remarried. These committee members reported that normally older Somali female disputants were receptive to this solution. They explained that these disputants, who often did not work, made use of the financial compensation for their own benefits.

The interviewees did not report any polygamy disputes involving young Somali women where such settlements were reached. In general, according to the committee members, couples from the young generation of Somali immigrants were even more reluctant than older couples and families to resort to the mosque. In addition, the findings from the interviews of the first author with Somali female informants showed that young women were increasingly inserting (or planning to) a stipulation against polygamy in their marriage contracts; and some of the older female informants also reported that if they had known of their right to negotiate for stipulations in the marriage contract, they would have entered one against polygamy. The stipulation against polygamy was normally phrased as the wife's right to divorce should the husband enter into a new marriage. And although this stipulation did not legally (according to Islamic law) forbid the husband from taking a new wife, it highlighted that these young women were contesting the ethical and religious acceptability and desirability of polygamy.

These young women were making a normative distinction between Somali cultural norms that perpetuate practices such as polygamy and gender hierarchy and Quranic emphasis on values such as affection, compassion, and justice in marital relations; this was a discursive strategy that these informants were using to renegotiate Muslim norms on spousal duties and rights (Al-Sharmani 2015). A similar discursive distinction between culture and religion was also employed by one of the mosques to challenge perceived problematic practices among some Muslim families,[5] which they saw as contributing to the stigmatization of Muslim families in the public discourse. One practice was husbands' lack of involvement in childcare. Another was men's adoption of a model of hierarchical spousal relations in which husbands were emotionally distant from their spouses and did not have relationships of sharing and reciprocity with them.

Linkages and Challenges with the Finnish Legal System and Welfare Sector

The mosques reported a number of challenges in their dispute resolution work. These were related to the relationship between the mosques and the Finnish legal system and institutions involved in family conflicts. The challenges included the mosques' lack of legal authority, particularly in divorce cases, the lack of mechanisms of coordination between mosques and Finnish institutions working with Muslim families during conflicts, and the lack of state support in terms of financial resources, adequate premises, and relevant training. In this section we examine these obstacles with the aim of locating the role and work of mosques and faith-based dispute resolution within the larger context of the Finnish legal system and family welfare institutions.

The role of the Finnish judicial system in family matters is twofold: on the one hand, legal recognition and confirmation are needed for creating and dissolving family relationships; on the other, the legal system is needed for conflict management and distributive purposes. In addition, outside the legal field or loosely connected to it, there are organizations of practitioners providing welfare services to families, such as counseling and conflict resolution. In their family work, the mosques in fact seem to play several different roles that in the secular sector would be occupied by a variety of actors.

Due to the delegation of state power regarding the performance of marriage ceremonies, religious and state authorities seem to complement one another rather well, which was also noted by the interviewees.[6] Divorce and family disputes, however, seem to raise concerns. Within the state legal framework (Marriage Act 1929/234, Section 25), divorce is automatically granted upon petition if the procedural requirements are fulfilled, including a reconsideration period of six months, during which the divorce petition is kept pending. If the spouses have lived separately for two years, the divorce is issued without a reconsideration period. The interviewees experienced this lack of legal authority as undermining their work. Women in particular need the religious divorce, and the mosque interviewees felt that legal authority would help them to deal more effectively with belligerent husbands. They were, however, unclear about the nature and scope of this authority. Some wanted the state to fully recognize the divorces they issued, whereas others thought that the kind of authority needed was more indirect and mostly related to the state's acknowledgment of their role—for example, by providing mosques with training, material resources, and mechanisms for coordination with relevant state institutions.

Granting religious communities legal authority to issue a divorce or legally recognizing religious divorces would require substantive legal reform and significant organizational changes. The "freedom of divorce" expressed by all Nordic marriage codes and the starting point that the state alone may possess the jurisdiction over divorce are considered fundamental and universal principles of the Finnish divorce law. If the systems of religious and secular divorce laws are indeed accommodated, one issue that would arise is the requirement of religious institutions to respect universalist principles such as full equality in divorce and the compatibility of this requirement with dominant doctrines on divorce in Islamic jurisprudence, which are generally upheld by mosques. Norwegian law, for example, has since 2003 required as a condition of marriage that the spouses grant each other an equal right to divorce (Norwegian Marriage Act, LOV-1991-07-04-47, 7.1 §). The reform was explicitly justified as strengthening the position of Muslim women (Ferrari de Carli 2008, 28).

The question of delegating legal authority from the Finnish legal system to mosques is further complicated by the specific legal character of family contracts within the Finnish legal system. While spouses are free to settle their disputes on a voluntary basis, they cannot efficiently make a binding agreement about, for example, which rules apply to their marriage or that their disputes over a certain matter are referred to a third party, such as a religious authority. This type of arbitration is not directly outlawed but rejected de facto, as family contracts in general are subject to specific legal requirements if they are to enjoy binding force. Should these contracts involve children, this threshold is set even higher. When parents separate, the issues that most immediately require legal action have to do with deciding upon the living arrangements, custody, and financing regarding children. A municipal child supervisor helps the parents reach an agreement on these issues, and the agreement confirmed by the child supervisor is legally enforceable. Having a confirmed agreement is also urgent in many other matters, as this document is required, for example, when separated families apply for social benefits and housing. The child supervisor is thus an important mediator of disputes of all separated parents, and usually the first person to whom they turn. In 2013, child supervisors confirmed fewer than 49,000 agreements on child support and more than 46,000 agreements on living arrangements, custody, and access rights (National Institute for Health and Welfare: Statistics 2013), whereas the number of cases in district courts barely reached 3,200 (Official Statistics of Finland 2013b).

A serious challenge that the interviewees emphasized was the lack of coordination between mosques and institutions dealing with families in conflict. The interviewees feared that when a family member who is experiencing a family conflict turns to official or secular institutions, such as state, municipal, or nongovernmental agencies that provide counseling and support to families, the conflict escalates and the possibilities for either reconciliation or just and amicable settlement are diminished. They saw the stigmatization of Islam and Muslims in Finnish public discourses as one factor that diminishes trust and cooperation and aggravates quarrels between Muslim spouses when family conflicts are taken to secular institutions before or without coordination with family and mosque. This view was corroborated by the interviews with individual immigrants of both genders. Female informants who took their disputes to Finnish agencies noted that they resorted to this step only when other mechanisms of dispute resolution had failed. The mosques believed that this challenge could be adequately addressed if these institutions would coordinate with them—for example, by putting in place an integrated framework in which the mosques' work would be incorporated into the larger official mechanisms for assisting families in dispute. For example, several imams suggested that practitioners providing counseling services, such as municipalities, NGOs, women's shelters, or the police, would contact mosques and involve them in the conflicts that were reported to them. The mosques believed that such an approach would encourage positive attitudes among the immigrants toward the work of these institutions and would accordingly improve the effectiveness of alternative mechanisms of dispute resolution.

The issue of domestic violence and abuse was mentioned by the interviewees, but they did not discuss the relevant cases in detail. They did, however, criticize secular institutions for not including them in the process of helping the victims of domestic violence. As a specific and difficult form of family crisis, domestic violence must be distinguished from other forms of family conflict and disputes. To provide a proper ground for analysis, these cases and practices of handling them would have to be specifically well documented. As our data do not include such detailed descriptions of these cases, we are not able to fully engage with this discussion here. As such, however, the interviewees' wish for enhanced cooperation between them and the other practitioners is understandable and might prove fruitful in fighting domestic violence in Finnish society. Indeed, previous research indicates that religious communities can be a valuable resource in this work (Taj 2013b). At the same time we must keep in mind that the victims might opt for a more selective engagement with religious authorities in violence cases. Taj (2013b, 74), for example, reports that women in her study rejected the idea of a more institutionalized role of the mosque in domestic violence cases and instead wished to resort to Norwegian law in these matters and to decide on a case-by-case basis how and when to engage with the mosque. Perhaps cooperation between religious and secular institutions could be based on interaction and joint education on a more general level.

The issue of coordination relates to the state's acknowledgement of the mosques' role in family work, also on a very practical level. The work in the mosques is currently carried out on a voluntary basis and with insufficient resources. According to the interviewees, the education and salaries of the people carrying out dispute resolution and arbitration are not secured, the premises are inadequate, and the lack of coordination between the mosques and other institutions renders their work inefficient in some respects. Support from the state in the form of financing, help in securing an adequate workplace, workshops for orienting mosques with regard to Finnish society and laws, and training in mediation skills and psychology indeed seem to be steps toward supporting the well-being of Finnish Muslims and increasing the integration between Muslim communities and wider society. The picture painted here should not, however, be interpreted as indicating a simplistic integration model in which the roles of the mosques should be fixed. Instead, the debates within communities on issues concerning the representation in mosques and how the committee members are chosen should be taken into account. Furthermore, important discussion about how much autonomy mosques can achieve in Finnish society has yet to unfold.

Our research shows that mosques in Finland are undertaking multiple roles. In addition to providing religious guidance and spaces for religious life, they function as a faith-based system for family dispute resolution. This latter role is important in that it relates to Muslim immigrants' religious need to organize their family lives according to Islamic law. Muslim family members, as residents and citizens of Finland, are also governed by the Finnish legal system. Their family relations and disputes are thus negotiated within two legal systems. However, the recent history of Muslim immigration to Finland, Muslims' diverse ethnic backgrounds, and the still unfolding trajectory of the establishment of these communities mean that relevant actors—immigrants, mosques, and the state legal and welfare system—have to grapple with the challenge of matching their work with the coexistence of these two systems: the Islamic religious one and the secular one. Our findings suggest that numerous challenges to the relationships between the two systems are hindering the effectiveness and limiting the scope of faith-based dispute resolution. A possible way to address these challenges, according to the mosques we studied, would be to create mechanisms for structured and sustained linkages between the two systems, although attempts to establish such linkages would necessarily also face obstacles. With limited research available on faith-based dispute resolution in Finnish society, our findings remain, for the time being, only tentative. They have to be corroborated by more extensive field research that would shed further light on the mosques' work and disputants' strategies for using faith dispute resolution. Such research would require observation of dispute resolution sessions and interviews with the disputants. Further research is also required from the point of view of the state and third-sector institutions dealing with Muslim families in conflict, such as organizations providing child welfare services, shelters for victims of domestic violence, organizations providing counseling to families, and civil courts handling divorce and child-custody and maintenance cases.

Furthermore, our findings, in agreement with the conclusions of some of the existing literature, confirm that the guiding principles, processes, and outcomes of faith-based dispute resolution cannot be understood in terms of mutually exclusive binaries such as individual versus community rights, or gender equality versus inequality, or religious versus secular. The mosque interviewees espoused and applied norms in multiple and mixed ways, such as blending Islamic juristic doctrines with cultural practices of particular ethnic communities and interpreting and applying Islamic law in varied ways. The outcomes for women were complex and mixed. Moreover, the interviewees articulated certain guiding values for their work that were clearly shaped by the experiences of Muslim immigrant communities in the Finnish context as the economic, cultural, and religious "other." We hope that our ongoing research projects will shed more light on these important issues that have a profound impact on the well-being of the immigrant populations as well as the development of Finnish welfare society in general.

Notes

1. The study was designed and led by the first author. It investigates marriage norms and practices of transnational Somali immigrants in Finland; the perspectives of the informants on these norms/laws and how they use them to organize their family life; and the interplay between informants' transnational family-based ties and their marriage practices. The field research was conducted by the first and third authors. The study is part of a larger project funded by the Academy of Finland titled "Transnational Muslim Marriages in Finland: Well-being, Law, and Gender," led by Dr. Marja Tiilikainen at the Department of Social Research, University of Helsinki. The goals of the project are to study how transnational Muslim immigrants in Finland organize marriage and family life in a transnational space and how the Finnish legal system meets the needs of the immigrants in regard to intimate relationships and family life, and facilitates (or not) their well-being.

2. The first and third authors conducted individual interviews with thirty-seven female and male immigrants of Somali background and five focus group discussions with a total of thirty-nine Somali immigrants. The first author has also been conducting ongoing participant observation of a mosque in a program titled "Muslim Family." This program advocates Islamic norms for Muslim marriages and family life through a series of annual seminars, dispute resolution work, and educational and recreational services.

3. In three of the interviews, the first author led the interview and the third author asked follow-up questions. The remaining two interviews were conducted separately by the first and third authors. The same interview guide, designed by the first author, was used in all interviews.

4. This is a divorce enacted according to the rulings of Islamic jurisprudence. *Talaq* is normally conducted extrajudicially through the pronouncement of the husband, while *tatliq and fasaq* are enacted by a court or religious authority applying Islamic law after a petition is submitted by the wife on specified grounds, which vary according to schools of Islamic jurisprudence.

5. This point was repeatedly made in the mosque seminars that were observed by the first author.

6. The five mosques were licensed to perform religious marriages and had in place mechanisms to inform state notary offices of these marriages.

Bibliography

Al-Sharmani, Mulki. (2015). "Striving against the 'Nafs': Revisiting Somali Muslim Spousal Roles and Rights in Finland." *Journal of Religion in Europe* 8(1): 101–20.

Bano, Samia. (2012). *An Exploratory Study of Shariah Councils in England with Respect to Family Law*. Reading: University of Reading.

Bano, Samia (2013). "Muslim Dispute Resolution in Britain: Towards a New Framework of Family Law Governance?" In Mavis Maclean and John Eekelaar (eds.), *Managing Family Justice in Diverse Societies*, 61–86. Oxford: Hart.

Blackstone, Laureve (2005). "Courting Islam: Practical Alternatives to a Muslim Family Court in Ontario." *Brooklyn Journal of International Law* 31(1): 207–51.

Borell, Klas and Gerdner, Arne (2011). "Hidden Voluntary Social Work: Nationally Representative Survey of Muslim Congregations in Sweden." *British Journal of Social Work* 41(5): 968–79.

Boyd, Marion (2004). "Dispute Resolution in Family Law: Protecting Choice, Promoting Inclusion." 20 December. http://www.attorneygeneral.jus.gov.on.ca /english/about/pubs/boyd/fullreport.pdf, accessed 26 March 2015.

Bredal, Anja and Wærstad, Tone Linn (2014). *Gift, men ugift: Om utenomrettslige religiøse vigsler*. Report 2014:6. Oslo: Institutt for samfunnsforskning.

Broyde, Michael J., Bedzow, Ira, and Pill, Shlomo C. (2014). "The Pillars of Successful Religious Arbitration: Models for American Islamic Arbitration Based on the Beth Din of American and Muslim Arbitration Tribunal Experience." *Harvard Journal on Racial & Ethnic Justice* 30: 34–76.

EU-MIDIS (2009). *European Union Minorities and Discrimination Survey: Main Results Report*. Vienna: European Union Agency for Fundamental Rights.

Ferrari de Carli, Eli (2008). *Religion, juss och rettigheter: Om skillsmisse, polygamy og shari'a-råd*. Report 2008:5. Oslo: Institutt for samfunnsforskning.

Grillo, Ralph, Ballard, Roger, Ferrari, Alessandro, Hoekema, Andre J., Maussen, Marcel, and Shah, Prakash (2009). *Legal Practice and Cultural Diversity*. Farnham: Ashgate.

Husa, Jaakko (2012). "Muhammed ja olkiukko." *Oikeus* 41: 139.

Jacobsen, Brian Arly (2014). "Denmark." In Jørgen S. Nielsen, Samim Akgönül, Ahmet Alibašić, and Egdūnas Račius (eds.), *Yearbook of Muslims in Europe*, 6: 189–209. Leiden: Brill.

Jänterä-Jareborg, Maarit (2014). "On the Cooperation between Religious and State Institutions in Family Matters: Nordic Experiences." In Prakash Shah with Marie-Claire Foblets and Mathias Rohe (eds.), *Family, Religion and Law: Cultural Encounters*, 79–101. Farnham: Ashgate.

Keskinen, Suvi (2011). "Troublesome Differences: Dealing with Gendered Violence, Ethnicity, and 'Race' in the Finnish Welfare State." *Journal of Scandinavian Studies in Criminology and Crime Prevention* 12: 153.

Ketola, Kimmo, Martinainen, Tuomas, and Salomaki, Hanna (2014). "New Communities of Worship: Continuities and Mutations among Religious Organizations in Finland." *Social Compass* 61(2): 153–71.

Kilpi, Elina (2010). "The Education of Children of Immigrants in Finland." Unpublished doctoral diss., Oxford University. http://citeseerx.ist.psu.edu /viewdoc/download?doi=10.1.1.696.1088&rep=rep1&type=pdf.

Larsson, Göran (2014). "Sweden." In Jørgen S. Nielsen, Samim Akgönül, Ahmet Alibašić, and Egdūnas Račius (eds.), Yearbook of Muslims in Europe, 6: 570–81. Leiden: Brill.

Leirvik, Oddbjørn (2014). "Norway." In Jørgen S. Nielsen, Samim Akgönül, Ahmet Alibašić, and Egdūnas Račius (eds.), Yearbook of Muslims in Europe, 6: 459–71. Leiden: Brill.

Liversage, Anika (2012). "Muslim Divorces in Denmark: Findings from an Empirical Investigation." In Rubya Mehdi, Werner Menski, and Jørgen S. Nielsen (eds.), Interpreting Divorce Laws in Islam, 179–201. Copenhagen: DJØF Publishing.

Liversage, Anika and Jensen, Tina Gudrun (2011). Parallelle rettsopfattelser I Danmark: Et kvalitativt studie af privatretlige praksisser blandt etniski minoriteter. Report 11:37. København: SFI-Det Nationale Forskningscenter for Velfærd.

Malik, Maleiha (2009). Muslim Legal Norms and the Integration of European Muslims. EUI Working papers, Robert Schuman Centre for Advanced Studies, Florence.

Mehdi, Rubya (2013). "Law versus Religion: State Law and Religious Norms." In Jan Klabbers and Touko Piiparinen (eds.), Normative Pluralism and International Law: Exploring Global Governance, 284–300. Cambridge: Cambridge University Press.

Muhammed, Husein (2011). "Islamilaisen Sharia-lain soveltaminen Suomessa?" Oikeus 40: 376.

Muhammed, Husein (2012). "Kyse ei ole Husasta vaan asiasta." Oikeus 41: 141.

National Institute for Health and Welfare: Statistics (2013). Child Maintenance and Custody 2013. https://www.julkari.fi/bitstream/handle/10024/116177/Tr10 _14.pdf?sequence=3, accessed 7 June 2016.

Official Statistics of Finland (2013a). Population Structure. Helsinki: Statistics Finland. http://www.stat.fi/til/vaerak/2013/02/vaerak_2013_02_2014-12-10 _tie_001_en.html, accessed 7 June 2016.

Official Statistics of Finland (2013b). Decisions by District Courts in Civil Cases. Helsinki: Statistics Finland. http://www.stat.fi/til/koikrs/2013/koikrs_2013 _2014-04-02_tau_001_en.html, accessed 7 June 2016.

OSF (2013). Somalis in Helsinki. New York: Open Society Foundations.

Pauha, Teemu and Martikainen, Tuomas. "Finland." In Jørgen S. Nielsen, Samim Akgönül, Ahmet Alibašić, and Egdūnas Račius (eds.), Yearbook of Muslims in Europe, 6: 218–28. Leiden: Brill.

Peltola, Marja (2014). Kunnollisia perheitä: Maahanmuutto, sukupolvet ja yhteiskunnallinen asema. Helsinki: Nuorisotutkimusseura.

Roberts, Marian (2008). *Mediation in Family Disputes: Principles of Practices,* 3d ed. Aldershot: Ashgate.

Shachar, Ayelet (2009). "Entangled: State, Religion, and the Family." *Harvard International Law Journal,* 49: 132–45.

Shachar, Ayelet (2010). "State, Religion, and the Family Law: The New Dilemmas of Multicultural Accommodation." In Rex Ahdar and Nicholas Aroney (eds.), *Shari'a in the West,* 115–33. Oxford: Oxford University Press.

Shah, Prakash with Foblets, Marie-Claire and Rohe, Mathias, eds. (2014). *Family, Religion and Law: Cultural Encounters in Europe.* Farnham: Ashgate.

Shah-Kazemi, Sonia N. (2001). *Untying the Knot: Muslim Women, Divorce and the Shariah.* London: Nuffield Foundation.

Shayan, Fatemeh (2013). "Ontological Anxiety among Shii Muslims in Finland: A Case Study of First Generation Immigrants in City of Tampere." *Islamic Perspectives: Journal of the Islamic Studies and Humanities* 9: 91–106.

Taj, Farhat (2013a). *Legal Pluralism, Human Rights and Islam in Norway: Making Norwegian Law Available, Acceptable, and Accessible to Women in Multicultural Setting.* Oslo: University of Oslo.

Taj, Farhat (2013b). "The Status and Role of the Norwegian-Pakistani Mosque: Interfaith Harmony and Women's Rights in Norway." In Esther Gallo (ed.), *Migration and Religion in Europe: Comparative Perspectives on South-Asian Experience,* 59–76. London: Ashgate.

Wolfe, Caryn Litt (2006). "Faith-Based Arbitration: Friend or Foe? An Evaluation of Religious Arbitration Systems and Their Interaction with Secular Courts." *Fordham Law Review* 75(1): 427–43.

12

Together Forever: Are You Kidding Me?

CATHOLICISM, SAME-SEX COUPLES, DISPUTES, AND DISPUTE RESOLUTION IN ITALY

Maria Federica Moscati

THIS CHAPTER ASKS whether Catholicism influences the resolution of disputes between same-sex partners in Italy and, if so, how. It argues that the relationship between dispute resolution, Catholicism, and being in a same-sex relationship in Italy is characterized by personal conflict and choices about identity as much as by compromise and intrusion by the Roman Catholic Church. Accordingly, the study described here represents a pioneering attempt to contribute to the current literature on family disputes and religion with regard to same-sex couples.[1]

Religion may influence disputes and the resolution of disputes to different extents and in different ways. Religion may be a source of dispute, or it may determine how and where a dispute is resolved (von Benda-Beckman et al. 2013), or religious diktats may be adopted to lead the parties toward an agreement. Particularly, the resolution of family disputes is often subject to the intrusive participation of religion (Bano 2007). And the resolution of intra-family disputes between same-sex partners is not an exception.

However, analysis of the nature of the disputes between, and the recourse to mediation by, same-sex partners adds a new dimension to the study of mediation adopted for the resolution of intra-family disputes. For instance, as my study shows with regard to Catholicism and dispute resolution between same-sex partners in Italy, the aim and function of religious instructions regarding the unity and indissolubility of marriage operate in a different way for same-sex partners than for different-sex partners. Indeed, as one of the interviewees in my study pointed out, "For the Roman Catholic Church the same-sex couple does not exist; and if it exists it must be dissolved."[2]

In addition, as explained further in this chapter, religious opposition to same-sex relationships, and Catholic values more generally, could be considered a way of resolving disputes through avoidance. On the other hand, as this chapter shows, there are cases in which same-sex couples decide to resolve their disputes through mediation, through counseling, or with the informal intervention of friends or members of Catholic associations created by gay and lesbian people. Therefore, the question arises as to whether and how the Catholic patriarchal approach to heterosexual marriage interacts—or actually negotiates—with the rights of same-sex partners.

The influence of religion on the resolution of disputes between same-sex partners is an issue largely unexplored in the literature. Therefore, given limited data and resources that deal specifically with the influence of Catholicism on disputes and dispute resolution between same-sex partners in Italy, this study relies mainly on empirical data collected by the author during fieldwork and semi-structured interviews with same-sex couples, counselors, psychologists, and LGBT (lesbian, gay, bisexual, transgender) rights activists in Italy.

This preliminary research on the influence of religion on dispute resolution between same-sex partners developed within a broader research project titled "Litigious Love: Same-Sex Couples and Mediation in the EU," which received funding from the DG Civil Justice of the European Commission.[3] The project aimed at broadening mutual understanding among judges, lawyers, and mediators with regard to the disputes and dispute resolution mechanisms involving same-sex partners. In addition, the project attempted to raise awareness of the rights of same-sex couples and of the direct impact that social disapproval and lack of legal protection of same-sex relationships have on the nature of disputes and on the process of resolution.

One facet of "Litigious Love: Same-Sex Couples and Mediation in the EU" was comparative research on the causes of dispute between same-sex partners and issues surrounding the resolution through mediation in Bulgaria, Croatia, Hungary, and Italy. More specifically, the research project investigated the sources of dispute between same-sex partners. In addition, it looked at the manner in which intra-family disputes are resolved through mediation and other dispute resolution processes. Finally, it analyzed selected issues surrounding the mediation process, including power imbalances between the partners, styles and models of practice adopted by mediators, the involvement of children during mediation, and inter-country recognition of mediated agreements.

As far as developments of alternative dispute resolution in Italy are concerned, arbitration, assisted negotiation,[4] and mediation are used for the resolution of several types of dispute. In particular, mediation is adopted for commercial, civil, family, employment, and criminal disputes (Lorenzetti and Viggiani 2015).[5] Legislative Decree 04/03/2010 no. 28, "Implementation of Article 60 of Law 18 June 2009 no. 69, Regarding Mediation Aiming at the Conciliation of Civil and Commercial Disputes,"[6] introduced norms regulating the use of mediation for civil and commercial disputes. The mediation is generally facultative for disputants. There are, however, specific types of dispute for which the law requires a compulsory attempt at mediation.[7] In addition, in presiding over court proceedings regarding civil and commercial disputes during the first and second instances, judges can suggest that parties attempt mediation (Lorenzetti and Viggiani 2015).[8]

With regard to divorce and dissolution, opposite-sex married couples and same-sex couples in registered civil unions[9] may resolve disputes through adjudication and assisted negotiation.[10] Same-sex couples may dissolve their relationship also through declaration sent to the registry office.[11] The recourse to mediation for the resolution of family disputes is not compulsory under Italian law[12]—it can be suggested by the judge, or disputants may decide to attempt it, and if an agreement is reached, this will become binding and enforceable through judicial approval.

For de facto same-sex and opposite-sex couples, the recourse to court is limited and almost possible only when the dispute concerns disposable rights (*diritti disponibili*) such as patrimonial rights and not personal rights such as dissolution. Other dispute resolution mechanisms that these couples may choose include assisted negotiation and mediation.[13] However, the legal consequences of a mediated or negotiated agreement will be limited to disposable rights.

The findings of the project "Litigious Love" suggest that same-sex couples in Italy use mediation only rarely. Such limited use of mediation is a result of meager awareness of and knowledge about the nature of mediation, preference for other forms of third-party intervention such as counseling and family therapy or confusion between mediation and family therapy, and fear of being discriminated against (Lorenzetti and Viggiani 2015).

The "Litigious Love" research represents the significant premise underpinning this chapter. As mentioned earlier, this study draws on semi-structured interviews with same-sex couples, as well as counselors and psychologists, in Italy. Among the fifteen interviewees, one was a counselor and one a psychologist; the others were same-sex partners. The counselor and psychologist were chosen for their significant experience with Catholic LGBT people in Italy. One of the interviewees was a former priest, who because of his homosexuality experienced ostracism and homophobia within the Roman Catholic Church and eventually left the clergy. The same-sex partners were all male and Catholic, and had some role, including that of founder, or some experience in independent groups of gay and lesbian Christians in Italy.

There are several such groups in Italy,[14] spontaneously formed by gay men and lesbian women of different Christian beliefs with the aim of supporting Christian LGBT people who are dealing with issues such as coming out, identity conflicts, same-sex relationships, and parenthood. Although they follow different approaches, all groups serve as places of "acceptance: where everyone can feel understood, loved and supported in the process of accepting his or her own identity; personal research: through prayer, the exchange of views, and communion, everyone can perceive and live his or her own sexual orientation as a gift of God; testimony: in order to contribute to the elimination of homophobia, including that within each church" (Gruppo Gionata).[15]

The groups are independent but often and in different ways collaborate with some of the Christian churches. For instance, the group of gay and lesbian Evangelicals called Rete Evangelica Fede e Omosessualita (Evangelical Network of Faith and Homosexuality) organizes activities with the Waldensian Evangelical and Methodist Churches and has given broad support to the LGBT community.[16] On the other hand, Catholic groups find more resistance to their attempts to involve the Roman Catholic Church. Even if monks, nuns, and priests have sometimes participated in some of the groups' activities, only two Catholic dioceses in Italy have developed specific pastoral care for homosexual people.

The groups' activities include research, the dissemination of data, meetings, prayer,[17] counseling with the help of professional counselors—such as those interviewed for this study—and psychologists. As far as the resolution of intra-family disputes is concerned, the research that is the basis for this chapter shows that so far the groups do not provide structured mediation services. Instead, members of the group—sometimes involving monks, nuns, or priests—may informally support and advise the partners who share their experience. As considered further in this chapter, there are other examples of mediation offered by religious family counseling services.

For the purpose of this study the interviewees were contacted via email first and then via Skype. Each interview was (with each respondent's full permission) audiotaped, transcribed, translated from Italian into English, and returned to each interviewee to ensure accuracy. Although Italian law does not criminalize homosexuality,[18] there are some environments where the heteronormative approach to sexual orientation influences human relationships and where being "out" would contribute to exclusion and discrimination. Therefore, for the sake of ethics and privacy, the names of some interviewees have been amended or avoided.

The study is divided into two main sections: the first section focuses on Catholicism as a source of dispute, and the second on Catholicism as a factor influencing the resolution of dispute. Both sections explore the diverse pressures and effects that personal conflict, choices about identity, compromise, and intrusion by the Roman Catholic Church have on the causes of dispute and on dispute resolution between same-sex partners in Italy.

Although Italy is a secular country and does not have a state religion,[19] and although several religious denominations are recognized by agreements with the Italian state, the present study takes into consideration only the influence of Catholicism and the impact of the Roman Catholic Church. This choice is based mainly on the evidence of the privileged role that the Vatican has long played within Italian political and social life (Moscati 2014). Overall, the Italian legal culture—and in particular politics—has been, and still is, strongly influenced in different ways by both Catholicism in general and the Vatican in particular (Moscati 2014; Zagrebelsky 2010; Politi 2009).

I have investigated elsewhere the relationship between the Vatican, the Roman Catholic Church, and Italy (Moscati 2014). A detailed account of this relationship is outside the scope of this study. Here it suffices to say that, on the one hand, general moral principles condemning homosexuality found in the Judeo-Christian tradition have infiltrated Roman law and have in turn permeated Italian law (Cantarella 1995; Moscati 2014). In particular, the Corpus Juris Civilis, inspired by the Christian condemnation of homosexuality, criminalized homosexuality, considering it contrary to nature and deeply offensive to God (Cantarella 1995). This negative conceptualization of homosexuality as an act against nature and against religion has since then characterized Roman law and subsequently Italian law (Cantarella 1995).

On the other hand, the Vatican, which is a tangible expression of the political power of the Roman Catholic Church, is located in Italy and has a political and economic relationship with the Italian state. The relations between the Vatican and the Italian state are regulated by the Lateran Pacts,[20] with the consequence that the Italian state has allowed the intrusion of the Vatican into its sovereignty and into secular settings (Gramsci 2006 [1929]). The result is that several aspects of society in Italy, including legal reforms regarding family life, have involved some compromise with the Vatican (Moscati 2014).

Generally speaking, since the drafting of the 1942 Italian Civil Code the norms regarding the nature of marriage, the role of women within family, and parenting issues tend to mirror the patriarchal and hierarchical Catholic conceptualization of family relationships. Indeed, in the Lateran Pacts the Italian state agreed to legislate according to Catholic values regarding marriage and family relationships. In addition, together with being responsible for primary and secondary education for several decades, and notwithstanding the revision of Lateran Pacts in 1984, the Roman Catholic Church has intervened in legislative developments concerning family relations in Italy (Moscati 2014). For instance, when in 2007 the Italian government presented a bill for the recognition of same-sex unions,[21] the draft of the bill was scrutinized by a number of legal experts within the Vatican and modified according to the wishes of the Roman Catholic Church (Politi 2009).

Catholicism as a Cause of Disputes

Catholicism may represent a source of disputes and disagreement for same-sex partners in Italy in three respects.[22] First, individual conflicts between being gay and being Catholic arise. Second, adherence to Catholicism may be a factor in creating disagreement between the partners in a same-sex relationship. Third, disputes between the partners and other persons—in particular parents and relatives—may well happen as a result of Catholic beliefs. All three dimensions involve personal conflicts and compromise in which a choice regarding identity—religious identity and sexual identity—is at the core of what is the issue in the disagreement and may need to be negotiated in the resolution of the dispute.

Regarding the first dimension, the literature shows that a conflict between religion and sexual identity is often experienced by gay and lesbian people (Couch et al. 2008; Buchanan et al. 2001). Research also reveals the manner in which these identity conflicts are resolved (Thumma 1991; Mahaffy 1996; Levy and Reeves 2011).[23]

It is not the purpose of this chapter to offer an in-depth discussion of the various psychological studies that to differing extents have examined the process of conflict resolution of identity conflicts. Suffice it to say that Catholic gay and lesbian individuals approach such conflicts in various ways. A first approach is to reconcile sexual orientation and religious beliefs. Second, a separation is made between being gay and being Catholic. The final option is avoiding the resolution of the conflict (Levy and Reeves 2011). The resolution of the conflict between religious identity and sexual identity may involve several stages, which in turn are influenced by other personal and social factors (Levy and Reeves 2011).[24]

A recent study demonstrates that Catholicism in Italy influences the way in which Catholic gay men and lesbian women perceive their homosexuality, often showing higher levels of internalized homophobia than homosexual people who are not religious (Petilli et al. 2010).[25] According to this research, a degree of internalized homophobia is related to the approach to religion taken by the family of the homosexual individual. The greater the extent to which Catholic beliefs are followed by the family, the higher is the level of internalized homophobia (Petilli et al. 2010).

In particular, as Arianna Petilli, a psychologist and one of the authors of the Italian study, pointed out during an interview for this study:

Italian Catholic gay men and lesbian women often experience a dramatic situation of identity conflict because of religion. There is an internal conflict as soon as individuals perceive themselves to be homosexual: if someone is educated according to Catholic doctrine (which says homosexuality is wrong) then once he/she becomes aware of his/her homosexuality an identity conflict arises. In fact, the levels of internalized homophobia of a Catholic are much higher than those of a non-Catholic background. Social disapproval and the approach of the Catholic Church to homosexuality strengthen the internal conflict for a Catholic person who discovers he/she is homosexual and as a consequence often increases the internalized homophobia.[26]

During the fieldwork carried out as part of my study, interviewees were asked: How do you reconcile being gay and being Catholic in Italy, and how do you cope with the Catholic doctrine opposing homosexuality and same-sex couples? Generally speaking, the answers offered by same-sex couples, the psychologist, and counselors represent a wide range of perspectives. These perspectives support the general view of sexuality as interconnected with diverse aspects of society (Munro and Stychin 2007), and as a consequence the decision regarding which identity to prioritize inevitably involves an internalized power imbalance between two apparently conflicting expressions of the same individual. As Arianna Petilli explained:

> It may happen that homosexual people think: I cannot be gay and Catholic; these two things are opposite. Therefore, some gay men and lesbian women may decide to choose between sexual identity and religious identity, renouncing one of them. Some other homosexual persons do not prioritize any aspects of their identity and continue to live [according to] both [their sexual and religious orientation] but without revealing their homosexuality in Catholic contexts or, conversely, showing their disagreement with the Roman Catholic Church when meeting with other LGBT people. Finally, there are several homosexual persons who balance and integrate being Catholic and being homosexual because a distinction is made between religious belief and what Catholic Church says.[27]

At either end of the continuum of interviewees' responses, the field-work confirmed findings from previous research in psychology showing that some gay men and lesbian women who follow Catholicism in Italy often make two types of choice. First, there are those who choose to avoid dealing with the conflict. For instance, as Davide described his experience: "How do I reconcile my sexual identity with my religious identity? Well, I do not reconcile. I just do not deal with it!"[28] Second, there are gay men and lesbian women who choose between the two identities. Often sexual identity is prioritized, and as reported by Petilli et al. (2010) and by several of my interviewees, same-sex partners often consciously decide to abandon their religious beliefs.

Navigating between being homosexual and being Catholic in Italy may be possible—and according to some of the interviewees it is possible—through an emotional and psychological separation of faith (*fede*) from spirituality or religion. According to Arianna Petilli:

> Many gay and lesbian people in Italy are able to reconcile their sexual orientation with their belief in Catholicism (or find a compromise). They can do so by applying various strategies that have a common characteristic: reducing the value that official documents of the Roman Catholic Church have and promoting a personal relationship with God. Such relationship with God does not need any mediation by the Roman Catholic Church. Therefore, there is a division between religion and spirituality, where religion is understood as a set of dogmas of Catholic institutions and spirituality is perceived as a personal relationship with God.[29]

Focusing on the importance of faith helps to minimize the influence that ideas of the Roman Catholic Church targeting homosexuality have on the self-confidence and self-acceptance of gay and lesbian believers in Italy. For instance, as Arianna Petilli suggested:

> Making a distinction between spirituality and religion helps to increase self-confidence. Some examples of this distinction include thoughts such as: if you consider that God created human beings in his image and likeness, being gay is not wrong and God does not oppose homosexuality; or if the Catholic Church in the past has

made several mistakes and has apologized, perhaps after two hundred or three hundred years the Vatican will apologize to all its homosexual victims and for the homophobia that the Roman Catholic Church promotes; or if I am in a same-sex relationship and I live my relationship following the values that the Roman Catholic Church imposes with regard marriage, where is the problem of having a same-sex relationship?[30]

Moving on to the issue of intra-family disputes between same-sex partners in which religion plays a causal role, it is clear that disputes occur between same-sex partners when both are religious or between one religious partner and his or her same-sex atheist or agnostic partner. When both partners are religious, the unresolved individual conflicts and the compromises that gay and lesbian believers make in order to adjust to the competing demands of sexual identity and religious identity can create disagreement and disputes between same-sex partners. As two same-sex partners, Vincenzo and Marco, agreed in their interview with me:

When partners do not share a similar understanding of the value, space, and importance that faith and the instructions of the Roman Catholic Church have in their lives, then disagreements arise.[31]

As a consequence, a first significant source of dispute is the nature of the feeling—the love—that same-sex partners have for each other. As Sergio told me:

There are disputes about being Catholic and at the same time about being in a same-sex relationship. The cause of disagreement is the nature of love between same-sex partners: is this kind of feeling real love and can it therefore be accepted and lived, or is it against nature . . . as the traditions and values of the Roman Catholic Church decree? If one of the partners gives greater attention to the instructions of the Roman Catholic Church, then the same-sex relationship is questioned and disputes arise. The partner who, although religious, does not agree with the Roman Catholic Church may be blamed for his/her disagreement and for his/her freedom to love someone of the same sex.[32]

Another source of dispute can lie in the partners' disagreement regarding sexuality—whether to have sex or whether to have sex following Catholic norms. All interviewees suggested that if one of the partners strictly follows Catholic instructions, which consider sexual intercourse between same-sex partners to be unnatural and wrong, he or she may require chastity during the relationship. The experience of Davide and his partner represents an example of such disagreement:

> I am religious and my partner is very religious. Since we started our relationship, my partner has questioned our love. More importantly, we are in disagreement about having a sexual relationship. After several discussions we decided that sex will be part of our relationship, but we will have sex in the Catholic manner, which means avoiding infidelity and promiscuity.[33]

During the fieldwork, interviewees shed light on intra-family religious disputes between same-sex partners when only one partner is religious. For instance, several respondents reported that an atheist or agnostic partner may not easily understand the sense of guilt that his or her Catholic partner feels in regard to his or her own homosexuality, being in a same-sex relationship, having sex with a person of the same sex, or lying about or failing to mention sexual experiences during confession with a priest.

The disputes described during the interviews mainly concerned the level of commitment that the Catholic partner has to religious activities and the time that the involvement in religious activities takes from the time shared with the partner. An example was given by a counselor who works with a group of religious gay men and lesbian women:

> A gay couple once asked me to help resolve their dispute. The two partners were married abroad and came back to Italy. One of the partners played guitar in the parish church every Sunday. At the beginning of the relationship, his playing guitar during the mass did not interfere with the couple's life. Indeed, the other partner— who was atheist—knew that on Sunday each of the partners could dedicate himself to his own hobbies. When the Catholic partner's involvement in the church increased, with that partner accepting more duties within the parish and spending three evenings at the parish for rehearsal, the couple had an argument. The partner who

was not religious felt excluded from the life of the other one and felt that religion "was stealing time" from the relationship.[34]

Davide described a similar experience:

I had two friends in a relationship. One was Catholic, and the other was not. They seemed to have found a good balance in their relationship. However, they had a very intense disagreement when the Catholic partner decided to join a group of LGBT Catholics, and they separated.[35]

Finally, it may well be that a disagreement arises because the Catholic partner challenges the nonreligious approach of his or her partner. The Catholic partner may question his or her same-sex partner's choice not to follow any religion or faith or may criticize the partner's decision to refuse or not to adhere to Catholic instructions. For instance, one of the interviewees described a dispute he had with his partner in the following terms:

I am very [religiously] observant, while my partner is atheist. However, my partner was baptized. One day he expressed the wish to formally renounce baptism. Of course I did not agree with this choice and we had a dispute. I was disappointed because in my view being atheist is acceptable, but deciding to renounce baptism is useless, illogical, and inconsistent with being atheist.[36]

Religion can be a source of dispute not only between partners but also between same-sex partners and their relatives. Disagreements may occur when parents learn that their son or daughter is in a same-sex relationship and is planning to get married. Vincenzo and Marco offer an interesting example:

Usually when you plan to get married you involve your parents, and your family. However, if you are gay and decide to go abroad and register your union or your marriage and wish to share this plan with your parents, religious problems may arise mainly because marriage has a social impact; it is a symbol that creates visibility. Many parents accept that their children are gay and have a companion (*fidanzatino*), but marriage is not acceptable because it will make homosexuality visible and, as a consequence, the entire family will be recognized through the homosexuality of one of the members.[37]

Catholicism and the Resolution of Disputes

Generally speaking, it is during the process of resolving disputes between same-sex partners in Italy that the intrusions of Catholic morality and of the Vatican are perhaps most significant. This section is informed by the argument that the encroachment of Catholic morality and the Vatican on secular debates regarding homosexuality and legal recognition of same-sex unions has an impact on the perception of grievance, on the decision regarding the mechanism of resolution, and on the process of resolution for same-sex couples who are Catholic in Italy.

In particular, for our purposes we should note the effects of the fierce ostracism of homosexuality and same-sex unions by the Roman Catholic Church in its teachings, and in its dealings with adherents, on the transformation of disputes and on the dispute resolution process.[38] It is well known that official documents of the Roman Catholic Church regard homosexuality as an *objective disorder* and chastity as the only solution to this problem (Congregazione per la Dottrina della Fede 1986). In addition, the Vatican has intervened in the debate about the legalization of same-sex unions in Italy and reiterated its disapproval of legal recognition of same-sex marriage (Congregazione per la Dottrina della Fede 2003).[39]

It is contended here that the Catholic disapproval of homosexuality and same-sex unions not only contributes to the creation of individual identity conflicts, as explained in the preceding section, but in addition has limited the range of available mechanisms for the resolution of disputes between same-sex partners in Italy. The intrusion of the Vatican into the debate about allowing same-sex unions in Italy has been one of the reasons for the lack of legal protection of same-sex unions in Italy until recently. The failure to secure legal recognition of these relationships has meant that same-sex partners had limited access to formal adjudication and its institutions—courts of law—for the resolution of their family disputes.

Moving next to the process of the transformation of a dispute, Felstiner et al. (1980–81) have offered a powerful general paradigm of the transformation of disputes. The paradigm is based on three stages: *naming*, as the perception of being victim of an injustice; *blaming*, as the identification of the offender; and *claiming*, as the request for compensation. In order for "disputes to emerge and remedial action to be taken, an unperceived injurious experience (unPIE) must be transformed into a perceived injurious experience (PIE)" (Felstiner et al. 1980–81, 631). However, the transformation from an unperceived to a perceived injurious experience is often limited by a variety of important personal and social factors that contribute to the recognition and perception of a wrong and to the subsequent request for compensation (Sarat 2000; Palmer 2014). Social factors limiting the perception of a wrong include, among others, differences in the social class of the perpetrator and the victim of the wrong and the use of violence.

In the case of Italian society, it could be argued that Catholic morality may well encourage "grievance apathy" (Felstiner et al. 1981). The combination of Catholic disapproval of homosexual relationships and Catholic principles informing the model of marriage may limit the level of perception of distress and injustice that Catholic same-sex partners have and encourage the tolerance of injury. One of the interviewees explains and supports such a conclusion:

> I am a counselor and I have been working with same-sex couples for several years. In my experience I have seen that Catholic morality brings some same-sex Catholic couples to accept and bear solutions that are often not feasible or suitable with respect to the dispute. It seems that these Catholic same-sex couples in their conduct manifest obsolete dynamics that were common to heterosexual couples several decades ago in Italy. In particular I refer, on the one hand, to the imposed patriarchal idea of the woman who has to accept all behaviors [and misconduct] of the husband and, on the other hand, to the indissolubility of marriage. Both contribute to a tolerance of disagreement and make notions of grievance and the need for resolution irrelevant.[40]

However, once an unperceived injurious experience is transformed into a perceived injurious experience, and the perpetrator of the wrong does not acknowledge that she or he has injured the complainant, the parties in the dispute move to the following stage of choosing the forum for resolving the dispute (Sander and Goldberg 1994; Sander and Rozdeiczer 2005).

As shown by Roberts and Palmer (2005), primary forms of dispute resolution include avoidance, self-help, negotiation, mediation, and public and private umpiring. With regard to dispute resolution processes chosen by Catholic same-sex partners in Italy, my fieldwork has shown that only self-help and umpiring are uncommon. Catholic third-party interventions may include informal help by Catholic gay and lesbian groups, meetings with members of the clergy or of a religious order or with a religious mediator, and mediation at diocesan family counseling associations (*consultori familiari diocesani*).

Before we look at third-party interventions more closely, it is important to consider how personal choices about the way disputes are resolved can be coerced by cultural attitudes toward homosexuality and same-sex unions. Decisions about which forum to use are not straightforward when religious directives are involved (von Benda-Beckman et al. 2013). Some of the same-sex partners who were interviewed explained that the choice of a mechanism of resolution involving third-party intervention—especially when the third party is a member of the clergy—may be limited by fear of being judged or discriminated against. Therefore, disputants may nevertheless ask for religious third-party intervention but decide to frame the dispute without making reference to their sexual orientation or to the intimate relationship they share. In particular, when Catholic same-sex partners consult a priest for advice about the relationship, frequently each partner meets the priest separately and does not mention his or her sexual orientation or being in a same-sex relationship.

In addition, as suggested, "Religious instructions often appeal to emotions in that they may have a calming, soothing or, by, contrast, rousing effect" (von Benda-Beckman et al. 2013, xiii). Indeed, several interviewees reported that Catholic values have such a calming effect on the partners, reducing antagonism in two respects. On the one hand, Catholic values encourage avoidance in two respects: Gulliver (1996) refers to these as *dispute avoidance*, in which parties refrain from communicating with each other after a dispute has occurred, and *conflict avoidance*, in which certain rules limit contact in order to prevent disputes from arising. In addition, my case study offers the opportunity to extend the concept of "moral minimalism" and "its aversion to conflict and its preference for restraint" developed by Baumgartner (1988, 129). Indeed, during the fieldwork, the counselor and the psychologist suggested that often partners do not attempt a resolution of the issues and prefer, instead, to just "forget and forgive" as taught by the Roman Catholic Church.

On the other hand, Catholic values shape bilateral negotiation between the parties, promoting a more problem-solving, cooperative resolution. It appears that if the partners have a mature approach to religion and follow their faith, Catholic values may teach them to listen to each other and support each other. In this way disputes are prevented or resolved. The experience of Innocenzo and Carlo offers a significant example:

> The faith in God may well be the instrument helping the resolution of family disputes between the partners. Our faith (we prefer faith and not religion) is what brings us together. We had a dispute some time ago: our faith and praying led us to be honest with each other—but without offending or hurt each other—and to listen to each other.[41]

As already indicated, attempts to resolve disputes between Catholic same-sex partners include Catholic third-party interventions. Here the focus is on interventions involving groups and associations of Catholic LGBT people, as well as mediation with monks, priests, or Catholic mediators. Implicated in the use of these third-party interventions is the question of how the third party employs Catholic values during the resolution of the dispute. These aspects will be analyzed in turn.

Interviewees affirmed that interventions by members of LGBT organizations usually occur informally.[42] In particular, Catholic LGBT groups have weekly meetings during which same-sex partners who have a dispute share their experience with other couples and attempt to find a solution to their problems. Some groups include counselors and psychologists. Two same-sex partners and a counselor describe their experiences:

> We meet every month and our meetings are open to everyone, not only Catholic couples. Of course, our faith and Catholic values inform our meetings, and therefore if a couple is separating we try to help the partners understand their conflict and listen to each other.

I am the counselor and I am an expert in couple counseling. I organize monthly workshops with the couples. I do not deal with the
religious aspect of the relationship that same-sex partners share.
My workshops follow a group-based path and involve several creative activities. If partners do have specific problems to deal with,
I suggest individual counseling or couples therapy.[43]

Third-party intercession involving monks, priests, or religious lay persons is subject to a certain degree of intrusion by the Roman Catholic
Church. In particular, the pastoral care of homosexual people is part of
the agenda of the Roman Catholic Church, and together with catecheti-
cal programs it "would include the assistance of the psychological, sociological and medical sciences, in full accord with the teaching of the
Church" (Congregation for the Doctrine of the Faith 1986, 7). Such assistance has sometimes entailed reparative therapy.[44]

A less radical approach, but still embedded in Catholic morality, often
includes the intercession of monks, priests, and mediators who are not
members of the clergy but are believers. My fieldwork so far has shown
that one of the first persons to be consulted may be the priest of the par-
ish attended by the partners or a monk or nun whom the partners trust.
Often the partners do not disclose their relationship, do not have joint
meetings, and approach the third party more as spiritual guide than as
a conventional mediator: the parties may look more for reassurance, suggestions, a space for venting emotions, and psychological support than
for resolution of the dispute.

Another example of Catholic third-party intervention is mediation
offered by diocesan family counseling associations. These are several
in Italy, and they have a very active role in supporting family members in
accordance with the values and principles of the Roman Catholic Church.
The services offered include family counseling, psychotherapy, mediation, legal assistance, and health and medical assistance. Professional
mediators are responsible for family mediation sessions, and mediation
starts with a one-on-one meeting with each of the parties and then proceeds to joint meetings. As suggested in the literature of diocesan family
counseling associations, Catholic values and principles regarding family,
marriage, divorce, and procreation inform and inspire all activities and
services offered by the associations—including mediation. As judged by
the websites of the diocesan associations, the family model recognized

and supported by these associations is that of the heterosexual family. Therefore, same-sex couples may find that the mediation service is not adequate for their needs. Indeed, some of the interviewees indicated that they would approach such services but without referring to homosexuality or to an intimate relationship with a partner of the same-sex.

Some of the interviewees described their experience of meeting with priests or monks for the resolution of family disputes and discussed the approach taken by monks and priests, which operates in two ways. First, on some occasions monks or priests invoked Catholic values—such as partners' respect for one another and their willingness to listen and talking to each other—to help the disputants adopt a problem-solving approach. Sergio shared his experience:

> A monk helped me and my partner to overcome a dispute we had. The monk listened to us and helped us to remember and apply the values of Catholicism, namely listening to each other, supporting each other, and being compassionate towards each other.[45]

In some other circumstances the third party may adopt a more radically literal interpretation of religious writing, suggesting separation of the couple or encouraging a chaste relationship.

A further inquiry arises as to whether and how the Catholic patriarchal approach to heterosexual marriage relates to and accommodates the rights of same-sex partners. To what extent does the value of indissolubility of marriage fit into the resolution of dispute between same-sex partners?

A reading of official documents of the Roman Catholic Church brings one to the conclusion that the union of two partners of the same sex is considered "deprived of their essential and indispensable finality, intrinsically disordered, and able in no case to be approved" (Congregazione per la Dottrina della Fede 1986). As a consequence, the indissolubility of marriage is not something that a religious third party would suggest to same-sex partners; instead, the party would most likely encourage the couple to separate. This is strikingly different from the situation of opposite-sex couples, in which monks and priests aim at reconciliation of the partners.

This was confirmed by all the interviewees, who pointed out that Catholic mediators or priests are not keen to consider the principle of indissolubility of marriage—simply because Catholic morality deems that same-sex partners cannot be a couple.

But to what extent does the value of indissolubility inform decisions that Catholic same-sex partners make with regard to their separation? The interviewees asserted that the idea indissolubility does not have as a great an influence on religious same-sex partners who have successfully integrated religious identity and sexual identity. These couples prioritize their faith and participate in the relationship according to their faith and not the words of the Roman Catholic Church. Conversely, the interviewees reported that the indissolubility of marriage seems to have a great influence on gay men who are Catholics, who are not "out," and who are involved in a heterosexual marriage. Marriage is a significant religious symbol, with strong religious meaning attached to it. Marriage is the way in which a Catholic who is gay but is not out perceives him- or herself.

The foregoing reflections and empirical analysis of disputes and dispute resolution involving Catholic same-sex partners in Italy demonstrate that both dimensions are influenced by a combination of identity conflict, compromise with religious beliefs, and intrusion by the Roman Catholic Church.

Catholic morality, its approach to homosexuality, and its disapproval of same-sex relationships have a direct impact on the sources of dispute, on the choice of the forum for the resolution of disputes, and during the resolution. In particular, such morality triggers identity conflict and disagreement between partners, which they often resolve by making a conscious distinction between faith and the instructions of the Roman Catholic Church. At the same time, Catholic instructions *successfully* promote grievance apathy and conflict avoidance.

However, when Catholic views permeate third-party interventions with regard to intra-family disputes between same-sex partners, a certain degree of *planned intolerance* (planned by the hierarchy of the Roman Catholic Church)—which is in fact contrary to the main Catholic value of compassion—shapes the resolution process. As a result, as the title of this study suggests, togetherness and indissolubility are apparently not a possibility for same-sex couples! Therefore, as suggested by all the interviewees, a genuine Catholic mediator aims at dividing same-sex partners!

Notes

The author wishes to thank Professor Michael Palmer for his suggestions on the first draft of this chapter. Gratitude goes to Arianna Petilli, Angela Infante, Gianni Geraci, Sergio Caravaggio, Mario Bonfanti, Innocenzo, Carlo, Vincenzo, Marco, and the other same-sex couples, who prefer to remain anonymous, for sharing their experiences with me.

1. The study, however, leaves to future research a critical evaluation of the influence that Catholicism has on disputes and dispute resolution involving different-sex partners as opposed to same-sex partners.

2. Interview with Sergio, 19 March 2015.

3. The project "Litigious Love: Same-Sex Couples and Mediation in the EU" began in May 2014 and ended in September 2015. The jurisdictions analyzed in the project are Bulgaria, Italy, Croatia, and Hungary. For information on the project's activities see www.litigiouslove.eu.

4. Legal Decree 12 September 2014 no. 132, implemented by law 10 November 2014 no. 162—"Urgent Measures for the De-processualization and Other Measures for the Limitation of the Delay in Civil Process" (*Misure urgenti di degiurisdizionalizzazione e altri interventi per la definizione dell'arretrato in materia di processo civile*)—has introduced assisted negotiation (*negoziazione assistita*) by one or more attorneys. Assisted negotiation consists of an agreement between the parties in which the disputants agree that they will resolve the dispute, cooperating in good faith and honesty (article 2). The parties are assisted by at least one lawyer.

5. In particular mediation is provided in the Juvenile Justice System by Decree of the President of the Republic 448, 22 September 1998: "Norms Regarding Criminal Proceedings against Child Offenders."

6. Hereinafter Legislative Decree 28/2010. The mediation procedure starts with an application that one or both disputants submit to one of the providers of alternative dispute resolution (ADR) registered with the Ministry of Justice (article 4). The ADR provider selects the mediator, and a preliminary meeting is held between the parties and the mediator. If settlement is not reached, the parties consider whether and how to proceed with mediation or adjudication (article 8). The mediation process should last three months (article 6). The legislative decree expressly opens the possibility for the mediator to offer options regarding the content of the agreement (article 11).

7. Article 5 of Legislative Decree 28/2010 provides that the attempt to mediate is compulsory for disputes concerning condominiums, real properties, division of goods, inheritance, agreements regarding family business, tenancy, loan, rent of business, request of damages resulting from medical liability or from defamation by the press or by other means of publicity, contracts regarding insurance, banking, and finance.

8. Article 5 (2) of Legislative Decree 28/2010.

9. Sections 23, 24, and 25 of Law 20 May 2016 no. 76, "Law on Civil Unions between Same-Sex Partners and Regulation of Cohabitation."

10. Article 6 of Legal Decree 132/2014 provides assisted negotiation for disputes regarding separation, dissolution of marriage, termination of civil consequences of marriage, and changes to the conditions of separation and divorce.

11. Article 12 of Decree 132/2014.

12. Family mediation is not regulated by Legislative Decree 28/2010. Italian law does not provide a specific legal framework for family mediation.

13. Mediation is compulsory for same-sex partners when the dispute concerns the division of common properties (article 5, Legislative Decree 28/2010).

14. At the moment of writing there are twenty-four volunteer groups of gay and lesbian Christians in Italy. The first group—called Guado—was created in 1980. A center for the study and documentation of faith and homosexuality started in 2007 with the aim of collecting research and data on homosexuality and faith in Italy. The name of the center is Centro Studi e Documentazione "Ferruccio Castellano" in Turin. A website on faith and homosexuality called "Progetto Gionata" was developed in 2007. For a detailed map of groups for gay and lesbian Christians in Italy see www.gionata.org.

15. www.gionata.org.

16. See, e.g., Document on Homosexuality of the Synods of the Methodist and Waldensian Churches; http://www.chiesavaldese.org, accessed 28 May 2015.

17. In this regard, particularly important is the ecumenical prayer for the victims of homophobia that the groups organize every year during the week before 17 May (International Day against Homophobia).

18. Italy decriminalized homosexuality in 1890. Discrimination based on sexual orientation and gender identity is prohibited under Decree 216/2003. Law 20 May 2016 has introduced same-sex civil unions. However, Italian legal culture does not provide a specific law against homophobia and trans-phobia.

19. The Italian Constitution recognizes at article 8, "All religious denominations are equally free before the law. Denominations other than Catholicism have the right to self-organization according to their own statutes, provided they do not conflict with Italian law. Their relations with the State are regulated by law based on agreements with their respective representatives." Moreover, the Italian Constitution recognizes the personal right to freely profess religious belief (article 9) and the right to create religious associations (article 20). To date, Italy has signed agreements with ten religious denominations.

20. The first Lateran Pacts were signed on 11 February 1929. They founded the Vatican State, regulated financial relations between the Italian state and the Vatican, and defined civil and religious relations between Italy and the Vatican. In particular, Catholicism was elected as the religion of the Italian state. The

Lateran Pacts were revised in 1984, and among other changes the new pacts eliminated reference to Catholicism as the religion of state. The Constituent Assembly discussed the inclusion of this provision in the postwar Italian Constitution. A major concern was whether to introduce in the Constitution the reference to the Lateran Pacts as a treaty between the Italian state and the Holy See. The fact that the Lateran Pacts were signed by Mussolini, who was the prime minister at that time, was considered to be against the principles of the new Constitution, as this document was considered to be anti-fascist. In the end the provision was approved, with the result that the influence of the Vatican on the Italian state was reinforced (Gramsci 2006 [1929]).

21. Bill 1339, "Rights and Duties of Cohabitants" (also known as DICO).

22. I have discussed elsewhere examples of religions other than Catholicism, and here two cases, described by a mediator during an interview, are worth reporting (Moscati 2015): "1) Date of marriage: in one case one of the spouses was a religious leader of an established religious community. She and her partner had gone through a religious ceremony about 15 years earlier, but they had only gotten married legally about 2 years earlier. The religious leader was the higher earner, and in [. . .], community property and spousal support only apply to the marital period, not the period of pre-marital cohabitation. The date of marriage was relevant with regard to the splitting of savings accrued pre-marriage (mostly earned by the religious leader), and the duration of support (which in [. . .] is typically half the length of the marriage, without regard to pre-marital cohabitation. So, in this case the religious leader felt obligated to honor the spirit of the religious ceremony, and accept an earlier date of marriage than the one legally mandated. 2) Schools for the children: the parties were each observant, but in different religions. They had agreed to send their 2 kids to a school aligned with the religion of one of them, but after they broke up, the one aligned with the religion of the kid's school became more devout—to the point where the kids didn't want to spend time with the other parent, as they felt they were being forced to choose that partner's religion. The alienated spouse felt that the ex was exaggerating the religious affiliation in order to 'win over' the loyalty of the kids."

The present study relies on a definition of dispute developed by Roberts and Palmer: First, in a dispute there are identifiable parties, one of whom at least has a grievance. Second, the grievance is based on a perceived breach of rule. Third, the perceived wrong is thought to be the responsibility of the other party. Fourth, the party held responsible disagrees with the characterization of the situation put forward by the first party. I believe that disagreement leads to dispute. However, because of the context and the factors influencing disputes and dispute resolution for religious same-sex partners in Italy, disagreement and dispute are often considered interchangeably. Indeed, the pressure of Catholic morality does not allow all disagreements to become disputes.

23. The study by Thumma (1999) shows how religious groups support gay men and lesbian women as they deal with identity conflict. In particular, Thumma analyses the work of a group called "Good News," the aim of which is to integrate religious identity with sexual identity through a positive interpretation of religious writing. The analysis of Mahaffy (1996) concerns self-reported dissonance between religion and sexual orientation experienced by lesbian women, and it concludes that outputs of the resolution of individual dissonance include exclusion of religious belief, revised interpretation of religious belief, or living with the dissonance.

24. The research carried out by Levy and Reeves (2011, 58) shows that the process for the resolution of identity conflict includes five stages: (1) awareness of the conflict; (2) initial response, which may embrace secrecy, increased religious involvement, or depression; (3) new knowledge; (4) working through conflict; (5) resolution, which proceeds through a renewed understanding of faith and acceptance of sexuality.

25. The study involved 366 homosexual persons and some religious groups in Italy.

26. Interview, 25 February 2015.

27. Ibid.

28. Interview, 28 February 2015.

29. Interview, 25 February 2015.

30. Ibid.

31. Interview, 12 March 2015.

32. Interview, 19 March 2015.

33. Interview, 26 February 2015.

34. Interview, 20 April 2015.

35. Interview, 26 February 2015.

36. Interview, 15 February 2015.

37. Interview, 2 April 2015.

38. Although the current pope, Francis, has shown some degree of acceptance—or at least less condemnation—of homosexuality, nevertheless the attitude of the Roman Catholic Church is still negative, and official documents concerning family or sexuality do not show any change in attitude toward homosexuality.

39. Clearly the Vatican has affirmed that "legal recognition of homosexual unions or placing them on the same level as marriage not only would mean not only the approval of the deviant behavior, with the consequence of making it a model in present-day society, but would also obscure basic values which belong to the common inheritance of humanity." In addition, "Catholics are obliged to oppose the legal recognition of homosexual unions" (Congregazione per la Dottrina della Fede 2003, 5). Such an approach has been recently reiterated by

Cardinal Parolin commenting on the Irish vote on same-sex marriage and defining it as a "defeat for humanity." See http://www.bbc.com/news/world-europe -32900426, accessed 29 May 2015.

40. Interviews, 2 and 20 April 2015.

41. Interview, 12 March 2015.

42. See Petilli et al. (2010) and www.gionata.org.

43. Interviews, 20 April 2015.

44. Reparative therapies aim at changing the sexual orientation of homosexual persons to heterosexuality. See American Psychological Association (2008).

45. Interview, 19 March 2015.

Bibliography

American Psychological Association (2008). *Answers to Your Questions: For a Better Understanding of Sexual Orientation and Homosexuality.* Washington, DC: American Psychological Association. http://www.apa.org/topics/lgbt/orientation.aspx, accessed 25 April 2015.

Bano, Samia (2007). "Muslim Family Justice and Human Rights: The Experience of British Muslim Women." *Journal of Comparative Law* 4: 1–29.

Baumgartner, Mary Pat (1988). *The Moral Order of a Suburb.* Oxford: Oxford University Press.

Buchanan, Melinda, Dzelme, Kristina, Harris, Dale, and Hecker, Lorna (2001). "Challenges of Being Simultaneously Gay or Lesbian and Spiritual and/or Religious: A Narrative Perspective." *American Journal of Family Therapy* 29(3): 435–49.

Cantarella, Eva (1955). *Bisexuality in the Ancient World.* New Haven, CT: Yale University Press.

Cogregazione per la Dottrina della Fede (1986). *Cura Pastorale delle Persone Omosessuali.* Milano: Edizioni Paoline.

Congregazione per la Dottrina della Fede (2003). *Considerations Regarding Proposals to Give Legal Recognition to Unions between Homosexual Persons.* http://www.vatican.va/roman_curia/congregations/cfaith/documents/rc_con_cfaith _doc_20030731_homosexual-unions_en.html, accessed 25 April 2015.

Couch, Murray, Muclare, Hunter, Pitts, Marian, Smith, Anthony, and Mitchell, Anne (2008). "The Religious Affiliation of Gay, Lesbian, Bisexual, Transgender and Intersex Australians: A Report from the Private Lives Survey." *People and Place* 16(1): 1–11.

Felstiner, William, Abel, Richard, and Sarat, Austin (1980–81). "The Emergence and Transformation of Disputes: Naming, Blaming, Claiming." *Law & Society Review* 15: 631–54.

Galanter, Marc (2009). "Access to Justice in a World of Expanding Social Capability." *Fordham Urban Law Journal* 37: 115–27.

Gramsci, Antonio (2006) [1929]. *Il Vaticano e L'Italia*. Edited by Elsa Fubini. Roma: Editori Riuniti.

Gulliver, Philip (1996). "On Avoidance." In David Parkin, Lionel Caplan, and Humphrey Fisher (eds.), *The Politics of Cultural Performance*, 125–43. London: Bergham Books.

Levy, Denise L. and Reeves, Patricia (2011). "Resolving Identity Conflict: Gay, Lesbian, and Queer Individuals with a Christian Upbringing." *Journal of Gay and Lesbian Social Services* 23: 53–68.

Lorenzetti, Anna and Viggiani, Giacomo (2015). "Italy." In Maria Federica Moscati (ed.), *Same-Sex Couples and Mediation in the EU*, 116–18. DG Justice, Specific Programme, Civil Justice, 2007–2013, Grant agreement JUST/2013/JCIV /AG/4667. London: Wildy, Simmonds & Hill.

Mahaffy, Kimberly A. (1996). "Cognitive Dissonance and Its Resolution: A Study of Lesbian Christians." *Journal for the Scientific Study of Religion* 35(4): 392–402.

Moscati, Maria Federica (2014). *Pasolini's Italian Premonitions: Same-Sex Unions and the Law in Comparative Perspective*. London: Wildy, Simmonds & Hill.

Moscati, Maria Federica (2015). *Same-Sex Couples and Mediation: A Practical Handbook*. European Union, DG Justice, Specific Programme, Civil Justice, 2007–2013, Grant agreement JUST/2013/JCIV/AG/4667. http://www.litigious love.eu/resources/, accessed 22 April 2015.

Munro, Vanessa and Stychin, Carl, eds. (2007). *Sexuality and the Law: Feminist Engagements*. New York: Routledge.

Palmer, Michael (2014). "Formalisation of Alternative Dispute Resolution Processes: Some Socio-Legal Thoughts." In Joachim Zekoll, Mortiz Balz, and Iwo Amelung (eds.), *Formalisation and Flexibilisation in Dispute Resolution*, 17–44. Leiden: Brill.

Petilli, Arianna, Dettore, Davide, Montano, Antonella, and Flebus, Giovanni Battista (2010). "Religion and Homosexuality: An Empirical Study about Internalized Homophobia of Homosexual People in Relation to the Degree of Religiosity." Paper presented at the Fifteenth Congress of EABCT (European Association for Behavioural and Cognitive Therapies), Milan, Italy. https:// waysoflove.files.wordpress.com/2014/09/articolo-inglese-conferenza-1.pdf, accessed 15 March 2015.

Politi, Marco (2009). *La Chiesa del No. Indagine sugli Italiani e liberta' di coscienza*. Milan: Mondadori.

Roberts, Marian (2014). *Mediation in Family Disputes: Principles of Practice*, 4th ed. Aldershot: Ashgate.

Roberts, Simon and Palmer, Michael (2005). *Dispute Processes: ADR and the Primary Forms of Decision Making*, 2d ed. Cambridge: Cambridge University Press.

Sander, Frank E. A. and Goldberg, Stephen B. (1994). "Fitting the Forum to the Fuss: A User-Friendly Guide to Selecting an ADR Procedure." *Negotiation Journal* 10(1): 49–68.

Sander, Frank E. A. and Rozdeiczer, Lukasz (2005). "Selecting an Appropriate Dispute Resolution Procedure: Detailed Analysis and Simplified Solution." In Michael Moffit and Robert Bordone (eds.), *The Handbook of Dispute Resolution*, 386–406. San Francisco: Jossey-Bass.

Sarat, Austin (2000). "Exploring the Hidden Domains of Civil Justice: 'Naming, Blaming and Claiming' in Popular Culture." *De Paul Law Review* 50(2): 425–52.

Thumma, Scott (1991). "Negotiating a Religious Identity: The Case of the Gay Evangelical." *Sociological Analysis* 52(4): 333–47.

von Benda-Beckman, Franz, von Benda-Beckman, Keebet, Ramstedt, Martin, and Turner, Bertram (2013). *Religion in Disputes: Pervasiveness of Religious Normativity in Disputing Processes*. New York: Palgrave Macmillan.

Zagrebelsky, Gustavo. *Scambiarsi la Veste. Stato e Chiesa al Governo dell'Uomo*, Rome: Editori Laterza, 2010.

ABOUT THE CONTRIBUTORS

Farrah Ahmed joined Melbourne Law School in July 2012. Before this, she was a Lecturer in Law at Queen's College, University of Oxford. Her research spans public law, legal theory, and family law. Her recent work on constitutional statutes, the doctrine of legitimate expectations, the duty to give reasons, social rights adjudication, and religious tribunals has been published by the *Cambridge Law Journal*, the *Oxford Journal of Legal Studies*, *Public Law*, and *Child and Family Law Quarterly*. Her book, *Religious Freedom under the Personal Law System*, was published by Oxford University Press in 2016. Farrah is currently a Chief Investigator on an Australian Research Council Discovery grant studying religious dispute resolution processes (http://www.ausmuslimfamlawproject.com/). She serves as Associate Director (India) of the Asian Law Centre, Melbourne Law School. Her educational history includes an LLB from the University of Delhi and a bachelor of civil law, an MPhil in law, and a DPhil in law from the University of Oxford.

Nazmin Akthar-Sheikh is the Vice-Chair of Muslim Women's Network UK (MWNUK), a national charity that works for the promotion of equality, diversity, and the empowerment of Muslim women within a framework of Islamic feminism. As well as tackling issues such as domestic violence and forced marriage, MWNUK has addressed issues on gender inequality in UK family laws and regularly deals with cases involving Muslim marriages and divorce through the MWN helpline. Nazmin is also a lawyer at a Legal 500–rated law firm specializing in real estate, social housing, and asset management.

Mulki Al-Sharmani is a Docent and Academy of Finland Research Fellow at the Faculty of Theology, Study of Religions Unit, University of Helsinki. Mulki researches and writes on modern Somali diasporas with a focus on transnational families; Muslim marriage norms and practices; Muslim family laws and Islamic jurisprudence;feminist legal activism; and Islamic feminism. She is the editor of *Feminist Activism: Women's*

Rights and Legal Reform (Zed books, 2013) and the coeditor of *Men in Charge? Rethinking Authority in Muslim Legal Tradition* (with Ziba Mir-Hosseini and Jana Rumminger) (Oneworld, 2015). She is also the author of the forthcoming *Gender Justice and Legal Reform in Egypt: Negotiating Muslim Family Law* (American University in Cairo Press).

Samia Bano is a Senior Lecturer in Law at the School of Oriental and African Studies, University of London. Prior to this appointment Samia taught at the University of Reading (2006–13) in Family Law, Gender and Law (LLB), and Research Methods in Law (LLM), where she was also appointed Deputy Director of Research. Samia's research interests include the practice of Muslim family law in the United Kingdom and Europe, multiculturalism, citizenship, Islamic jurisprudence and human rights, and issues concerning the rights of Muslim women and gender equality. She has published widely in this field and is the author of *Muslim Women and Shariah Councils: Transcending the Boundaries of Community and Law* (Palgrave Macmillan, 2012) and the coeditor of *Personal Narratives, Social Justice and The Law* (*Feminist Legal Studies*, special issue) and a research project for the Ministry of Justice entitled "An Exploratory Study of Shariah Councils in England with Respect to Family Law" (2013). Samia has also worked as a researcher on a number of social and policy projects and acted as an adviser for a number of working groups.

Sarah Beskine practices family and divorce law in London. She is a Director of Hopkin Murray Beskine, a specialist family, human rights, and property litigation law practice. Sarah is a recognized expert in divorce/relationship breakdown, including complex financial disputes and international child abduction, regarding which she is on the panel of the International Child Abduction and Contact Unit. Sarah is also a qualified collaborative lawyer and an accredited resolution specialist. Her opinion is often sought by the media. An experienced family mediator, Sarah set up and manages Hopkin Murray Beskine's mediation service.

Shaista Gohir is a leading Muslim women's rights activist in Britain and Chair of Muslim Women's Network UK, which works to improve social justice and equality for Muslim women and girls through research, a helpline, training, advocacy, and campaigning. She is also a member of Musawah's International Advisory Group, its highest policy and decision-making body. Musawah is a global movement for equality and justice in the Muslim family.

Abdirashid A. Ismail is a postdoctoral researcher at the Department of Social Research, University of Helsinki. He is also an Economics Policy Fellow with the Heritage Institute for Policy Studies (HIPS) in Somalia. Ismail studies immigration and diaspora, with a particular focus on transnational migration and child well-being. Furthermore, Ismail's areas of interest include the political economy of conflict and state formation.

Wendy Kennett is a Lecturer in Law at Cardiff University, having previously taught in Nottingham, Cambridge, and Keele and at University of Central Lancashire, Cyprus. Her field of research is international and comparative dispute resolution and the historical, cultural, and structural differences between legal systems. Although her main body of work is in the civil and commercial sphere, she has recently been investigating the use of arbitration as a method of resolving family law disputes. Wendy's research on Muslim and Jewish family dispute resolution thus fits into this broader framework of research and scholarship. It explores the relationship between religious and secular modes of dispute resolution—including the recognition of any resulting decision or agreement—both in the domestic context (local legal pluralism) and transnationally (private international law).

Ghena Krayem is a Senior Lecturer at the Faculty of Law, University of Sydney, teaching and researching in the areas of constitutional and public law, legal ethics, the application of Sharia in Australia, Muslim women, and Islamic family law. She is the author of *Islamic Family Law in Australia: To Recognise or Not to Recognise* (Melbourne University Publishing, 2014). Ghena is a regular commentator on issues relating to the Muslim community. She is also a family dispute resolution practitioner.

Maria Federica Moscati is a Lecturer in Family Law at the University of Sussex and an Italian advocate. Her main research interests lie in issues relating to alternative dispute resolution, access to justice, comparative family law, human rights with a focus on children and LGBTI people, and law in context. She has published in those areas and is the author of *Pasolini's Italian Premonitions: Same-Sex Unions and the Law in*

Comparative Perspective. Her latest research project, "Litigious Love: Same-Sex Couples and Mediation in the European Union," has been awarded financial support by the EU Commission.

Sanna Mustasaari earned a master of laws at the University of Helsinki and is a doctoral student at the Faculty of Law at that university. Her doctoral research focuses on transnational families and the questions of belonging and recognition of relationships in the fields of family law, private international law, and immigration law. She is a member of the research project "Transnational Muslim Marriages: Wellbeing, Law and Gender," led by Marja Tiilikainen and funded by the Academy of Finland, and the research project "The Legal Language of Moral Struggles," led by Samuli Hurri and funded by the University of Helsinki.

Rehana Parveen qualified as a solicitor in 1995 and has worked in both Birmingham and London. As a solicitor, Rehana specialized in family law, criminal law, and general litigation. While in practice, Rehana was a member of the Family Law Panel and a Duty Solicitor. In 1999 she became a partner in her own firm, which she set up with another solicitor, in Tooting, London. Rehana continued to work as a partner until 2002, when she joined the College of Law, teaching a range of courses, including the Graduate Diploma in Law, Legal Practice Course, and Bar Professional Training Course, as well as a range of skills, such as advocacy, client interviewing, legal research, and drafting of court documents. She joined the University of Birmingham in 2012 as a Postgraduate Teaching Assistant and as a PhD candidate. She began working on her PhD thesis, examining whether Sharia councils meet the needs of Muslim women. Rehana is currently employed as a Teaching Fellow at the University of Birmingham (teaching the Law of Adult Relationships and Equity and Trusts Law). She won an Excellence in Teaching award from the University of Birmingham in 2014, as voted for by students.

Pragna Patel is a founding member of the Southall Black Sisters and Women Against Fundamentalism. She worked as a coordinator and senior case worker for SBS from 1982 to 1993, when she left to train and practice as a solicitor. In 2009 she returned to SBS as its Director. She has been centrally involved in some of SBS's most important cases and campaigns around domestic violence, immigration, and religious fundamentalism. She has also written extensively on race, gender, and religion.

Gopika Solanki is Associate Professor of Political Science at Carleton University in Canada. Her research interests include religion and politics, multiculturalism, and legal pluralism, indigeneity and the law, and feminist theory. She is the author of *Adjudication in Religious Family Laws: Cultural Accommodation, Legal Pluralism, and Gender Equality in India* (Cambridge University Press, 2011) and the coauthor (with Anjali Dave) of *Journey from Violence to Crime: A Study of Domestic Violence in the City of Mumbai* (Tata Institute of Social Sciences, 2001). She is currently working on a book project on legal pluralism and indigenous politics, *The Split Personality of Law: Political Decentralization, Gender, and Adivasi Legal Mobilization in India.*

Saher Tariq was called to the bar but later qualified as a solicitor and cofounded YHM Solicitors. Having been involved in community work since her early twenties, she has a strong interest in woman's issues and woman's rights. Saher recently set up a panel of Muslim scholars that aims to provide women with an efficient and professional *khula* (Islamic divorce).

Lisa Webley is Professor of Empirical Studies at the University of Westminster and Senior Research Fellow at the Institute of Advanced Legal Studies, University of London. She undertakes research on the legal profession, the civil justice system, and dispute resolution as well as family law, equality, and diversity. She is a member of the Law Society of England and Wales' Equality, Diversity and Inclusion Committee and the Civil Mediation Council's Academic Committee.

INDEX